Internet Business Foundations:
Student Guide

prosofttraining ™

Chairman and Chief Executive Officer

Robert Gwin

Vice President of Certification and
Product Development

James Stanger, Ph.D.

Product Development Manager

Todd Hopkins

Managing Editor

Susan M. Lane

Senior Editor

David Oberman

Editor

Sarah Skodak

Publishers

Joseph Flannery, Tina Strong

Customer Service   ComputerPREP, Inc.
A division of ProsoftTraining
410 N. 44th Street, Suite 600
Phoenix, AZ 85008
(602) 275-7700

Internet Business Foundations

Developers

Irina Amstutz and Ken Kozakis

Contributors

James Stanger, Ph.D., and Patrick T. Lane

Editors

Sarah Skodak and Susan M. Lane

Publisher

Tina Strong

Project Manager

Todd Hopkins

Trademarks

Prosoft is a trademark of ProsoftTraining. All product names and services identified throughout this book are trademarks or registered trademarks of their respective companies. They are used throughout this book in editorial fashion only. No such use, or the use of any trade name, is intended to convey endorsement or other affiliation with the book. Copyrights of any screen captures in this book are the property of the software's manufacturer.

Disclaimer

ProsoftTraining makes a genuine attempt to ensure the accuracy and quality of the content described herein; however, ProsoftTraining makes no warranty, express or implied, with respect to the quality, reliability, accuracy, or freedom from error of this document or the products it describes. ProsoftTraining makes no representation or warranty with respect to the contents hereof and specifically disclaims any implied warranties of fitness for any particular purpose. ProsoftTraining disclaims all liability for any direct, indirect, incidental or consequential, special or exemplary damages resulting from the use of the information in this document or from the use of any products described in this document. Mention of any product or organization does not constitute an endorsement by ProsoftTraining of that product or corporation. Data used in examples and labs is intended to be fictional even if actual data is used or accessed. Any resemblance to, or use of real persons or organizations should be treated as entirely coincidental. ProsoftTraining makes every effort to ensure the accuracy of URLs referenced in all its material, but cannot guarantee that all URLs will be available throughout the life of a course. When this course/CD-ROM was published, all URLs were checked for accuracy and completeness. However, due to the ever-changing nature of the Internet, some URLs may no longer be available or may have been redirected.

Copyright Information

Table of Contents

Course Description..xi
Courseware xii
Course Objectives...xiv
Classroom Setup xiv
System Requirements xiv
Conventions and Graphics Used in This Book xviii

Lesson 1: Information Technology and the Internet 1-1
Pre-Assessment Questions 1-2
Overview of Information Technology (IT)...1-3
IT Job Roles 1-3
Overview of Networks 1-14
Overview of the Internet 1-16
Connecting to the Internet...1-18
Internet Protocols..1-24
Domain Name System (DNS) 1-27
Case Study..1-33
Lesson 1 Review..1-35

Lesson 2: Web Browsing 2-1
Pre-Assessment Questions 2-2
Introduction to Web Browsing 2-3
Basic Functions of Web Browsers..2-3
Installing a Web Browser 2-3
Web Addresses...2-6
How Browsers Work 2-10
Browser Choices...2-14
Resources for Technical Data 2-15
Browsers in the Business World 2-19
Browsing Techniques 2-22
Configuring Web Browser Preferences...2-25
Cookies 2-35
Configuring Browser Security 2-41
Proxy Servers 2-44
Troubleshooting Internet Client Problems..2-46
Case Study..2-47
Lesson 2 Review..2-49

Lesson 3: Multimedia on the Web 3-1
Pre-Assessment Questions 3-2
Introduction to Multimedia on the Web 3-3
Objects, Active Content and Languages 3-3
Objects and Security Issues 3-6
Introduction to Plug-in Technology...3-6
Data Compression and Decompression..3-8
Plug-in Installation..3-9
Types of Plug-ins 3-9
Types of Viewers..3-20
Miscellaneous File Formats 3-23
Downloading Files with a Browser 3-26
Case Study..3-30
Lesson 3 Review..3-31

Lesson 4: Databases and Web Search Engines 4-33
Pre-Assessment Questions 4-34
Introduction to Data Searching Tools 4-35
Overview of Databases..4-35
Introduction to Web Search Engines...4-40
Registering a Web Site with a Search Engine 4-41
Types of Web Searches 4-42

Basic Web Searching Techniques 4-45
Boolean Operators.. 4-49
Advanced Web Searching Techniques 4-51
Using Web Searches to Perform Job Tasks 4-54
Unexpected Web Search Results... 4-55
Web Search Strategies... 4-56
Citing Copyrighted Web Site References.. 4-58
Case Study... 4-60
Lesson 4 Review 4-62

Lesson 5: E-Mail and Personal Information Management **5-1**
Pre-Assessment Questions 5-2
Introduction to Electronic Mail (E-Mail) 5-3
How E-Mail Works.. 5-3
E-Mail Configuration Requirements... 5-8
E-Mail Message Components... 5-15
Creating and Sending E-Mail Messages 5-16
Receiving and Viewing E-Mail Messages 5-23
E-Mail in the Workplace 5-26
E-Mail Problems and Solutions... 5-30
Personal Information Management (PIM).. 5-35
Case Study... 5-38
Lesson 5 Review 5-40

Lesson 6: Internet Services and Tools **6-1**
Pre-Assessment Questions 6-2
Internet Resource Tools.. 6-3
Newsgroups... 6-3
Telnet.. 6-8
File Transfer Protocol (FTP).. 6-12
Managing Downloaded Files 6-21
Virtual Network Computing (VNC) and Microsoft Terminal Services 6-26
Instant Messaging 6-30
Peer-to-Peer Networks 6-34
Lightweight Directory Access Protocol (LDAP) 6-35
Concurrent Versions System (CVS) 6-35
Communicating Effectively over the Internet.. 6-36
Troubleshooting Using TCP/IP Tools 6-39
Case Study... 6-41
Lesson 6 Review 6-43

Lesson 7: Internet Security **7-1**
Pre-Assessment Questions 7-2
Introduction to Internet Security 7-3
Encryption 7-3
Authentication 7-6
Firewalls 7-6
Malware (Malicious Software) 7-10
Virus Detection and Prevention 7-12
Spyware 7-14
Updates and Patches... 7-18
Screen Savers.. 7-19
List Servers and Listserve Groups 7-20
Security-Related Ethical and Legal Issues.. 7-23
Case Study... 7-28
Lesson 7 Review 7-30

Lesson 8: IT Project Management **8-1**
Pre-Assessment Questions 8-2
Overview of IT Project Management 8-3
Project Management Fundamentals.. 8-3
Project Management Skills 8-4
Project Management Phases 8-6

The Project Triangle..8-10
Project Management Software...8-10
Creating Project Schedules..8-12
Documenting Projects 8-16
Planning and Scheduling Meetings 8-17
Reviewing Projects..8-17
Quality Assurance...8-18
IT Business Implications 8-18
Project Management Institute (PMI) 8-22
Case Study...8-23
Lesson 8 Review...8-25

Appendixes .... **Appendixes - 1**

CIW Foundations Glossary... **CIW Foundation Glossary - 1**

Index .... **Index - 1**

Supplemental CD-ROM Contents .... **Supplemental CD-ROM Contenets - 1**

List of Labs

Lab 1-1: Reviewing basic Web site design concepts 1-4
Lab 1-2: Conducting a basic Web site analysis..1-9
Lab 1-3: Using Internet protocols in Microsoft Internet Explorer.....................................1-30
Lab 2-1: Installing the Netscape 7.1 browser..2-4
Lab 2-2: Browsing Web pages using various browsers...2-8
Lab 2-3: Accessing statistics, and accessing secure and non-secure Web pages 2-16
Lab 2-4: Using browser features to enhance your browsing experience..............................2-23
Lab 2-5: Configuring font size in Microsoft Internet Explorer...2-27
Lab 2-6: Setting a browser home page in Microsoft Internet Explorer 2-27
Lab 2-7: Managing the History folder in Microsoft Internet Explorer.................................2-28
Lab 2-8: Configuring the browser cache in Microsoft Internet Explorer.............................2-33
Lab 2-9: Controlling image loading in Microsoft Internet Explorer 2-34
Lab 2-10: Setting automatic cookie handling in Internet Explorer 2-38
Lab 2-11: Configuring Internet Explorer to display cookie warnings 2-38
Lab 2-12: Setting safety levels in Microsoft Internet Explorer 2-42
Lab 3-1: Using Macromedia Shockwave and Flash with Microsoft Internet Explorer 3-10
Lab 3-2: Using the RealPlayer plug-in 3-13
Lab 3-3: Downloading, installing and demonstrating Apple QuickTime...............................3-15
Lab 3-4: Updating and demonstrating Windows Media Player 3-18
Lab 3-5: Using Adobe Reader with Microsoft Internet Explorer 3-21
Lab 3-6: Downloading and storing Web site content using Microsoft Internet Explorer 3-27
Lab 4-1: Performing a directory search using Yahoo!...4-46
Lab 4-2: Performing a keyword search using AltaVista 4-47
Lab 4-3: Using the plus sign (+) and minus sign (-) operators in AltaVista 4-50
Lab 4-4: Performing an advanced search in AltaVista..4-52
Lab 4-5: Using the Internet to perform job tasks 4-54
Lab 4-6: Retrieving unexpected Web search results using Google 4-56
Lab 5-1: Configuring Outlook Express as your e-mail client 5-11
Lab 5-2: Configuring a Web-based e-mail account using Hotmail......................................5-14
Lab 5-3: Creating and sending e-mail messages using Outlook Express 5-17
Lab 5-4: Creating and sending e-mail messages using Hotmail 5-18
Lab 5-5: Creating e-mail signatures in Outlook Express and Hotmail................................5-20
Lab 5-6: Attaching files to e-mail messages 5-22
Lab 5-7: Receiving and viewing e-mail messages 5-25
Lab 5-8: Setting up a spam filter in Outlook Express 5-32
Lab 6-1: Configuring and using Outlook Express as a news client.....................................6-6
Lab 6-2: Accessing a library database using Telnet 6-9
Lab 6-3: Installing the FileZilla FTP client 6-14
Lab 6-4: Downloading files using command-line FTP...6-15
Lab 6-5: Downloading files using the Internet Explorer FTP client 6-16
Lab 6-6: Downloading files using the FileZilla FTP client 6-17

Lab 6-7: Uploading files to an FTP site using FileZilla...6-19
Lab 6-8: Defining MIME types..6-22
Lab 6-9: Compressing and decompressing files using bzip2 and bunzip2 6-24
Lab 6-10: Using the TightVNC remote administration application...6-26
Lab 6-11: Using Remote Desktop Connection 6-29
Lab 6-12: Using the Windows Messenger instant messaging client 6-31
Lab 6-13: Using TCP/IP diagnostic tools 6-40
Lab 7-1: Enabling your desktop firewall 7-8
Lab 7-2: Installing and using spyware detection software 7-16
Lab 7-3: Activating a screen saver...7-20
Lab 7-4: Exploring LISTSERV 7-21
Lab 7-5: Exploring Topica 7-22
Lab 8-1: Installing Java and the GanttProject project management tool....................................8-11
Lab 8-2: Creating a project schedule 8-13

List of Figures

Figure 1-1: Web site design — plain Web page 1-4
Figure 1-2: Web site design — more interesting Web page 1-4
Figure 1-3: Viewing Web page for design qualities 1-5
Figure 1-4: Inserting HTML code 1-6
Figure 1-5: Improved Web page..1-6
Figure 1-6: Web site usage report — graphical format 1-8
Figure 1-7: Web site usage report — tabular format 1-8
Figure 1-8: Client/server model 1-14
Figure 1-9: Multiple connections among servers...1-16
Figure 1-10: Typical domain name 1-28
Figure 1-11: CIW Web site home page in Microsoft Internet Explorer.......................................1-31
Figure 2-1: Netscape 7.1 Setup Wizard..2-4
Figure 2-2: Specifying Netscape setup type 2-5
Figure 2-3: Specifying additional Netscape setup components 2-5
Figure 2-4: Typical Uniform Resource Locator (URL) 2-6
Figure 2-5: CIW Certified home page..2-9
Figure 2-6: Properties dialog box — Microsoft Internet Explorer 2-17
Figure 2-7: Certificate dialog box — Microsoft Internet Explorer 2-18
Figure 2-8: Page Info dialog box — Netscape Navigator 2-19
Figure 2-9: CIW extranet login page 2-20
Figure 2-10: Webinar session...2-21
Figure 2-11: Netscape Navigator Bookmarks..2-22
Figure 2-12: Microsoft Internet Explorer Favorites 2-22
Figure 2-13: Add Favorite dialog box 2-23
Figure 2-14: Adding to Favorites 2-23
Figure 2-15: Internet Options dialog box — Microsoft Internet Explorer...................................2-26
Figure 2-16: Preferences dialog box — Netscape Navigator 2-26
Figure 2-17: Navigator Preferences dialog box — Popup Windows card 2-29
Figure 2-18: Settings dialog box — Microsoft Internet Explorer 2-31
Figure 2-19: Cache Preferences — Netscape Navigator 2-31
Figure 2-20: Configuring browser cache in Microsoft Internet Explorer....................................2-33
Figure 2-21: Controlling image loading in Microsoft Internet Explorer 2-35
Figure 2-22: Internet Options dialog box — Privacy tab 2-37
Figure 2-23: Advanced Privacy Settings dialog box — Microsoft Internet Explorer..................2-39
Figure 2-24: Privacy Alert — Microsoft Internet Explorer 2-39
Figure 2-25: Cookie Manager — Netscape Navigator...2-40
Figure 2-26: Internet Options dialog box — Security tab 2-41
Figure 2-27: Microsoft Internet Explorer Medium-level security warning 2-42
Figure 2-28: Microsoft Internet Explorer High safety level...2-43
Figure 2-29: Security warning — Microsoft Internet Explorer 2-43
Figure 2-30: Proxies card of Preferences dialog box — Navigator...2-45
Figure 2-31: Internet Options dialog box, Connections tab — Internet Explorer 2-45
Figure 2-32: Local Area Network (LAN) Settings dialog box 2-46
Figure 3-1: Embedded RealPlayer video...3-7

Figure 3-2: Downloading Shockwave and Flash players in Microsoft Internet Explorer 3-11
Figure 3-3: Downloading Shockwave Player 3-11
Figure 3-4: Installation Complete dialog box 3-12
Figure 3-5: Testing plug-in installation 3-12
Figure 3-6: QTVR sequence 3-15
Figure 3-7: QuickTime File Download dialog box 3-16
Figure 3-8: QuickTime Save As dialog box 3-16
Figure 3-9: Windows Media Player interface 3-18
Figure 3-10: Adobe Reader download page 3-21
Figure 3-11: Browse For Folder dialog box 3-22
Figure 3-12: Optimizer dialog box 3-22
Figure 3-13: Viewing PDF file in Adobe Reader window 3-23
Figure 3-14: Saving Web pages in Internet Explorer 3-28
Figure 3-15: Save Picture dialog box 3-28
Figure 3-16: Save A Copy dialog box 3-29
Figure 4-1: Sample database table 4-35
Figure 4-2: Sample relational database 4-36
Figure 4-3: Related tables 4-36
Figure 4-4: One-to-many database table relationship 4-38
Figure 4-5: Many-to-many database table relationship 4-38
Figure 4-6: Yahoo! keyword search field 4-43
Figure 4-7: Yahoo! static directory 4-44
Figure 4-8: AltaVista home page 4-47
Figure 4-9: AltaVista Advanced Web Search page 4-52
Figure 4-10: Google home page 4-55
Figure 5-1: Outlook Express Properties dialog box — General tab 5-8
Figure 5-2: Outlook Express Properties dialog box — Servers tab 5-9
Figure 5-3: Mail & Newsgroups Account Settings dialog box — Account Settings panel 5-10
Figure 5-4: Mail & Newsgroups Account Settings dialog box — Server Settings panel 5-10
Figure 5-5: Mail & Newsgroups Account Settings dialog box — Outgoing Server (SMTP)
    Settings panel 5-11
Figure 5-6: Microsoft Outlook Express main window 5-12
Figure 5-7: Configured e-mail account in Outlook Express 5-13
Figure 5-8: Hotmail account registration 5-15
Figure 5-9: Creating message in Outlook Express 5-17
Figure 5-10: Creating message in Hotmail 5-18
Figure 5-11: Delivery confirmation in Hotmail 5-19
Figure 5-12: Outlook Express window sections 5-24
Figure 5-13: New Mail Rule dialog box 5-32
Figure 5-14: Specifying words for spam filter in Outlook Express 5-33
Figure 5-15: PIM calendar entries in Outlook 5-35
Figure 5-16: PIM contact information window in Outlook 5-36
Figure 6-1: Hits for Visual Studio .NET in comp.lang.basic.visual.misc newsgroup on Google Groups ... 6-5
Figure 6-2: Newsgroup Subscriptions dialog box — Outlook Express 6-7
Figure 6-3: Accessing library database using Telnet 6-9
Figure 6-4: Sample SSH session 6-10
Figure 6-5: Using command-line FTP 6-16
Figure 6-6: Using Internet Explorer FTP client 6-17
Figure 6-7: Using FileZilla FTP client 6-18
Figure 6-8: WinSCP client 6-21
Figure 6-9: File with undefined MIME type 6-21
Figure 6-10: File Types tab — Folder Options dialog box 6-22
Figure 6-11: WinVNC Current User Properties dialog box 6-27
Figure 6-12: Connection Details dialog box 6-27
Figure 6-13: VNC display on client computer 6-28
Figure 6-14: Remote Desktop Connection dialog box 6-29
Figure 6-15: Signing in to Windows Messenger 6-32
Figure 6-16: Adding Windows Messenger contact 6-32
Figure 6-17: Receiving instant message 6-33
Figure 6-18: Using TCP/IP diagnostic tools 6-40
Figure 7-1: Web page personal information form 7-3

Figure 7-2: Network Connections window 7-9
Figure 7-3: Advanced Settings dialog box 7-9
Figure 7-4: Ad-aware 6.0 Personal spyware detection application 7-17
Figure 7-5: Display Properties dialog box — Screen Saver tab 7-19
Figure 7-6: L-Soft home page 7-21
Figure 7-7: Topica home page 7-22
Figure 8-1: Organizational structure — project team members 8-9
Figure 8-2: Sample Gantt chart... 8-12
Figure 8-3: GanttProject application window... 8-13
Figure 8-4: GanttProject toolbar.. 8-13
Figure 8-5: GanttProject Properties dialog box for task.. 8-14
Figure 8-6: Task list and Gantt chart 8-15
Figure 8-7: Task list and Gantt chart — final 8-16

List of Tables

Table 1-1: Common speeds for dial-up Internet connections 1-20
Table 1-2: Common speeds for direct Internet connections... 1-23
Table 2-1: Internet Explorer Privacy level effects on cookies 2-37
Table 4-1: Types of Web searches... 4-43
Table 4-2: Boolean operators 4-50
Table 5-1: E-mail message components.. 5-16
Table 5-2: E-mail response options 5-27
Table 6-1: SSH-based utilities... 6-11
Table 6-2: Popular file types found on FTP servers 6-13
Table 6-3: Compression applications and common file name extensions............................ 6-24
Table 7-1: Computer virus types 7-11

Course Description

Internet Business Foundations prepares students to work effectively in today's business environment. In this course, you will learn about the tasks involved in various Information Technology (IT) job roles. You will also learn about Internet connection methods, Internet protocols and the Domain Name System (DNS). You will study the basic functions of Web browsers, the components of Web addresses and the use and control of cookies. You will learn how plug-ins can improve your Web-browsing experience, and you will use browsers to download and manage files.

You will learn about databases as they relate to Web search engines, and you will use search engines to conduct basic and advanced Web searches. This course also teaches you to configure e-mail clients and use e-mail, and it provides guidelines for communicating effectively over the Internet via e-mail and other methods such as instant messaging and newsgroups.

You will learn about the risks associated with being connected to the Internet, and about the security measures that can keep your computer system and your personal information secure. Finally, you will study the fundamental elements of project management and the importance of acquiring these skills for all IT job roles.

All CIW Foundations courses offer Case Studies for class discussion about real-world skills applications, and updated topics such as project management and the relationship between technology and business operations. The CIW Foundations courses prepare students to take the CIW Foundations certification exam.

Guided, step-by-step labs provide opportunities to practice new skills. You can challenge yourself and review your skills after each lesson in the Lesson Summary and Lesson Review sections. Additional skill reinforcement is provided in Activities, Optional Labs, Lesson Quizzes and a Course Assessment that are available from your instructor.

This coursebook includes a supplemental CD-ROM containing the lab files used in class. To practice the skills presented in class or to perform any labs that were not completed, refer to the Classroom Setup section for information about system requirements and using the lab files.

Series

Internet Business Foundations is the first course in the CIW Foundations series. CIW Foundations consists of the following courses:

* *Internet Business Foundations*

* Site Development Foundations

* Network Technology Foundations

Prerequisites

No prior experience using the Internet, developing Web pages or configuring networks is necessary. However, students should be familiar with an operating system such as Microsoft Windows XP before taking this course. The CIW Foundations courseware does not provide entry-level computer literacy. Rather, it builds upon computer literacy training and certifications such as Microsoft Office Specialist (*www.microsoft.com*) and IC[3] (*www.certiport.net*).

Certification

The CIW Foundations series of courses prepares students to take the high-stakes CIW Foundations certification exam. Those who pass the CIW Foundations exam earn the highly respected CIW Associate certification, which is recognized throughout the industry as validating essential Internet skills for the workplace. The CIW Associate certification proves that an individual has evolved from being an Internet consumer to an Internet producer, capable of producing real-world Internet applications. A CIW Associate certificant can use common Internet-ready applications, can create properly formed HTML/XHTML documents, knows CGI and database essentials, and can troubleshoot networks. For information about taking the Foundations exam, visit *www.CIWcertified.com*.

Courseware

This coursebook was developed for instructor-led training and will assist you during class. Along with comprehensive instructional text and objectives checklists, this coursebook provides easy-to-follow hands-on labs and a glossary of course-specific terms. It also provides Internet addresses needed to complete some labs, although due to the constantly changing nature of the Internet, some addresses may no longer be valid.

The student coursebook is organized in the following manner:

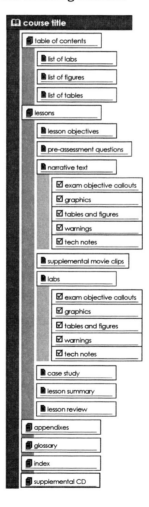

When you return to your home or office, you will find this coursebook to be a valuable resource for reviewing labs and applying the skills you have learned. Each lesson concludes with questions that review the material. Lesson review questions are provided as a study resource only and in no way guarantee a passing score on the CIW Foundations certification exam.

Coursebook versions

The CIW Foundations courseware is designed for various classroom environments: academic, learning center and corporate. These coursebooks are available in both instructor and student versions. Student versions are available for both the academic environment and the learning center/corporate environment. Check your book to verify which version you have.

- **Instructor (Academic, Learning Center and Corporate)** — Example syllabi for 10-week and 16-week instruction periods are included on the instructor supplemental CD-ROM. Learning centers can teach this series at an accelerated pace; consult the implementation tables on the supplemental CD-ROM. The supplemental CD-ROM also includes an appendix listing the CIW Foundations certification exam objectives and locations of corresponding material in the coursebook. The instructor version of this book includes Instructor Notes in the margin, which provide additional tips and commentary for the instructor to supplement course narrative. Margin callouts also direct instructors to material that relates directly to specified CIW Foundations objectives. The instructor book and supplemental CD-ROM contain all answers to Activities (pen-and-paper-based), Optional Labs (computer-based), Lesson Quizzes and the Course Assessment. This book also includes handout versions of all Activities, Optional Labs, Lesson Quizzes and the Course Assessment, which the instructor can photocopy and assign during class or as homework. Lesson Quizzes and Course Assessments are provided as study and course-grading resources only; success on these materials in no way guarantees a passing score on the CIW Foundations certification exam.

- **Student (Academic)** — The student book and supplemental CD-ROM include Pre-Assessment and Lesson Review questions for each lesson. However, the student book does not provide answers to these questions. It also does not include any Activities, Optional Labs, Quizzes or the Course Assessment. Students can obtain these elements and answers only from the instructor. The student supplemental CD-ROM contains appendixes and files used to perform many of the labs in the coursebook. The supplemental CD-ROM also includes an appendix listing the CIW Foundations certification exam objectives and locations of corresponding material in the coursebook. Lesson Quizzes and Course Assessments are provided as study and course-grading resources only; success on these materials in no way guarantees a passing score on the CIW Foundations certification exam.

- **Student (Learning Center/Corporate)** — Designed for the learning center/corporate environment, this student book includes Pre-Assessment and Lesson Review questions. The student supplemental CD-ROM contains appendixes; files used to perform many of the labs in the coursebook; and answers to the Pre-Assessment Questions, Lesson Review Questions, Course Assessment, Activities, Optional Labs and Lesson Quizzes. The supplemental CD-ROM also includes an appendix listing the CIW Foundations certification exam objectives and locations of corresponding material in the coursebook. Lesson Quizzes and Course Assessments are provided as study and course-grading resources only; success on these materials in no way guarantees a passing score on the CIW Foundations certification exam.

Course Objectives

After completing this course, you will be able to:

- Define Information Technology (IT) job roles.
- Define networks, the Internet, Internet connection methods, Internet protocols and the Domain Name System (DNS).
- Identify the basic functions of Web browsers and the components of Web addresses.
- Identify the use and control of cookies.
- Define and use multimedia and plug-ins.
- Use browsers to download and manage files.
- Define databases and database components.
- Define Web search engines, and conduct Web searches using Boolean operators and advanced search techniques.
- Install and configure e-mail clients, use e-mail effectively, and identify e-mail problems and solutions.
- Identify the functions of personal information management (PIM) software.
- Use a news client, Telnet, FTP, VNC and Microsoft Terminal Services.
- Troubleshoot Internet client issues using TCP/IP tools.
- Identify topics related to Web security such as encryption, authentication, firewalls, malware, spyware, patches and updates.
- Identify project management skills and phases.
- Discuss the business implications of IT decisions.

Classroom Setup

Your instructor has probably set up the classroom computers based on the system requirements listed in the following sections. Most software configurations on your computer are identical to those on your instructor's computer. However, your instructor may use additional software to demonstrate network interaction or related technologies.

System Requirements

This section lists the hardware, software and connectivity requirements to implement this course.

Hardware

Each classroom should be equipped with an individual computer workstation for each student and the instructor. The following table summarizes the hardware requirements for all courses in the CIW program.

Note: The CIW hardware requirements are similar to the minimum system requirements for Microsoft Windows XP Professional implementation except that CIW requires increased hard disk space (8 GB).

Hardware Specifications	Minimum Requirements
Processor	Intel Pentium III processor (or equivalent) with 300-MHz processor clock speed recommended; 233-MHz minimum required (single or dual processor system)
L2 cache	256 KB
Hard disk	8 GB
RAM	128 MB
CD-ROM	32X
Network interface card (NIC)	10BaseT or 100BaseTX (10 or 100 Mbps)
Sound card/speakers	Required for instructor station, optional for student stations
Video adapter	4 MB
Network hubs	Enough 10-port 10BaseT or 100BaseTX (10 or 100 Mbps) hubs to allow classroom computers to communicate
Monitor	Super VGA (800 x 600) resolution video graphics card and monitor with 256 colors

Software

If you are teaching all three CIW Foundations courses sequentially, there is no need to reformat your computers for each course. The recommended software configurations for computers used to complete the labs in this book are as follows.

Internet Business Foundations

To be installed before class:

- Microsoft Windows XP Professional (typical installation)

- Microsoft Internet Explorer 5.5 or later with Outlook Express (typical installation)

To be installed by students during course labs:

- Netscape 7.1 (binary provided in the C:\CIW\Internet\LabFiles\Lesson02 folder)

- Adobe Reader 6.0.1 (binary provided in the C:\CIW\Internet\LabFiles\Lesson03 folder)

- Aethera (binary provided in the C:\CIW\Internet\LabFiles\Lesson05 folder)

- TightVNC, Bzip2 and Bunzip2 (binaries provided in the C:\CIW\Internet\LabFiles\Lesson06 folder)

- Ad-aware 6.0 (binary provided in the C:\CIW\Internet\LabFiles\Lesson07 folder)

- GanttProject (binary provided in the C:\CIW\Internet\LabFiles\Lesson08 folder)

- Java 2 Runtime Environment (binary provided in the C:\CIW\Internet\LabFiles\Lesson08 folder)

Site Development Foundations

To be installed before class:

- Microsoft Windows XP Professional (typical installation)

- Microsoft Internet Explorer 5.5

To be installed by students during course labs:

- Lynx (binary provided in the C:\CIW\SDF\LabFiles\Lesson01 folder)

To be installed by instructor for instructor-led demonstration:

- Apache2Triad (C:\CIW\SDF\LabFiles\Lesson11\apache2triad)

You can also install Netscape Navigator or another browser (e.g., Mozilla or Opera) if you prefer

Network Technology Foundations
To be installed before class:

- Microsoft Windows XP Professional (typical installation)

- Microsoft Internet Explorer 5.5 or later with Outlook Express (typical installation)

To be installed by students during course labs:

- Java 2 Runtime Environment (binary provided in the C:\CIW\Network\LabFiles\Lesson01 folder)

- Phex (binary provided in the C:\CIW\Network\LabFiles\Lesson01 folder)

- FineCrypt (binary provided in the C:\CIW\Network\LabFiles\Lesson05 folder)

Connectivity

Internet connectivity is required for this course. You will experience optimal performance with a dedicated Internet connection (e.g., a cable/DSL modem or a T1 line). However, you can teach the course using slower connections (e.g., 56-Kbps modem).

CIW Master Supplemental CD-ROM

Each coursebook includes a supplemental CD-ROM. The files on the CD-ROM are referenced and used throughout the course.

When you insert the CIW Master Supplemental CD-ROM, you will see a list of courses. Select the appropriate course, and you will be prompted to unzip an executable file. This executable file will create a directory of all supplemental materials for the course. You can choose to download the directory to the default location, which is C:\CIW\[Course_Title]. Optionally, you can select another location. After you choose the location and unzip the file, a directory will be created on your hard drive. All supplemental files for the course will be downloaded to this directory. You can then create a shortcut to this directory on your Desktop. As you conduct the course labs, you can use this shortcut to access your lab files quickly.

CIW Foundations Movie CD-ROM

The CIW Foundations courses offer optional movie files from LearnKey that discuss selected technology topics. You must purchase the CIW Foundations Movie CD-ROM separately. To order the CIW Foundations Movie CD-ROM, call (800) 228-1027 or send an e-mail message to *info@ciwcertified.com*.

To view the movies from the optional CIW Foundations Movie CD-ROM:

- You need a Windows Internet Explorer 5.5 (or later) browser.

- You need Windows Media Player 9 and all necessary codecs.

- You can use Windows Update to obtain the latest versions of Internet Explorer and Media Player.

- You can visit *www.onlineexpert.com/elearning/gettingstarted/sys.php* if you need more information about playing LearnKey movies.

Note that students will install Windows Media Player software on their systems during an Internet Business Foundations course lab.

Consider the following points about the CIW Foundations Movie CD-ROM:

- The movies provide supplementary instruction in a multimedia format, and enhance the coursebook narrative and labs. However, movie content does not comprehensively address CIW Foundations exam objectives and is not intended to replace coursebook content.

- CIW Foundations coursebooks include Movie Time alert boxes that signal appropriate points at which to view the supplemental movies.

- Instructors in a classroom environment are strongly encouraged to present movies to the entire class using a computer screen projector. Group presentations enable instructors to present and discuss movie content when appropriate. Controlling the presentation of movies also minimizes distractions from course material, and essential lecture or lab time.

- Students are strongly encouraged to purchase the CIW Foundations Movie CD-ROM so they can watch the movie clips at their convenience. Owning the Movie CD also allows students to reference the movie clips after completing the course.

- Do not distribute unlicensed copies of this copyrighted material.

Conventions and Graphics Used in This Book

The following conventions are used in these coursebooks.

Terms   Technology terms defined in the margins are indicated in **bold type** the first time they appear in the text. However, not every word in bold type is a term requiring definition.

Lab Text   Text that you enter during a lab appears in ***italic bold type***. Names of components that you access or change in a lab appear in **bold type**.

Notations   *Notations or comments regarding screenshots, labs or other text are indicated in italic type.*

Program Code or Commands   Text used in program code or operating system commands appears in the Lucida Sans Typewriter font.

The following graphics are used in these coursebooks.

Tech Notes point out exceptions or special circumstances that you may find when working with a particular procedure. Tech Notes that occur within a lab are displayed without the graphic.

Tech Tips offer special-interest information about the current subject.

Warnings alert you about cautions to observe or actions to avoid.

This graphic signals the start of a lab or other hands-on activity.

The Movie Time graphic signals appropriate points in the course at which to view optional movie clips. All movie clips are © 2004 LearnKey, Inc.

Each lesson summary includes an *Application Project*. This project is designed to provoke interest and apply the skills taught in the lesson to your daily activities.

Each lesson concludes with a summary of the skills and objectives taught in that lesson. You can use the *Skills Review* checklist to evaluate what you have learned.

This graphic indicates a line of code that is completed on the following line.

Lesson 1: Information Technology and the Internet

Objectives

By the end of this lesson, you will be able to:

- Define Information Technology (IT) job roles.
- Define networks.
- Define the Internet.
- Identify Internet connection methods.
- Define Internet protocols.
- Define the Domain Name System (DNS).

Pre-Assessment Questions

1. What is the purpose of Transmission Control Protocol/Internet Protocol (TCP/IP)?

   a. It maps hosts on the Internet.
   b. It directs a packet along a prescribed route.
   c. It passes information from one computer to another.
   d. It downloads incoming messages.

2. A domain name server performs which function?

   a. It resolves machine addresses to domain names.
   b. It resolves domain names to machine names.
   c. It resolves IP addresses to Web URLs.
   d. It resolves domain names to IP addresses.

3. What is the main difference between Internet Protocol version 4 (IPv4) and Internet Protocol version 6 (IPv6)?

   _____

   _____

   _____

   _____

   _____

Overview of Information Technology (IT)

Information Technology (IT)
The management and processing of information using computers and computer networks.

Information Technology (IT) refers to all aspects of managing and processing information using computers and computer networks. Because computers are vital to information management in all organizations and companies, most organizations have dedicated computer personnel referred to as IT departments. IT departments generally deal with computer, telecommunications, network and other related technologies and services to provide employees with the resources necessary to reach their organizations' goals.

Information Technology is one of the fastest-growing career fields in the world today. IT skills are essential in all industries and are necessary in many different job roles.

IT Job Roles

OBJECTIVE:
1.1.1: Individual IT job roles

The following sections will identify the various job roles in the IT industry, including the responsibilities, tasks and skills they encompass. As you will see, many of the responsibilities and skills overlap, so distinctions between job roles are not always precise.

Many of the job roles listed in this section are integral components of most organizations. However, many are outsourced to contractors in the United States or, increasingly, sent offshore to be performed by qualified personnel in developing countries. By incorporating business and project management skills into your skill set, you will make yourself more marketable for employment in the U.S. IT industry.

Web site designers

OBJECTIVE:
1.1.2: Web site designer job role

Web site designers create the "look and feel" that visitors will see when they access a site on the World Wide Web. Web site designers determine the most effective site layouts, color schemes, navigational links and fonts to maintain visitor interest in the site. Site designers primarily establish the organization, mood and tone of the site relative to its content. In short, Web site designers are responsible for developing the user interface and aesthetics of a Web site.

Web site designer
An individual responsible for the organization and appearance of a Web site.

Web site designers must understand Web development technology and be proficient in Web languages such as Hypertext Markup Language (HTML), VBScript or JavaScript, and graphics applications such as Flash, Photoshop, Illustrator or Dreamweaver. They must also possess good communication, organizational and visual design skills. Web site designers work closely with other departments within organizations and with potential site viewers to determine the information and format that the site will present online.

Figures 1-1 and 1-2 show two different designs for the same Web site. Figure 1-1 shows a Web page with rudimentary formatting applied. A Web site designer may look at this page, determine that the page will not effectively grab the attention of potential viewers, and change the formatting and color scheme to make the page more interesting, thereby increasing viewer awareness of and participation in the Web site.

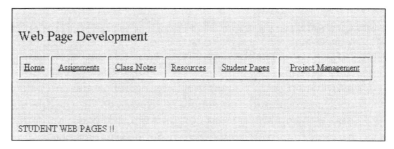

Figure 1-1: Web site design — plain Web page

Figure 1-2 shows the same Web page with additional formatting applied. Notice that this Web page is more interesting and easier to read than the preceding Web page.

Figure 1-2: Web site design — more interesting Web page

In the following lab, you will review basic Web site design concepts. Suppose you are the Web site designer for your company. Your project manager has asked you to prepare several prototypes of the Summer Youth Blitz Web page. What formatting attributes or images would you use to increase the page's visual appeal?

 Lab 1-1: Reviewing basic Web site design concepts

In this lab, you will modify an HTML page to make it more aesthetically pleasing and informative.

1. First, you will view the existing HTML page and consider ways to improve it. Open **Windows Explorer** and navigate to the **C:\CIW\Internet\LabFiles\Lesson01** folder.

2. Double-click the **Lab_1-1** folder, then double-click **blitz.html**. This step opens your default browser and displays the Web page shown in Figure 1-3.

    *Note: If you want to display file name extensions in Windows Explorer, select **Tools | Folder Options**, then click the **View** tab. Deselect **Hide Extensions For Known File Types**, click the **Apply To All Folders** button, click the **Yes** button, then click **OK**.*

Figure 1-3: Viewing Web page for design qualities

Consider the following points about this Web page:

- The page provides a clear explanation of the Habitat for Humanity project of building a home, and offers an application form.

- The page contains some graphical content, such as the side bar. The World Wide Web lends itself to graphical content. If you add the right image, you will better convey the page's message. An image can also increase the attractiveness of the page.

Suppose that as a Web site designer, you have decided to add an image. Working with a graphic artist, you have created an image and want to insert this image into the page.

3. Next, you will change the HTML file so that it is more aesthetically pleasing. Close your browser window.

4. In Windows Explorer, double-click **SYBcollage.jpg** to display the image that you will add to enhance the existing Web page.

5. Close the image file.

6. In Windows Explorer, right-click **blitz.html**, then click **Properties**. The Properties dialog box will display.

7. Verify that the **Read-only** check box is deselected, then click **OK**. This step ensures that you will be able to edit the HTML file.

8. From your Desktop, select **Start | Run** to display the Run dialog box.

9. In the Open text box, type *Notepad*, then click **OK**. This step opens the Notepad application.

10. In Notepad, select **File | Open** to display the Open dialog box.

11. Display the Files Of Type drop-down list, then click **All Files** to display all file types in the dialog box.

12. Navigate to the **C:\CIW\Internet\LabFiles\Lesson01\Lab_1-1** folder if necessary, then double-click **blitz.html**. You will see the HTML code display in the Notepad window.

13. Scroll down approximately halfway until you see the following line:

```
<td valign="top" width="435" rowspan="2">
```

14. In the white space between <td valign="top" width="435" rowspan="2"> and the next line of code, type the following code:

<img src="sybcollage.jpg" width="432" height="154" border="0" alt="Do something real this summer - build a home for a family" />

Note: Ensure that the above code displays as a single line.

The HTML code (including your newly inserted code) should match Figure 1-4.

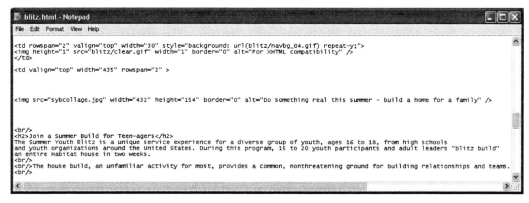

Figure 1-4: Inserting HTML code

15. Press **CTRL+S** to save the changes, then close the Notepad window.

16. Open **blitz.html** in your Web browser. The modified Web page should appear as shown in Figure 1-5.

Figure 1-5: Improved Web page

17. Position the mouse pointer over the inserted graphic. Notice that a pop-up box with the text "Do something real this summer - build a home for a family" displays for several seconds.

18. Consider ways that adding this new image helps convey the message contained in this page's text. You have just helped enhance the design of this page.

19. Close the browser window.

In this lab, you considered Web site design issues and modified a page. You now have a better understanding of the Web site designer job role.

Web application developers and Web architects

Web application developer
An individual who develops primarily server-side Web applications.

Web architect
An individual who is responsible for creating the overview plan of a Web site's development.

Web application developers use Web programming languages or products to develop Web sites, generally for Web server applications. Web application developers design, build and test the Web pages and hyperlinks that form the site. Web application developers must be proficient in programming and scripting languages such as Java, JavaScript, C++, Perl and others.

Web application developers may also lead project teams that design Web applications, so strong project management and analytical abilities are desirable skills for this job role.

Web architects are responsible for the overview plan of a Web site's development. They consult with management and Web site users to design and implement the plan for developing and maintaining an organization's Web site. They often manage Web site designers and Web application developers to design, develop, document and maintain an organization's Web presence. Web architects must have solid project management, organizational and communication skills in order to provide technical leadership to an application development staff.

Web site analysts

Web site analyst
An individual who analyzes Web site statistics to determine the site's effectiveness.

Web site analysts are responsible for analyzing Web site effectiveness from the viewpoints of both the organization and the end user. Analysts may design and conduct user surveys to obtain feedback about Web site features, then provide recommendations to improve the site's effectiveness. Analysts may also develop and monitor Web site tracking methods to determine the number of visitors, or "hits," a site receives.

Good analytical and communication skills are required for Web site analysts. Analysts gather and analyze statistical data, and often work with IT and marketing departments to recommend ways to increase a Web site's effectiveness. An analyst can also spend a considerable amount of time writing HTML, as well as creating graphics and writing client-side code such as JavaScript and VBScript.

The following two figures show examples of Web site usage summary reports generated by a Web site analyst. The reports indicate that Web traffic remained relatively steady for several months, then declined dramatically in August. A Web site analyst would use these statistics, along with other research, to provide information to marketing and sales departments about their efforts. For example, if data shows that traffic increases with concentrated marketing efforts, then the Web site can be used to measure marketing success. Figure 1-6 is a graphical representation of the site usage data.

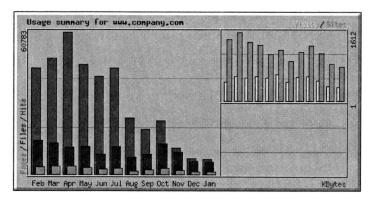

Figure 1-6: Web site usage report — graphical format

Figure 1-7 shows the same data in tabular format.

Summary by Month										
Month	Daily Avg				Monthly Totals					
	Hits	Files	Pages	Visits	Sites	KBytes	Visits	Pages	Files	Hits
Jan 2004	217	175	37	10	805	0	318	1119	5273	6533
Dec 2003	221	175	38	10	856	0	334	1185	5434	6867
Nov 2003	377	311	55	15	1108	0	476	1651	9343	11325
Oct 2003	740	416	79	18	1288	0	567	2470	12912	22969
Sep 2003	644	288	63	18	1148	0	555	1902	8647	19338
Aug 2003	778	234	42	14	933	0	438	1303	7284	24121
Jul 2003	1459	377	77	20	1198	0	623	2409	11713	45251
Jun 2003	1391	289	77	17	1092	0	530	2315	8677	41752
May 2003	1507	385	87	18	1312	0	567	2712	11953	46739
Apr 2003	2026	384	113	18	1378	0	541	3419	11544	60783
Mar 2003	1602	430	108	18	1612	0	570	3350	13353	49664
Feb 2003	1617	516	116	15	1437	0	438	3273	14463	45282
Totals						0	5957	27108	120596	380624

Figure 1-7: Web site usage report — tabular format

A Web site analyst will probably be called to examine the data further to see whether decreased traffic has translated into decreased profitability for the company. Data analysis also has technical uses. For example, you can review usage statistics to help the IT department plan for increases in Web activity that accompany concentrated marketing efforts. It may become necessary to obtain a larger server or plan for more bandwidth if Web traffic is anticipated to increase dramatically.

dead link
A hyperlink that, when clicked, sends a Web site visitor to a page or resource that does not exist on the server.

Finally, an analyst may be asked to make technical changes to the site. Such changes may include modifying HTML, updating server-side scripts to eliminate errors, and fine-tuning database connectivity. One common activity of a Web site analyst is to look for evidence of locations at which visitors become confused, or get sent to missing pages, called **dead links**. One possible indicator of a dead link is the "404 – Page Not Found" error, which you may see in a Web server log file. Regardless of the specific activities you undertake, if you are an effective Web site analyst, your Web site will operate more efficiently, from both a sales-and-marketing perspective and a technical perspective.

In the following lab, you will conduct a basic Web site analysis. Suppose that you are a Web site analyst for your company. Your project manager has asked you to prepare a report illustrating Web site usage trends over the past year. Do you think it would be worthwhile for the Web site designer to review the site and determine whether design issues are contributing to the decreasing hit rate?

Lesson 1: Information Technology and the Internet
1-9

 Lab 1-2: Conducting a basic Web site analysis

In this lab, you will analyze traffic from a Web site log to determine usage patterns.

1. In Windows Explorer, navigate to the **C:\CIW\Internet\LabFiles\Lesson01** folder, double-click **Lab_1-2**, then double-click **index.html**. You will see a report of activity on a Web site from the Web server of a fictional company. The server is named *www.company.com*.

2. In the table, click the **Jan 2004** link in the Month column. This step displays monthly statistics for January 2004.

3. Scroll down, if necessary, and view the Hits By Response Code section of the first table. Find the **Code 404 – Not Found** error count. Notice that 304 instances of the 404 error have occurred. As a Web site analyst, you would want to reduce this count for the following reasons:

   • From a technical perspective, your site should not contain dead links.

   • From a business perspective, you do not want to frustrate customers as they browse the Web site.

Not all 404 errors result from dead links, but this error is an example of one statistic that a Web site analyst would consider.

4. After you have reviewed the report, consider the following concepts and discuss them as a class:

   • In both this lab and the preceding lab, you worked with a Web server. However, in this lab, you are not creating a Web page or working directly with Web design issues. You are considering statistics and trying to determine trends. You are more interested in how well the Web site as a whole is functioning, and the ways it contributes to a company's overall business. A Web site analyst is interested in marketing issues and visitor statistics, rather than design issues.

   • Working with various members of the Web team, you can use these statistics to modify pages, or even change the structure of the entire Web site to increase its effectiveness.

5. Close the browser window.

6. Close the **Windows Explorer** window.

In this lab, you analyzed traffic to determine usage patterns, and you learned more about the job role of a Web site analyst.

OBJECTIVE:
1.1.5: Web site
manager job role

Web site manager
An individual who
manages a Web
development team.

Web site managers

A **Web site manager** in a large organization generally manages the Web development team. A Web site manager in a small company could perform all the Web development job roles discussed previously. In short, Web site managers provide organizational leadership for Web site content and all related initiatives.

Web site managers are typically involved in standardizing the content, style, design and development procedures required to create and maintain an organization's Web site. Site

© 2004 ProsoftTraining, All Rights Reserved.
Version 1.0

managers also assess the costs and benefits of implementing these standards. Site managers may also evaluate alternative Web technologies and standards, and train Web designers and application developers.

Web site managers do not necessarily need to possess highly technical skills. However, they must demonstrate the ability to remain up-to-date in their knowledge and understanding of current Web technologies and processes. Site managers must also possess the ability to analyze, interpret and integrate a wide variety of data, evaluate Web resource utilization, forecast customer and organizational site needs, and anticipate and resolve ethical issues related to site content and design.

Database administrators

OBJECTIVE:
1.1.6: Database administrator job role

database administrator
An individual responsible for the maintenance and security of an organization's database resources and data.

Databases store and manage information. Databases are used in all areas of an organization to store information related to employees, vendors, customers, inventory, resources, and so on. The power of databases lies in their ability to organize, sort and access information to meet specific user requirements.

Database administrators are responsible for the maintenance and security of an organization's database resources and data. They are also responsible for researching and analyzing the latest database technologies and developments, and for providing recommendations to senior management about database use and information management procedures and standards.

Database administrators develop and implement database maintenance plans to check the integrity of the data, manage the physical resources necessary to store and manipulate the data, administer and enforce data usage standards, and audit database systems to maintain system performance. Database administrators also manage backup and recovery procedures to prevent data loss, and apply database software upgrades and repairs as needed.

Database administrators must be able to judge system effectiveness and efficiency, analyze information to propose solutions and solve problems, evaluate the impact of resource allocations, and communicate effectively with senior management when discussing the benefits and risks of proposed technology solutions.

Server administrators

OBJECTIVE:
1.1.7: Server administrator job roles

server administrator
An individual responsible for managing and maintaining network servers.

Server administrators are responsible for designing, implementing, managing and maintaining network servers, and associated applications and peripheral devices. Server administrators may also implement policies and procedures for ensuring the security and integrity of the servers and network, and protect the network from viruses and other intrusion threats, such as hacking. Other responsibilities include providing technical assistance and training to IT staff and system users, troubleshooting server and network problems, implementing cost-effective solutions, suggesting and implementing system improvements, and providing data backup services.

Server administrators should be proficient in a variety of network operating systems and applications, such as Windows, UNIX/Linux, Microsoft Internet Information Services (IIS), Microsoft SQL Server and Microsoft Exchange. They should also be familiar with Web technologies such as HTML, Extensible Markup Language (XML) and File Transfer Protocol (FTP), and applications such as Macromedia Dreamweaver. In addition to possessing strong technical skills, server administrators must display strong communication skills so they can distill complex server and network issues into understandable concepts upon which senior management can make decisions and users can take action. Communication skills also include project management skills, as you will learn later in this lesson.

Server administrators can be classified into subcategories, such as Web server administrators or e-mail/groupware administrators. Web server administrators are responsible for servers that act as gateways between the organization and the Internet. E-mail/groupware administrators are responsible for network servers upon which e-mail clients and groupware (software that enables groups of people in a local area network [LAN] to organize their activities) are located. E-mail/groupware administrators install and maintain e-mail clients, develop and maintain security procedures to protect the integrity of electronic data transfers, and analyze and recommend improvements for e-mail utilization, capacity and performance.

Convergence technologies and server administration

Traditionally, telephone networks have been limited to sending voice data (e.g., telephone calls). Over the past 10 years, however, telephone networks have increasingly transported network-based data. Any equipment used to carry voice/data and run by telephone companies is called a telephony network. Similarly, data networks have traditionally been limited to sending standard network data (such as files from a Windows client to a Windows server via TCP/IP). Increasingly, however, voice and data networks have been combined, creating convergent networks. It has been estimated that by 2007, more than 75 percent of voice data will travel over networks formerly reserved for standard network data, according to a Frost and Sullivan report cited by CommWeb (*www.commweb.com*), ItWeb (*www.itweb.co.za*) and the University of California at Berkeley (*www.sims.berkeley.edu*).

Convergent networks can help reduce cost to companies and organizations. Increasingly, Internet connections are used to carry voice communication. Server administrators and network engineers are often asked to manage these networks.

Network engineers

OBJECTIVE:
1.1.8: Network
engineer job role

network engineer
An individual
responsible for
managing and
maintaining a
network
infrastructure.

Network engineers focus on the design, implementation, delivery and support of network components, policies and procedures used by an organization. Network engineers are responsible for configuring and testing network devices, and setting up and maintaining the network infrastructure. Network engineers also analyze, design and implement networking technologies to better meet the needs of the organization and the network users. Network engineers support and maintain network devices such as Web servers, e-mail servers, routers, connecting cables, and so forth. Network engineers may also be responsible for system security, data backup, disaster recovery planning and virus protection.

Network engineers must be able to implement LANs and wide area networks (WANs), and be proficient in a variety of networking skills, such as routing and switching, network traffic analysis, and device configuration and testing. Network engineers must also be knowledgeable in a variety of network technologies and protocols, such as network communication media, Virtual Private Network (VPN), firewalls, Internet Protocol version 4 (IPv4) and Internet Protocol version 6 (IPv6). Network engineers must also possess excellent communication skills to be able to present technical information in an understandable way to management, non-technical associates and customers.

Security managers and security analysts/consultants

OBJECTIVE:
1.1.9: Security
manager vs.
security
analyst/consultant

security manager
An individual
responsible for
managing the
security measures
used to protect
electronic data.

**security
analyst/consultant**
An individual
responsible for
examining an
organization's
security
requirements and
determining the
necessary
infrastructure.

Security managers are responsible for managing the security measures used to protect electronic data. They maintain the software and procedures necessary to protect the confidentiality and integrity of information, and legitimate access to it. Security managers perform security risk assessments, prepare for disaster recovery, monitor security control systems to ensure that appropriate security clearances and information access levels are maintained, and work with other departments to maintain secure data and information flow. Security managers may also implement and document the organization's security policies and procedures, provide security training to management and employees, and monitor and recommend advancements in information security technologies.

Security analysts/consultants are responsible for examining an organization's security requirements and determining the hardware, communications and software capabilities needed to satisfy the requirements. Security analysts/consultants may lead project teams that perform risk assessment, information security program development and implementation, network security architecture review and design, product reviews, and security solution deployments.

In addition to the technical skills related to information security, security analysts/consultants should have strong project management, consulting and communication skills. They will often manage security-related projects, write technical reports understandable to non-technical readers and communicate recommendations to senior management.

Security managers and analysts/consultants should possess knowledge of server operating systems (Windows, UNIX, etc.), firewall technology, virus-scanning software, security management software, security assessment software, intrusion-detection systems, VPN, and so forth.

PC repair technicians

OBJECTIVE:
1.1.10: PC repair
technician job role

PC repair technician
An individual
responsible for
installing, modifying
and repairing
personal computer
(PC) hardware
components.

Personal computer (PC) repair technicians install, modify and repair personal computer hardware components, such as PCs, disk drives, CD/DVD drives, tape devices, monitors, keyboards, data input devices and other peripheral equipment. PC repair technicians also install software, such as PC operating systems and application programs. PC technicians should be familiar with operating system and application program functionality in order to test and modify system functions to ensure proper performance.

PC technicians need to possess communication skills in order to provide technical assistance and training to end users, answer user inquiries regarding PC operations, diagnose hardware problems, and provide solutions. In addition, PC technicians must be able to use standard shop tools, such as soldering equipment, power tools and hand tools. PC technicians also need to be aware of standard safety procedures associated with the repair and maintenance of electronic equipment.

Help desk technicians

OBJECTIVE:
1.1.11: Help desk
technician job role

**help desk
technician**
An individual
responsible for
diagnosing and
resolving users'
technical hardware
and software
problems.

Help desk technicians diagnose and resolve users' technical hardware and software problems. Help desk technicians typically receive questions from users who are having problems using computer hardware or software, or who want to know how to use a specific software application. Technicians must use their knowledge of hardware, operating systems, applications and any relevant procedures to determine the sources of problems and provide solutions. Technicians may need to research problems with co-workers, programmers, IT staff, hardware vendors or software vendors in order to provide solutions. Technicians may also be involved in testing hardware and software to evaluate their ease of use, and to determine their applicability to the current work environment.

Help desk technicians must possess knowledge of the hardware, operating systems and software used by the organization. They must also possess strong communication skills to effectively troubleshoot and solve user problems, usually by telephone. Help desk technicians may also be responsible for documenting their troubleshooting and problem-solving activities, escalating problems they cannot solve that require immediate resolution, and making recommendations to senior management to streamline or improve help desk functions.

Project management and IT responsibilities

The following additional skills are necessary to become a successful IT professional:

- The ability to plan projects, which includes estimating costs for software, hardware and labor, as well as working with management to obtain project approval

- Writing skills, so that plans can be distributed to all relevant individuals

- The ability to work with vendors to obtain cost and time estimates for the proper software and equipment

All IT workers must have some project management skills to excel at their positions and lead projects.

IT job skills in the future

In most organizations, the current IT career model approximates a pyramid with many entry-level positions at the bottom, and fewer positions available as you move up the hierarchy. Many IT managers believe that the future IT career model will be diamond-shaped: few entry-level jobs (because of offshore outsourcing of many IT positions), many mid-level positions, and few high-level positions.

In the diamond-shaped model, managers foresee a lack of experienced professionals to fill the mid-level positions. Smaller companies that do not outsource due to scale may be the source of mid-level IT jobs required in larger organizations. It is increasingly important that IT professionals possess general business knowledge, negotiating skills, intercultural skills and project management skills. As an IT professional, you must be able to make informed decisions and fulfill commitments. If your company has outsourced some of its positions and you are working with foreign personnel, you may be able to avoid typical cross-cultural problems by doing the following:

- Learning common greetings or phrases in other languages

- Learning about common cultural misunderstandings so you can avoid them

- Developing good listening skills to better understand processes, issues, and so forth that may be communicated to you in various ways

- Developing good communication skills to better disseminate information to those with whom you work

Overview of Networks

network
A group of two or more computers connected so they can communicate with one another.

A **network** is a group of two or more computers connected so they can communicate, share resources and exchange information with one another. In a networked environment, computers are connected to a network server, which acts as the central repository of programs and data to which all users connected to the network have access. Networks allow users to:

- Simultaneously access the same programs and data.

- Transfer data from one computer to another.

- Share peripheral devices, such as printers.

- Share data storage devices for backup.

- Use electronic mail (e-mail) to communicate with each other.

- Access the Internet.

OBJECTIVE:
1.2.1: Client vs. server

node
Any entity on a network that can be managed, such as a system, repeater, router, gateway or firewall. A computer or other addressable device attached to a network; a host.

client
An individual computer connected to a network. Also, a system or application that requests a service from another computer (the server), and is used to access files or documents (such as a Web browser or user agent).

server
A computer in a network that manages the network resources and provides, or serves, information to clients.

The client/server model

Many networks are structured using the client/server model, in which individual computers and devices, called **nodes**, interact with one another through a central server to which they are all connected. The client/server model divides processing and storage tasks between the **client** and the **server**. The server is more powerful than the individual computers, or clients, connected to it. The server is responsible for storing and presenting information. The client/server model processes information as follows:

1. A client requests information from a shared file stored on the server.

2. The server processes the request, locates the requested information and sends the information to the client.

3. The client uses or processes the data as needed.

Figure 1-8 illustrates the client/server relationship.

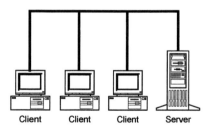

Figure 1-8: Client/server model

In a client/server environment, client programs run on the computer nodes and interact with a server program running on the server. The client software is the interface that enables users to communicate with and request information from the server. The client and server are able to communicate because they follow the same rules, or protocols, established for the client/server model. Therefore, a client can access information from any server if both the client and server understand the protocol.

A network can accommodate more than one server. Specific servers can be dedicated to making certain resources available to clients. These resources can include printers, applications and documents. Types of servers include:

- Network servers, which manage the flow of data between them and client nodes.

- Print servers, which manage network printers.

- File servers, which store shared data.

- Web servers, which manage access to the World Wide Web.

- E-mail servers, which manage electronic mail.

Client/server model example

E-mail is a technology that uses the client/server model. If you want to use e-mail, you must install and configure an e-mail client program on your computer. You can type an e-mail message, edit it repeatedly before sending it, and work offline until you are ready to access the network (or Internet) connection to send the message. When you send the message, the e-mail client computer connects to the network or Internet, transmits the message to an e-mail server, and closes the connection. The message recipient can connect to his or her e-mail server through a network or the Internet to retrieve the message.

LANs and WANs

The two main types of network structures are local area networks (LANs) and wide area networks (WANs).

Local area networks (LANs)

local area network (LAN)
A group of computers connected within a confined geographic area.

A **local area network (LAN)** is a group of computers connected within a confined geographic area. A LAN can consist of as few as two computers, or any number up to hundreds of computers and various types of servers. LANs are commonly used for intraoffice communication. They can extend over several yards or several miles, but are generally confined to one building or a group of buildings, such as a corporate office in Phoenix, Arizona, United States, for example.

It is often useful to connect one LAN to other LANs if different divisions or departments within a large business have their own LANs. By connecting the LANs to one another, the divisions or departments can communicate with each other to share data and resources.

Wide area networks (WANs)

wide area network (WAN)
A group of computers connected over an expansive geographic area so their users can share files and services.

A **wide area network (WAN)** consists of two or more LANs that span a wide geographic area. For example, a large business may have offices in several locations across the country or around the world. Each site has its own LAN with which to share resources and data locally, but it also needs to communicate with the other sites. By connecting the LANs via public networks (such as high-speed telephone lines, leased lines such as T1 lines, or satellites), the company creates a WAN. The largest WAN is the Internet.

In addition to geographic distance, the main difference between LANs and WANs is data transmission cost. In a LAN, the organization owns all components. In a WAN, an organization typically leases some of the necessary components needed to transmit data, such as high-speed telephone lines or wireless transmissions via microwave antennas and satellites.

Internet
A worldwide
network of
interconnected
networks.

Overview of the Internet

The **Internet** is a vast network of LANs and WANs that electronically connects millions of people worldwide. Every computer that connects to the Internet is (for the time that it is connected) part of the Internet. These LANs and WANs are able to communicate with each other because of standardized Internet guidelines and procedures, such as the use of Internet protocols and standard Internet addresses. Using the Internet, it is possible to "surf" the World Wide Web, use e-mail, and send real-time messages to friends using instant messaging and Internet Relay Chat (IRC) applications.

The Internet was formed in 1969 when the U.S. Department of Defense's **Advanced Research Projects Agency (ARPA)** funded what would become the first global computer network, the **Advanced Research Projects Agency Network (ARPANET)**. The ARPANET allowed university and government engineers to research and work from any location on the network. ARPANET's design featured multiple servers, or hosts, and multiple connections — in the form of telephone lines — among those servers. If one part of the network became incapacitated, other parts would remain functional, thereby reducing the chances of total network failure. Figure 1-9 illustrates ARPANET's decentralized design.

Advanced Research Projects Agency (ARPA)
A U.S. Department of Defense agency that created the first global computer network.

Advanced Research Projects Agency Network (ARPANET)
A computer network, funded by ARPA, that served as the basis for early networking research and was the backbone during the development of the Internet.

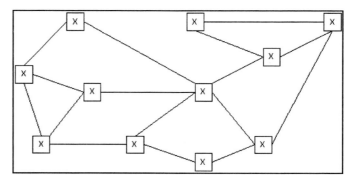

Figure 1-9: Multiple connections among servers

National Science Foundation (NSF)
An independent agency of the U.S. government that promotes the advancement of science and engineering.

In the late 1980s, the Department of Defense decommissioned the ARPANET, and all sites switched over to the **National Science Foundation (NSF)** network, called NSFnet. The NSF added access to more networks, expanding the range of sites to businesses, universities, and government and military installations. The connections among ARPANET, NSFnet and the other networks became what is now known as the Internet.

backbone
The highest level in the computer network hierarchy, to which smaller networks typically connect.

NSF did not permit users to conduct private (i.e., commercial) business over the NSFnet. As a result, private telecommunications companies developed their own high-speed data lines, called **backbones**, which used the same protocols as NSFnet and connected to it through **gateways**. These private networks did not restrict network use, so the Internet became usable for commercial purposes.

gateway
A node on a network that serves as a portal to other networks.

In the early 1990s, the Internet began to expand rapidly. Today it connects thousands of networks and hundreds of millions of users around the world. The Internet has no centralized control or ownership, which makes it available for anyone to access and use. Through the Internet, any computer can exchange data, e-mail and programs with potentially any other computer anywhere in the world.

The World Wide Web

World Wide Web (WWW)
A set of software programs that enables users to access resources on the Internet via hypertext documents.

The **World Wide Web (WWW)**, also called the Web for short, was created in 1989 at the European Particle Physics Laboratory in Geneva, Switzerland. The Web was designed to enable scientists studying high-energy physics to share information more efficiently by using hypertext documents. A hypertext document is created using Hypertext Markup Language (HTML), a system of code that enables the author to include **hypertext links** (also called hyperlinks or links) in documents.

hypertext link
Highlighted or underlined text in a Web page that, when clicked, links the user to another location or Web page.

Hyperlinks show as highlighted or underlined text in a hypertext document, or **Web page**. You can click a hyperlink and immediately move to another location in the same Web page or to another Web page that can reside anywhere on the Internet. Any Web page is a potential destination for a hyperlink. A collection of related Web pages is called a **Web site**. Web sites are located on Web servers, which are host computers on the Internet.

Web page
An HTML document containing one or more elements (text, images, hyperlinks) that can be linked to or from other HTML pages.

Unlike the Internet, the World Wide Web is not a network. The Web is a set of software programs that enables users to access resources on the Internet. However, the Web was used almost exclusively by scientific researchers until the introduction of Web browsers, whose graphical user interfaces (GUIs) made them easy to use.

Web site
A World Wide Web server and its content; includes multiple Web pages.

Web browsers

Web browsers (or browsers) are software applications that enable users to easily access, view and navigate Web pages on the Internet. Examples of Web browsers are Microsoft Internet Explorer, Netscape Navigator, and Opera.

Web browser
A software application that enables users to access and view Web pages on the Internet.

A browser displays the elements of a Web page according to the HTML code used to create the page. The HTML code provides the browser with information, such as:

- The fonts and font sizes used in the Web page.

- The location of the graphical, animated, audio or video content.

- The format for displaying graphical, animated, audio or video content.

- The location of hyperlinks.

- Other formatting elements such as content alignment, page and text color, and so forth.

A Web page may not appear the same in different browsers because each browser interprets HTML somewhat differently. For example, different browsers may use different default fonts and layouts, or support different table formatting commands.

Transmission Control Protocol/Internet Protocol (TCP/IP)
A suite of protocols that turns data into blocks of information called packets, which are then sent across the Internet. The standard protocol used by the Internet.

Web browsers often have more capabilities than simply reading HTML pages and downloading files. Web browsers often support additional Internet protocols, which are discussed in the following section.

How the Internet works

Every computer connected to the Internet uses a protocol called **Transmission Control Protocol/Internet Protocol (TCP/IP)**, which enables computers to communicate with one another. TCP enables two computers to establish a communication link and exchange **packets** of data; IP specifies the format and addressing scheme of the packets. Dissimilar systems can then communicate and exchange data provided that both use TCP/IP.

packet
Data processed by protocols so it can be sent across a network.

Most client computers are connected to the Internet through gateways, which connect their LANs to the Internet backbone. Thus, computers access information from the Internet in the following sequence:

You request data through your LAN from a server connected to the Internet.

1. The request is divided into packets of data.

2. The packets are routed through your LAN, and potentially through other networks, to the Internet backbone.

3. The packets are routed from the Internet backbone through one or more networks until they reach the destination server containing the requested information.

4. The destination server sends information in response to your request using the same process, although possibly following a different route.

router
A device that routes packets between networks based on network-layer address; determines the best path across a network. Also used to connect separate LANs to form a WAN.

Thus, your original request and the subsequent response may travel through several networks and servers, each forwarding the packets toward their final destination. Your software does not have a map of the entire Internet and does not know the route your transmission will take. In essence, all paths through the Internet lead to your destination. A network device called a **router** determines the best path across a network.

TCP/IP ensures that your information is transferred quickly and reliably. If a packet is lost, all your data is not re-sent; TCP/IP re-sends only the missing packet. The destination computer collects the packets and reassembles them into your original data.

If one of the connections, or routes, between two computers is not working, the nearby computers simply stop using that route until the connection is repaired. Routers recognize damaged connections and send data through other routes. The routing flexibility of TCP/IP software ensures an accurate and steady flow of information.

Connecting to the Internet

OBJECTIVE:
1.2.3: Internet client infrastructure

Six elements are required to connect to the Internet:

- **Computer** — PC, WebTV, mobile phone, Internet phone or handheld device

- **Operating system** — Windows XP Professional, Linux/UNIX, Macintosh, etc.

- **TCP/IP** — protocol software used to communicate with the Internet

- **Client software** — Web browser, e-mail or news client program

- **Internet connection** — dial-up or direct connection to an Internet Service Provider (ISP)

- **Internet address** — Web address (e.g., *www.CIWcertified.com*), e-mail address (e.g., *student1@class.com*) or server address (e.g., *ss1.prosofttraining*)

The first three items are generally acquired when you buy a computer. When you arrange to connect your computer to the Internet, you must install client software, implement a connection method, and identify the addresses of servers you can use. Within the business environment, the corporate IT department may set up your system for you. Because of the high cost of connecting directly to the Internet backbone, most businesses and individuals obtain access through ISPs, which provide the backbone connection. The ISP, in effect, acts as the gateway connecting your LAN to the Internet backbone.

If you are connecting your computer yourself, client software is available from ISPs. The installation CD-ROM that you receive from an ISP contains customized software, including Web browser, e-mail and news programs. ISPs also provide instructions for connecting to the Internet, and Internet addresses for configuring your client software.

The following sections will discuss ISPs, and dial-up and direct Internet connections.

Internet Service Providers (ISPs)

Internet Service Provider (ISP)
An organization that maintains a gateway to the Internet and rents access to customers on a per-use or subscription basis.

An **Internet Service Provider (ISP)** is an organization that provides access to the Internet, such as America Online (AOL) (*www.aol.com*), Microsoft Network (MSN) (*www.msn.com*) and many others. Many ISPs offer other online services in addition to Internet access and e-mail. For instance, when users log on to AOL, they access the self-contained network of AOL servers. AOL servers provide content exclusively to their users so users need not navigate the entire Internet. AOL can also filter Internet content to make it safer and more relevant for the intended audience. Most ISPs charge a flat monthly rate. Some basic-service ISPs offer Internet connectivity for free, such as NetZero (*www.netzero.net*) and Juno (*www.juno.com*) in the United States.

ISPs offer two principal options for connecting to the Internet: dial-up and direct. You must check with each ISP to see which connection types it offers.

Dial-up Internet connections

OBJECTIVE:
1.2.4: Hardware and software connection devices

modem
Abbreviation for modulator/demodulator. An analog device that enables computers to communicate over telephone lines by translating digital data into audio/analog signals (on the sending computer) and then back into digital form (on the receiving computer).

Many individual users connect to the Internet through telephone lines by using a **modem**, which is a device that enables computers to transmit data over standard analog telephone lines. A modem converts digital data from a computer into an analog signal to be transmitted through the telephone line to another modem. The receiving modem converts the analog signal back into digital code and transmits it to the receiving computer.

 The term modem is widely used, but does not always assume an analog-to-digital translation. For instance, DSL and ISDN modems (presented later in this lesson) are used on all-digital networks — no translation to analog is required. In this sense, DSL and ISDN modems are not actually modems. In many cases, the term modem has been used to describe any device that adapts a computer to a phone line or cable TV network, whether it is digital or analog. The term analog modem is often used to indicate a traditional modem.

You gain access to the Internet by dialing a phone number that connects your computer with an ISP, which in turn connects your computer to the Internet. When finished, you disconnect from the ISP. The speed with which you can access the Internet is determined primarily by the speed capability of the modem.

Integrated Services Digital Network (ISDN)
A communication standard for sending voice, video or data over digital telephone lines.

channel
The cable or signal between two network nodes that enables data transmission.

To gain faster dial-up connections, you can go through a local phone company to install an **Integrated Services Digital Network (ISDN)** line, which is a digital telephone line. The typical ISDN line is called an ISDN Basic Rate Interface (BRI) line. This type of ISDN line is often called a "two-B-plus-D line" because it provides two 64-Kbps B **channels** for use with data, as well as a 16-Kbps D channel that carries signaling and is used to manage the 64-Kbps lines. ISDN BRI lines were originally intended for home users and small businesses. The advent of cable and DSL services has mostly superseded ISDN in North America, whereas many countries in Europe still use ISDN. ISDN Primary Rate Interface (PRI) is another form of ISDN that is much more powerful. In North America, an ISDN PRI line provides 23 64-Kbps B channels (for use with data and/or voice), and one 64-Kbps D channel (to carry signaling). In Europe, ISDN PRI lines have 30 64-Kbps channels and one 64-Kbps D channel.

An ISDN "modem," which is technically not a modem but a digital terminal adapter, is attached to a computer that transfers data over the digital phone line. With an ISDN line, you can connect a computer, telephone and fax machine into a single line and use them simultaneously.

 Connectivity speeds are measured in bits per second (bps). A thousand bits per second is referred to as kilobits per second (Kbps). A million bits per second is referred to as megabits per second (Mbps).

Table 1-1 lists common speeds for dial-up connections.

Table 1-1: Common speeds for dial-up Internet connections

Speed	Description
128 Kbps	Two 64-Kbps ISDN BRI channels combined to increase the connection speed
64 Kbps	Typical ISDN BRI speed
56 Kbps	Fastest theoretical dial-up speed available using an analog modem
33.6 Kbps	Moderately fast dial-up modem speed
28.8 Kbps	Standard dial-up modem speed in the mid-1990s
14.4 Kbps	Moderately slow dial-up modem speed; may not support streaming audio and video

The least expensive method of obtaining access to the Internet is to use existing standard phone lines and an analog modem, which connects to an ISP that serves your area.

WebTV also utilizes dial-up connections to access the Internet. Even though a WebTV box rests on your television and uses your television as the monitor, it usually uses an analog modem and a standard phone line to connect to the Internet.

Direct Internet connections

OBJECTIVE:
1.2.4: Hardware and software connection devices

1.2.5: Cable/ADSL and wireless connections

1.3.2: Internet bandwidth technologies

bandwidth
The amount of information, sometimes called traffic, that can be carried on a network at one time. The total capacity of a line. Also, the rate of data transfer over a network connection; measured in bits per second.

Direct connections provide continuous access to the Internet through permanent network connections. Unlike dial-up connections, direct connections do not require activation for each usage period. Direct connections are convenient and fast because permanent network connections are generally capable of handling high **bandwidth**.

Direct connections can be obtained in a number of ways: high-speed data links, wireless connections, T and E carriers, fractional T and E lines, LAN connections, cable modems and Digital Subscriber Lines (DSLs), which will be discussed shortly. If your company's network is connected to the Internet, or you have a cable or DSL modem installed, then your computer has a direct connection to the Internet.

High-speed data links
Analog modem capacity is limited to a data transfer rate of 56 Kbps, the maximum theoretical data transfer rate of a standard telephone line. Although analog modems are sufficient to transmit text, they are impractical for transmitting large audio and video files. Telephone companies, cable TV services and other suppliers provide high-speed data links, such as fiber-optic cables and wireless connections, that offer faster Internet connections than those provided by analog modems.

Wireless connections

Wireless network connections are usually implemented in a hybrid environment, in which wireless components communicate with a network that uses cables. For example, a laptop computer may use its wireless capabilities to connect with a corporate LAN that uses standard cabling.

The only difference between a wireless network and a cabled network is the medium itself; wireless systems use wireless signals (high-frequency radio waves) instead of a network cable. A standard system that uses a wireless **network interface card (NIC)** is called an end point. Two types of wireless modes exist:

- **Ad-hoc** — wireless mode in which systems use only their NICs to connect with each other

- **Infrastructure** — wireless mode in which systems connect via a centralized access point, called a wireless access point (WAP)

A **wireless access point (WAP)** is a device that enables wireless systems to communicate with each other, provided that they are on the same network.

The 802.11 **standard**, developed by the Institute of Electrical and Electronics Engineers (IEEE), refers to a family of specifications for wireless network technology. The 802.11 standard includes 802.11a, 802.11b and 802.11g. The 802.11b standard is the most common type of wireless network, and usually operates at speeds between 5.5 Mbps and 11 Mbps, though some can reach speeds of up to 20 Mbps. The 802.11b networks are often called "WiFi" (Wireless Fidelity) networks, and support common Ethernet networks (Ethernet is a LAN standard that allows computers in a network to communicate). The 802.11b networks operate at the 2-gigahertz (GHz) range, the same level as common wireless 2-GHz phones and other devices, and are subject to interference.

The 802.11a networks are capable of reaching speeds up to 54 Mbps. Although the 802.11a standard also uses Ethernet, it is not compatible with the 802.11b standard because 802.11a operates in the range of 5 GHz to 6 GHz. The 802.11a wireless networks are often used to connect municipal networks and large campuses. The 802.11g standard also operates at 54 Mbps, but is compatible with 802.11b networks, making 802.11g a popular alternative to 802.11b in home and office networks.

T and E carriers

T carriers refer to T1 and T3 lines, which are dedicated digital telephone lines that have much greater bandwidths than ISDN lines. T1 lines can transmit data at 1.544 Mbps, and T3 lines can transmit data at 44.736 Mbps. Many businesses lease T1 lines from phone companies to connect to ISPs. The ISPs use T3 lines to connect to the Internet backbone, which is composed of T3 lines.

E carriers refer to E1 and E3 lines, which are the European equivalents of T1 and T3 lines, respectively. E1 lines can transmit data at 2.048 Mbps, and E3 lines can transmit data at 34.368 Mbps.

Fractional T and E lines

T and E carriers consist of channels, or transmission paths. Each channel is capable of supporting 64 Kbps. A T1 line consists of 24 channels, and a T3 line consists of 672 channels. Most telephone companies will allow you to purchase one or a number of these individual channels, rather than the entire T1 or T3 line. The resulting line is known as a fractional T1 or fractional T3 line. Likewise, in Europe, you can purchase fractional E1 and E3 lines.

Fractional T and E lines provide less bandwidth than their undivided counterparts, but are much less expensive to purchase.

LAN connections

A LAN can be connected to the Internet by a router, provided that the LAN uses TCP/IP. The LAN router is connected to another router at the ISP by a high-speed data link. The line between the LAN and the ISP is leased monthly, and can cost from US$250 or less per month for a small-business connection to $40,000 or more per month for a large corporation, depending on the speed and the amount of traffic. If LANs do not use TCP/IP, they can be connected to the Internet by gateways, which convert the protocol used by a LAN to and from TCP/IP.

Cable modems

Cable television systems use coaxial cables, which can transmit data and streaming audio and video images at much faster speeds than are possible using standard telephone lines. You can connect to the Internet through your cable TV system by attaching a cable modem to the computer's NIC and to a cable television outlet. By so doing, the computer becomes connected to the cable TV system's Internet server, which is in turn connected to the Internet backbone.

Another option you can use to connect to the Internet is cable Internet. Cable Internet is a technology that uses your television as the monitor by connecting your TV to the Internet with an enhanced set-top cable box. The cable box accesses the Internet through the cable TV line.

Digital Subscriber Line (DSL)

Digital Subscriber Line (DSL)
A high-speed direct Internet connection that uses all-digital networks.

xDSL
Collectively, the variations of Digital Subscriber Line (DSL), which include ADSL, RADSL and HDSL.

Another direct connection method is **Digital Subscriber Line (DSL)**, a high-speed connection that uses digital phone lines and an xDSL modem. Several variations of the DSL modem exist, hence the term **xDSL**. Some of the more popular versions include Asymmetric Digital Subscriber Line (ADSL), which is used primarily in homes and small businesses. Rate-Adaptive DSL (RADSL) is a version of ADSL that allows the transmission rate to vary depending on your phone line capabilities. High-bit-rate Digital Subscriber Line (HDSL) was the original version of DSL. It was used for wideband digital transmissions between the phone company and a customer, as well as within large corporations. DSL is similar to but much faster than ISDN, with speeds up to 10 Mbps.

You must check whether your local phone company supports xDSL. If so, its technicians may need to visit your location to install xDSL, depending on the type it offers. You will also need an xDSL modem and possibly a NIC to attach your computer to the xDSL modem. xDSL may eventually replace ISDN; it also competes directly with cable modems.

Cable modem and DSL limitations

Both cable modem and DSL connections are subject to various limitations, as follows:

*   **Service limitations** — Your connection speed may be limited, depending upon the type of plan you purchased. With cable modems, connection speeds often become slower when many people are online. For example, some cable customers perceive a significant slowdown in access during peak hours (for example, between 5 and 8 p.m.).

*   **Upload and download limitations** — DSL and cable modems often have different upload and download speeds. Upload speeds are generally slower than download speeds. Typically, download speeds range from 512 Kbps to 1.544 Mbps, and upload speeds are about 128 Kbps. Providers of high-speed Internet service assume that most home and small-business users download far more than they upload. Usually,

uploading is used only to establish and maintain connections. Therefore, larger businesses may need to upload files more often.

Upload connections are often called upstream connections, and download connections are often called downstream connections.

Direct connection speeds

Transmission speeds can vary greatly for direct connections based on distance, wire and equipment type, ISP capabilities, and so forth. Table 1-2 lists the connection speeds associated with direct connections.

Table 1-2: Common speeds for direct Internet connections

Connection Type	Speed
Fiber-optic cable	Up to 100 Gbps.
T3 line	44.736 Mbps. Commonly used by North American ISPs to connect to the Internet backbone. Extremely fast and one of the most costly types of access.
E3 line	34.368 Mbps. European equivalent of T3.
T1 line	1.544 Mbps. Commonly used by North American corporate LANs to connect to ISPs.
E1 line	2.048 Mbps. European equivalent of T1.
Cable modem	512 Kbps to 52 Mbps.
xDSL modem	512 Kbps to 32 Mbps.

Cable and xDSL modems are usually limited to 10 Mbps because of the NIC. Only ISPs are capable of achieving the maximum rates. Also, many cable modems must share the cable network with other users in their neighborhoods. The speed of the cable modem depends on how many users are online at a given time. Likewise, the speed of an xDSL modem depends on the distance between the xDSL modem and the phone company's main distribution frame. Speeds less than 512 Kbps are common on both cable and xDSL modems.

Connecting cable and DSL modems

When connecting a home office or small business to the Internet using a cable or DSL modem, you will need the following equipment:

- **A modem** — This modem is actually a router that connects your home computer or network to the Internet. The ISP offering digital access to the Internet often supplies this modem. You can purchase or rent the modem from the ISP. You can also purchase your own router at a store. However, make sure that this router is compatible with your ISP's network.

- **Network cables** — If you are using a DSL modem, you will use two standard Ethernet cables (for example, a category 5, 5e or 6 cable) with RJ-45 connectors. An RJ-45 connector is similar to a standard North American telephone cable connector (an RJ-11), but the RJ-45 is larger. You will attach one cable from the wall of your home to the modem, and attach another cable from the modem to your computer. If you are using a cable modem, you will attach a coaxial cable from the wall to the modem, then connect a computer to the modem using a standard networking cable (for example, a category 5 cable).

It is also possible to obtain equipment that combines wireless connections with modems that are compatible with your ISP. In these cases, you must also equip each of your computers with a wireless NIC, or connect your wireless router to a hub.

Movie Time!

Insert the CIW Foundations Movie CD to learn even more about this topic.

Introduction to the Internet (approx. playing time: 06:00)

All movie clips are © 2004 LearnKey, Inc.

Internet Protocols

Internet Protocol (IP)
The data transmission standard for the Internet. Every computer connected to the Internet has its own IP address, which enables a packet of data to be delivered to a specific computer.

Protocols are the rules that describe how clients and servers communicate across a network. Protocols are similar in concept to the rules of diplomatic interaction that dictate who speaks first, who bows to whom, and so forth. **Internet Protocol (IP)** is the protocol by which data is sent from one computer to another on the Internet. Each computer on the Internet has at least one IP address that uniquely identifies it from all other computers on the Internet. When you send or receive data on the Internet (for example, when you send or receive an e-mail message or retrieve information from a Web site), the Internet gateways route the packets of information from your source address to the destination address.

In the following sections, you will examine the standard protocols used in network and Internet communication.

Internet Protocol version 4 (IPv4)

OBJECTIVE:
1.2.2: Internet history and protocols

1.4.5: Internet addresses

The creators of the Internet recognized the need for a flexible addressing system powerful enough to accommodate the enormous number of current and future users. They decided that every device on the Internet would be given an IP address, just as every house and business is given a street address. Instead of a street address format, such as 123 Main Street, a 32-bit address format is used, such as the following:

12.42.192.73

This IP address format is also referred to as a "dotted quad" because the series of numbers is divided into four segments, each separated by a period, or dot. Each segment is a number between 0 and 255. Some number values are reserved, but roughly 256 x 256 x 256 x 256 different IP addresses are possible — approximately 4 billion. Nevertheless, the current supply of IP addresses will eventually be depleted because IP address demand continues to increase. The most widely used version of IP today is Internet Protocol version 4 (IPv4), which supports the dotted quad IP address format.

In an IP address, the first set of numbers on the left represents the largest network. As you move from left to right, the networks get smaller and more specific. The last number in the address (on the far right) identifies the specific computer.

Using your computer to connect to others on the Internet is similar to using your telephone to connect to other telephones through the phone system. You need not know how a signal goes through switching systems in order to connect to the person you want to reach; you need only dial the correct set of numbers. Similarly, when you use the

Internet, you need not know how the networks connect; you only need a computer's IP address to connect to it.

Internet Protocol version 6 (IPv6)

OBJECTIVE:
1.2.2: Internet history and protocols

1.4.5: Internet addresses

hexadecimal
A base-16 number system that allows large numbers to be displayed by fewer characters than if the number were displayed in the regular base-10 system. In hexadecimal, the number 10 is represented as the letter A, 15 is represented as F, and 16 is represented as 10.

Work is under way to improve TCP/IP so it can handle the phenomenal growth that the Internet is experiencing. Internet Protocol version 6 (IPv6), also known as Internet Protocol Next Generation (IPng), will meet the increasing demand for IP addresses.

IPv6 supports approximately 4 trillion IP addresses by using a 128-bit address format. This format uses **hexadecimal** numbers instead of decimals. Following is an example of an IPv6 address:

    2E22:4F00:000E:00D0:A267:97FF:FE6B:FE34

In addition to solving IP address shortages, IPv6 is more efficient and requires less overhead than IPv4 because it uses routers more efficiently.

IPv6 is now included as part of IP support in many products, including major computer operating systems such as Microsoft Windows XP. IPv6 is expected to gradually replace IPv4, with the two coexisting for a number of years during a transition period. Any server that can support IPv6 packets can also support IPv4 packets.

Remote access protocols

OBJECTIVE:
1.3.1: Remote access protocols

Point-to-Point Protocol (PPP)
A protocol that allows a computer to connect to the Internet over a phone line.

Point-to-Point Protocol over Ethernet (PPPoE)
A protocol that implements PPP over Ethernet to connect an entire network to the Internet.

Remote access protocols refer to dial-up and direct Internet connections that you can establish from a remote computer, such as your PC, and that can operate independently of a network or the Internet.

When you use a phone line and modem to connect to the Internet, you are using a dial-up connection. Most dial-up connections use **Point-to-Point Protocol (PPP)**. Multilink Point-to-Point Protocol (MLPPP) can be used to combine two PPP connections into one, thereby enabling a higher transmission speed.

Many direct Internet connections, such as LAN, cable modem and DSL connections, are established using **Point-to-Point Protocol over Ethernet (PPPoE)**. PPPoE uses the PPP that is commonly used for dial-up networks and implements it over Ethernet. Ethernet is a LAN standard that allows computers in a network to communicate. Therefore, PPPoE can connect an entire network to the Internet. PPPoE is also used by cable modem and DSL ISPs. The protocol uses the same methods as PPP; however, it allows the point-to-point connection to establish itself on the Ethernet architecture, allowing much faster connection speeds.

Hypertext Transfer Protocol (HTTP)

OBJECTIVE:
1.3.3: Protocols for business services

Hypertext Transfer Protocol (HTTP)
The protocol for transporting HTML documents across the Internet.

Hypertext Transfer Protocol (HTTP) is the protocol used to transfer Web pages from a Web server to a Web client, usually a Web browser. Specifically, HTTP is the set of rules required to exchange files, such as text, images, video and multimedia content, across the Web. An essential concept of HTTP is that files contain references to other files, so they are linked to one another. HTTP transfers HTML files and other file formats that it can serve. Web servers are often called HTTP servers. HTTP requires a client program on one end (a browser) and a server on the other, both running TCP/IP.

HTTPS is a secured version of HTTP used to transfer Web pages from a secure Web server to a Web client. When you use HTTPS, your Web session is managed by a security protocol, which encrypts and decrypts your requests as well as the information that is returned by the Web server. You will learn more about HTTPS later in this course.

File Transfer Protocol (FTP)

OBJECTIVE:
1.3.3: Protocols for
business services

**File Transfer Protocol
(FTP)**
An Internet protocol
used to transfer files
between
computers.

File Transfer Protocol (FTP) is a TCP/IP suite protocol that enables the transfer of files between two computers on the Internet. Some sites allow guests to transfer files without an account on the remote site. These sites are called anonymous FTP sites and are available to the public. To obtain access to files through an anonymous FTP server, you use the general user ID "anonymous" and provide your e-mail address as the password. Many major universities have reliable anonymous FTP servers on the Internet. Most business FTP servers require user names and passwords because the data is confidential.

Businesses have discovered many uses for FTP servers as efficient information access and distribution points. For instance, when you download software programs and documents from Web sites, you are usually transferred to FTP sites for the download. This process takes place transparently (that is, the user is unaware of the protocol that is downloading the program). FTP is also used to publish Web pages to a Web server. You simply upload your Web page files to an FTP server. After the upload is complete, Web browsers using HTTP can access your Web pages.

Files on FTP sites can include text, graphics or software. Often, a site index lists the site's available files. Unlike the Web, where you browse for information as you move from one Web page to another, FTP sites are organized by topic. Navigating an FTP site is similar to navigating a hard drive's directory structure. You start at the top by selecting a directory name close to your general topic. You then continue to select directory names that are more specific to the topic you are seeking, until you find the file you want. This navigation process may take you many levels into an FTP server's hard drive. Most FTP servers are structured similarly, and when you become familiar with FTP servers, navigating their contents becomes easy.

Electronic mail (e-mail) protocols

OBJECTIVE:
1.3.3: Protocols for
business services

**Simple Mail Transfer
Protocol (SMTP)**
The Internet
standard protocol
for transferring
e-mail messages
from one computer
to another.

**Post Office Protocol
(POP)**
A protocol that
resides on an
incoming mail
server. The current
version is POP3.

**Internet Message
Access Protocol
(IMAP)**
A protocol that
resides on an
incoming mail
server. Similar to
POP, but is more
powerful. Allows
sharing of mailboxes
and multiple mail
server access. The
current version is
IMAP4.

E-mail involves two mail servers: outgoing and incoming. The outgoing and incoming servers use various protocols to handle sending, receiving and storing e-mail messages.

You send e-mail to others with an outgoing server using **Simple Mail Transfer Protocol (SMTP)**. SMTP is the Internet standard protocol for transferring e-mail messages from one computer to another. It specifies how two e-mail systems interact. SMTP is responsible solely for sending e-mail messages, and is part of the TCP/IP suite.

You receive mail from an incoming mail server using **Post Office Protocol (POP)** or **Internet Message Access Protocol (IMAP)**. POP and IMAP are used to store and access e-mail messages.

The current version of POP is version 3 (POP3). POP3 stores incoming e-mail until users authenticate and download it. POP3 is the more accepted and widely used protocol for receiving and managing e-mail. POP3 servers store and forward e-mail messages to the host. For example, if you were to send an e-mail message, the message would be stored in the appropriate mail server until the recipient downloaded it from the server. The POP3 server responds to a request, asks for a password, then forwards the messages immediately.

The current version of IMAP is version 4 (IMAP4). IMAP4 handles messages in a more sophisticated manner than POP3 because it allows you to browse and manage e-mail messages while they reside on the server. A POP3 server forces you to download e-mail messages before reading, deleting or otherwise managing them.

You can use separate servers for outgoing and incoming e-mail, or a single server for both tasks. You need an account and password to receive e-mail, and tightened Internet security measures now require an account and password to send it as well. Internet creators thought that e-mail would be a minor tool and were amazed that it immediately became the primary source of Internet traffic.

Network News Transfer Protocol (NNTP)

Usenet (User Network) is a public-access worldwide network to which users can submit messages or notes about any conceivable subject. Usenet consists of newsgroups and mailing lists, which are organized into topics. Usenet can be accessed from various Internet sources such as Web pages or Usenet readers. Usenet has no central moderator; it is a cooperative environment.

A **newsgroup** is a group of messages about a particular subject that is posted to a central Internet site (a news server) and redistributed through Usenet. A news server uses the **Network News Transfer Protocol (NNTP)**. Like an e-mail server, a news server provides text output that users can access at their convenience. However, like a conference call, it has multi-person input, allowing users to post information in an easily accessible location. Web browsers, such as Netscape Navigator, Microsoft Internet Explorer and Opera, include an NNTP client. You may also use a separate client program called a newsreader, such as Knews, to access a news server.

Newsgroup articles are generally unofficial, rapidly updated and informal. They tend to provide timely, significant and often spirited information. They do not usually discuss current news events. They tend to be focused on goods and services, events, people, pets, topics, concepts, ideas, and so forth. Newsgroups are usually excellent informal sources of information. Because users participate by choice, newsgroups tend to be tightly focused and the data tends to be reliable.

You can think of a newsgroup as a vast e-mail system in which everyone has access to all messages. Unlike e-mail, which sends messages to your computer from a server, newsgroup messages remain on the server so everyone can see them. Newsgroup participants exchange views and ideas by writing messages that are transmitted automatically to news servers in the network. Articles posted to news servers can be read by anyone who can access the network.

Domain Name System (DNS)

To access any resource on the Internet (for example, a Web or FTP server), you must enter its address in the client (for example, a Web browser or FTP application). One way to do this is to provide the IP address. However, IP addresses can be difficult to remember because they consist of a series of numbers separated by periods. The **Domain Name System (DNS)** remedies this problem.

DNS resolves IP addresses into easily recognizable text-based names. For example, you can access the CIW Web server at IP address 12.42.192.73 by typing *www.CIWcertified.com* in your browser's Address box. In other words:

12.42.192.73 = *www.CIWcertified.com*

OBJECTIVE:
1.3.3: Protocols for business services

Usenet (User Network)
A collection of thousands of Internet computers, newsgroups, and newsgroup members using Network News Transfer Protocol (NNTP) to exchange information.

newsgroup
On Usenet, a subject or other topical interest group whose members exchange ideas and opinions. Participants post and receive messages via a news server.

Network News Transfer Protocol (NNTP)
The Internet protocol used by news servers that enables the exchange of Usenet articles.

OBJECTIVE:
1.4.1: Purpose of DNS

1.4.5: Internet addresses

Domain Name System (DNS)
A system that maps uniquely hierarchical names to specific Internet addresses.

Both the domain name and the IP address refer to the same resource (for example, an FTP or Web server), but the domain name is much easier to remember. Without DNS, users would be forced to enter IP addresses every time access was needed to any resource on the Internet.

One way to remember a domain name is to understand its structure, which can reveal information about the site. Businesses choose their domain names carefully so other businesses and users will be able to recall them.

Each domain name is unique and registered with the Internet Corporation for Assigned Names and Numbers (ICANN). When a name within a domain category (such as .com) is assigned, no other organization or individual can use that name within that category. For example, no other Web server can use *CIWcertified.com*. However, *CIWcertified.org* is still available, as is *CIWcertified.net*.

Figure 1-10 shows a domain name, which consists of letters (and numbers) separated by periods. A domain name usually indicates the server name, the registered company domain name and the domain category, also called a top-level domain.

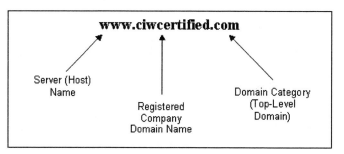

Figure 1-10: Typical domain name

 It is possible for DNS to use protocols other than TCP/IP. Additional protocols include IPX/SPX. However, DNS is most often used with TCP/IP.

OBJECTIVE:
1.4.3: Hierarchical
DNS structure

Domain name syntax

A domain name, read right to left, signifies general divisions, then specific companies, then departments within the company and even individual computers (such as a Web server or an e-mail server). For example, reading right to left, the domain name *www.CIWcertified.com* can be interpreted as follows:

- **com** — a commercial site

- **CIWcertified** — the name registered by the company that manages the CIW program, chosen because it accurately represents the purpose of the Web site

host
A computer that other computers can use to gain information; in network architecture, a host is a client or workstation.

- **www** — the name of the Web server at the company, also called the Web site **host**

Some companies further subdivide their domain names into departments or individual computers. For example, if a company wants to divide the domain *companyname.com* by department, it might use *finance.companyname.com* and *sales.companyname.com*. Or it might use *tokyo.companyname.com* and *london.companyname.com*, dividing by geography. For example, *www.research.microsoft.com* can be interpreted as follows:

- **com** — a commercial site

- **microsoft** — Microsoft Corporation

- **research** — the research division of Microsoft

- **www** — Web site host for the research division

Some sites name each computer on the LAN and give each a unique domain name, such as *sales1.companyname.com*, *sales2.companyname.com*, and so forth.

Fully qualified domain names (FQDN)

fully qualified domain name (FQDN)
The complete domain name of an Internet computer, such as *www.CIWcertified. com*.

A **fully qualified domain name (FQDN)** is the complete domain name of an Internet computer. The FQDN provides enough information to convert the domain name to an IP address. For instance, *www.CIWcertified.com* is an FQDN. The FQDN must include the server (host) name, the registered domain name and the top-level domain.

Root-level servers

root-level server
A server at the highest level of the Domain Name System.

The Domain Name System is hierarchical. **Root-level servers** are at the highest level of the Domain Name System. They provide foundational naming services; if these servers were to become unavailable, then name resolution would no longer occur. To learn more about root-level servers, visit *www.ripe.net.*

OBJECTIVE:
1.4.2: Internet domain names

Top-level domains

top-level domain
The group into which a domain is categorized, by common topic (company, educational institution) and/or geography (country, state).

The right-side component of a domain name categorizes domains into groups by common type (company, educational institution) or geography (country, state). These categories are called **top-level domains**. The original top-level domains categorize domains by common type and signify the type of site you are visiting. These original top-level domains are as follows:

- **com** — commercial or company sites

- **edu** — educational institutions, typically universities

- **org** — organizations; originally clubs, associations and nonprofit groups; currently various types of organizations

- **mil** — U.S. military

- **gov** — U.S. civilian government

- **net** — network sites, including ISPs

- **int** — international organizations (rarely used)

Other top-level domain names use a two-letter abbreviation to indicate states and countries. These domain names often correspond to postal codes. Examples of geographic domain names include the following:

- **au** — Australia

- **ca** — Canada

- **ch** — Switzerland (Confédération Helvétique)

- **dk** — Denmark

- **fr** — France

- **gr** — Greece

- **jp** — Japan

- **mx** — Mexico

- **uk** — United Kingdom

- **us** — United States

Domain names that end with country codes may feature categories or further geographical divisions before the company or organization name. For example, commercial sites in Australia all have domain names that end with *.com.au*, and university sites use *.edu.au* for their domain names.

Other countries use other abbreviations. In the United Kingdom, names ending with *.ac.uk* are universities (ac stands for academic), and names ending in *.co.uk* are companies. In Canada, many names feature province abbreviations such as *.on.ca* or *.mb.ca* (for Ontario and Manitoba, respectively). Reading from right to left, you will eventually reach the organization name.

Additional domain categories were selected in the year 2000. They are categorized by topic and include the following:

- **aero** — travel industry

- **biz** — businesses

- **coop** — cooperatives

- **info** — content and research-related sites

- **museum** — museums

- **name** — personal Web addresses

- **pro** — professional

In the following lab, you will use IP addresses and DNS to access different hosts on the Internet. Suppose that you are a help desk technician and you have been asked to teach new sales interns some techniques they can use to access Web sites. You show the interns how to access Web sites using various protocols, IP addresses and domain names. Note the differences in domain name syntax as you visit different servers and server types.

 Lab 1-3: Using Internet protocols in Microsoft Internet Explorer

In this lab, you will use Internet protocols in the Microsoft Internet Explorer browser.

1. Select **Start | All Programs | Internet Explorer** to start the Internet Explorer browser.

2. Click anywhere in the **Address** box at the top of the browser window to select the text.

3. Type *www.CIWcertified.com*, then press **ENTER**. This step accesses the CIW Web site and displays its home page in the browser window, as shown in Figure 1-11.

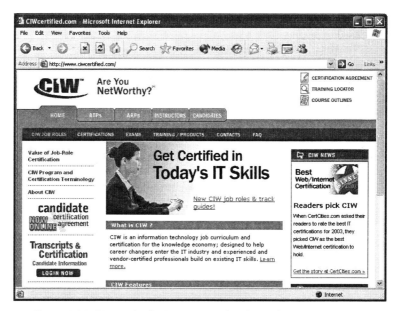

Figure 1-11: CIW Web site home page in Microsoft Internet Explorer

4. In the browser toolbar, click the **Home** button to display the browser's default Web site.

   Note: The Home button in the browser toolbar displays the browser's specified default Web site, not the home page of the site you are visiting.

5. Click anywhere in the **Address** box, type *12.42.192.73*, then press **ENTER**. This step also accesses the CIW Web site and displays its home page in the browser window.

6. Click anywhere in the **Address** box, type *www.research.microsoft.com*, then press **ENTER**. This step accesses Microsoft Corporation's research division Web site.

7. Click anywhere in the **Address** box, type *www.icann.org*, then press **ENTER**. This step accesses the ICANN Web site.

8. Click anywhere in the **Address** box, type *ftp://ss1.prosofttraining.com*, then press **ENTER**. This step accesses the CIW FTP site, which you can use to transfer files between it and your computer.

9. Form teams of two people each with your classmates.

10. **Partner A:** Go to *www.microsoft.com* and learn about the newest operating systems sold by Microsoft.

11. **Partner B:** Go to *www.redhat.com* and *www.sun.com* to learn about UNIX-based operating systems.

12. **Both partners:** Go to *http://dnsmon.ripe.net/dns-servmon* and review the statistics about the root DNS servers that exist on the Internet.

13. Close the **Internet Explorer** window.

Domain name servers

OBJECTIVE:
1.4.4: Domain name
server roles

**domain name
server**
A server that
resolves domain
names into IP
addresses.

Domain name servers are servers on the Internet whose sole function is to resolve human-readable domain names into their computer-readable IP addresses. For example, when you enter *www.CIWcertified.com* into your browser's Address box, the browser contacts a domain name server to obtain the IP address related to this domain name. When the browser receives the IP address 12.42.192.73 from the domain name server, the CIW Web site displays on your screen.

Reverse DNS

Domain name servers can also be programmed to resolve IP addresses into domain names. This function is called reverse Domain Name System (reverse DNS).

Virtual and shared domains

virtual domain
A hosting service
that allows a
company to host its
domain name on a
third-party ISP
server.

A **virtual domain** is a hosting service in which one domain name server hosts multiple domain names. For example, if you register your domain name *yourcompany.com*, users can enter *www.yourcompany.com* to access your site, even if your Web site is hosted by a third-party ISP whose domain name is *webserver.com*. Users enter only your domain name, not the domain name of the third party.

If you hosted your Web site with a third-party ISP using a non-virtual domain, you would not need to register your company's domain name. Instead, users might access your site at *www.webserver.com/yourcompany*.

OBJECTIVE:
1.4.6: Shared
domains

A virtual domain allows your Web address to be shorter. It also gives your company the prestige of its own Web address for branding purposes, even though a third party is hosting your Web site.

shared domain
A hosting service
that allows multiple
entities to share
portions of the same
domain name.

Rather than a single domain name server hosting multiple domain names, a **shared domain** occurs when multiple companies, organizations or people share portions of the same domain name. Multiple entities can use your registered domain name *.yourcompany.com* as their domain name as long as you elect to sell the domain name and make it available to others. For example, you could sell the domain name *company1.yourcompany.com* to company1, the domain name *company2.yourcompany.com* to company2, and so forth. The Web sites for each respective company would then be hosted by the *.yourcompany.com* domain.

Case Study
Improving a Company Web Site

Suzanne is the newly hired Web site designer for a scientific organization that conducts seismic research about "hot spots" worldwide. The organization was formed only recently; its Web site was hurriedly developed by an outside contractor and contains only rudimentary information about the organization. The organization's sponsors have asked Suzanne to make the Web site more informative and appealing to viewers.

Suzanne decides to upgrade the Web site by performing the following tasks:

* She adds introductory text and diagrams about the science of seismology and other geophysical processes to illustrate how scientists study earthquakes, volcanoes and the earth's mantle.

* She uploads and creates links to photographs of the most visually stunning hot spots around the world, such as those in Yellowstone National Park in the United States; the mid-Atlantic ridge; Iceland; Hawaii; and so forth.

* She uploads and creates links to scientific papers and studies conducted by the resident team of seismologists.

* * *

As a class, discuss other improvements Suzanne can make to the Web site to increase viewer interest and provide additional information. Because few people have in-depth knowledge about seismology, the Web site should be as visually interesting and informative as possible. What design elements would you incorporate to achieve this goal?

Lesson Summary

Application project

Consider the following situations, and compare your solutions to those of your classmates.

- The Internet is composed of many systems that are connected using the client/server architecture. What other computer interactions occur during your business day that might use client/server architecture?

- A friend needs your assistance connecting to the Internet. She uses a Windows XP computer at home with a modem and a standard analog phone line. Determine the connection type she should use and suggest several ISPs she could use.

- You are hired by a nonprofit organization that promotes cultural exchanges among youths from countries that are politically estranged from one another. The organization wants you to establish a domain name and create a Web site. Determine a domain name and the domain name category that will best suit your customer.

Skills review

In this lesson, you learned about the responsibilities, tasks and skills required for various job roles in the Information Technology (IT) industry.

You learned about networks, the client/server network model, and the differences between LANs and WANs. You also learned about the history of the Internet, the difference between the Internet and the World Wide Web, and the way the Internet works.

You learned about the elements required to connect to the Internet, Internet Service Providers (ISPs), and how to connect to the Internet through dial-up and direct connections.

You learned about Internet protocols such as IPv4, IPv6, PPP, PPPoE, HTTP, HTTPS, FTP, SMTP, POP, IMAP and NNTP, and about the business services to which they refer. You also learned about the Domain Name System (DNS), the hierarchical structure of DNS, top-level domains, domain name servers, and virtual and shared domains.

Now that you have completed this lesson, you should be able to:

✓ Define Information Technology (IT) job roles.

✓ Define networks.

✓ Define the Internet.

✓ Identify Internet connection methods.

✓ Define Internet protocols.

✓ Define the Domain Name System (DNS).

Lesson 1 Review

1. What IT job role would most likely be responsible for managing and maintaining a network infrastructure?

   _____

2. What term describes a group of two or more computers connected so that they can communicate, share resources and exchange information?

   _____

3. Briefly describe the client/server model.

   _____

   _____

4. What is the difference between a local area network (LAN) and a wide area network (WAN)?

   _____

   _____

5. What is the difference between the Internet and the World Wide Web?

   _____

   _____

   _____

6. What is the difference between an Integrated Services Digital Network (ISDN) line and a Digital Subscriber Line (DSL)?

   _____

   _____

   _____

7. Describe the difference between a dial-up Internet connection and a direct Internet connection.

   _____

   _____

   _____

8. Why are IP addresses also called dotted quads?

   _____

   _____

   _____

9. What is the function of Hypertext Transfer Protocol (HTTP)?

    _____

    _____

10. How are domain names structured?

    _____

    _____

    _____

11. How are domain names resolved to IP addresses?

    _____

    _____

    _____

    _____

Lesson 2:
Web Browsing

Objectives

By the end of this lesson, you will be able to:

- ✿ Identify the basic functions of Web browsers.
- ✿ Install a Web browser.
- ✿ Identify the components of Web addresses.
- ✿ Use browsers to authenticate and encrypt.
- ✿ Identify considerations in selecting a browser.
- ✿ Identify and locate resources for technical data.
- ✿ Identify how businesses use browsers.
- ✿ Use various browsing techniques.
- ✿ Configure Web browser preferences.
- ✿ Define and use cookies.
- ✿ Configure browser security settings.
- ✿ Identify the function of proxy servers.
- ✿ Troubleshoot common Internet client problems.

Pre-Assessment Questions

1. If you disable image loading in a browser, then:

   a. Web pages load in text mode only.
   b. Web pages download more slowly.
   c. you can view Web pages without storing them in a disk cache.
   d. it is impossible to accept cookies from a Web site.

2. What is a cookie?

   a. A harmful piece of code
   b. A helper application
   c. A published privacy policy
   d. A small text file

3. How can you ensure that you are viewing the latest information on a Web page?

Introduction to Web Browsing

Web browsing is the process of viewing Web pages over the Internet. Millions of people browse the Web every day for research, shopping, job duties and entertainment, and most take their Web browsers for granted. Just about anybody can open a browser and surf the Web.

On the other hand, an IT professional can evaluate a browsing session and identify the processes, technology and potential risks involved therein. Understanding the process, and the tools that enable it, will help you (or someone who has called for your assistance) use your Web browser to your advantage.

As you learn about the processes involved in browsing, consider that there are always trade-offs. For example, enforcing strong browser security may protect your organization from dangerous content, but also may inhibit the work of employees who need to download content. Balance is usually the key to maintaining employee productivity and preventing frustration in the IT department; however, the way to achieve that balance may not be obvious.

Basic Functions of Web Browsers

As you have already learned, the primary function of a Web browser is to retrieve pages from a Web server and display those pages on your screen. Browsers enable users to easily use the World Wide Web by:

- Providing a way for users to access and navigate Web pages.

- Displaying Web pages properly.

- Providing technology to enable multimedia features.

- Providing access to Internet services other than Web pages (such as FTP, Telnet, news servers and e-mail).

- Performing authentication and encryption for the secure exchange of information.

Not all Web browsers are the same. The first Web browsers were text-based; they displayed only text, and not graphics or other multimedia features of a Web page. Lynx is an example of a text-based browser. Graphical browsers, such as Microsoft Internet Explorer and Netscape Navigator, display the multimedia features of Web pages, including graphics, animation and video content.

You will learn about modern browser choices and guidelines for choosing the best browser for your business later in this lesson.

<table>
<tr><td>**OBJECTIVE:**
1.5.6: Common Web
browser
applications</td></tr>
</table>

Installing a Web Browser

Windows XP Professional comes with the Microsoft Internet Explorer 6.0 browser, which is automatically installed when you load the operating system. To install other browsers, you can request the installation CD from browser vendors, or even download the browsers directly from the Web.

To download a free copy of Netscape Navigator 7.1, go to
http://channels.netscape.com/ns/browsers/default.jsp.

wizard
A tool that assists users of an application in creating documents and/or databases based on styles and templates.

The process for installing a browser is the same as the process for installing any other software application. Generally, a **wizard** will guide you through the necessary steps. A wizard is a tool that assists users of an application in creating documents and/or databases based on styles and templates.

In the following lab, you will install Netscape 7.1. Suppose you work for your company's IT department, and your manager has instructed you to install new browsers on all employee computers.

 Lab 2-1: Installing the Netscape 7.1 browser

In this lab, you will install Netscape 7.1.

1. Right-click the **Start** button, then click **Explore** to open Windows Explorer. Navigate to the **C:\CIW\Internet\LabFiles\Lesson02** folder, then double-click **NSSetup-Full.exe** to launch the Netscape 7.1 Setup Wizard, as shown in Figure 2-1.

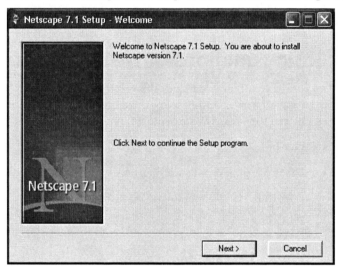

Figure 2-1: Netscape 7.1 Setup Wizard

2. Click **Next** to display the license agreement. Read the agreement.

3. Click **Accept** to accept the license agreement and display the screen that lets you choose the Setup Type, as shown in Figure 2-2.

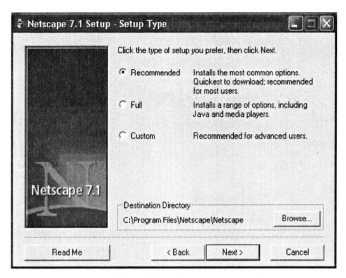

Figure 2-2: Specifying Netscape setup type

4. Verify that the **Recommended** setup is selected, and then click **Next**.

5. You will see a box that asks if the Installation Wizard can create a destination directory. Click **Yes** to create the destination directory and display the dialog box that lets you select additional components (Figure 2-3).

    Note: If the C:\Program Files\Netscape\Netscape directory already exists, you will not see the box that asks if the Installation Wizard can create a destination directory; the dialog box in Figure 2-3 will display instead.

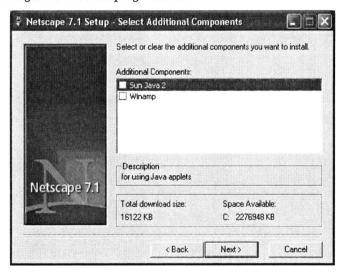

Figure 2-3: Specifying additional Netscape setup components

6. Ensure that neither component is selected, then click **Next**. You will see a dialog box that asks if you want to enable the Quick Launch feature, which speeds the loading of the browser by keeping portions of the program resident in memory.

7. Deselect **Use Quick Launch For Faster Startup Times When Possible**. This step declines the use of Quick Launch. Click **Next**.

8. You will see the Additional Options dialog box, which allows you to designate the Netscape.com page as your home page.

9. Click **Next** to specify the Netscape.com page as your home page and to display a dialog box that lets you review your current installation settings. If you want to make changes, you can click the **Back** button.

10. Click the **Install** button to begin the installation.

    Note: If the Netscape Network Registration dialog box displays, click **Cancel***, then click* **Yes** *to complete the installation without registering for the Netscape Network.*

11. When installation is complete, the browser will open to the Netscape.com home page, and a dialog box will ask if you want to make Netscape 7.1 your default browser. Click **No** to specify that you do not want to make Netscape your default browser.

12. Close any open browser windows, pop-up windows, or Windows Explorer windows. Notice that the installation program created Desktop shortcuts for Netscape 7.1, Netscape Mail & Newsgroups, Netscape Instant Messenger, and AOL for Broadband.

Web Addresses

As you have already learned, every Web page has a unique address. To access a particular Web site, you must know its Web address or click a hyperlink that takes you to that address. Some Web addresses take you to the top level, or domain level (home page) of a Web site, whereas others take you deep into a Web site.

Understanding URIs and URLs

OBJECTIVE:
1.5.1: URLs/URIs

Uniform Resource Identifier (URI)
A standardized method of referring to a resource.

Uniform Resource Locator (URL)
A text string that specifies an Internet address and the method by which the address can be accessed.

A **Uniform Resource Identifier (URI)** is a way to refer to information or resources, whether they are on the World Wide Web, on a personal computer system or elsewhere. A URI is a text string that can refer to documents, resources or people.

Web addresses are called **Uniform Resource Locators (URLs)**. A URL is a text string that specifies an Internet address and the method by which the address can be accessed. A URL is a specific type of URI.

The components of a typical URL include the protocol, the Internet resource (server or host name) and the domain name, as shown in Figure 2-4.

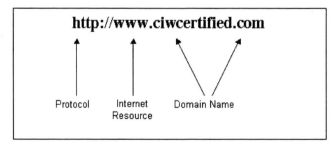

Figure 2-4: Typical Uniform Resource Locator (URL)

In a URL, the protocol component identifies the Internet protocol used to send information from the server to a user's computer, and thus indicates both the type of server and Internet service being used. HTTP is used to transfer Web pages and other information over the World Wide Web. FTP is used to transfer files to and from FTP sites.

NNTP is used by news servers and news readers. Note that in a URL, the protocol is indicated in lowercase letters.

The use of a secure protocol, such as HTTPS, indicates that a secure session is in progress and that authentication has occurred. Authentication and secure protocols will be discussed later in this lesson.

The Internet resource is the name of the server on which the page resides. In the example shown in the preceding figure, the Internet resource is a server named *www*. Web servers usually (but not always) have names beginning with *www*. The Web server for the Netscape home page is named *home*, and its URL is *home.netscape.com*.

Remember that a domain name server translates a domain name into an IP address, and that your browser uses the IP address to connect to a host. The network administrator for a given domain is in charge of mapping the names in the domain to specific computers and their IP addresses. In cases in which you can connect to a Web site without typing the "www" prefix, the domain administrator has assigned the IP address of the Web server to names that do not include a prefix.

As you have already learned, the domain name (which includes the top-level domain, such as *.com* or *.org*) identifies the site owner's registered site name and organization type. The *www.CIWcertified.com* Web site is a commercial site that offers information about CIW certification.

home page
The first Web page that displays when you access a domain.

When you enter the URL *http://www.CIWcertified.com*, you access the CIW Certified domain, which is the top level of the CIW Certified Web site. When you access a domain, the first page you see is the Web site's **home page**. Home pages are usually named *home*, *default* or *index*. The specific file name of the CIW home page is *default.asp*, but you do not need to specify the name of the home page in order to access it.

The domain (*www.CIWcertified.com*) is the system root on the Web server.

deep URL
A URL that includes a path past the domain into the folder structure of a Web site.

A URL that goes deeper into a Web site than the home page, such as *www.CIWcertified.com/jobroles/aboutCIW.asp*, is called a **deep URL** because it includes a path that penetrates the folder structure of the Web site. URLs can go many layers into a Web site's folder structure to point to a specific resource (such as an HTML page, a PDF document or an executable file).

On some servers, the portion of a deep URL that comes after the domain may be case-sensitive. For example, on UNIX systems running Apache Web server, deep URLs are case-sensitive by default. If you do not enter the URL with exact letter case, you will receive some version of a Page Not Found error.

absolute URL
A URL that gives the full path to a resource.

A URL can be absolute or relative. An **absolute URL** includes the full path from the system root (or domain, which includes the server name) to a specific page or resource. Any URL that you type into your Web browser's Address box will be an absolute URL. Domain-level URLs (e.g. *www.CIWcertified.com*) and deep URLs (e.g. *www.CIWcertified.com/jobroles/aboutCIW.asp*) are both absolute.

Sometimes Web page file names change, or Web site structure changes. If you get an error when specifying a deep URL, try accessing the domain and then following links to get to the deep page you want.

relative URL
A URL that gives an abbreviated path to a resource using the current page as a starting position.

A **relative URL** gives a path to a resource using the current page as an origin. In a relative URL, the system root is implied but not specified. A relative URL is also known as an abbreviated URL, and it is always referenced from within the page currently loaded into the Web browser. The URL */jobroles/aboutCIW.asp* (without the preceding domain portion) is an example of a relative URL. The system root is implied by the slash (/) that begins the URL.

You would use relative URLs when coding a Web site in HTML/XHTML. The use of relative URLs in Web site coding makes it possible to move an entire site from one server to another without having to edit the pages, which saves a lot of time. You would not enter a relative URL into your browser's Address box when browsing the Web.

Entering URLs

As you learned earlier, a URL includes a protocol, an Internet resource and a domain name. You can access any Web page by entering its URL in your browser's Address box. After you launch your browser, click in the Address field, type the URL of the Web site you want to visit, and then press ENTER.

Netscape Navigator and Microsoft Internet Explorer both assume that HTTP is the protocol being used because you generally use a browser to access Web pages. You can include the *http://* when you enter the URL, or you may omit it. If you want to use your browser to access an FTP site, or any site that uses a protocol other than HTTP, you must include the protocol when you type the URL.

Most users manually enter a URL only when first starting an Internet session or when first accessing a specific Web site. After that, they generally use links or other techniques to navigate Web pages and browse the Web.

Using links

Although you can specify a URL for every page that you want to visit on the Internet, it is easier and faster to click hyperlinks on Web pages to visit other pages, or other areas on the same page. Links can be either text or graphics. It is a standard Internet convention to use underlined text to represent a hypertext link.

Most Web sites include a navigation section that displays across the top or along one side of their Web pages. The options in the navigation section are links to other pages and areas in the site. Each link automatically enters a new URL into the browser's Address box.

Clicking a hyperlink sends you to a linked page. You can click hyperlinks on successive pages to navigate deeper into a Web site. Clicking your browser's Back button will return you to the previously visited page. You may also find hyperlinks that lead back to a previously viewed page or portion of a page. For example, you may find a link back to the home page or a link that reads "Back To Top" that will return you to the top of the current Web page.

In the following lab, you will browse the Web using Internet Explorer and Navigator. Suppose your project manager has asked you to evaluate the navigation capabilities of these two popular Web browsers so your company can choose whether to standardize on one browser or use both because each has relevant strengths.

 Lab 2-2: Browsing Web pages using various browsers

OBJECTIVE:
1.5.2: Navigate Web sites

In this lab, you will access Web pages using various browsers.

1. First, you will use Microsoft Internet Explorer. From your Desktop, click **Start**, then click **Internet Explorer** to launch Microsoft Internet Explorer 6.0. Notice that the Microsoft Network (MSN) home page displays by default.

2. Click in the **Address** box. Type *www.CIWcertified.com*, then press ENTER to access the CIW Certified home page, as shown in Figure 2-5. Notice that you do not need to enter "http://" to specify HTTP as the protocol. Web browsers assume this protocol.

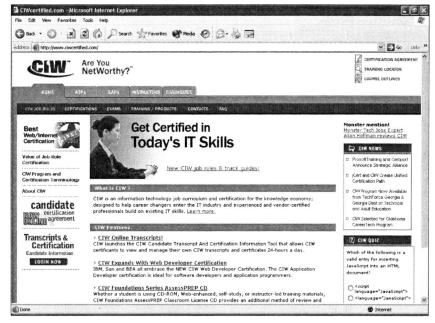

Figure 2-5: CIW Certified home page

3. In the navigation section across the top of the Web page, click **FAQ** to access the Frequently Asked Questions page. Notice that the URL in the browser Address box now reads *http://www.CIWcertified.com/faq/ciwfaq.asp?comm=home&llm=6*.

4. In the Quick Links section on the top of the FAQ page, click **How Do I Get Certified** to access another section of the FAQ page.

5. Scroll down the Web page until you see Back To Top, then click the **Back To Top** link to return to the top of the FAQ page.

6. On the left side of the Web page, click **Privacy Policy** to access the privacy policy.

7. In the navigation section across the top of the page, click **Home** to return to the CIW home page.

8. In the browser toolbar, click the **Back** button to return to the Privacy Policy page.

9. In the browser toolbar, click the **Forward** button to return to the CIW home page.

10. In the browser toolbar, click the **Home** button (image of a house) to access the MSN home page, then minimize the **Internet Explorer** window.

11. Next, you will use Netscape Navigator. On the Desktop, double-click the icon for **Netscape 7.1** to launch the browser and display the Netscape home page. Close any pop-up windows that display by clicking the Close button (X) in the upper-right corner of the window.

12. Notice that a tab displays in the browser window and that *Netscape.com* displays in the tab. Netscape Navigator offers tabbed browsing, which you will investigate in a later lab.

13. Click in the **Location** box, type ***www.CIWcertified.com***, then press **ENTER** to display the CIW Certified home page. Notice that the page displays almost exactly as it does in Internet Explorer.

Note: In Navigator, the place where you enter URLs is called the Location box, whereas Internet Explorer calls it the Address box.

14. Click in the **Location** box, type ***www.google.com***, then press **ENTER** to access the Google search engine.

15. In the browser toolbar, click the **Home** button to redisplay the Netscape home page.

16. In the browser toolbar, click the **Go Back One Page** button to redisplay the Google page.

17. Click in the **Location** box, type ***www.amazon.com***, then press **ENTER** to access the Amazon.com home page. Notice that a deep URL displays in the Location box.

18. Now you will change the case-sensitive portion of a deep URL. Position the mouse pointer over the Location box, select the text ***exec*** in the URL, type ***EXEC*** to replace the selected text, then press **ENTER**.

19. Notice that you are redirected to a page that says the Web address you entered is not a functioning page. Notice also that the tab in the browser window reads "404 – Document Not Found."

Tech Note: The default display for the 404 error is "Not Found 404." This message indicates that the server could not find a page matching the URL specified. Most Web page designers embellish their Error 404 page and offer links back to the home page. To view original and creative Error 404 pages, go to www.404Lounge.net.

20. Click the **Go Back One Page** button to return to the Amazon home page.

21. In the browser toolbar, click the **Home** button, then minimize the **Navigator** window.

22. If any pop-up windows display, close them.

How Browsers Work

In the previous lab, you accessed the CIW Certified Web site. You entered a URL and the browser displayed the Web site home page. How does that happen?

The basic series of steps in the functioning of a Web browser is as follows:

1. You enter the URL *www.CIWcertified.com* in your browser.

2. Your browser breaks the URL into three parts: the protocol (*http*), the server and domain name (*www.CIWcertified.com*), and the name of the file you want to view. In this case, the default or home page (*default.asp*) is implied because you are visiting the top level of a Web site.

3. Your browser communicates with a domain name server to translate the server name into an IP address (in this case, 12.42.192.73).

4. Your browser uses the IP address to form a connection with the CIW Web server.

5. Your browser uses HTTP to request the default page from the server.

6. Some level of authentication takes place.

7. The server sends the requested Web page (coded in HTML) to your browser.

8. Your browser reads and interprets the HTML and displays the Web page.

Authentication

Authentication is the process of verifying the identity of a user who logs on to a system, or the integrity of transmitted data. Before providing (or "serving") pages, servers require authentication. Browsers must be able to engage in the authentication process.

General authentication types include the following:

- **Anonymous logon** — No user name or password is required, and authentication is handled automatically and transparently by the browser and the server. Whenever you "hit" a site, an anonymous logon takes place, and the Web server will count each instance as an anonymous logon.

- **Basic authentication** — A user name and a password are required. You are prompted to enter your information before you can access the Web page, and that information is sent across the Internet as plain text. Anyone who intercepts the data with packet-sniffing software will be able to read it.

- **Secure authentication** — A user name and password are required, and that information is encrypted before it is sent across the Internet, so that anyone who intercepts the data will not be able to read it. Encrypted authentication can be performed by various methods, which will be discussed shortly. In basic and secure authentication, knowledge of the user name and password are assumed to guarantee that the user is authentic.

- **Digital certificates** — You must have the proper digital certificate to gain access. A user name or password may not be required to access the site. Digital certificates will be discussed in detail shortly.

Encryption

Encryption is the process of converting data into an unreadable form of text. **Decryption** is the process of converting the encrypted data back to its original form. Encryption and decryption are performed through keys. A key is a mathematical algorithm. The more complex the encryption algorithm, the harder it is to decipher the encrypted message without access to the key.

Although encryption is often used in the process of authentication, it is not the same as authentication. Authentication occurs before an encrypted session can begin, but authentication does not ensure that the ensuing session will be encrypted.

Businesses use authentication and/or encryption for a variety of reasons. Generally, organizations use authentication to prevent unauthorized users from accessing company documents and data. Authentication is also used to protect company intranets and extranets, which will be discussed later in this lesson. Encrypted data transmissions prevent unauthorized users from intercepting and/or modifying data. Remember that the Internet is a public network, and people with malicious or criminal intent can intercept non-encrypted transmissions of data.

Password Authentication Protocol (PAP)

Password Authentication Protocol (PAP) is used to authenticate dial-up sessions for remote users. Although user names and passwords can be encrypted, systems that use

OBJECTIVE:
1.5.5: SSL/TLS and encryption protocols

authentication
The process of verifying the identity of a user who logs on to a system, or the integrity of transmitted data.

OBJECTIVE:
1.5.5: SSL/TLS and encryption protocols

encryption
A security technique to prevent access to information by converting it to a scrambled (unreadable) form of text.

decryption
The process of converting encrypted data back to its original form.

PAP to verify user identity are still vulnerable to attack because user names and passwords are static and can be determined by unauthorized users.

Challenge Handshake Authentication Protocol (CHAP)

Challenge Handshake Authentication Protocol (CHAP) authenticates by generating a challenge phrase, which is a randomly generated text string. The challenge phrase is sent to the client requesting a connection, and the client responds with a value created through the use of a one-way hash function. A hash function uses an algorithm to generate a number from a string of text, in this case, from the challenge phrase sent to it by the server. The server compares the client response (hash value) with its own calculation of the expected hash value. If the values match, then the client is authenticated and the session proceeds. CHAP is a more secure procedure than PAP because the server can request authentication at any time during the session.

Microsoft Challenge Handshake Authentication Protocol (MS-CHAP)

Microsoft developed a proprietary version of CHAP called Microsoft Challenge Handshake Authentication Protocol (MS-CHAP). Microsoft Internet Information Services (IIS) uses MS-CHAP for authentication, and until recently, Microsoft Internet Explorer was the only browser that could authenticate with a server running IIS. Now Mozilla 1.6 and Netscape Navigator 7.1 have the ability to authenticate with IIS. However, older versions of these browsers cannot authenticate with IIS.

Digital certificates

OBJECTIVE:
1.5.5: SSL/TLS and encryption protocols

A digital certificate proves the identity of an individual or company over the Web. A digital certificate is equivalent to an ID card and is digitally signed by the certificate creator.

Software developers use certificates to digitally sign the programs they develop. Digital signatures provide positive identification of the sending and receiving parties to ensure that programs downloaded from the Internet are original and safe. The browser can check the information in a certificate to see whether the program is valid or whether it has been tampered with since the certificate was signed. When you receive a certificate during a download, you can be relatively certain that the sender's identity is legitimate. You are offered the option to view the certificate, and you can cancel the download if you do not trust the authenticity of the sender of the digital certificate.

Both Navigator and Internet Explorer allow digital certificate use; these browsers enable you to obtain a personal certificate or a certificate for your business, and to view certificates from other companies.

The Web server administrator creates a digital certificate. The first step in creating a digital certificate is to create a certificate request. This certificate request is then signed by a trusted third party, called a certificate authority (CA). Commercial CAs such as VeriSign (*www.verisign.com*) are organizations that verify the credentials of a server or company that has submitted a certificate request. Once the CA trusts the information provided by the party that submitted the request, the CA signs the certificate request, thereby creating a digital certificate.

The server always possesses the digital certificate. When a client begins an encrypted session, the server sends the certificate to the client. The client (Web browser or e-mail client) checks the signature on the certificate against its own list of CAs (which is loaded in your browser software). If the signature is recognized, then authentication occurs, because the client now knows that a trusted authority has verified the information provided by the server. After authentication occurs, encryption can begin.

Certificates provide a strong level of prevention against fraudulent use or misrepresentation of your personal or company information, and that of other Internet-based entities. Because the password method of authentication has inherent weaknesses (passwords can be stolen, forgotten or inadvertently revealed), the use of digital certificates seems likely to become the standard authentication method over the Internet.

Secure Sockets Layer (SSL) and Transport Layer Security (TLS)

OBJECTIVE:
1.5.5: SSL/TLS and encryption protocols

Secure Sockets Layer (SSL)
A protocol that provides authentication and encryption, used by most servers for secure exchanges over the Internet. Superseded by Transport Layer Security (TLS).

Transport Layer Security (TLS)
A secure protocol based on SSL 3.0 that provides encryption and authentication.

Most servers use the **Secure Sockets Layer (SSL)** protocol for secure exchanges. The SSL protocol authenticates using digital certificates and provides for data encryption. Netscape originated SSL, and version 3.0 is the current standard. All major browsers, such as Netscape Navigator, Microsoft Internet Explorer, NCSA Mosaic and Lotus Personal Web Browser, support SSL 3.0.

Transport Layer Security (TLS) is the successor to SSL and is becoming more common. The Internet Engineering Task Force (IETF), which defines standard Internet operating protocols, developed TLS. Because TLS was developed by the IETF, you can read Requests for Comments (RFCs) about it. RFCs are public documents of interest to the Internet community that include detailed information about standardized Internet protocols. RFCs are identified by number. RFC 2246 explains TLS 1.0. In contrast, no RFCs about SSL exist because a private company developed SSL.

SSL/TLS can be used to encrypt any type of TCP-based service (e-mail, instant messaging, Web/HTTP, NNTP, FTP, etc.).

SSL/TLS sessions can use 40-bit encryption or 128-bit encryption. The size refers to the length of the session key generated by each SSL transaction. Again, the longer the key, the more difficult it is to break the encryption code. Most browsers support 40-bit SSL sessions, and the latest browsers can encrypt in 128-bit sessions.

In the United States and Canada, the use of 128-bit encryption is standard. Some countries restrict encryption strength to 40-bit, fearing that the use of 128-bit encryption might enable terrorists to conduct secure, unbreakable communications and evade authorities. Many governments, including the U.S. government, want to set up a key-escrow arrangement that would require everyone who uses strong encryption to provide the government with a copy of the key. This topic has caused considerable controversy.

Secure protocols

OBJECTIVE:
1.5.5: SSL/TLS and encryption protocols

Various protocols in the TCP/IP suite (such as HTTP, FTP, IMAP and POP3) can be made more secure by running them over SSL. Secure protocols increase safety when sending sensitive data such as confidential company information or credit card numbers over the Internet, thus making e-commerce possible.

For example, HTTP over Secure Sockets Layer (HTTPS) is a protocol developed by Netscape that is now supported by most browsers. HTTPS encrypts and decrypts information sent from the browser to the server and information sent from the Web server.

Suppose you browse the Amazon.com site for a book about e-mail security. While you are looking at Amazon's offerings, you are using HTTP. However, once you begin the process of purchasing a book online with a credit card number, you are sent to a Web page with a URL that starts with *https://*. When you submit (send) your credit card information to the server, your browser will encrypt the data transmission. The confirmation you receive from the server will also be encrypted and will display on a page with an *https://* URL. Your browser will decrypt the information and display it for you.

FTP over SSL (S/FTP) provides a more secure mode of file transfer to and from FTP sites. You can also use e-mail protocols (SMTP, POP3, IMAP) over SSL for more secure e-mail.

Internet Explorer and Navigator allow you to view information about sites that use secure protocols. When you visit a secure site, the site sends you its digital certificate. In addition to displaying the *https://* protocol in the Address box, Internet Explorer displays a lock icon in the status bar. You can click this icon to view details about the digital certificate. Navigator also displays the secure protocol in the Location box and a lock icon in the status bar when you access a secure page. Both browsers include features that allow you to view details about the secure session.

Browser Choices

Many different Web browsers are available today. Several are free or relatively inexpensive. Both mainstream and alternative browsers are described in the next sections.

Widely used browsers

Currently, the most widely used browsers are Microsoft Internet Explorer and Netscape Navigator, which are graphical browsers. Both are distributed free over the Internet, and Internet Explorer comes bundled with the Microsoft Windows XP Professional operating system.

Many versions of these browsers exist, and older versions do not support some of the Web features considered standard today. For example, Netscape Navigator versions prior to 2.0 (March 1996) and Microsoft Internet Explorer versions prior to 3.0 (August 1996) do not support frames sites, which structure pages into independent panes. Generally, you can view all Web sites if your browser from either vendor is version 3.0 or later.

Netscape Navigator 7.1 offers a few features not found in Microsoft Internet Explorer 6.0, such as pop-up window control and tabbed browsing, which allows the user to open several pages at once and toggle between the pages. However, subsequent releases of Internet Explorer will probably include similar features.

Most Web pages display almost identically in Navigator and Internet Explorer. The toolbar features vary between the browsers, but these differences have little effect on your Web-browsing experience.

The reason a Web page may not appear the same in different browsers is because each browser interprets some HTML elements differently. For example, online order forms may not appear or print the same because each browser may use some different default fonts and layouts for forms. Web page tables, which display information in rows and columns, may not appear the same because each browser supports some different table formatting commands.

Also, some browsers support some proprietary HTML tags that are not standard. In this case, only the browsers that understand the proprietary code will display the Web page properly. Web page authors should test their Web pages in as many browsers as possible to make sure the pages display properly.

Alternative browsers

OBJECTIVE:
1.5.13: Alternative
browsers

You are not limited to using Microsoft Internet Explorer or Netscape Navigator. Additional browsers exist, including the following:

- **Mozilla (*www.mozilla.org*)** — the open-source version of Netscape Navigator.

- **Opera (*www.opera.com*)** — an alternative browser that supports Windows systems, Linux, OS/2, Macintosh/Mac OS, smart phone/PDA, Solaris, FreeBSD and QNX.

- **Konqueror (*http://konqueror.kde.org*)** — a browser found in the KDE desktop environment for UNIX workstations.

- **Lynx (*http://lynx.browser.org*)** — a text-only browser that runs on UNIX, VMS, Windows 3.x/9x/NT, 386DOS and OS/2 EMX. Lynx supports HTTP, Telnet, Gopher, FTP and NNTP.

- **Arachne (*http://arachne.browser.org*)** — a graphical browser for DOS systems, with a beta version (i.e., a version in the final stages of development and testing) available for Linux.

Selecting a browser for your business

OBJECTIVE:
1.5.13: Alternative
browsers

While selecting a browser for use on a home computer may be purely a matter of personal preference, selecting one browser standard to implement across an organization requires careful consideration.

Many businesses prefer one browser to others for standardization and easier upkeep by their IT departments. Therefore, all computers in the company may have the same browser (and perhaps only that browser) installed.

While it may be tempting to use the one browser that the majority of employees already have installed, or to use the browser that the CEO likes best, IT personnel should consider all the ripple effects that implementing a browser standard may produce.

If your company hosts an intranet or extranet, you will want to authenticate the users. To implement authentication, both the server and the client (browser) must be able to handle the authentication type. Your authentication method could affect your browser choice. For example, if your server is running Microsoft Internet Information Services (IIS), your employees should probably use Microsoft Internet Explorer, or the latest version of Mozilla or Netscape Navigator. Any alternative browser must be researched carefully to ensure that it will authenticate with your server.

Alternative browsers also may have benefits and drawbacks specific to your organization. For example, a text-only browser may run on the Windows 3.x systems in your office, allowing Internet access on limited resources. However, employees who are accustomed to a graphical browser may have a difficult time adjusting.

IT personnel should consider all potential benefits and drawbacks before making a decision to implement one browser as a company standard. One way you can learn about the current trends in server software is to locate and review technical data on the Web.

Resources for Technical Data

You should be aware of the available resources for technical data. The following list suggests a few Web sites you can visit to learn about current technology and Internet trends. You will visit some of these resources during this course.

- *www.netcraft.com*

- *www.whatis.com*

- *www.howstuffworks.com*

- *www.learnthenet.com*

- *www.microsoft.com/technet*

If you visit these sites on your own, be sure to follow the links to related sites. The best way to learn about available resources is to visit and browse them.

Netcraft.com is a site that performs market research and analyzes current trends in Internet business. The site provides a wide variety of Internet-related information, including data about the fastest-growing hosting companies, statistics on widely used server software, and trends in e-commerce.

In the following lab, you will view Web statistics. Suppose the IT manager has instructed you to compile statistics about the latest trends in server software for an upcoming meeting in which the software to implement on the new server will be chosen. You should be familiar with at least a few of the technical resources available.

 Lab 2-3: Accessing statistics, and accessing secure and non-secure Web pages

In this lab, you will visit the Netcraft site and examine Internet statistics. You will also access secure and non-secure pages, and display security properties for each.

1. First, you will visit the Netcraft site. Restore the **Internet Explorer** window, click in the **Address** box, type *www.netcraft.com*, then press **ENTER** to access the Netcraft home page.

2. In the left margin, click the **Web Server Survey Archive** link to open another browser window that displays the survey archives.

3. In the sentence that reads *The Current Web Server Survey Report Is Always Here*, click the **Here** link to access the current report. After viewing the graph, can you tell which is currently the most popular Web server?

    Note: Apache Server has traditionally been the most popular Web server, and Microsoft IIS has been second most popular.

4. Scroll down and read the statistics. What else can you learn about common Web servers?

5. Close the window with the survey report. This step redisplays the Netcraft home page.

6. In the upper-left corner of the Web page, click in the text box that displays below *What's That Site Running*. You can enter a URL into this text box to learn the Web server software being used at the specified site.

7. Type *www.CIWcertified.com*, then press **ENTER**. If a message box displays, click **Yes** to continue to submit the URL.

*Tech Note: Depending on your current security settings, Internet Explorer may display a message informing you that others might view data you send over the Internet. This message appears because you are not using a secure connection. Notice that the **In The Future, Do Not Show This Message** option in the message is selected by default. It is safe to submit non-sensitive data to the server across a non-secure connection.*

8. Netcraft displays the results of your site software inquiry in a separate browser window. Notice that the CIW Certified Web site runs Microsoft IIS 4.0. Notice also that the results include information about the operating system used on the server.

9. Close the second browser window, select the text in the **What's That Site Running** text box, type ***www.amazon.com***, then press **ENTER** to submit the URL for Amazon. Notice that Amazon runs Apache 1.3.6 and several other programs on the Linux operating system.

10. Close the second browser window.

11. Next, you will access secure and non-secure pages and view security properties for each. Click in the **Address** box, type ***www.desertschools.org***, then press **ENTER** to display the home page for Desert Schools Federal Credit Union.

12. Select **File | Properties** to display the Properties dialog box shown in Figure 2-6. Notice that the connection is not encrypted, indicating that the home page for Desert Schools Federal Credit Union is not a secure page.

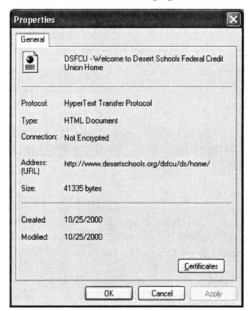

Figure 2-6: Properties dialog box — Microsoft Internet Explorer

13. Click **OK** to close the Properties dialog box.

14. In the navigation section at the top of the Web page, click the **ePAL/Online Banking** button. Internet Explorer displays a Security Alert box informing you that you are about to view pages on a secure connection.

15. Click **OK** to close the alert box and access the secure page in a separate browser window. Notice that *https://* displays in the Address box, and that a closed lock icon displays in the status bar, informing you that you are on a secure page.

16. Read the page. Notice that the credit union recommends you use Netscape 4.7 or Internet Explorer 5.x or later, both of which include 128-bit encryption capabilities.

17. Display the **Properties** dialog box for the secure page. Notice that the connection uses SSL 3.0 with 128-bit encryption.

18. Close the **Properties** dialog box, then position the mouse pointer over the closed lock icon in the status bar to display a pop-up box that reads *SSL Secured (128 Bit).*

19. Double-click the **closed lock** icon to display the Certificate dialog box shown in Figure 2-7, in which you can examine details about the digital certificate received from the Web site.

Figure 2-7: Certificate dialog box — Microsoft Internet Explorer

20. You can click the various tabs of the Certificate dialog box to view details about the digital certificate. Click the **Details** tab. Notice that the value for the Version is V3, indicating SSL 3.0.

21. Click **OK** to close the Certificate dialog box.

22. Click the **VeriSign** logo on the page to display information from the CA regarding EPAL.DESERTSCHOOLS.ORG. After you have seen the information, close all **Internet Explorer** windows.

23. Restore the **Navigator** window, click in the **Location** box, type *www.desertschools.org*, and then press **ENTER** to access the Desert Schools home page. Notice that an open lock icon displays in the status bar.

24. Click the **open lock** icon to display the Page Info dialog box shown in Figure 2-8. Notice that the page is not encrypted.

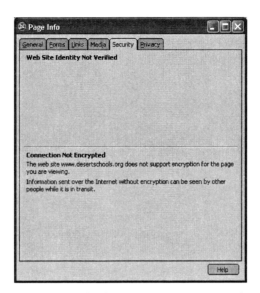

Figure 2-8: Page Info dialog box — Netscape Navigator

25. Close the **Page Info** dialog box, and then click the **ePAL/Online Banking** button. Navigator displays a security warning that you have requested an encrypted page from the server.

26. Click **OK** to close the warning and display the ePAL page. Notice that the open lock icon has changed to a closed lock icon.

27. Position the mouse over the closed lock icon to display a pop-up box with the message "Signed by VeriSign, Inc."

28. Click the **closed lock** icon to display the Page Info dialog box again. Notice that the current page uses 128-bit encryption.

29. Click the **View** button in the dialog box to display the Certificate Viewer window, which displays information about the digital certificate received from the server.

30. Close the **Certificate Viewer** dialog box, close the **Page Info** dialog box, then close all **Navigator** windows.

Browsers in the Business World

You already know that millions of people use browsers at work daily to find information, conduct transactions, send e-mail and transfer files. You also know that thousands of businesses have Web sites. However, many companies use browsers for local functions, such as maintaining intranets and extranets, and conducting training and conferences.

Internet, intranets and extranets

OBJECTIVE:
1.5.8: Intranet,
extranet, Internet

What are the differences among the Internet, an intranet and an extranet? Intranets and extranets can be considered subsets of the Internet. They use Internet technology and protocols, but are smaller networks that allow corporations and organizations to exclude the general Internet public.

Intranets

intranet
An internal network based on TCP/IP protocols, accessible only to users within a company.

An **intranet** is an internal, or in-house, Web site and network used only by employees within a company. Employees use Web browsers to access files and documents. Security features (such as user names and passwords) prevent the Internet public from accessing a company intranet, but allow employees who use the intranet to access the Internet. An intranet could be described as a mini-Internet within a company.

Intranets are popular because they provide a standard method for accessing resources, regardless of the operating systems used. For example, an intranet allows Macintosh, Windows and UNIX/Linux systems to access the same data because all these operating systems can use TCP/IP. They can access the same resources as if they were on the Internet. Intranets can save a company from buying extra computers to standardize all the operating systems because employees can continue to use their existing computers. This consideration is important because different types of computers are required for specific tasks.

Extranets

extranet
A network that connects enterprise intranets to the global Internet. Designed to provide access to selected external users.

An **extranet** is an internal network designed to provide access to selected external users, and is not available to the Internet public. Extranets are an efficient way for business partners to share and exchange information. Customer support tasks can also be performed using an extranet. For example, if customers need to access a sales report generated by your company, they will first access the Internet, then enter in their browsers the URL of your company's extranet Web server. Once they access the Web server, they must log on to the Web server with user names and passwords. When they are logged on, customers access your company's extranet, which appears as a normal Web site and provides all the same services. The only difference is that the extranet provides security to exclude the Internet public. Customers can then download the sales report instead of calling your office and asking someone to fax or mail the report to them.

The CIW Community Login page shown in Figure 2-9 is an example of an extranet. CIW Authorized Training Providers can click a link to access a logon page. Once a user's identity has been authenticated, he or she has access to a Web site containing support materials.

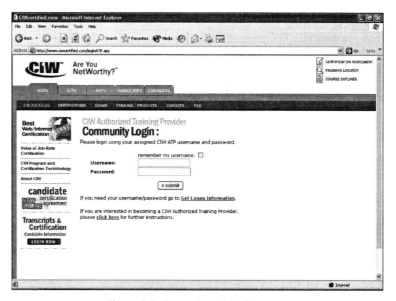

Figure 2-9: CIW extranet login page

Webinars and Web conferences

OBJECTIVE:
1.5.12: Business uses
of Web clients

Companies can also use browsers for conducting Webinars and Web conferences. Webinars and Web conferences reduce travel expenses because they enable employees or customers to attend training sessions remotely, without having to travel to the location where the training is being conducted.

Webinar
An interactive Web-based seminar or training session.

A **Webinar** (short for Web-based seminar) is training — usually a PowerPoint presentation and/or lecture — that is delivered over the Web. Webinars are usually interactive, enabling participants to communicate with the presenter and with each other via online chat.

OBJECTIVE:
1.7.12: Internet
conferencing

Figure 2-10 shows the presentation and interactive elements of a Webinar session.

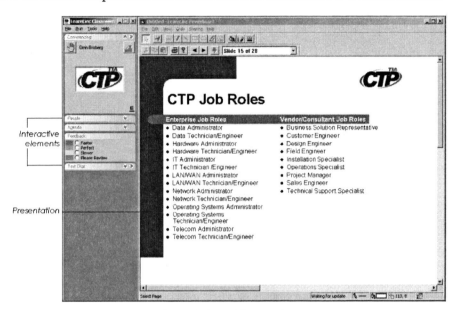

Figure 2-10: Webinar session

To attend a Webinar or Web conference, you need access to the Internet. Depending upon the setup in your company, you may need to phone in to a conference call to hear the presentation. You may also need to install an application that will allow you to interact during the presentation. Some packages allow for online chat with fellow participants and the presenter.

Generally, participants must register for a specific Webinar or Web conference, and are assigned a user name and password. Participants enter the Webinar's home page URL in the browser, log on, dial the phone number and wait for the presentation to begin.

Movie Time!

Insert the CIW Foundations Movie CD to learn even more about this topic.

Web Conferencing (approx. playing time: 05:15)

All movie clips are © 2004 LearnKey, Inc.

Browsing Techniques

Now that you have done some browsing, you will learn about browsing techniques that can make your time on the Internet more efficient.

Using Bookmarks and Favorites

OBJECTIVE:
1.9.1: Browser
preference
configuration

Instead of manually entering a URL each time you visit a Web site, you can create Bookmarks for Web pages you visit often or add links to those pages to your Favorites folder. If you work in Navigator, saved links are called Bookmarks. If you work in Internet Explorer, saved links are entries in your Favorites folder.

Bookmarks display in Navigator as shown in Figure 2-11.

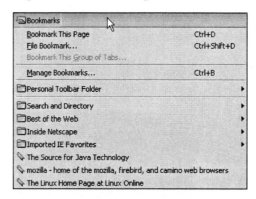

Figure 2-11: Netscape Navigator Bookmarks

Favorites display in Microsoft Internet Explorer as shown in Figure 2-12.

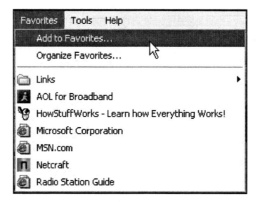

Figure 2-12: Microsoft Internet Explorer Favorites

As you add Bookmarks and Favorites, you can rearrange the structure of the folders to quickly and easily find the sites you want.

Using multiple windows

OBJECTIVE:
1.5.3: Multiple
browser windows

Sometimes as you follow links throughout the World Wide Web, you may lose track of the path back to a page you want to revisit. Or you may find yourself looking for information on disparate topics at the same time.

You can open multiple browser windows, and then follow one path of hyperlinks in one window and another path of hyperlinks in the other window. By keeping both windows open, you have simultaneous access to two Web pages.

To use multiple browser windows in Internet Explorer, you must launch the application twice (or use the File | New | Window command, which launches the browser again). Press ALT+TAB to switch between open browser windows.

Navigator supports tabbed browsing, which means you launch the browser once, and then open new tabs for multiple windows. Click a tab to activate the window you want.

In the following lab, you will use various browser features. Suppose your supervisor often calls you for immediate information regarding technical issues. By adding Bookmarks and Favorites to your browser, you can access technical information quickly. You can also use various browser features to help you work efficiently.

Lab 2-4: Using browser features to enhance your browsing experience

OBJECTIVE:
1.5.2: Navigate Web
sites

In this lab, you will use various browser features to enhance your browsing experience.

1. First, you will add Favorites in Microsoft Internet Explorer. Start **Internet Explorer** and go to ***www.netcraft.com***.

2. In the browser Menu bar, select **Favorites | Add To Favorites** to display the Add Favorite dialog box, shown in Figure 2-13.

Figure 2-13: Add Favorite dialog box

3. Click **OK** to add the site to your Favorites folder.

4. In the toolbar, click the **Favorites** button to display the Favorites folder in a separate pane along the left side of the browser window, as shown in Figure 2-14. Notice that Netcraft displays at the bottom of your Favorites list.

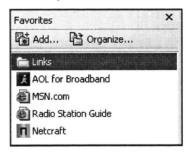

Figure 2-14: Adding to Favorites

5. In the Address box, type ***www.howstuffworks.com***, and then press **ENTER** to access the HowStuffWorks Web site.

6. Close the pop-up window that explains how to use the site.

    *Tech Note: While you are viewing the HowStuffWorks site, a security warning dialog box may display asking if you want to download and install Macromedia Flash. If the dialog box displays, click **No**. You will download Flash later in this course.*

7. In the Favorites pane, click the **Add** button, and then click **OK** to add the HowStuffWorks Web site to your Favorites folder.

8. In the Address box, type ***www.microsoft.com***, press ENTER, select **Favorites | Add To Favorites**, and then click **OK** to add the Microsoft site to your Favorites folder.

9. In the Favorites pane, click **Netcraft** to return to the Netcraft Web site.

10. In the Favorites pane, click **HowStuffWorks** to return to the HowStuffWorks Web site.

11. Minimize the **Internet Explorer** window, and close any pop-under windows that may display.

12. Next, you will create Bookmarks in Netscape Navigator. Start **Navigator**, and then go to ***www.java.com***.

13. Select **Bookmarks | Bookmark This Page** to create a Bookmark for the Web site.

14. In the toolbar, click the **Bookmarks** button to display the current Bookmarks. Notice that the Bookmark for the Java site displays at the bottom of the Bookmarks list.

15. Click anywhere outside the Bookmarks list, then go to ***www.mozilla.org***.

16. Select **Bookmarks | Bookmark This Page** to create a Bookmark for the Web site.

17. Go to ***www.linux.org***, and then add a Bookmark for the Linux site.

18. In the toolbar, click the **Bookmarks** button to display the list of Bookmarks you have created, then click the **Mozilla** Bookmark to go to the Mozilla Web site.

19. Display the **Bookmarks** list, and then click the **Linux** Bookmark to return to the Linux Web site.

OBJECTIVE:
1.5.3: Multiple
browser windows

20. Next, you will use tabbed browsing in Navigator. Select **File | New | Navigator Tab** to open a new tab.

21. In the **Location** box, type ***www.adobe.com***, then press ENTER to access the Adobe Systems Web site in a second Navigator tab.

22. Select **File | New | Navigator Tab** to open a new tab, click the **Bookmarks** button, then click the **Java** Bookmark to access the Java Web site in a third Navigator tab. All of Navigator's tools are available in all open tabs.

23. In the Java tab, click in the **Location** box, type ***www.yahoo.com***, and then press ENTER to access the Yahoo! Web site in the third tab.

24. In the Yahoo! tab, click the **Classifieds** link to display the Yahoo! Classifieds.

25. In the Yahoo! Classifieds page, click the **HotJobs** link to display the Yahoo! HotJobs page.

26. Click the **Adobe Systems Incorporated** tab, scroll down to the bottom of the page, and then click the **Get Adobe Reader** button to display the Adobe Reader download page.

27. Bookmark this page.

28. Right-click the **Linux Home Page** tab, then click **Close Tab** to close that tab in Navigator. Now two tabs are open.

29. Right-click the **Adobe Reader - Download** tab, then click **Close Other Tabs** to close the Yahoo! Classifieds tab.

30. Close **Navigator** and any pop-under windows that might display.

OBJECTIVE:
1.5.3: Multiple
browser windows

31. Finally, you will use multiple browser windows in Microsoft Internet Explorer. Restore the **Internet Explorer** window. In the toolbar, click the **Favorites** button to close the Favorites pane.

32. Select **File | New | Window** to open another Internet Explorer window.

33. Enter the URL ***www.msn.com*** in the new window's Address box to access the MSN Web site.

34. In the Windows taskbar, click the **HowStuffWorks** button to display the HowStuffWorks Web site.

35. Press **ALT+TAB** to view the MSN Web site.

36. In the navigation section on the left side of the MSN home page, click **Encarta** to display the MSN Encarta page.

37. Click a link on the Encarta page.

38. In the Windows taskbar, click the **HowStuffWorks** button to restore the HowStuffWorks Web site.

39. In the navigation section at the top of the page, click **ComputerStuff**.

40. Press **ALT+TAB** to view the Encarta page.

Note: If a pop-up or pop-under window displays, close it.

41. Close all **Internet Explorer** windows.

OBJECTIVE:
1.9.1: Browser
preference
configuration

Configuring Web Browser Preferences

Browsers in their default configurations are easy to use. But you can configure your browser to accommodate your working style, or so it complies with standards implemented by your organization.

Both Navigator and Internet Explorer allow you to customize your browser. Both browsers allow you to configure the same basic preferences, or options, although the methods to set preferences differ.

In Internet Explorer, you use the various tabs of the Internet Options dialog box (Figure 2-15) to configure most of your browser settings. Some options can be set through other menu commands.

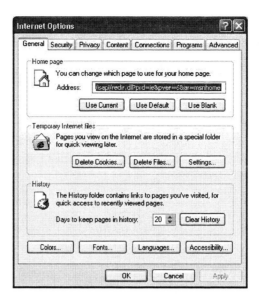

Figure 2-15: Internet Options dialog box — Microsoft Internet Explorer

In Navigator, you use the Preferences dialog box (Figure 2-16) to customize your browser.

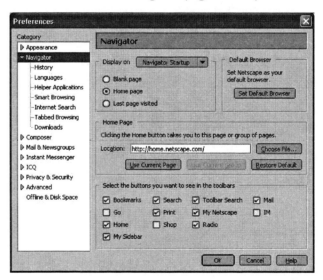

Figure 2-16: Preferences dialog box — Netscape Navigator

In the following labs, you will learn to configure your browser's preference settings.

OBJECTIVE:
1.9.1: Browser
preference
configuration

Browser fonts

Both Internet Explorer and Navigator allow you to set the size of the fonts used within the browser window. This preference is important for users who have high-resolution monitors, such as 1024 x 768, 1280 x 1024 or larger. Adjusting font size can improve readability on any monitor.

In the following lab, you will configure font size in Internet Explorer. Suppose a new employee who is visually impaired has recently joined your project team. Your supervisor has asked you to configure Internet Explorer so that the new employee can conduct research on the Web comfortably.

Lab 2-5: Configuring font size in Microsoft Internet Explorer

In this lab, you will change the font size settings in Internet Explorer.

1. Open **Internet Explorer** and enter the URL ***www.yahoo.com***. Note the font sizes used on the Yahoo! Web site.

2. In the Internet Explorer menu bar, select **View | Text Size | Smallest** to decrease the font size. Look at the page and note the differences.

3. Select **View | Text Size | Largest** to increase the font size. Again view the page, and consider your preferences.

4. Set the font to the size that is most comfortable for you, and then minimize the **Internet Explorer** window.

OBJECTIVE:
1.9.1: Browser
preference
configuration

Browser home page

When you install and open a browser, the first Web page that appears is the default browser home page. In Internet Explorer, the default home page is the MSN page. In Navigator, the default home page is the Netscape page.

Many corporations prefer that employees set their browser home pages to the company's Web site, especially if the employees need to access the company's intranet frequently. Many users set their home pages to search engines or favorite Web sites.

In the following lab, you will set the browser home page in Internet Explorer. Suppose the IT supervisor has assigned you the task of setting the home page for all corporate systems to the company intranet.

Lab 2-6: Setting a browser home page in Microsoft Internet Explorer

In this lab, you will set your Internet Explorer home page to your company's Web site or to a search engine of your choice.

1. Restore the **Internet Explorer** window, then select **Tools | Internet Options** to display the Internet Options dialog box.

2. Click the **General** tab if necessary.

3. In the Home Page section, select the text in the Address text box if necessary, then enter your company's URL, or a search engine URL such as *www.altavista.com*.

4. If a drop-down list displays, click in a blank area of the Internet Options dialog box to close it. Click **OK** to save your settings.

5. In the Internet Explorer toolbar, click the **Home** button to access your new home page. After you have accessed your new browser home page, minimize the **Internet Explorer** window.

   Note: You can also restart Internet Explorer to access your new home page.

OBJECTIVE:
1.9.1: Browser
preference
configuration

History folder

The History folder allows easy access to previously viewed Web pages. It stores the URLs of sites you have accessed within a defined period of time. The History folder is a convenient tool for revisiting Web sites, especially if you cannot remember the exact URL. The History folder can usually be accessed by a History toolbar button or by selecting the Address box drop-down menu.

Many people view the History folder as "evidence" of sites they have been browsing, and fear that employers may use the History folder to spy on employees. Anyone can view the contents of your History folder.

The default amount of time to keep pages in History for Microsoft Internet Explorer is 20 days. A History folder can grow very large; sometimes so large it is difficult to use. You can set time limits for files in the History folder, and you can empty the History folder manually.

In the following lab, you will manage the History folder in Internet Explorer. Suppose one of the managers in your company has contacted the IT department because her browser does not seem to work as quickly as it used to. The IT manager has assigned you to check the browser settings and make necessary changes to enable the browser to work as quickly as possible.

 Lab 2-7: Managing the History folder in Microsoft Internet Explorer

In this lab, you will set a time limit for pages in the History folder, and then manually empty it.

1. Restore the **Internet Explorer** window.

2. Click the **History** button on the Internet Explorer toolbar to display the History folder in its own window on the left side of the screen.

3. Notice that several folders display in the History window. Each folder displays a domain that you have visited, such as *www.desertschools.org* or *www.netcraft.com.* Also notice that each folder contains links to specific Web pages that you have viewed.

4. Open a folder and click a link to revisit a Web site.

5. Close the **History** window.

6. Select **Tools | Internet Options**, and then click **General** to display the General tab of the Internet Options dialog box, if necessary.

7. In the History section, change the expiration for the History folder to **2** days.

8. In the History section, click the **Clear History** button, then click **Yes** to delete the contents of the History folder.

9. Click **OK** to close the Internet Options dialog box.

10. In the Internet Explorer toolbar, click the **History** button to display the History folder and verify that the contents have been deleted.

11. Close the **History** window, and then minimize the **Internet Explorer** window.

Now that you have completed the lab, how important is it to you that you regularly empty your History folder? You may find that emptying your History folder frequently is worthwhile because it is easy and conserves memory.

Controlling pop-up and pop-under windows

OBJECTIVE:
1.5.4: Pop-up and pop-under browser windows

pop-up window
A small browser window that appears in front of the browser window you are viewing.

pop-under window
A small browser window that appears behind the browser window you are viewing.

As you browse various Web pages, one or more small windows may suddenly open in front of the page you are viewing. These devices are called **pop-up windows**. Pop-up windows have been used in Windows applications for years, offering specialized commands and options that must be selected before a user can continue with the current task. On the Web, pop-ups can be used to remind a visitor to log on or to enter required information. Pop-up windows are also used extensively for advertising on the Web, and many users find them obtrusive.

A **pop-under window** appears behind the browser window of a Web site that a user has visited, and it displays after you close the current browser window. Pop-under windows may be less intrusive than pop-up windows but are still often unwelcome.

Pop-up and pop-under windows display on their own, and remain open until a user clicks an option inside or closes them. Sometimes closing a pop-up or (most often) a pop-under window triggers a chain reaction of numerous additional windows that open automatically and must be closed. You can try to avoid activating pop-ups and pop-unders by not clicking inside any that display, by avoiding sites that contain adult content, and by not clicking on banner ads. However, be aware that it is becoming more difficult to avoid them.

Because pop-up windows can be annoying, several pop-up-blocking applications are available for purchase (STOPzilla, Popup Begone, Popup Killer) or for free download (Popup Stopper 2.0, FilterGate Popup Killer 5.20).

Although blocking pop-up and pop-under windows may seem like a great idea, keep in mind that it may prevent vital features of some Web sites (such as logon windows) from displaying.

Netscape Navigator 7.1 allows you to block pop-ups in the Popup Windows card of the Preferences dialog box, shown in Figure 2-17.

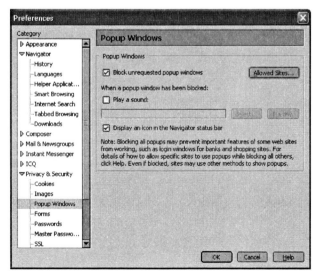

Figure 2-17: Navigator Preferences dialog box — Popup Windows card

Because blocking pop-up windows may prevent logon screens from appearing, Navigator is configured to display an icon in the status bar whenever pop-up windows are blocked. You can also click the Allowed Sites button to specify sites from which you will allow pop-up windows. Notice that Navigator includes a disclaimer in this dialog box stating that some sites may use methods to evade pop-up blocking methods.

OBJECTIVE:
1.9.1: Browser
preference
configuration

1.9.3: Browser
caching

1.9.4: Configuring
the Desktop

Browser cache

The browser cache is a folder on your hard drive that stores downloaded files (such as Web pages, images, fonts, etc.). The cache improves the performance (speed) of your browser because it allows you to view previously accessed Web pages without having to request them from the server again.

When you enter a URL, your browser checks the cache to see if the page is already stored there. If the cache contains a recent version of the page, it will display the cached version instead of downloading the page from the Web again. Loading cached pages is much faster than downloading them from a server.

Cached files are stored in several locations on the hard drive. Some are stored in a folder named Cookies, and some are stored in folders named Temp or NS_Temp. In Navigator, most of your cached files are stored in a folder named Cache. In Internet Explorer, most cached files are stored in a folder named Temporary Internet Files.

Locating the browser cache

The location of the browser cache varies among operating systems. In Windows XP, the following default location is used by Navigator to write cached files:

C:\Documents and Settings\<username>\Application Data\ Mozilla \Profiles\default\ <variable>\Cache

In Windows XP, the following default location is used by Internet Explorer to write cached files:

C:\Documents and Settings\<username>\Local Settings\Temporary Internet Files

In Internet Explorer, you can specify a different folder for storing your temporary Internet files. In Navigator, you can specify a different directory, under which a subfolder named Cache will be written.

Setting options for the browser cache

The two most significant settings for browser cache control are the size of the browser cache and frequency with which the browser will compare a cached page to the page on the server. Both of these settings affect performance. Figure 2-18 shows the Settings dialog box in Internet Explorer.

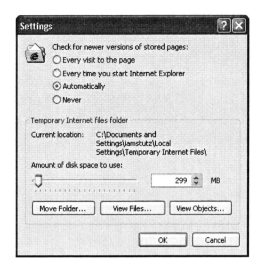

Figure 2-18: Settings dialog box — Microsoft Internet Explorer

Figure 2-19 shows the Cache card of the Preferences dialog box in Navigator.

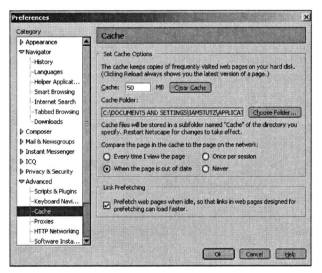

Figure 2-19: Cache Preferences — Netscape Navigator

Frequency of browser cache checking for newer pages

The default setting for both Microsoft and Netscape browsers specifies that the browser will compare a cached page to the page on the server only when you revisit a page that was viewed in a previous browser session; it will not compare when you return to a page during the current session. If the browser determines that the page changes infrequently, then it will compare less frequently.

Generally, the default setting is the most efficient. Following is a summary of the options in Internet Explorer:

- **Every Visit To The Page** — This option slows down performance because the browser compares cached pages to pages on the server every time you return to a page. The comparable selection in Navigator is Every Time I View The Page.

- **Every Time You Start Internet Explorer** — This option speeds up performance because the browser will compare pages that were viewed in earlier sessions, but not the current session. The comparable selection in Navigator is Once Per Session.

- **Automatically** — This option speeds up performance because pages that change infrequently are compared less often. The comparable selection in Navigator is When the Page Is Out Of Date.

- **Never** — This option can speed performance, but you can never be sure that you are viewing current information. The comparable selection in Navigator is Never.

When dealing with cached pages, it is important to remember that you may get outdated information from them. In fact, a cached Web page may display even if the server is not running.

The currentness of a Web page becomes especially important when you view pages that contain dynamically generated content. Consider the following example:

A Web site named uBid.com allows site visitors to place bids on various merchandise. Every couple of seconds, the uBid.com server dynamically calculates the current high bid and the amount of time remaining to place bids on a given product, then places this information into a file named (for example) *latest_bid.html*. Suppose you visit uBid.com and your browser caches *latest_bid.html*. Then you browse Web for an hour and revisit uBid.com. Your browser will display the cached page, which now contains old information.

Regardless of the setting you have specified for checking for new pages, you can click the Refresh button in Internet Explorer, or the Reload button in Navigator to download the latest page from a server anytime.

In previous releases of Navigator, clicking the Reload button would cause the browser to refresh the page from the cache. You could force a download of the page from the server by pressing and holding ENTER while clicking the Reload button.

You can also ensure that you always get the most current pages by clearing the cache before you begin browsing. You can disable caching altogether, but that can considerably slow down browsing, especially on a dial-up connection.

Size of the browser cache

Another browser cache setting that affects performance is the cache size. If your cache size is set to a large number and you work extensively on the Web, you may soon have an overwhelming number of files in your browser cache.

It is difficult to determine a universal optimal size for a browser cache. Optimal size will differ among systems. Connection speed, hard disk size and frequency of browsing sessions should be considered. You may also want to consider other applications on the system. Do they require disk space to run? Do they write temporary files? How much hard disk space do you need to run all your necessary computer processes without affecting performance? Determining the best size for your browser cache may be a matter of trial and error.

If your cache is too small, you will sacrifice performance because you will spend a lot of time waiting while pages download from the server. Increasing the size of your browser cache can improve performance while browsing, but if your cache is too large, it may slow performance because the browser must search though hundreds of cached files to locate a specific page. A cache should be large enough to speed your browsing experience, yet not so large that it slows down your computer.

A cache that is too large may also slow other computer processes. For example, disk defragmentation and virus scans can take a very long time on a large hard disk, especially if the disk is full of cached Internet files. Also, when you quit Navigator, the browser performs cache maintenance. The larger the size of the cache, the longer it takes to complete the maintenance tasks.

Emptying the cache

When your browser cache is full, the browser automatically deletes old cached files as you continue to browse the Web. In theory, it is not necessary to empty the cache.

However, there are certain advantages to emptying the cache.

- Emptying the cache before beginning a browser session will ensure you get the most current pages.

- Emptying the cache before running a virus scan, disk defragmentation or other disk maintenance can speed those processes.

- Emptying the cache can free disk space.

In the following lab, you will configure the browser cache in Internet Explorer. Suppose your IT supervisor has assigned you the task of defragmenting the hard drives on 10 systems in your corporate office. The systems are used for extensive Internet research. To speed the defragmentation process, you want to empty the browser cache before beginning disk maintenance.

 Lab 2-8: Configuring the browser cache in Microsoft Internet Explorer

In this lab, you will view, configure and empty the browser cache of Internet Explorer. The Internet Explorer browser cache is named Temporary Internet Files.

1. First, you will view the files in the browser cache. Restore the **Internet Explorer** window, then select **Tools | Internet Options** to display the Internet Options dialog box.

2. In the Temporary Internet Files section, click the **Settings** button to display the Settings dialog box, as shown in Figure 2-20.

Figure 2-20: Configuring browser cache in Microsoft Internet Explorer

3. Click the **View Files** button, then scroll through the contents of the Temporary Internet Files folder. Notice that cookies are stored in this folder. You will learn about cookies later in this lesson.

4. Close the **Temporary Internet Files** window.

5. Next, you will configure the size of the browser cache. Select the value in the Amount Of Disk Space To Use box, and then type **25** to change the size of the browser cache to 25 megabytes (MB).

6. Click **OK**. This step applies your new settings, closes the Settings dialog box and redisplays the Internet Options dialog box.

7. Next, you will empty the cache. In the Temporary Internet Files section, click the **Delete Files** button and click **OK** at the prompt to confirm that you want to delete the files.

8. Click **OK** to close the Internet Options dialog box.

9. Minimize the **Internet Explorer** window.

OBJECTIVE:
1.9.1: Browser
preference
configuration

Image loading

When images are loaded into your browser, the loading process consumes bandwidth and slows the transfer of information between the Web server and your computer. After images have been downloaded, they are stored in the disk cache and consume space.

Disabling image loading

Most browsers allow users to disable the image-loading function. When images are disabled, only the text appears in the browser window. An X or a No Image Available icon specified by the browser replaces each image. It makes sense to disable image loading in the following situations:

- **When conducting research** — If you research a topic on the Internet, you may not need to view graphics or active content because you are probably seeking only text about a subject.

- **With a slow Internet connection** — If you do not have a high-speed, permanent Internet connection, disabling image loading is advantageous. Slower analog modems, such as 14.4-Kbps and 28.8-Kbps connections, require much more time to download images. Disabling image-loading functions saves time (and telephone charges, if applicable).

In the following lab, you will disable image loading in Internet Explorer. Suppose the project manager for a research project at your university has asked you to help make the research team's computers work more quickly. The researchers are using dial-up connections and do not want to wait for graphics to load because they only need to see the text.

 Lab 2-9: Controlling image loading in Microsoft Internet Explorer

In this lab, you will control content in Internet Explorer by disabling image loading.

1. Restore the **Internet Explorer** window.

2. Select **Tools | Internet Options**, then click the **Advanced** tab.

3. Scroll down to the Multimedia section and deselect the **Show Pictures** check box, as shown in Figure 2-21.

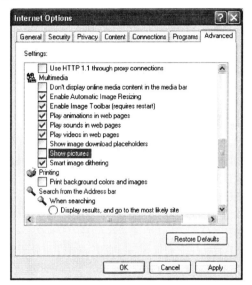

Figure 2-21: Controlling image loading in Microsoft Internet Explorer

4. Click **OK** to save your settings.

5. Click the **Refresh** button to download the current Web page from the server again.

6. View the Web page without images.

7. Select **Tools | Internet Options**, and click the **Advanced** tab. Scroll down to the Multimedia section, select **Show Pictures**, then click **OK** to restore your settings.

8. Click the **Refresh** button to display the images on the Web page.

9. Minimize the **Internet Explorer** window.

Cookies

cookie
A text file that contains information sent between a server and a client to help maintain state and track user activities. Cookies can reside in memory or on a hard drive.

Cookies are small text files placed on Web site visitors' computers so Web site managers can customize their sites to their visitors' preferences. For example, a cookie might be used to store information about your actions, such as the options you clicked on the Web page.

Cookies are sent to the client the moment a visitor accesses a Web site, and are usually used for identification. Cookies are connected to a database entry on the server site. These cookies enable the issuing cookie authority to customize distribution of its Web content to the visitor's operating system and browser.

Cookies can also be used to gather visitor information that could be used for marketing purposes, such as contact information (e-mail address, home address or phone number) or the operating system and browser you use. Unless you register with a site and provide this personal information, cookies do not have access to any data about you.

There are different types of cookies. A persistent cookie is one stored as a file on your computer and which remains there after you end your browser session. A session cookie is stored only during the current browsing session, and is deleted from your computer when you close your browser. A first-party cookie comes from the Web site you are currently viewing. A third-party cookie comes from a Web site other than the one you are currently viewing. Generally, third-party Web sites provide advertising content on the Web site you are currently viewing.

If a user configures his or her browser to allow cookie downloads from Web sites, then each time the user revisits that site, the user's computer will send the cookie to the Web server. The cookie can inform the Web server of the visitor's preferences, such as selection for local news and favorite stocks, as well as the sections of the site the visitor has navigated. Once a cookie is saved on a computer, only the Web site that created the cookie can read it.

A persistent cookie is stored in a specific directory on your computer. Cookies are considered to be so useful to both end users and the companies that build Web servers that both Navigator and Internet Explorer allow them by default. However, both browsers allow you to control cookie functions. Depending on security settings, the browser warns users before accepting a cookie, and then allows users to view, restrict or disable cookies completely.

Privacy issues with cookies

OBJECTIVE:
1.9.2: Cookies

Web sites publish privacy policies in both human-readable form (which you can view on the Internet) and as a file that can be interpreted by your browser. For example, Internet Explorer looks for a compact policy, or a condensed computer-readable privacy statement, before accepting cookies.

Many Web sites publish privacy statements based on the Platform for Privacy Preferences (P3P) standard. P3P is a protocol developed by the World Wide Web Consortium (W3C) to specify information that should be disclosed in a privacy policy.

A Web site's privacy policy should disclose the types of information the site collects, the ways that information may be used, and the parties to whom that information may be given. Once your information has been collected, the site can use the information for its own purposes (which may or may not include sharing that information with others). Some sites will share your information without your consent.

After reading a Web site's privacy policy, you can decide whether you want to provide that site with your personal information. Consider that there is no guarantee that a Web site will adhere to its own published privacy policy.

Setting automatic cookie handling

In Internet Explorer, you can control when and from whom cookies are accepted (called automatic cookie handling) by specifying the level of privacy you want to maintain. Use the Privacy tab of the Internet Options dialog box (shown in Figure 2-22) to control cookies.

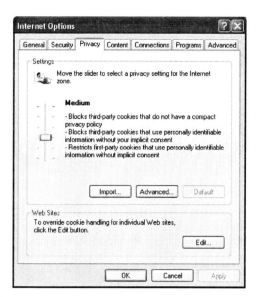

Figure 2-22: Internet Options dialog box — Privacy tab

You use the slider bar to adjust the level of privacy to your specifications. Table 2-1 shows the effects each privacy level has on cookies.

Table 2-1: Internet Explorer Privacy level effects on cookies

Privacy Level	Effect on Cookies
Block All Cookies	Blocks cookies from all Web sites, and existing cookies on your computer cannot be read by Web sites.
High	Blocks cookies from all Web sites that do not have a compact policy, and blocks cookies from all Web sites that use your personal information without your explicit consent.
Medium High	Blocks cookies from third-party Web sites that do not have a compact policy and/or that use your personal information without your consent. Also blocks cookies from first-party Web sites that use your personal information without your consent.
Medium	Blocks cookies from third-party Web sites that do not have a compact policy and/or that use your personal information without your consent. Also deletes cookies from first-party Web sites that use your personal information without your consent when you close Internet Explorer.
Low	Blocks cookies from third-party Web sites that do not have a compact policy, and deletes cookies from third-party Web sites that use your personal information without your consent when you close Internet Explorer.
Accept All Cookies	Saves all cookies on your computer and allows existing cookies to be read by the Web site that created them.

In the following lab, you will set automatic cookie handling in Internet Explorer. Suppose a manager in your company has read that cookies store personal information, and he asks you to adjust his browser to reject all cookies.

 Lab 2-10: Setting automatic cookie handling in Internet Explorer

In this lab, you will control cookies in Internet Explorer.

1. Restore the **Internet Explorer** window.

2. Select **Tools | Internet Options**, then click the **Privacy** tab.

3. Drag the slider up to **Block All Cookies**. Read the description for this level of privacy.

4. Drag the slider down to **Low** and read the description for this level of privacy. How do the two levels compare to one another?

5. Drag the slider to **Medium** to restore the default setting. Click **OK**, then minimize the **Internet Explorer** window.

Viewing cookie warnings

Instead of setting automatic cookie handling, you can configure your browser to override automatic cookie handling, and instead display warnings, or accept or block first-party and third-party cookies.

Configuring your browser to prompt you when cookies are sent can show you how extensively cookies are used.

In the following lab, you will configure Internet Explorer to display cookie warnings. Suppose that the manager who asked you to block all cookies on his browser is now complaining that he cannot access various Web sites and cannot find information that he needs. You tell him that by setting his browser to display cookie warnings, you will demonstrate to him how useful and common cookies are. You tell him that he can then choose the level of cookie control he prefers.

 Lab 2-11: Configuring Internet Explorer to display cookie warnings

In this lab, you will configure Internet Explorer to view cookie warnings that are sent to your computer.

1. Restore the **Internet Explorer** window.

2. Select **Tools | Internet Options**, then click the **Privacy** tab.

3. In the Privacy tab of the Internet Options dialog box, click the **Advanced** button to display the Advanced Privacy Settings dialog box.

4. Select **Override Automatic Cookie Handling** to make the options available.

5. Select **Prompt** for both first-party and third-party cookies, as shown in Figure 2-23. This step specifies that you want to be notified when a Web site is requesting to send a cookie to your computer.

Figure 2-23: Advanced Privacy Settings dialog box — Microsoft Internet Explorer

6. Click **OK** twice. This step closes the Advanced Privacy Settings dialog box and the Internet Options dialog box.

7. Click in the **Address** box, type *www.thetimes.co.uk*, then press ENTER. Before the page loads, a Privacy Alert displays, similar to the one shown in Figure 2-24.

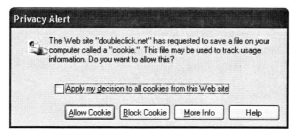

Figure 2-24: Privacy Alert — Microsoft Internet Explorer

8. In the Privacy Alert dialog box, click the **Allow Cookie** button to accept the cookie and display the page.

9. Select **Tools | Internet Options**, click the **Privacy** tab, and click the **Advanced** button. Deselect **Override Automatic Cookie Handling**, then click **OK** twice.

10. Minimize the **Internet Explorer** window.

Viewing cookie content

You can view the file content of cookies sent to browsers. Cookie files are partially encrypted; you will not be able to read them easily, but you can see information about the Web site that sent them to you.

Navigator's Cookie Manager lets you view cookies and displays information about them, as shown in Figure 2-25.

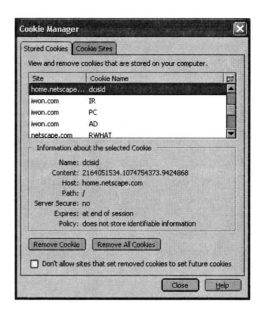

Figure 2-25: Cookie Manager — Netscape Navigator

To access the Cookie Manager, select Tools | Cookie Manager | Manage Stored Cookies. In the Stored Cookies tab, click on a cookie to display information about it. Notice that the cookie's expiration date, as well as the privacy policy of the Web site that set the cookie, are displayed.

You can also use Windows Explorer to view cookies. Different operating systems and browsers store cookie files in different locations. In Windows 95/98/Me, cookies are normally saved on your hard drive and set to expire after a period of time. Cookies are saved in the following folders, depending on the browser:

- Netscape Navigator — C:\Program Files\Netscape\Users\<username>

- Microsoft Internet Explorer — C:\Windows\Cookies_folder or C:\Windows\Temporary_Internet_Files

In Windows 2000 installed on a C:\ drive:

- Navigator cookies are stored in the C:\Documents and Settings\<user name>\ Application Data\Mozilla\directory.

- Internet Explorer cookies are stored in the C:\User Name\Local Settings\Temp\Cookies\ directory.

In Windows XP Professional installed on a C:\ drive:

- Navigator cookies are stored in the C:\Documents and Settings\<user name>\Application Data\Mozilla\Profiles\Default directory. You can also view stored cookies from within the browser.

- Internet Explorer cookies are stored in the C:\Documents and Settings\<username>\Cookies folder.

Note: You can also view Internet Explorer cookies in the C:\Documents and Settings\<username>\Local Settings\Temporary Internet Files folder. However, you must sort through all downloaded files from the Web page, such as images and HTML files.

Configuring Browser Security

You can configure your browser for added security by controlling active content downloading. Active content consists of any active, or moving, objects on a Web page, such as ActiveX controls and Java applets.

Both ActiveX controls and Java applets allow information to be downloaded and run on your system. However, some content can cause problems ranging from inconvenience to data loss. Professional developers have created hostile applets and ActiveX controls simply to demonstrate the possible security breaches in both technologies. You probably will not inadvertently browse a page with a hostile applet or ActiveX control because most are clearly labeled and meant only to demonstrate this possibly dangerous technology. But the danger is remotely possible, so you need to know how to shield your system from such problems.

To protect your system from incursions, both Internet Explorer and Navigator provide control options to enable or disable the execution of Java programs and other active content.

Some corporate IT departments ask that employees disable active content on their browsers. Disabling these features in a corporate environment reduces bandwidth use over networks, and protects the corporate servers and computers from possible security compromises.

If you disable Java programs, you will not see applets run, nor see any indication that an applet would have been running, and you will not receive an error message. If you enable Java programs, you will see the effects of the applet or an applet error message, if any exist.

OBJECTIVE:
1.9.1: Browser
preference
configuration

Internet Explorer safety levels

Internet Explorer provides several settings that allow you to determine whether potentially dangerous content can be downloaded to your computer automatically, with a warning, or not at all. These settings will often determine whether you can download active content, such as Java applets or ActiveX controls.

You use the Security tab of the Internet Options dialog box (Figure 2-26) to set safety levels in Internet Explorer.

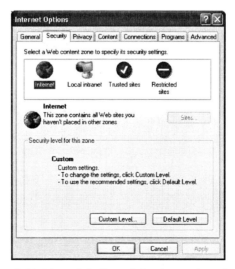

Figure 2-26: Internet Options dialog box — Security tab

Each safety level performs certain actions or requests, depending on the content of the Web page. For example, if the High setting is selected as the security level, and a Web page with active content is encountered, the active content will not display and a notification message will appear. The High safety level does not give you the option to view the active content.

If the Medium safety level setting is selected, you may receive a warning message (such as the one shown in Figure 2-27) when you start to download a file. When you see such a message, you are given the option to open the file in its current location, save it to your disk, cancel the download or request more information.

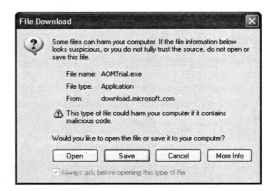

Figure 2-27: Microsoft Internet Explorer Medium-level security warning

If Low is selected for the safety level, you will not be warned or receive any confirmation messages, and you will not be protected from most active content. You will still be prompted when downloading unsigned and unsafe ActiveX controls. The content that prompted the warning in the preceding figure is deemed safe, so with a Low safety level setting, you would not be prompted with a warning.

If you are not denied access or prompted, then active Web content will download and operate in your browser automatically.

In the following lab, you will set safety levels in Internet Explorer. Suppose your company's security manager has established a security policy stating that safety levels in Microsoft Internet Explorer should be set to High on all corporate systems. You are assigned to ensure that this setting is put into effect.

 Lab 2-12: Setting safety levels in Microsoft Internet Explorer

In this lab, you will change the security level for downloading active content with Internet Explorer.

1. Restore the **Internet Explorer** window.

2. Select **Tools | Internet Options**, then click the **Security** tab.

3. Verify that the **Internet** zone is selected, then click the **Custom Level** button to specify your security settings. By default, your security settings are set to Medium, which warns you before running potentially damaging content.

4. In the Reset Custom Settings section, display the **Reset To** drop-down list, click **High**, and click the **Reset** button.

5. Click **Yes** when prompted to confirm that you want to change the security zone. The High setting prohibits you from downloading content that could damage your computer; this includes all ActiveX controls and plug-ins, as shown in Figure 2-28.

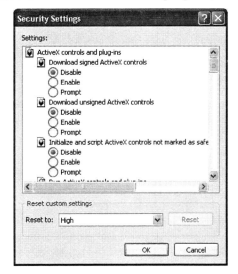

Figure 2-28: Microsoft Internet Explorer High safety level

6. Scroll down the list to examine the settings, then click **OK** twice to return to your browser.

7. Access ***http://moneycentral.msn.com/investor/home.asp***.

8. Locate and click the **Open Streaming Stock Ticker** hyperlink. You are unable to download the ActiveX object.

9. On the browser menu bar, select **Tools | Internet Options**, and click the **Security** tab. Click the **Custom Level** button, display the **Reset To** drop-down list, then click **Medium.** Click **Reset**, then click **Yes** to reset the safety level back to Medium.

10. Click **OK** twice to return to your browser.

11. Click the **Open Streaming Stock Ticker** hyperlink again. This time the warning shown in Figure 2-29 displays. Now that the safety level is set to Medium, you are warned and given the option to download and install potentially harmful content.

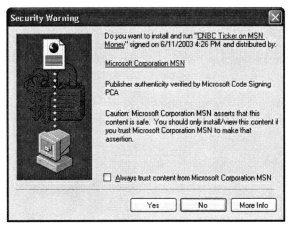

Figure 2-29: Security warning — Microsoft Internet Explorer

12. Click **Yes** to install the content and display the streaming stock ticker in its own window at the bottom of the browser window.

13. Close the **streaming stock ticker** window and the **Internet Explorer** window.

Which security method will you use when you return to your workplace? Does your IT department require you to use the highest security levels?

Safety levels are important for all Web users. With the rapid growth of the Internet, and the number of files and active programs transferred over it, security awareness has become increasingly important. You may find it disruptive to be warned for every cookie or active content item you encounter, but the warnings will serve as a constant reminder of the importance of Web security.

OBJECTIVE:
1.9.4: Configuring
the Desktop

Proxy Servers

Many organizations use proxy servers as "middlemen" between their corporate networks and the Internet. The main function of a proxy server is to enhance the corporate network's security and increase its Internet access speed by providing caching server functions for frequently used documents. The caching function is similar to your browser cache, except it caches Web sites for an entire network.

In a network setting, a proxy server replaces the network IP address with another, contingent address. This process effectively hides the actual IP address from the rest of the Internet, thereby protecting the entire network.

Proxy servers can provide the following services:

- **Web document caching** — If corporate users access information from a Web server from the Internet, that information is cached to the local proxy server. This caching allows anyone in the corporate intranet to access the same information from the local system instead of repeatedly downloading the files from the Internet. This feature reduces the amount of network traffic, which leads to improved performance for the corporate intranet and the Internet.

- **Corporate firewall access** — A proxy server can provide safe passage for corporate users through a firewall. You will learn more about firewalls in a later lesson.

Configuring applications to work with a proxy server

If your company network uses a proxy server, all users must be properly configured. For example, to browse the Web, the user (or IT personnel) must configure the browser to address the proxy server. Otherwise, the proxy server will ignore any requests and employees will be unable to access the Internet.

Furthermore, you must configure every application you want to use (such as Telnet and FTP programs) to work with your proxy server. Otherwise, those applications will not be able to access outside networks.

Browsers from both Netscape and Microsoft provide proxy server configuration, and you can obtain third-party programs that allow almost any application to work properly with a proxy server.

Netscape Navigator and proxy servers

In Netscape Navigator, you specify settings for a proxy server on the Proxies card of the Preferences dialog box, as shown in Figure 2-30. Notice that by default, Navigator assumes your computer has a direct connection to the Internet.

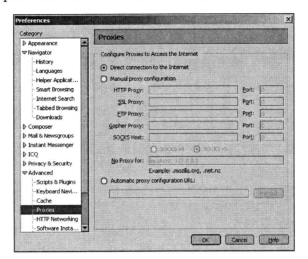

Figure 2-30: Proxies card of Preferences dialog box — Navigator

If you need to enter a manual configuration, select Manual Proxy Configuration, and enter the IP address and port number for each service that will use the proxy server.

If the system administrator has set up a proxy configuration file, Navigator can connect to the proxy server's URL automatically. You simply select Automatic Proxy Configuration URL, and enter the URL.

Microsoft Internet Explorer and proxy servers

Internet Explorer can use a configuration script, or automatically scan, for a proxy server. A configuration script is an executable file (or batch file) written by the server administrator. You run the script, and it will automatically load the necessary settings for the proxy server. To scan for a proxy server, click the Setup button on the Connections tab of the Internet Options dialog box, as shown in Figure 2-31.

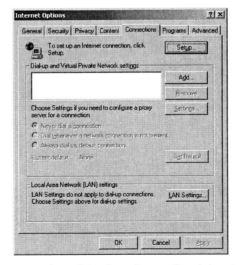

Figure 2-31: Internet Options dialog box, Connections tab — Internet Explorer

Clicking the Setup button will launch the Internet Connection Wizard.

You can also click the LAN Settings button to display the Local Area Network (LAN) Settings dialog box (Figure 2-32), in which you can manually configure a proxy server.

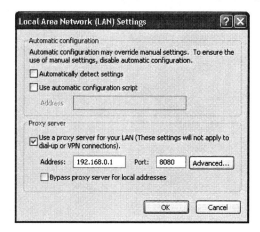

Figure 2-32: Local Area Network (LAN) Settings dialog box

Enter the IP address and port number used by the proxy server. By default, Internet Explorer automatically detects your proxy server.

Troubleshooting Internet Client Problems

OBJECTIVE:
1.9.5:
Troubleshooting
connectivity issues

You are now familiar enough with browser functions and settings to effectively troubleshoot some of the most common Internet client problems, including the following:

- **Poor rendering** — If the text on the screen is unreadable, you can adjust the font setting to help compensate for lower-resolution monitors.

- **Slow connection** — To improve the performance of computers with slow connections, you can increase the size of the browser cache, change the frequency with which the browser compares cached pages to those on the Web, and disable image loading.

- **No connection** — If your computer is unable to connect to any Web site and your company uses a proxy server, verify that the browser is correctly configured to use the proxy server.

- **Inability to render images** — If the browser will not display images, check to see if image loading has been disabled. If it has, deselect the Show Pictures check box in order to restore image loading.

- **Slow browser and other system functions** — Check the size of the browser cache to see whether it is too large. Empty the cache and reset the cache size if necessary to improve system performance.

Case Study

Working the Help Desk

Melissa is the IT person working the help desk, and several employees call her with various issues. Following are some of the complaints she receives:

- Maria says that any and every URL she types in the Address box returns a 404 — Page Not Found error.

- Jake is working on a system that uses a dial-up connection, and he is conducting extensive research on the Web. Jake says that whenever he visits a new site, it takes "forever" for the pages to load.

- Susan is trying to log on to a partner's extranet. Although she is using the user name and password assigned to her, she cannot log on.

- Ivan is a new employee, and his vision is poor. He needs to work extensively on the Web, but he cannot read most of the text on the Web pages.

Melissa takes the following steps to help these four employees:

- To help Maria, Melissa first verifies that the company network is allowing requests to go out. On another computer, Melissa visits a URL and refreshes the page. Because Maria could not access that same page, Melissa checks her connection settings and discovers that the browser is not configured properly to use the company proxy server.

- To help Jake, Melissa asks whether he must see graphics while conducting his research. He does not need to see graphics, so Melissa disables image loading to speed up page downloading.

- To help Susan, Melissa needs to see whether her system has an authentication problem. Melissa accesses www.netcraft.com and finds that the server software running on the partner site is IIS version 4. Susan is using an old version of Netscape Navigator, which is not compatible with IIS. Melissa recommends that Susan update her browser to the latest version.

- Melissa demonstrates to Ivan the way to adjust his font settings so that he can comfortably read the pages.

Melissa always remembers that she is part of a team, and that each person on that team is important. She always treats each person with respect, and avoids speaking to anyone in a condescending way. Even though Melissa is the expert, her primary job is to help and support the rest of the company.

* * *

As a class, discuss what additional steps, if any, Melissa can take to help these employees. What other types of calls might be commonly received by a help desk?

Lesson Summary

Application project

Suppose you are the network administrator for a company, and you want to standardize all employee browsers. Each employee computer should use the same browser, default opening page and links to competitors in the Favorites or Bookmarks menu. Choose a company and configure your computer to meet these standards. For example, suppose your company is Nike. Select your preferred browser and configure it to open by default to *www.nike.com.* Set your competitor links to the Reebok, Adidas and Puma Web sites. In what other ways can you standardize your employees' browsers?

If you are conducting research on the Internet, why might it help to disable image loading? Do you think it is equally important to control image loading if your company has a high-speed Internet connection?

Skills review

In this lesson, you learned about the basic functions of browsers, and you installed a browser and browsed the Web. You looked at the components of Web addresses, investigated ways that browsers authenticate and encrypt data for secure transmission, and identified considerations in selecting a browser. You also examined ways that businesses use browsers, used different browsing techniques, and located resources for technical information on the Web. You configured browser preferences, reviewed the use of cookies, set policies for accepting and blocking cookies, configured browser security settings, and reviewed the use of proxy servers.

Now that you have completed this lesson, you should be able to:

✓ Identify the basic functions of Web browsers.

✓ Install a Web browser.

✓ Identify the components of a Web address.

✓ Use browsers to authenticate and encrypt.

✓ Identify considerations in selecting a browser.

✓ Identify and locate resources for technical data.

✓ Identify how businesses use browsers.

✓ Use various browsing techniques.

✓ Configure Web browser preferences.

✓ Define and use cookies.

✓ Configure browser security settings.

✓ Identify the function of proxy servers.

✓ Troubleshoot common Internet client problems.

Lesson 2 Review

1. What are the two most popular browsers used on the World Wide Web today?

   _____

2. What is the purpose of the History folder?

   _____

   _____

3. What is contained in the browser cache?

   _____

4. What features are the same in various Web browsers? What features are different?

   _____

   _____

5. What is the purpose of disabling active content?

   _____

   _____

   _____

   _____

Lesson 3: Multimedia on the Web

Objectives

By the end of this lesson, you will be able to:

✿ Define objects and their relationships to multimedia.

✿ Explain the fundamentals of C, C++, Java, JavaScript, ActiveX, JScript and VBScript, and describe the relationships among them.

✿ Define the purpose of plug-ins.

✿ Identify plug-ins and viewers, including RealNetworks RealPlayer, Macromedia Shockwave and Flash players, Apple QuickTime and Adobe Reader.

✿ Listen to and view multimedia objects within your browser.

✿ Identify various file formats, such as MPEG, MP3, MOV, AIFF, AU, WAV, EPS, TIFF and RTF.

✿ Download files and store them on your computer.

Pre-Assessment Questions

1. Briefly describe C++.

    _____

2. Which statement about vector graphics is true?

    a. Vector graphics are saved as sequences of vector statements.
    b. Vector graphics have much larger file sizes than raster graphics.
    c. Vector graphics are pixel-based.
    d. GIFs and JPGs are vector graphics.

3. Name at least two examples of browser plug-ins.

    _____

    _____

Introduction to Multimedia on the Web

In recent years, the Internet has become much more than a text-based research tool. Many Web sites, including corporate sites, now feature multimedia content and interactive objects. For instance, employee orientation sessions, audio and video memos, and training materials are often placed on the Internet or corporate intranets.

To view interactive multimedia online, you need a sound card, speakers and a video card. You also need small applications called plug-ins that allow you to experience simulated three-dimensional worlds, play streaming audio and video, and interact with multimedia objects over the Internet. As an IT professional, you should understand the elements required for browsers to view these items.

This lesson will introduce you to multimedia content and the plug-in technology that allows you to view it. It will also teach you to install and operate some of the most widely used plug-ins. You will also learn how to download and store various types of files from the Internet.

Objects, Active Content and Languages

object
An element on a Web page that contains data and procedures for how that item will react when activated. On a Web page, an object is typically a multimedia presentation.

Objects enable Web authors to include multimedia effects, also called active content, on their sites. These objects can play sounds, show video clips and animation sequences, or demonstrate ideas in 3-D virtual reality simulations. In addition to making the user's Web experience more enjoyable, these multimedia capabilities can greatly enhance a site's educational value. Many businesses expect to profit from this active approach to Web site design and construction. The following sections discuss various types of programming and scripting languages used to create objects and active content, and their relationships to one another.

C

object-oriented programming (OOP)
Programming concept based on objects and data and how they relate to one another, instead of logic and actions; C++ and Java are OOP languages.

C is a programming language used primarily to create operating systems and applications. For instance, many UNIX operating systems have been developed using C. Because **object-oriented programming (OOP)** is becoming popular, C is being replaced by C++ and Java. In object-oriented programming, a program is handled as a collection of individual objects that perform separate functions, rather than as a sequence of statements that performs a specific task.

C++

C++ is a superset of the C language that uses object-oriented programming. Although the names are similar, C++ uses a completely different set of programming concepts than C uses and is considered the best language for creating large applications.

Java

Java
An object-oriented programming language developed by Sun Microsystems that is fully cross-platform functional.

Java is based on C++ and is also an object-oriented programming language. However, Java concentrates on distributed objects over a network (for example, the Internet) and is not as complex.

When the Web first became popular, HTML was the only language available for creating Web page content. It delivered a static page of text and/or graphics but offered limited interactivity.

graphical user interface (GUI)
A program that provides visual navigation with menus and screen icons, and performs automated functions when users click command buttons.

The increased demand for interactivity led to the development of Java, which provided cross-platform Internet applications. Now most computer users, whether they use Windows, Macintosh or UNIX systems, are accustomed to **graphical user interfaces (GUIs)** for their applications. They click buttons to execute commands, enter values into text boxes and choose from menu lists. This increase in user abilities and expectations has caused the continual improvement of Web programming and scripting languages, which includes the advent of Java **applets** and the powerful scripting language **JavaScript**.

Java applets

applets
Small programs written in Java, which are downloaded as needed and executed within a Web page or browser.

Java applets are programs written in the Java language and designed to run within a Web browser when accessed. Applets were the first technology developed for bringing program objects to the Web. Similar to ActiveX objects (discussed later in this lesson), applets animate pages, add functionality and interactivity, access multimedia services, and provide active content.

JavaScript
An interpreted, object-based scripting language developed by Netscape Communications that adds interactivity to Web pages.

Java applets are miniature Java programs downloaded into a Web browser when a user requests a Web page. They are treated the same way as other Web-embedded objects and are displayed in the browser's content area. Your Web browser must be Java-enabled to run applets. Both Netscape Navigator and Microsoft Internet Explorer support Java applets.

Unlike static objects, such as non-animated GIF and JPEG images or hyperlinks, Java applets can be **dynamic** and **interactive**. Their special effects include the following:

- **Inline video, changing text, and animation** — dynamic objects that can be embedded in Web pages without the need for external helper applications or plug-ins.

- **Audio** — sound files played either when an applet is invoked or in response to user action.

- **User interaction**— action and responses between a user and the displayed applet. Examples of interactive applets include user-interface controls that allow the user to interact with an on-screen element, such as in a computer game.

dynamic
Always changing.

interactive
The characteristic of some hardware and software, such as computers, games and multimedia systems, that allows them to respond differently based on a user's actions.

- **Real-time data feeds**— transmissions that maintain an open connection between the server and an applet on a Web page, or periodically poll the server to update information displayed in the browser. Examples of real-time data feeds are online clocks and up-to-the-minute stock market tickers.

Applets can combine these properties to create complex but easy-to-use Internet applications.

JavaScript

event-driven
Reacting to particular user actions or the browser's completion of a specific task.

The Web is **event-driven**. For example, when you click or select an element on a Web page, you have caused an event. Events include: a mouse click, a mouse drag, text entered or a page loaded (or unloaded) in the browser. JavaScript is an event-driven scripting language because it is designed to react whenever an event occurs.

Traditional programming languages, such as C, cause events to happen, rather than reacting to events. By contrast, scripting languages are used within existing programs to extend those programs' capabilities. If you have ever written a macro in Microsoft Excel or used WordBasic to perform a task in a Microsoft Word document, you have already used a scripting language.

JavaScript was the first scripting language developed exclusively for online content design. JavaScript syntax resembles that of traditional programming languages. These scripts are placed within your Web document. When your browser retrieves a page that incorporates JavaScript, it runs the scripts and performs the appropriate operations.

JavaScript vs. Java

Although the names are similar, JavaScript and Java are different languages. Java is an object-oriented programming language, whereas JavaScript (as the name suggests) is an object-based scripting language.

Java, developed by Sun Microsystems, can create stand-alone applications and Java applets.

LiveScript
The Netscape-developed scripting language that was the predecessor to JavaScript.

JavaScript, developed by Netscape Communications, has its origins in a scripting language called **LiveScript**. Unlike Java, JavaScript is not a stand-alone programming language: It must reside within HTML documents to run. JavaScript adds interactivity to Web pages without the need for specialized server-based programs.

JavaScript complements Java by supporting most of Java's expression syntax and basic program flow controls. It also exposes useful properties of Java applets to JavaScript programmers.

JScript

JScript is the Microsoft version of JavaScript. Though similar in functionality, it is merely a subset of the full JavaScript language. JScript is built into Microsoft Internet Explorer; JavaScript is built into Netscape Navigator. Because of the slight differences between JavaScript and JScript, programs written in JavaScript may not function properly within Internet Explorer, and programs written in JScript may not function properly within Netscape Navigator.

ActiveX

ActiveX was first developed by Microsoft, but was then turned over to an independent organization, The Open Group. ActiveX is a strategic initiative that incorporates object-oriented programming tools and technologies. ActiveX is Microsoft's response to Java.

ActiveX
An open set of technologies for integrating components on the Internet and within Microsoft applications.

ActiveX technology enables authors to place interactive objects on their Web sites based on a common standard, and allows the objects to work together. With ActiveX, Web pages can include animation, audio, video and virtual reality. Web content can be dynamic, providing current information on any topic, customized to the user's profile and preferences.

ActiveX is used to create ActiveX controls, which are self-contained programs that can be run anywhere on a network, including within a browser from the Internet. ActiveX controls are similar to Java applets.

Visual Basic Script (VBScript)
Scripting language from Microsoft, derived from Visual Basic; used to manipulate ActiveX scripts.

Visual Basic
The Microsoft graphical user interface (GUI) programming language used for developing Windows applications. A modified version of the BASIC programming language.

Visual Basic Script (VBScript) *(.vbs)*

Visual Basic Script (VBScript) is an object-based scripting language that Microsoft derived from its more powerful **Visual Basic** programming language.

VBScript can manipulate two types of objects. The first type is called a standard HTML object, which is an intrinsic object such as those found on a form: a display button, radio button, check box or password field. The second type of object, the ActiveX control, is more powerful and flexible. The ActiveX functions of an object are invoked by user action.

Most commonly used to write virus

> Microsoft VBScript is a vendor-specific scripting language. Unlike JavaScript, VBScript may not be supported by browsers other than Microsoft Internet Explorer.

Objects and Security Issues

To work with downloadable active content such as Java applets and ActiveX objects, you need to understand the security issues involved and know how to protect yourself from hostile incursions.

Both ActiveX and Java applets allow information to be downloaded and run on your system. However, some content can cause problems ranging from inconvenience to loss of data.

You learned earlier in this course that both Internet Explorer and Navigator provide control options to enable or disable the execution of Java programs and other active content. You also learned how to disable active content entirely. This knowledge will allow you to choose the appropriate security setting for your personal computer or your company, and shield your system from dangerous content.

Introduction to Plug-in Technology

plug-in
A program installed in the browser to extend its basic functionality. Allows different file formats to be viewed as part of a standard HTML document.

As browsers have evolved, features that enhance their functionality have been included to support a large range of objects. Users can access the active content directly from the browser with **plug-ins**, such as Apple QuickTime and Macromedia Shockwave and Flash players. Plug-ins, also called players, extend the capabilities of Web browsers. When you visit a Web site that requires a plug-in (or a more recent version of a plug-in that you already have installed), you may be prompted to download and install or reinstall the application so that you can view the Web page content properly.

What are plug-ins?

Plug-ins are applications associated with a specific platform (such as Windows or Macintosh) and sometimes with a specific browser (such as Navigator or Internet Explorer). The primary goal of a plug-in is to provide efficient integration of multimedia formats with the browser and computer. Without this integration, a user would have to download multimedia files and play them back later with a separate application. Plug-ins allow multimedia data types to execute directly from a browser, allowing immediate viewing and listening, thus enhancing your Web experience.

How do plug-ins work?

When a browser encounters a file type that is not directly supported, it launches a plug-in application that retrieves the multimedia files from a server, similar to the way a browser retrieves standard Web pages. The files are then delivered to the client system for playback.

disk cache
Storage space on a computer hard disk used to temporarily store downloaded data.

streaming media
A continuous flow of data, usually audio or video files, that assists with the uninterrupted delivery of those files into a browser.

Instead of loading the entire file at once, many plug-ins retrieve a small portion at a time and store the data in the local **disk cache**. Using a cache, the plug-in delivers just enough information to build a continuous stream of data, called **streaming media**, which eliminates transfer delays. For instance, when you listen to a Web audio file, you may be hearing one part of the file while the next part downloads in the background. If you download an entire file before playing it, you are playing non-streaming media.

Plug-in appearance

Files that have been interpreted by a plug-in appear in one of three ways, depending on the file type and additional HTML tags. Some files will not function if additional HTML attributes are set. Following are the three appearance modes:

- **Full-screen** — The multimedia will completely fill the browser window's inner frame.

- **Embedded** — The multimedia appears as part of a larger document, in which the media or media player is visible as a rectangular sub-portion of a page. This mode resembles an embedded GIF or JPEG image, except the media can be live and/or dynamic, and may have its own embedded functionality. Many videos, such as RealPlayer and Shockwave videos, are embedded files. Plug-ins play them within the browser window, as shown in Figure 3-1.

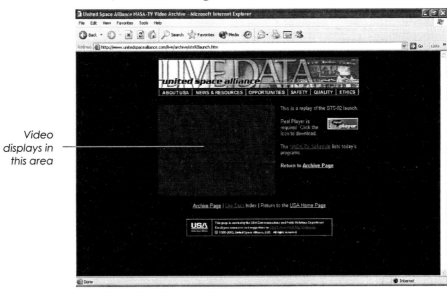

Video displays in this area

Figure 3-1: Embedded RealPlayer video

Musical Instrument Digital Interface (MIDI)
A standard computer interface for creating and playing electronic music. It allows computers to re-create music in digital format for playback.

- **Hidden** — The multimedia and its players are not visible in the browser and run in the background. An example of a commonly hidden plug-in is a **Musical Instrument Digital Interface (MIDI)** player.

The browser appears largely the same despite the plug-in. Basic browser operations (such as navigation, history, file opening, and so forth) apply to all pages, regardless of which plug-ins are required to view each page.

Data Compression and Decompression

Before exploring particular audio and video player plug-ins, you should acquaint yourself with the basic principles of data compression. Compression is the reduction in size of data files. Audio and video files are compressed before they are transferred across the Internet to shorten the amount of time required to download them. Once files are received at the client system, they are decompressed so that they can be played (viewed and/or heard).

There are various ways to compress data, and many types of data can be compressed. You are probably already familiar with popular "zip" programs that compress text and images. Some image file formats such as GIF and JPEG are designed to reduce the size of image files.

 Do not confuse zipped file formats with proprietary Iomega Zip drives.

lossless compression
A type of data file compression in which all original data can be recovered when the file is decompressed.

lossy compression
A type of data file compression in which some file information is permanently eliminated.

codec
A compression/ decompression algorithm used by modern video and audio player plug-ins.

Compression can be either lossy or lossless. With **lossless compression**, all the original data can be recovered when the file is decompressed. Lossless compression is used for compressing text and spreadsheet files, for example. The Graphics Interchange File (GIF) format provides lossless compression.

Lossy compression permanently eliminates some of the information (especially redundant information). When the file is decompressed, only part of the original information is still there. Lossy compression is used for video and sound files, where certain amounts of information loss is hard to detect and is therefore not noticeable. The JPEG file format, which is used extensively for photographs on the Web, uses lossy compression. When you save an image file in JPEG format, you can specify how much loss you want to allow. Generally, you must find a balance between image quality and file size.

Compression is performed by a program that uses an algorithm to specify compression or decompression instructions for a given file. Multimedia players (such as RealPlayer, Windows Media Player and QuickTime player) use special algorithms called **codecs** to create streaming media.

Codec is an abbreviation for compression/decompression. Media files on the Web are compressed, and when you download them, they must be decompressed so that you can play them. Several standard codec schemes are employed on the Internet today, and new ones are added regularly. Players are equipped with these standardized codec schemes; as new codecs become popular, you can update your player's store of codecs. The store of codecs is updated when you upgrade your plug-in.

Movie Time!

Insert the CIW Foundations Movie CD to learn even more about this topic.

Plug-ins (approx. playing time: 06:50)

All movie clips are © 2004 LearnKey, Inc.

Plug-in Installation

OBJECTIVE:
1.5.10: Plug-ins, add-ons and viewers

Although plug-in installation procedures are quickly becoming standardized, unpredictable results can occur. This uncertainty exists because so many different configurations are possible depending on the user's choice of browser, operating system and plug-in. The two ways to install plug-ins are online and offline.

Online installation

Online installation usually occurs with the browser open. Although certain Navigator plug-in installation files support online installation, many must be installed offline. Internet Explorer also installs many plug-in types without prompting the user when unsupported file types are encountered.

Offline installation

Offline installation requires the user to download the plug-in file, quit the browser and start the installation file. When installation is complete, the computer may need to be restarted before the changes take effect. In the case of offline installation, you must read the installation instructions carefully before starting the download.

Installing and updating plug-ins

Internet Explorer and Navigator both include several native plug-ins. The plug-ins are automatically installed with the browser. As mentioned earlier, when you visit a Web site that requires a plug-in (or a more recent version of a plug-in you already have), you may be prompted to download and install it. To avoid interrupting your Web browsing to download a plug-in every time you need one, you can visit several download sites in advance and install the most recent versions of popular plug-ins.

It is advisable to occasionally upgrade plug-ins from the appropriate vendor's site. Upgrades usually include increased functionality and security updates.

Types of Plug-ins

For many years, technology has allowed users to download and play back high-quality audio and video from the Internet. In the following pages, you will learn about several types of multimedia and their required plug-ins.

Various plug-ins are available, and each one can handle different file types, with some overlap. For example, both RealPlayer and Windows Media Player can play MP3 files. Most of these applications will prompt you to associate certain file types with the plug-in by default. The default association will display the plug-in icon next to the files of the associated type in Windows Explorer, and double-clicking an associated file will launch the default plug-in. However, you can still open a file using the non-default application.

Macromedia Shockwave and Flash players

Macromedia Shockwave is a group of multimedia players designed to deliver several types of multimedia, including animation, sound, graphics and streaming video. The Shockwave Player displays interactive games, multimedia user interfaces and audio, including live concerts and radio. Since Shockwave was introduced in 1995, many sites have been designed with its multimedia capabilities.

Macromedia developed another player called the Flash Player. The Flash Player allows browsers to view movies created with the Flash application. Flash movies offer full-screen navigation interfaces, are resizable to various display sizes and resolutions, and they can play as they download.

vector graphics
Resizable images that are saved as a sequence of vector statements, which describes a series of points to be connected.

The Flash authoring software allows you to create animation by using **vector graphics**. Think of vector graphics as mathematical shapes. A vector graphic is saved as a sequence of vector statements, which describes a series of points to be connected. The graphics you are probably most familiar with, GIFs and JPEGs, are raster graphics, which are images that map bits directly to a display space (think of a grid of x and y coordinates on a display space). Raster graphics are pixel-based, and as such are much larger files than vector graphics. When the vector images are downloaded, they are rasterized (converted into raster images) as they arrive and the animation displays in the player.

The advantages of using vector graphics are that the files are small (resulting in shorter download time) and they are easily resized without affecting image quality. Flash files have an .swf file name extension.

When you download Shockwave Player, you should also download Flash Player. Flash is ideal for the Internet; complex animations can be downloaded quickly because of their small file sizes.

In the following lab, you will use Shockwave and Flash with Internet Explorer. Suppose the marketing manager of your company wants to view Shockwave files and Flash movies in his browser so he can decide whether to invest time and money to create similar products for the company Web site. You can download and install these players so that he can view the files.

 Lab 3-1: Using Macromedia Shockwave and Flash with Microsoft Internet Explorer

In this lab, you will navigate to the Macromedia Web site and download and install the Macromedia Shockwave Player and Flash Player plug-ins.

Note: You may require access to an account with administrative permissions to install this software.

1. First, you will download and install the plug-ins. Open **Microsoft Internet Explorer**.

2. Enter the URL *www.macromedia.com/downloads/*. Your screen will resemble Figure 3-2.

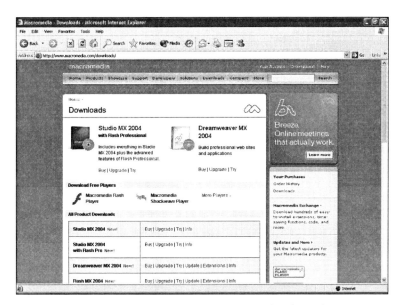

Figure 3-2: Downloading Shockwave and Flash players in Microsoft Internet Explorer

3. Click the **Macromedia Shockwave Player** link to access the Shockwave Player download page.

4. Click the **Install Now** button, and click **Yes** in response to the security warning. Shockwave Player displays a progress box (shown in Figure 3-3) while the program is downloading.

    Note: If you were using Navigator, you would click a Download Now button, and the installation files would be copied to your hard drive. You would then quit the browser and install the plug-ins in separate steps.

Figure 3-3: Downloading Shockwave Player

Note: The specific screens displayed during the download and installation may differ from the ones shown here.

5. Complete each dialog box that displays by providing the requested information and clicking **Next**. When you complete the registration for the free product, the Installation Complete dialog box appears (Figure 3-4).

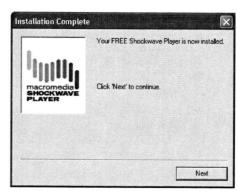

Figure 3-4: Installation Complete dialog box

6. Click **Next**. Your browser will play a Shockwave demo (such as the one shown in Figure 3-5) to ensure proper installation.

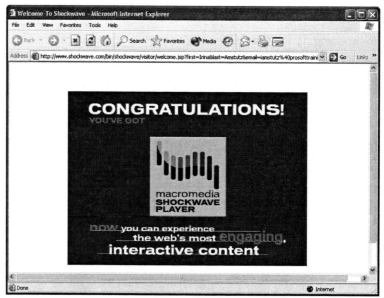

Figure 3-5: Testing plug-in installation

7. Close the Welcome To Shockwave window.

8. Click the Downloads link in the navigation bar at the top of the open Web page to return to the Downloads page.

9. Click the Macromedia Flash Player link.

10. Click the Install Now button and click Yes in response to the security warning. When the Installation Complete message flashes on the Web page, the installation is complete.

11. Next, you will explore the capabilities of the Shockwave and Flash players. Enter the URL ***www.macromedia.com/showcase/***. Explore the showcase to see examples of Web sites using this technology. What did you think of each site you visited? Does multimedia enhance your Web-viewing experience?

12. Click the link to view the **Site Of The Day**. Does this site use the animation technologies well?

13. Close the browser windows.

RealNetworks RealPlayer

RealNetworks (*www.real.com*) developed the streaming media format and introduced RealAudio in 1995. Soon after, RealVideo, which uses the same streaming format as RealAudio, was invented. The audio and video format features were combined in one application called RealPlayer. Additional capabilities were added, such as recording, mixing and burning CDs, and RealPlayer was renamed RealOne. However, many people still refer to the player as RealPlayer. In fact, some versions of the player are named RealOne Player, whereas other versions are named RealPlayer. Throughout this course, the player will be referred to as RealPlayer.

RealPlayer is easy to configure and use. It displays the name of the sound or video file and the play time remaining on the track. It allows users to play, stop, pause, rewind and fast-forward media files. RealPlayer sound files can be grouped into clips and then played in a specified sequence, similar to a jukebox playlist. The user can skip ahead or return to any part of the file. RealPlayer can also function as an external application.

The file name extensions normally associated with RealPlayer are .ra (RealAudio for streaming audio files) and .ram (RealMedia for streaming video files that include sound). RealPlayer also handles several other file types, which will be discussed later in this lesson. Although it will run from your browser, RealPlayer can also be run as a stand-alone application that can be launched from the Windows Start menu.

In the following lab, you will install the RealPlayer plug-in. Suppose a product development manager in your company needs RealPlayer to be installed on the computer system in the conference room for an upcoming meeting during which she will play a RealMedia (.ram) movie that highlights the company's new product.

 Lab 3-2: Using the RealPlayer plug-in

In this lab, you will use RealPlayer to listen to audio streams and view data streams in Microsoft Internet Explorer and Netscape Navigator.

Note: Conduct this lab only if you have sufficient bandwidth. Systems must have speakers to listen to audio streams. Students may require an account with administrative permissions to install this software.

1.   Verify that your computer has speakers, and that they are turned on and set to a suitable volume.

2.   Start **Microsoft Internet Explorer** and access the RealNetworks Web site at *www.real.com*. Click the necessary links to download the latest free version of RealPlayer.

3.   Click the **Yes** button at the security warning to proceed with the download.

4.   When the product download is finished, read the license agreement and accept it by clicking the **Accept** button.

5.   Follow the directions in the Installation Wizard (accept the default configuration) to install the product on your system.

6.   Respond to the prompts in the Product Setup Wizard. When RealPlayer is installed and configured, multimedia will stream into your browser.

7. Visit the following sites to listen to audio streams:

- The National Public Radio home page (***www.npr.org***).

- The Radio Locator home page (***www.radio-locator.com***). Specify your ZIP code and state to find a radio station in your area that broadcasts over the Internet.

When you reach one of these sites, search for links that allow you to begin streaming audio.

8. Stop all audio streams. Visit any of the following sites to view streaming video:

- Real Movies page (***http://movies.real.com***)

- The Reuters site (***www.reuters.com***)

- The CNN site (***www.cnn.com***), registration required.

9. Close **Internet Explorer**.

10. Start **Navigator** and use RealPlayer to listen to streaming audio and view streaming video.

11. Close all browsers, as well as RealPlayer windows and/or download manager windows.

Apple QuickTime

QuickTime
A plug-in developed by Apple Computer for storing movie and audio files in digital format.

QuickTime is a plug-in created by Apple Computer for storing video and audio files in digital format. QuickTime is available for both Windows and Macintosh systems. This plug-in lets you see and hear QuickTime content in your browser window. It can be downloaded from *www.apple.com/quicktime*. Many samples, such as movie previews, can be viewed at the site after you download the product.

The QuickTime plug-in works with existing QuickTime movies and other movies that can use its fast-start feature. This feature presents the first frame of the movie almost immediately and begins playing the movie before it has been completely downloaded, much like a streaming format.

QuickTime Movie (MOV)

QuickTime Movie (MOV)
Standard file format for Apple QuickTime; uses the .mov, .moov or .qt file name extension.

The **QuickTime Movie (MOV)** file format was created by Apple and is supported by all QuickTime versions. Video, animation, text and sound are combined into one file. QuickTime files are identified by a .mov, .moov or .qt file name extension.

QuickTime Virtual Reality (QTVR)

QuickTime Virtual Reality (QTVR) is a virtual reality product from Apple. It expands a two-dimensional photograph into a three-dimensional world, without cumbersome virtual reality headgear. The 3-D environment can be explored in 360 degrees and can include interactive elements. You will learn more about virtual reality plug-ins shortly. QTVR is automatically installed when you install Apple QuickTime. Figure 3-6 shows a QTVR sequence.

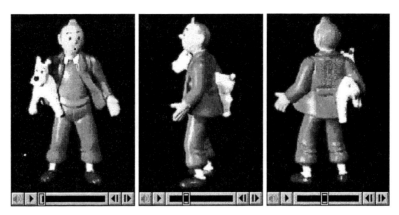

Figure 3-6: QTVR sequence

For more information about QTVR, including instructions for creating QTVR sequences, visit *www.apple.com/quicktime/qtvr*.

In the following lab, you will install the QuickTime plug-in. Suppose that the marketing team wants to compare QuickTime movies with RealMedia movies in order to decide which movie format to support on the corporate Web site. RealPlayer is already installed on all corporate computers, but QuickTime is not.

 Lab 3-3: Downloading, installing and demonstrating Apple QuickTime

In this lab, you will download and install QuickTime, and view a QuickTime movie. Unlike Macromedia Flash and Shockwave players, the QuickTime plug-in will be copied to your computer and then installed from a desktop folder.

Note: Conduct this lab only if you have sufficient bandwidth. Students may require an account with administrative permissions to install this software.

1. First, you will download the plug-in. Start **Microsoft Internet Explorer**. Enter the URL *www.apple.com/quicktime/*.

2. Click the **QuickTime Player** link to display the QuickTime page, which includes options for downloading the free player and purchasing other products. In the Download section of the page, you have an option to download the player or the stand-alone installer.

3. Click the **Standalone Installer** link to display the download page.

4. Ensure that the correct operating system is specified. The operating system in your classroom should be Windows XP.

5. Scroll down the page and click the **Download QuickTime** button to display the Congratulations page and start the download.

    Note: If your download does not begin automatically, click the specified link on the page.

6. You should see the File Download dialog box, shown in Figure 3-7.

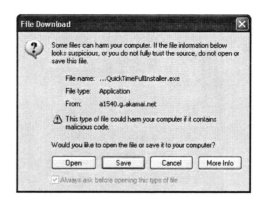

Figure 3-7: QuickTime File Download dialog box

7. You use the File Download dialog box to specify whether to run an application from its location, save it to your computer, or cancel the download. Click the **Save** button to display the Save As dialog box, shown in Figure 3-8. This dialog box specifies the location in which to save the downloaded file.

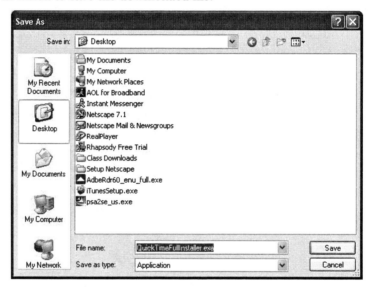

Figure 3-8: QuickTime Save As dialog box

8. Click the **Desktop** icon in the Save As dialog box if necessary, then click the **Create New Folder** button to create a new folder on the Desktop into which you will save the downloaded file.

9. Type *Class Downloads* and press **ENTER** to name the new Desktop folder. Double-click the **Class Downloads** folder to open it. *Class Downloads* should now display in the Save In text box at the top of the Save As dialog box.

10. Click the **Save** button to begin downloading the file to the specified Desktop folder. The Percent Completed dialog box may or may not close when the download is complete. If it does not close, close it. The Congratulations page will redisplay in the browser window.

11. Next, you will install the plug-in. Minimize the browser window to redisplay the Desktop. Double-click the **Class Downloads** folder on the Desktop, then double-click **QuickTimeFullInstaller.exe** to start the installation.

A series of dialog boxes will guide you through the installation and setup process.

12. Click **Next** twice to view the license agreement, click **Agree** to accept the license agreement, then click **Next** four more times to accept the defaults and install the plug-in.

13. Next, you will specify settings for the plug-in. These settings include specifying your connection speed, configuring the browser and associating file types with the QuickTime application. When the QuickTime Settings dialog box displays, click **Next**, display the Connection Speed drop-down list, and select the connection speed specified by your instructor.

14. Click **Next** twice, then click **Finish** to accept the remaining default settings.

Note: If your system has been reconfigured for class using the Windows Restore feature, the wizard screens that display may differ from those indicated in Steps 13 and 14. For example, you may not need to specify a connection speed, and fewer wizard screens may display.

15. When the Finished dialog box displays, deselect **Yes, I Want To View The QuickTime README File**, then click **Close**. This step will complete the setup and launch the QuickTime Player.

16. Now you will view movies with QuickTime Player. Close any open Windows Explorer windows, then restore the **Internet Explorer** window.

17. In the navigation bar at the top of the Congratulations page, click the **Movie Trailers** link to display the Movie Trailers page.

18. Click and view several items on the page. Depending on the movie trailer you select, you may be able to specify a screen size (small, medium or large) for viewing.

19. Click your browser's **Back** button once or twice as required to return to the Movie Trailers page.

20. Close your browser window and any QuickTime windows.

Windows Media Player

The Microsoft Windows Media Player is a popular standards-based plug-in that plays streaming audio and video. It can display both live and on-demand content. One benefit it offers is FM-quality audio. New features involve pay-per-view applications and increased piracy protection for owners of the downloaded content. The Windows Media Player interface is shown in Figure 3-9.

Figure 3-9: Windows Media Player interface

Windows Media Player is available for Windows and Macintosh systems. Windows Media Player includes a feature that will automatically look for available updates, which can be found at *www.microsoft.com/windows/windowsmedia*. You can also go directly to the Web site to download and install the update.

The file name extensions normally associated with Windows Media Player include .wma (Windows media audio) and .wmv (Windows media video), and the player also supports several video and audio file formats (such as .avi, .mpeg, .midi, .wav) discussed later in this lesson.

In the following lab, you will update the Windows Media Player plug-in. Suppose your company's marketing manager wants to view a competitor's Web site movies, which are in WMV format. The IT supervisor has assigned you to update the version of Windows Media Player currently installed on the marketing manager's computer so that the plug-in will support all the latest technologies.

 Lab 3-4: Updating and demonstrating Windows Media Player

In this lab, you will update Windows Media Player and use it to view movies.

Note: Conduct this lab only if you have sufficient bandwidth. Students may require an account with administrative permissions to install this software.

1. Start **Microsoft Internet Explorer** and enter the URL *www.microsoft.com/downloads/*.

2. In the navigation section on the left side of the page, click **Windows Media** to access the Windows Media download page.

3. Click the link for the most recent version of Windows Media Player for your operating system (your classroom computer should be running the Windows XP operating system).

4. On the download page for the version you selected, click the **Download** button to display the File Download dialog box.

5. Click the **Save** button in the File Download dialog box, navigate to the **Desktop\Class Downloads** folder if necessary, then click the **Save** button in the Save As dialog box to start the download.

6. The Percent Completed dialog box may or may not close when the download is complete. If it does not close, close it. The download page will redisplay in your browser.

7. Minimize the browser window to display the Desktop, double-click the **Class Downloads** folder, and then double-click **MPSetupXP.exe** to begin installing the Windows Media Player upgrade.

8. When the license agreement displays, read it, then click the **I Accept** button to continue the installation.

9. When the setup windows display, click **Next** twice to accept the defaults, then click **Finish** to launch the updated version of Windows Media Player.

10. Close any **Windows Explorer** windows.

11. Restore the **Internet Explorer** window, then enter the URL *www.windowsmedia.com/MediaGuide/Home* to display available movie clips at the Windows Media site.

12. Explore the site and click the free movie clips to view in Windows Media Player. How does viewing movie clips in Windows Media Player compare with viewing clips in QuickTime and in RealPlayer?

13. Close **Windows Media Player** and any open browser windows.

Virtual Reality Modeling Language (VRML) plug-ins

Virtual Reality Modeling Language (VRML)
A three-dimensional graphic authoring language.

Virtual Reality Modeling Language (VRML) extends your Web browser into the three-dimensional realm. With VRML plug-ins, you can visit 3-D spaces with lifelike, fully animated objects. You can also walk, fly or explore 3-D worlds.

Users can interact in real time with text and images, animation, sound, music and video, as well as with embedded mini-applications. VRML has potential for educational, training and commercial applications, from 3-D training centers to geographical information systems to interactive advertisements.

VRML features include:

- **High-performance VRML viewing** — 3-D spaces can be accessed at high speeds.

- **Animation** — VRML accommodates objects with lifelike behaviors.

- **Navigation** — VRML enables 3-D navigation via simulated walking, flying or pointing. Selectable camera viewpoints, sliding, optional gravity and sound add flexibility and realism.

Several VRML viewers are available. Netscape Live3D (*www.netscape.com*) is available for Windows. Computer Associates WorldView and Cosmo Player (*www.cai.com/cosmo*) are available for Macintosh and Windows.

Types of Viewers

viewer
A scaled-down version of an application; designed to view and print files.

A **viewer** is necessary to retrieve certain files when the program needed to open a file type is not installed on your computer. Viewers are scaled-down versions of applications and are usually available free of charge. They do not have the full application's functionality. Often, the viewer will allow you to view and print documents, but not edit them. Because viewer files are much smaller than program files, they are helpful when disk space is limited, or when the full program is unavailable. In this section, you will learn about two important viewers.

Microsoft PowerPoint Viewer

The Microsoft PowerPoint Viewer is a helpful tool for businesspeople who give slide presentations from laptop computers, or for users who have earlier versions of PowerPoint on their computers and must present slide shows created in newer versions. Installing the most recent version of PowerPoint Viewer ensures the ability to present a slide show created with any version of PowerPoint. PowerPoint Viewer can be downloaded and distributed freely from the Microsoft Web site at the following URL:

http://office.microsoft.com/assistance/9798/viewerscvt.aspx

You can also view PowerPoint slides directly within your browser. These file types are typically associated with your browser upon installation of either the browser or a new program.

You can download Netscape browser plug-ins and viewers from the Netscape download center:

http://cgi.netscape.com/plugins/presentations.html

These viewers allow you to read Microsoft Office files (such as Word, Excel and PowerPoint files) in your Netscape Navigator browser. Netscape Navigator must be configured to open the slides in the browser, whereas Microsoft Internet Explorer automatically opens the Microsoft PowerPoint file within the browser.

Adobe Reader

Adobe Systems Incorporated offers a free viewer that can read files created in Adobe Acrobat. Because many files on the Web have been created in Adobe Acrobat, this viewer can be found on thousands of corporate Web pages.

Portable Document Format (PDF)

Portable Document Format (PDF)
A file format that can be transferred across platforms and retain its formatting; designated by the file name extension .pdf.

Adobe created the **Portable Document Format (PDF)**, a general file format that can be created and read on any computer, regardless of the local operating system. These files are suitable for transmission over the Web. Because of their high compression and platform independence, PDF files take minimal time to download, even with slower connections. They also retain formatting information through all platforms. In the following lab, you will download and install Adobe Reader and view a PDF file.

In the following lab, you will use Adobe Reader with Internet Explorer. Suppose the manager for a new research and development project wants all the department personnel to be able to download and read PDF files. You can install Adobe Reader on the research and development team's computers to enable team members to do this.

Lab 3-5: Using Adobe Reader with Microsoft Internet Explorer

In this lab, you will download and install the current version of the free Adobe Reader, then use it to view PDF files directly in Internet Explorer.

Note: If you have a slow Internet connection, install Adobe Reader from the **C:\CIW\Internet\LabFiles\Lesson03** *folder. Double-click* **AdbeRdr60_enu_full.exe** *to launch the optimizer and installer, then skip to Step 9 of this lab. Students may require an account with administrative permissions to install this software.*

1. First, you will download and install the reader. Start **Microsoft Internet Explorer**.

2. Enter the URL **www.adobe.com**.

3. Scroll down the Adobe home page and click the **Get Adobe Reader** link to display the Download Adobe Reader page, as shown in Figure 3-10.

Figure 3-10: Adobe Reader download page

4. In the Step 1 of 2 section, display the **Platform** drop-down list and click **Windows XP**, then display the **Connection Speed** drop-down list and select an option as directed by your instructor.

5. Scroll down the page to view the Step 2 of 2 section, and ensure that **Download The Full Version Of Adobe Reader** is selected.

6. Deselect **Also Download Free Photoshop Album 2.0 Starter Edition Software**. You will download only the reader in this lab.

7. Click the **Download** button to begin the download. This step displays the Browse For Folder dialog box, as shown in Figure 3-11.

Figure 3-11: Browse For Folder dialog box

You use the Browse For Folder dialog box to specify the location in which to store downloaded files. Notice that the Temp folder is selected by default, but you can specify any folder you choose.

8. Click **OK** to start downloading the free Adobe Reader. The Optimizer dialog box, shown in Figure 3-12, may display before setup begins.

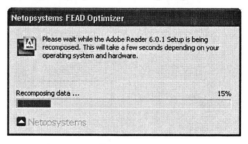

Figure 3-12: Optimizer dialog box

9. When the download and recomposition are complete, the Adobe Reader 6.0.1 Setup Wizard launches automatically. Click **Next** three times to accept the defaults, click **Install** to begin the installation, then click **Finish** to exit the wizard.

10. If a second, smaller Internet Explorer window is open, close it.

11. Next, you will read a PDF file in your browser window using Adobe Reader. Enter the URL *www.ComputerPREP.com* to visit the ComputerPREP Web site. ComputerPREP sells courseware for various certifications, including CIW, CTP and Microsoft Office.

12. In the navigation section on the left side of the page, locate the Desktop Applications heading, then click **MS Office 2003** to display the Web page for Microsoft Office 2003 products.

13. Scroll down the page and click the link for the **Excel 2003 Specialist Academic Student Guide** to display its specific details. Then click the **Course Description** link to launch Adobe Reader and display the course description in the Adobe Reader window, similar to the one shown in Figure 3-13.

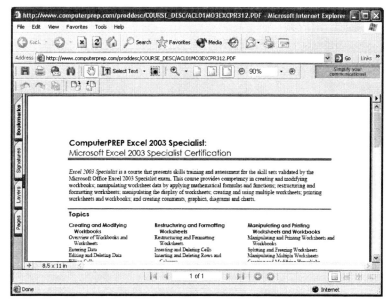

Figure 3-13: Viewing PDF file in Adobe Reader window

14. Use the Adobe Reader toolbar buttons to navigate through the document. Try to edit the document. Can you?

15. Close the **Adobe Reader** window, then close **Internet Explorer**.

Miscellaneous File Formats

OBJECTIVE:
1.5.11: Document and multimedia file formats

Files that you might download or use with plug-ins and streaming technologies include the following:

- Video

- Sound

- Graphics

- Documents

Video files

Audio Video Interleave (AVI)
Standard Windows file format for video files.

Moving Picture Experts Group (MPEG)
High-quality video file compression format.

Some of the most commonly used video files on the Web today include (but are not limited to) files with the following file name extensions:

- **.avi** — **Audio Video Interleave (AVI)** files are standard video files for Windows. They are supported by Windows Media Player in Internet Explorer and by LiveVideo in Navigator. LiveVideo allows users to instantly view AVI movies embedded in Web pages, without downloading the files for later playback.

- **.mov** — The standard format for QuickTime movies, and the Macintosh native movie platform. You can use Sparkle or MoviePlayer to view them on a Macintosh computer, or QuickTime for Windows.

- **.mpg or mpeg** — A standard format for movies on the Internet. The **Moving Picture Experts Group (MPEG)** is a standard for digital audio and video compression that provides extremely high quality and resolution. MPEG files are large and do not stream well on slower connections.

- **.qt** — Another file name extension for QuickTime movies.

- **.ram** — A video file formatted for RealPlayer streaming video.

Sound files

Audio Interchange File Format (AIFF)
High-quality audio format developed by Apple Computer.

AU
Audio file format used by UNIX servers, the majority of Web servers. Most Web browsers can read AU.

Waveform (WAV)
Windows standard format for audio files.

MPEG-1 Audio Layer-3 (MP3)
Compression standard for audio files; maintains original sound quality.

Navigator and Internet Explorer include native, or built-in, support for standard audio formats such as **Audio Interchange File Format (AIFF)**, **AU**, MIDI (discussed earlier in this lesson) and **Waveform (WAV)**. Users can play sound files embedded in HTML documents using their browsers, which automatically identify and play most major formats embedded in or linked to a Web page. Through connections to applications such as RealPlayer and Windows Media Player, browsers can also play MP3 files and other formats.

The sound files you are likely to encounter on the Web include:

- **.au** — audio format used by UNIX servers. Most browsers provide built-in support for AU files.

- **.aiff** — Audio Interchange File Format (AIFF), developed by Apple Computer, offers high-quality audio. Most browsers provide built-in support for AIFF files. The same programs that play AU files can be used to play AIFF files.

- **.mp3** — (abbreviation for **MPEG-1 Audio Layer-3**), a format for compressing audio files that uses the MPEG-1 standard. The MP3 format compresses audio files to one-twelfth the original size, shortening download times considerably. The original sound quality is preserved throughout the compression and decompression process. MP3 files are non-streaming (you must download them before you can play them). To listen to an MP3 file, you must download an MP3 player. Windows 98/Me/2000/XP have built-in MP3 players. Many MP3 players are available as shareware and freeware on the Web. Any time a developer creates an application that uses the MP3 format, he or she must pay a license fee to use this format.

- **.ogg** — Ogg Vorbis, a free alternative to the MP3 format (which is proprietary and licensed). In addition to not requiring a license, the Ogg Vorbis format uses a somewhat more efficient compression algorithm. Also, the creators of this format determined that certain frequencies can be dropped (lost) without affecting sound quality. Therefore, files are smaller, download faster, and sound as good as other formats. On Windows systems, the following players support Ogg Vorbis files: Winamp 2, Winamp 3, foobar2000 and Zinf. On UNIX/Linux, use XMMS or Zinf (formerly FreeAMP). For more information about the Ogg Vorbis format, consult the Xiph.org site (*www.xiph.org*) and the Ogg Vorbis site (*www.vorbis.com*).

- **.ra** — a proprietary streaming audio format developed by RealNetworks. You need RealPlayer to play this format.

- **.wav** — Waveform (WAV), the native sound format for Windows. Most browsers provide built-in support for WAV files.

Following is a brief list of software applications that can play audio files:

- **Nullsoft Winamp** (*www.winamp.com*) — plays a variety of formats

- **Windows Media Player** (*www.microsoft.com*) — also supports many formats

- **XMMS** (*www.xmms.org*) — for UNIX-based systems (e.g., Red Hat Linux)

- **Vorbix** (*http://winvorbis.stationplaylist.com*) — for the Ogg Vorbis format on UNIX systems

Converting media file formats

For many types of video and audio files, proprietary formats are not cross-compatible. For instance, you cannot play a RealMedia file with Windows Media Player. Several shareware programs can convert various types of files.

Video type conversions include (but are not limited to) DVD to AVI, or AVI and MPEGs to Flash movies. StreamTranscoder (*www.oddsock.org/tools/streamTranscoder/*) converts streaming media from various types of files (MP3, Vorbis, WMA) to other types.

Audio type conversions are numerous. A few examples are MP3 to WAV, WAV to various compressed formats, or even one compressed format to another, such as MP3 to Ogg. For example, oggdec (an Ogg Vorbis tool) decodes an Ogg Vorbis file to a WAV file.

Note: Converting file formats that use lossy compression does not yield the best sound quality.

Visit *www.tucows.com* or *www.freshmeat.net* to explore other tools you can use to convert media files.

Graphics files

Standard formats for graphics files use the following file name extensions. All of these formats can be viewed in browsers, and you can use several graphics programs (such as Photoshop or Paint Shop Pro) to modify and convert these files to other formats.

- **.gif** — Graphics Interchange Format (GIF), one of the most common graphics file formats on the Internet. GIF is a bitmap format that uses lossless compression. It supports various resolutions, but is limited to 256 colors and is used most effectively for drawings and illustrations, rather than for photographs.

- **.jpg or .jpeg or .jfif** — Joint Photographic Experts Group (JPEG), a format widely used for photographs and complex graphics. This format supports 16 million colors and uses lossy compression. JPEG files can be relatively small. However, the developer must decide how much compression to use. The more compression, the smaller the file size, but the lower the image quality. The JPEG format does not work well with line drawings because not much data can be discarded during the lossy compression process, and the images lose sharpness and clarity.

Tagged Image File Format (TIFF)
Commonly used graphic file format, developed by Aldus Corporation; uses the .tif or .tiff file name extension.

- **.tif or tiff** — developed by the Aldus Corporation, which is now Adobe Software. **Tagged Image File Format (TIFF)** is a popular, customizable graphic format commonly used for medical imaging and desktop publishing. TIFF supports grayscale, 8-bit and 24-bit color, and monochrome formats. TIFF files are high-resolution and very large in file size.

Document files

Some of the common document file formats you may download from the Internet (or your company's intranet) use the following file name extensions:

- **.txt** — a plain (ASCII) text file. These files can be viewed in your browser, or with a Word processor or text editor.

- **.pdf** — As you learned earlier in this lesson, PDF files can be read on any computer, regardless of the operating system. You need Adobe Reader to view PDF files, and a full version of Adobe Acrobat to create or modify PDF files.

- **.doc** — These files are usually created with Microsoft Word or WordPerfect for Windows.

- **.ps** — PostScript (PS) files are written in a page description language so they are unreadable, and are designed for printing on PostScript printers.

Encapsulated PostScript (EPS)
File format used for importing and exporting graphics.

- **.eps** — **Encapsulated PostScript (EPS)** is a file format that you can use to import and export graphic files between operating systems and applications. Whereas a PostScript file only has the instructions that determine the display of the graphic, an EPS file actually contains the bitmap information for the graphics file. This additional data allows EPS files to display an alternative bitmap graphic for previewing.

Rich Text Format (RTF)
Portable text file format created by Microsoft that allows image insertion and text formatting; an almost universal format.

- **.rtf** — **Rich Text Format (RTF)** was developed by Microsoft. Using RTF, you can insert images and format text. RTF is compatible with many operating systems and applications, including most Macintosh and Windows word processors. Most applications allow you to save files in Rich Text Format easily. For example, in Microsoft Word, you can select File | Save As, then select RTF as the document type.

EPS formats

EPS provides three preview formats for graphics: PICT for Macintosh systems, TIFF for Windows-compatible computers, and the platform-independent EPSI.

Most of the time, the EPSI format is used to transfer a graphic from a graphics-editing application (such as Adobe Photoshop) into a page-layout application (such as Adobe PageMaker). EPSI is necessary because each application tends to use its own format. EPSI acts as an intermediary that ensures no information will be lost during conversion from one format to another.

RTF benefits and drawbacks

RTF is a nearly universal format. Applications running on Windows, Linux and Macintosh can read and write RTF files. Applications that support RTF include Microsoft Word, Corel WordPerfect and Lotus WordPro. Although many PDF files created for Adobe Reader PDF are much richer, you can only create them using the full Acrobat application sold by Adobe. Even then, you must obtain Adobe Reader to view the file. The RTF format can deliver fairly rich, portable files without the need to obtain a separate application. However, RTF files can quickly become very large and, therefore, less useful. For instance, if a company wanted to provide RTF customer forms on its Web site, it must have ample hard drive space on the Web server and ensure that customers do not mind downloading large files. If customers have slow connection speeds, they may become impatient and leave the site.

Downloading Files with a Browser

OBJECTIVE:
1.5.7: Files and Web browsers

You can use various methods to download files from the Web using your browser. You can download Web pages (HTML files), image files, compressed files (ZIP files), various document types, MIDI files, and so forth. Keep in mind that copyright laws protect original works of authorship online as well as in print. Works of authorship include literary works (including computer programs); musical works; pictorial, graphical and sculptural works; motion pictures and other audiovisual works; sound recordings; and architectural works. Downloading songs and movies from the Internet is an illegal use of copyrighted material.

Copyright infringement

Many photos and other images found on Web sites include copyright information or a request that you do not copy the work. If you want to use someone's copyright-protected material, you must contact the copyright owner and ask for permission. If you are granted permission to use the copyrighted work, the copyright holder determines the terms of use. For instance, there may be no cost, but you may be required to credit the owner for the work. If you use someone else's copyrighted material without obtaining permission, you are committing copyright infringement, which is a punishable crime.

Saving Web site content

You can save entire Web pages or elements of a Web page to your hard disk. You can choose different Save options depending on the elements you want to save. For example, you would use different commands to save an entire Web page than you would to save a graphic from a Web page.

To save an entire Web page, use the File | Save As command in Internet Explorer or the File | Save Page As command in Navigator. When saving a Web page to hard disk, most browsers save all related images, fonts and scripts referenced by the HTML/XHTML on the page. You can open the page in your browser even when you are not connected to the Internet.

To save an image in Internet Explorer, right-click the image, then click Save Picture As to display the Save Picture dialog box. To save an image in Navigator, right-click the image, then click Save Image As to display the Save Picture dialog box.

When you download files to your hard disk, you are able to specify a destination directory. Be sure to remember where you store your downloaded files so that you can easily locate them when you are offline. In the next lab, you will save downloaded files to the Class Downloads folder.

Note: You can also copy and paste text and images from a Web page into various types of documents, such as word-processing files or graphics files. Select the text and images you want to copy, then select Edit | Copy to copy them to the Clipboard. Open the application into which you want to paste the text and/or images, then select Edit | Paste to paste them into a new document.

In the following lab, you will download and store Web site content using Internet Explorer. Suppose the marketing director of your company wants to study a page from a competitor's Web site on his laptop over the weekend without having to access the Internet to do so. You can download and save the Web page to the laptop's hard drive, giving the manager access to all the images, fonts and scripts.

 Lab 3-6: Downloading and storing Web site content using Microsoft Internet Explorer

In this lab, you will use Microsoft Internet Explorer to save Web site content using various methods.

1. First, you will save an entire Web page. Start **Internet Explorer** and enter the URL *www.ComputerPREP.com* to visit the ComputerPREP Web site.

2. Select **File | Save As** to display the Save Web Page dialog box, as shown in Figure 3-14.

Figure 3-14: Saving Web pages in Internet Explorer

3. Display the **Save In** drop-down list, navigate to the **Desktop\Class Downloads** folder, then click the **Save** button to save the Web page as a file on your hard drive.

4. Next, you will save an image from the Web site to your hard drive. Right-click any image on the page, then click **Save Picture As** to display the Save Picture dialog box, shown in Figure 3-15.

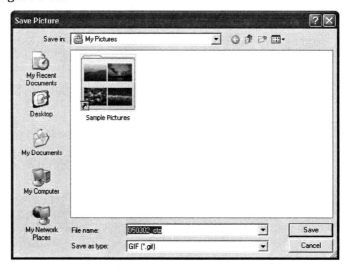

Figure 3-15: Save Picture dialog box

5. Display the **Save In** drop-down list, navigate to the **Class Downloads** folder, then click the **Save** button to save the image file to your hard drive.

6. Next, you will view and then download a PDF file. In the navigation section along the left side of the page, under the heading Desktop Applications, click the **MS Office 2003** link. Scroll down the page and click the link for **Excel 2003 Specialist Student Guide** to display the product details.

7. In the box that appears at the top of the course description page, click the **Table Of Contents** link to launch Adobe Reader and display the Table Of Contents PDF.

8. In the Adobe Reader window, click **File** to display the File menu. Notice that the Save As command is unavailable, but the Save command is available.

9. In the File menu, click **Save** to display the Save A Copy dialog box, shown in Figure 3-16.

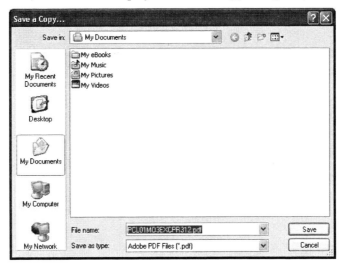

Figure 3-16: Save A Copy dialog box

10. Navigate to the **Class Downloads** folder, then click the **Save** button to save the PDF file to your hard drive.

11. Close the Adobe Reader window.

12. Next, you will download a PDF file without viewing it first. Right-click the **Course Description** link, then click **Save Target As** to display the Save As dialog box and the File Download dialog box. Notice that the course description PDF file has the same file name as the table of contents PDF file. These documents are stored in separate folders on the server. To save both to your hard drive, you will need to rename one.

13. Type *Course_Description* in the File Name text box, then click the **Save** button to save the PDF file with a new name to your hard drive.

14. In the Download Completed dialog box, click the **Close** button.

15. Finally, you will examine downloaded files. Close **Internet Explorer**.

16. On the Desktop, double-click the **Class Downloads** folder. Notice that in addition to the image file, the PDF files and the HTML file for the Web page, you now have a folder named ComputerPREP – The Learning Solutions Company_files. This folder contains files used on the Web site.

17. Double-click **Course_Description.pdf** to open the file in an Adobe Reader window. Notice that the reader functions outside your browser.

18. Close the **Adobe Reader** window.

19. Double-click the **ComputerPREP – The Learning Solutions Company_files** folder. What types of files are contained within it?

20. Close all windows and redisplay the Desktop.

Case Study

The Right Tools for the Job

Tomas is responsible for setting up and maintaining employee workstations at his company. Next week, Amanda will begin working for the company. In addition to the standard company setup, Amanda needs the equipment necessary to view and hear animations so that she can evaluate their quality. Also, she will routinely review PDF files that are posted to the company extranet.

As Tomas set up Amanda's workstation, he installed the following components and plug-ins:

* A sound card and speakers so she can hear sound files

* Macromedia Shockwave and Flash to allow her to view animation and movies

* Adobe Reader to allow her to view PDF files

                                          *   *   *

As a class, discuss any additional components or plug-ins Tomas can install to help Amanda perform her job functions.

Lesson Summary

Application project

What similarities and differences do you notice between the Netscape Navigator and Microsoft Internet Explorer browsers when using plug-ins such as QuickTime? Do you prefer one browser to the other? Could plug-ins help your company's Web-based clients? What other types of multimedia files might you use that require plug-ins?

Another popular plug-in is the MP3 player. Locate, download and install an MP3 player, then download license-free MP3 content and play it. Is the MP3 player you installed similar to other plug-ins you used in this lesson? Would you consider it a plug-in or a stand-alone application?

Skills review

In this lesson, you learned about active content and the programming and scripting languages used to create it, such as C, C++, Java, JavaScript, ActiveX, JScript and VBScript. You were introduced to several widely used Web browser plug-ins, and you saw how they can enhance browser performance and interactivity. You also gained hands-on experience downloading and installing plug-ins, and you navigated to several sites on the Web that contained functional plug-in demonstrations. Finally, you downloaded and stored files to your hard drive using your browser.

Now that you have completed this lesson, you should be able to:

✓ Define objects and their relationships to multimedia.

✓ Explain the fundamentals of C, C++, Java, JavaScript, ActiveX, JScript and VBScript, and describe the relationships among them.

    ✓   Describe the purpose of plug-ins.

    ✓   Identify plug-ins and viewers, including RealNetworks RealPlayer, Macromedia Shockwave and Flash players, Apple QuickTime and Adobe Reader.

    ✓   Listen to and view multimedia objects within your browser.

    ✓   Identify various file formats, such as MPEG, MP3, MOV, AIFF, AU, WAV, EPS, TIFF and RTF.

    ✓   Download files and store them on your computer.

Lesson 3 Review

1. What was the first scripting language developed exclusively for online content design?

    _____

2. Briefly describe Java.

    _____

    _____

3. Name some of the functions of Java applets.

    _____

4. What are the three ways in which a plug-in can appear within a browser?

    _____

5. What is Virtual Reality Modeling Language (VRML)?

    _____

Version 1.0

Lesson 4:
Databases and
Web Search Engines

Objectives

By the end of this lesson, you will be able to:

- Define databases and database components.

- Define relational database concepts.

- Define Web search engines and explain Web search types.

- Register a Web site with a search engine.

- Conduct basic and advanced Web searches.

- Define Boolean operators.

- Use Web searches to perform job tasks.

- Explain Web search strategies and unexpected Web search results.

- Identify Web search relevancy.

- Evaluate Web site information and cite copyrighted Web site information as a resource.

Pre-Assessment Questions

1. How is a many-to-many database table relationship established?

   _____

   _____

   _____

   _____

2. What distinguishes an information portal from a search engine?

   _____

   _____

   _____

   _____

3. Using the Boolean OR operator with keywords in a search means that the search results:

   a. may include a particular keyword.
   b. must include a particular keyword.
   c. may include at least one of the keywords.
   d. must include at least one of the keywords.

Introduction to Data Searching Tools

With so much data on the Internet, finding the exact information you need can be difficult and frustrating. Many tools are available for navigating the Internet. This lesson will focus on the various Web search engines and the search techniques you can employ to find the information you are seeking.

A Web search engine is a large database containing information about Web pages that have been registered with it. To understand search engines, you must understand basic database concepts and the manner in which data is organized and accessed.

Overview of Databases

This section will provide an overview of database components, relational databases, table keys, table relationships, database queries and common database vendors.

Database components

A **database** is a collection of data that can be sorted and searched using search algorithms. Databases are useful for storing, manipulating, managing and querying large amounts of data.

database
A collection of data that can be sorted and searched using search algorithms.

Database components are referred to as database objects and are each stored separately within the database. In a database structure, data values are stored in **tables**. A table can contain data such as personnel information, product inventories, customer lists, sales figures, and so forth. A database can consist of multiple tables, depending on the complexity of the data being stored.

table
A collection of data about a limited topic, organized into rows and columns in a database.

A **field** is a category of information in a table. Each column in a table represents a field. A **record** is a collection of information consisting of one or more related fields about a specific entity, such as a person, product or event. Each row in a table represents a record.

field
A category of information in a database table.

Figure 4-1 shows a sample database table containing technical specifications for three aircraft.

record
A collection of information in a database table consisting of one or more related fields about a specific entity, such as a person, product or event.

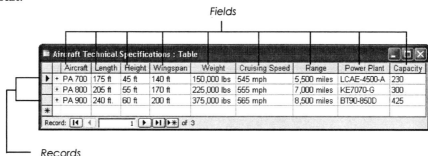

Figure 4-1: Sample database table

Relational databases

A **relational database** contains multiple tables of information that are related through **common fields**. Conversely, a non-relational database consists of multiple tables of information that are not related through common fields. When multiple tables have a field in common, they can be joined to form a **relationship** to access the table data as needed.

To understand the relational database concept, consider a simple database designed for an aircraft manufacturer with three new aircraft that will enter production soon. The manufacturer wants to keep track of aircraft orders, as well as technical information about each aircraft. Figure 4-2 is an example of a relational database.

relational database
A database that contains multiple tables related through common fields.

common field
A field contained in two or more database tables that forms a connection between the tables.

relationship
A connection between two or more database tables that is based on a field that the tables have in common.

Common field

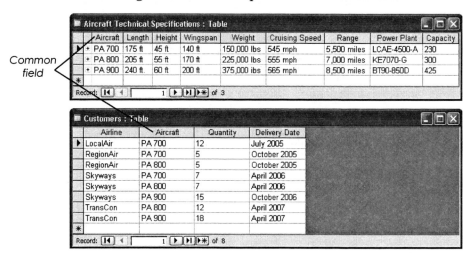

Figure 4-2: Sample relational database

The Customers table contains information only about the aircraft ordered by each airline; it does not contain information about the aircraft. The Aircraft Technical Specifications table contains information only about the aircraft. The only field the two tables have in common is the Aircraft field; the tables are related through this common field.

Relating the two tables can save time and eliminate data duplication. For example, storing customer and technical specification data in separate tables and creating a relationship between the tables through the common field Aircraft eliminates the need to enter the aircraft information every time you want information about the planes a customer ordered.

Figure 4-3 shows the aircraft ordered by each customer, the quantity ordered and the expected delivery dates.

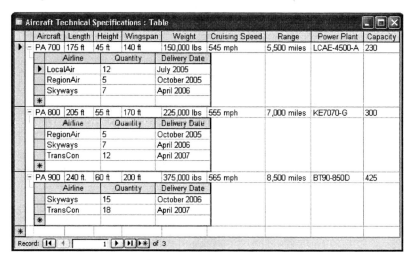

Figure 4-3: Related tables

The design of a relational database is usually determined by four factors:

- The purpose of the database

- The number of tables needed to store information without duplicating data

- The fields needed in each table

- The fields common to more than one table

Whether a database consists of a single table or multiple related tables depends on the data requirements of the database users.

Database table keys

primary key
A field containing a value that uniquely identifies each record in a database table.

foreign key
A field in a related database table that refers to the primary key in the primary table.

A table relationship is established by matching data in key fields between two database tables. Usually, the fields have the same name in both tables; however, the names can be different. In any given relationship, the table in which the common field is the **primary key** is called the primary table. The other table in the relationship is called the related table. The common field in the related table is called the **foreign key**. A database table can have only one primary key.

The previous figure depicting a sample relational database shows the common field, Aircraft. The Aircraft field is the primary key in the Aircraft Technical Specifications table because the data contained in the field is unique; that is, no duplicate data can be contained in the field. The Aircraft field is the foreign key in the Customers table.

Relating database tables

OBJECTIVE:
1.16.3: Database table relationships

Three types of relationships can be established between database tables: one-to-one, one-to-many and many-to-many. This section will discuss each of these table relationship types.

One-to-one relationship

one-to-one relationship
In databases, a relationship in which each record in Table A can have only one matching record in Table B, and vice versa.

A **one-to-one relationship** is a database table relationship in which each record in Table A can have only one matching record in Table B, and vice versa. The relationship is established only if the common field is the primary key in both tables.

One-to-one table relationships are unusual because most data related in this way would be stored in the same table. However, a one-to-one relationship might be used to divide a large table, to isolate part of a table for security reasons, or to store information that applies to a subset of the main table. For example, several sales representatives in your organization might be part of a training program, and that information could be stored separately.

One-to-many relationship

one-to-many relationship
In databases, a relationship in which a record in Table A can have multiple matching records in Table B, but a record in Table B has only one matching record in Table A.

A **one-to-many relationship** is a database table relationship in which a record in Table A can have multiple matching records in Table B, but a record in Table B has only one matching record in Table A. The relationship is established only if the common field is the primary key in Table A and the foreign key in Table B.

A one-to-many relationship is the most common type of table relationship. For example, a one-to-many relationship can exist between aircraft customers and the aircraft's technical specifications. Each aircraft can have only one set of specifications, but multiple customers can order the same type of aircraft.

Figure 4-4 shows two tables with a one-to-many relationship, joined by the Aircraft field. A record in the Aircraft Technical Specifications table can have several matching records in the Customers table, but a Customers record can have only one matching record in the Aircraft Technical Specifications table.

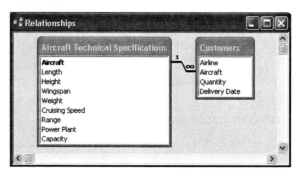

Figure 4-4: One-to-many database table relationship

Many-to-many relationship

A **many-to-many relationship** is a database table relationship in which one record in Table A can relate to many matching records in table B, and vice versa. A many-to-many relationship between two tables is established by creating two one-to-many relationships with a third table, called a **junction table**. For example, a many-to-many relationship can exist between airlines and aircraft technical specifications. An airline can order several types of aircraft, and the technical specifications for each aircraft can be combined with the data for each airline.

Figure 4-5 shows a many-to-many relationship between the Aircraft Technical Specifications table and the Airlines table. The Customers table is the junction table that establishes the two required one-to-many relationships. In this example, a one-to-many relationship also exists between the Aircraft Technical Specifications table and the Power Plants table, which provides information about the engines used by each type of aircraft.

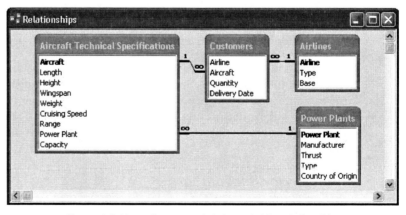

Figure 4-5: Many-to-many database table relationship

many-to-many relationship
In databases, a relationship in which one record in Table A can relate to many matching records in Table B, and vice versa.

junction table
A database table containing foreign-key fields that refer to the primary-key fields from the primary tables in a many-to-many relationship.

Querying databases using Structured Query Language (SQL)

query
A question posed by
a user to a database
to request database
information. The
database returns the
query results based
on the criteria
supplied by the user
in the query.

**Structured Query
Language (SQL)**
A language used to
create and
maintain
professional, high-
performance
corporate
databases.

Users input queries to selectively view and analyze data from a database. A **query** isolates and displays only the information you want to examine by specifying the fields and records you want to see. For example, you can use a query to display only the cruising speed, range and capacity of the aircraft that TransCon ordered.

There are three general types of queries:

*   **Menu query** — You are offered a list of options in a menu from which to choose.

*   **Query by example** — You specify the fields and data values to be used in a query.

*   **Query language** — You use a specialized language called **Structured Query Language (SQL)** to retrieve and manipulate information in a database.

SQL (pronounced "sequel") was developed by IBM in 1974 and was originally called Structured English Query Language (SEQUEL). Oracle Corporation released the first commercial SQL application in 1979.

SQL has become the standard interactive and programming language for accessing information from and updating information in a database, particularly large relational databases. SQL command statements are used for interactively querying information from a database and accumulating data for reports.

Common database vendors

**database
management
system (DBMS)**
A program used to
store, access and
manipulate
database
information.

A **database management system (DBMS)** is a program used to store, access and manipulate database information. IT professionals commonly use a DBMS to work with corporate database information. Originally, corporate databases were stored on large mainframe computers. More recently, client/server databases have become more popular and are able to work with smaller networks. Common database vendors and their DBMS products (in parentheses) include the following:

*   IBM (DB2)

*   Computer Associates (Advantage)

*   Oracle (Oracle Database 10g)

*   Microsoft (SQL Server, Microsoft Access)

*   Sybase (Sybase Adaptive Server Enterprise, SQL Anywhere Studio, Sybase IQ)

Databases and Internet servers

An Internet server can be connected to a database to provide information via the Web. In this case, the Web server provides HTML pages that act as the front end, which is another term for the interface that end users see. The database server then acts as the back end, which includes the database and the technologies that enable the front end to communicate with the database. In fact, most companies rely upon such connectivity. Following are examples of ways that an Internet server can use a database:

*   **Company sales data** — A company can store sales and marketing data in a centralized database. Employees can then conduct searches of this data when formulating a marketing plan. This process is also called "mining" data. An example of this type of database is Goldmine (*www.goldmine.com*). Such databases can be accessed via a proprietary client, such as one provided by Goldmine, or via a Web server.

- **Banking** — Banks store user account information in databases. Users can then access the databases through the banks' Web servers. Deutsche Bank (*www.db.com*), Citibank (*www.citibank.com*) and Wells Fargo (*www.wellsfargo.com*) are examples of companies that use Web servers and database technology to provide services to their customers.

- **Web storefronts** — Small, medium and large businesses have Web-enabled databases that allow customers to buy and sell goods. Well-known Web storefronts include Amazon.com (*www.amazon.com*), Travelocity (*www.travelocity.com*) and FTD.com (*www.ftd.com*).

- **Web search engines** — Web search companies, such as Google (*www.google.com*) and AltaVista (*www.altavista.com*), populate their databases with information about resources on the Internet, including the World Wide Web. Search engine companies strive to populate their databases with useful information so that people will find value in their services. In turn, they sell space to advertisers to generate revenue. Web search engines will be discussed in greater detail in the following sections.

Open Database Connectivity (ODBC)

Common Gateway Interface (CGI)
A program that processes data submitted by the user. Allows a Web server to pass control to a software application, based on user request. The application receives and organizes data, then returns it in a consistent format.

The Open Database Connectivity (ODBC) standard was created by The Open Group (*www.opengroup.org*). ODBC was designed to enable an operating system to access databases from various vendors (for example, Oracle, Microsoft and IBM). Using ODBC, a server (for example, a Goldmine or Web server) can access any type of database. ODBC provides a standard database interface.

An alternative to ODBC is Java Database Connectivity (JDBC), which is similar to ODBC except that JDBC uses the Java language and thus is capable of running on any platform. Another alternative to ODBC is the UnixODBC Project (*www.unixodbc.org*), which aims to implement ODBC on UNIX systems.

Anytime you conduct a database search, the database may be using ODBC, as well as a **Common Gateway Interface (CGI)** application to connect the front end (e.g., the Web server) to the back end (e.g., the database). When you click a hyperlink to access a Web page, the Web server retrieves the requested page. However, when you submit an online form, the Web server typically forwards the form information to an application program that processes the data. CGI is the method by which data is passed back and forth between the server and the application program. CGI uses languages and technologies, including Personal Hypertext Preprocessor (PHP), Perl and Microsoft Active Server Pages (ASP).

Introduction to Web Search Engines

search engine
A powerful software program that searches Internet databases for user-specified information.

Search engines are powerful software programs that make it easy to find information on the Internet. A search engine consists of a large database that contains information about Web pages that have been registered with the search engine. Most search engines allow you to browse general categories, search for specific topics or find detailed information based on narrowly defined criteria.

keyword
A word that appears on a Web page and is used by search engines to identify relevant URLs. Some words, such as "the" or "and," are too common to be used as keywords.

Using **keywords**, you can find information on the Internet about any subject you want to investigate. A search engine database typically contains information about the site such as the title, the URL, a short description of the site contents, and keywords to help the search engine reference the page. When a Web site manager registers a Web page with a search engine, the URL and associated information are added to the search engine database.

Not every Web site is registered with every search engine. Some Web site managers register their sites only with particular search engines, neglecting others. Because of this selectivity and the large number of search engines, you may receive different results using the same keywords on different search engines.

OBJECTIVE:
1.11.7: Search engine spiders

Some search engines are highly automated and initiate a robot or "spider" program that searches the Web and indexes Web sites. Search engines that use spider programs are sometimes called spider search engines. These programs gather information about Web sites and newsgroups as determined by certain parameters. In some cases, only the page title and URL are indexed. In others, partial or full-page text is also indexed from the site. In addition, spiders check the validity of the URL entered in the database to ensure accuracy.

OBJECTIVE:
1.11.6: Meta search engines

Registering a Web Site with a Search Engine

Many popular search engines require that you register your Web site for it to be accessible to Web users. Each search engine has its own registration process.

Many search engines, such as Excite, Lycos and WebCrawler, require you to register by completing online forms and entering the URL of your site. The search engines then use the robot or spider programs to visit your site and search it for relevant source code embedded in the page, often in the <meta> tag.

The <meta> tag is an HTML element used in a Web page to embed information for use by search engines. This information is placed near the top of the HTML document so search engines can quickly access it. The more descriptive the information included in the <meta> tag, the more likely the Web site is to rank high in search results. The <meta> tag includes information about a document, such as:

• Keywords to be used by some search engines.

• A description of the site's content for display in some search engines.

• An expiration date for the document.

• The document's author.

meta search engine
A search engine that scans Web pages for <meta> tag information.

Most search engines scan Web pages for <meta> tag information. These search engines are sometimes called **meta search engines**. The <meta> tag identifies data in the following format:

<meta name="keywords" content="*keyword1 keyword2 keyword3*"/>

The search engine spider program inspects pages that use the "keywords" value of the *name* attribute. The values specified by the *content* attribute are then ranked against keywords that users entered in the search engine.

You separate keywords in the <meta> tag with spaces or commas. Do not use keywords redundantly when creating <meta> tags for your site; multiple occurrences of the same word will cause the tag to be ignored.

Another useful attribute for search engines is the "description" value of the *name* attribute:

<meta name="description" content="This site provides aircraft technical data."/>

In the preceding tag, the *content* attribute value will appear in some search engines instead of the first few lines of the Web page. The description should be brief. Not all search engines recognize the *content* attribute.

Spiders can also search for word occurrences, titles, heading text and images within Web pages. Unfortunately, each search engine spider gathers different information, so no method guarantees a top listing.

Most search engine sites offer a link, such as Add Your Site or Suggest A Site, which you can access for more information about registering your site. You can visit each search engine's Web site and locate the registration link to submit your site's URL. Submitting your site to a search engine increases your chances for higher placement in the search results.

Not all search engines index the same number of sites. Some have fewer than a million site references, while others have hundreds of millions of references. When you search for topics using a Web search engine, you are never searching the entire Web, only an index or database of referenced sites.

Search engines vs. information portals

OBJECTIVE:
1.11.4: Search sites vs. information portals

The term search engine is used loosely in the Web community to include both search engines and information portals. A search engine, such as AltaVista or Google, uses a robot or spider program to browse the Web (by following hyperlinks) and index the content that it finds. Therefore, a search engine will eventually find your page, assuming that a link to your site exists somewhere on the Web. However, it is impossible to determine how long it will take for your site to be discovered. Therefore, it is important to submit your site to the search engines. Submitting your site speeds the process and increases your chances for higher placement in search results, thus allowing you as the Web site manager some control over placement.

An information portal differs from a search engine in that it will only find Web sites based on manual submissions. Thus, if you do not manually submit your site to the information portal, it will never know about or index your site, and never list your site in search results. Some information portals, such as Yahoo! and Magellan, visit your Web site after you register it to determine the content and its relevance to the submitted topic. After the review, you may receive an e-mail message requesting additional information so a Web site description can be created before the site is placed in the portal.

The advantage of information portals is that search results are more likely to contain high-quality content matches to each query. However, increasing the chances for a higher placement in search results is usually not within the control of the Web site manager.

Types of Web Searches

OBJECTIVE:
1.11.3: Keyword searching

Index
A catalog of the contents of a database. Each entry identifies a unique database record.

Search engines consist of large databases that allow you to query **indexes**. A search index is an enormous catalog that a specific search engine site has compiled, consisting of millions of Web page references.

You can perform two types of searches with search engines: directory searches and keyword searches. In a directory search, the engine displays a list of categories and subcategories that you can browse. At each level, the items are arranged from general to specific. In a keyword search, you enter one or more keywords into the engine, and the search engine finds specific topics by locating those keywords or phrases in registered Web pages.

You can access a search index using a search engine, or you can manually navigate through an index's structured directory using an information portal. Table 4-1 describes

the types of Web searches that users can perform using a search engine, as well as the
related indexing method the search engine uses to enable the search type.

Table 4-1: Types of Web searches

User Search Type	Search Engine Indexing Method	Description
Directory search	Static index/site map	Enables users to manually search information portals to locate indexed information. Some portals are presented as directory trees of all indexed pages. Many Web sites present site maps, which allow users to view the site contents without visiting each page. Examples include Yahoo! and most major Web sites.
Keyword search	Keyword index	Enables users to enter keywords in a search engine to query an index. The entered keywords are then compared to the keywords in the index. If the keywords match, the search engine will provide the indexed information. Keywords can consist of one word, several words or a phrase enclosed in quotation marks (e.g., search string). Examples include Yahoo!, AltaVista, Google, Excite and Lycos.
	Full-text index	Enables a user to enter any search string into the search engine. This type of search requires the full contents of every page to be indexed for results, rather than only the page title or URL. AltaVista and Google are examples of full-text index search engines.

Some search engines are indexed to allow either static directory searching or keyword
searching, whereas other search engines offer both. Yahoo! is an example of a search
engine site that offers both keyword and directory searching. Figure 4-6 shows the Yahoo!
keyword search field.

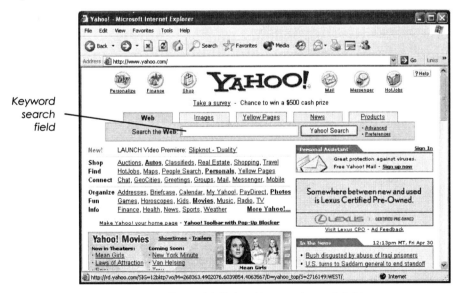

Figure 4-6: Yahoo! keyword search field

Figure 4-7 shows the Yahoo! static directory that appears when you scroll down the home page.

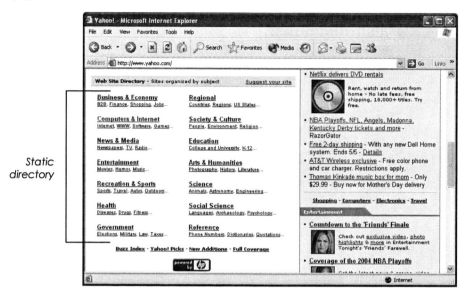

Static directory

Figure 4-7: Yahoo! static directory

Both directory searches and keyword searches are valuable. The search method you should use depends on the type of information you need. After browsing directories to find general categories, you can use keyword searches to narrow the results. For example, you could use directories to find a Web site about general project management principles, then use keywords to find specific information about the planning phase of a project.

Search engines vary greatly. Some search only the Web, and others (such as Google) also search for articles in newsgroups. Some engines provide links to sites, and others specify URLs. Some engines may give brief descriptions of the site contents, and others may include paragraph summaries of the sites.

File types searched

Traditionally, the search engines from various sites (such as Google and AltaVista) focused on indexing HTML pages. However, search engines now have the ability to search for and index the contents of additional file types, including the following:

- **ASCII** — files that are in plaintext format

- **Rich Text Format (RTF)** — files that contain simple formatting (bolding, italics, and so forth)

- **Portable Document Format (PDF)** — files that can be transferred across platforms and retain formatting

- **PostScript** — files that can be printed to PostScript printers, or read by various applications such as GhostView (commonly found in Linux systems)

- **Proprietary file formats** — files made by specific vendors' applications, such as Microsoft Word and Excel

Basic Web Searching Techniques

To conduct basic Web searches, you typically enter a keyword or a short phrase within quotation marks into a search field. Basic searches are useful when a simple, distinguishable topic is requested. In the following sections, you will perform basic Web searches with Yahoo! and AltaVista. You will also be introduced to Google, Lycos, WebCrawler and Excite.

Yahoo!

One of the oldest and most basic search engines is Yahoo! (*www.yahoo.com*). It was created in 1994 by two students at Stanford University as a way to track their personal interests on the Internet. They realized its usefulness, and soon customized their search utility into the hierarchical directory to the Internet that it has become. It was not intended to be a search engine, but rather an index providing several links relating to each topic. Originally, its database of links was very selective, including only carefully chosen and verified links. It is now one of the Internet's major search engines.

The Yahoo! interface provides hyperlinks to help narrow your search, such as Classifieds, Travel, Maps, Yellow Pages, Games, Finance, Health, News, Sports, Weather, and so forth. It also offers a hypertext listing by alphabetical categories, such as Arts & Humanities, Business & Economy and Society & Culture. Each of these topics contains subtopics. For example, under the larger topic of Computers & Internet, you will find hypertext links to Communications And Networking, Information Technology, Telecommunications, and World Wide Web.

If you select Information Technology, Yahoo! displays a more advanced search page that offers both a search field and further-categorized hypertext links.

Yahoo! searches titles, categories and text to find results that contain all of your keywords. Yahoo! is not case-sensitive. For example, the keywords "Project Management" would be read the same as "project management."

Yahoo! finds and retrieves three types of information for each search. The searches are based on:

- The alphabetized hypertext categories that match your keywords.

- Web sites that match your keywords.

- Yahoo! categories that list sites that match your keywords.

Yahoo! identifies its categories in bold type. Referenced sites are displayed in plain text. To navigate down the subject hierarchy, select a category, and the next lower level of the hierarchy will display.

In the following lab, you will perform a directory search. Suppose you are a newly hired help desk technician. You have been asked by your IT manager to join an IT association and attend several of its meetings to expand your skill set. What method would you use to find an appropriate organization?

Lab 4-1: Performing a directory search using Yahoo!

In this lab, you will use Yahoo! to perform a directory search.

1. Start **Microsoft Internet Explorer**.

2. Click anywhere in the **Address** box, type ***www.yahoo.com***, then press **ENTER**. The Yahoo! search engine home page will display.

3. Scroll down to the Web Site Directory section, then click **Computers & Internet**. You will see the subtopics of the Computers & Internet topic.

4. Click **Information Technology**@ to display hyperlinks related to Information Technology.

5. In the Categories section, click **Organizations** to display hyperlinks to Information Technology organizations.

6. In the Site Listings section, click Info**rmation Technology Association of America (ITAA)** to display that organization's Web site.

7. In the toolbar, click the **Home** button to return to your browser's home page.

Tech Note: There are several ways to arrive at the ITAA Web site. Many hyperlinks arrive at the same destination.

Static directory searches may require more steps than keyword searches. However, when you do not know which keywords to use, the static directory search is an excellent tool.

AltaVista

AltaVista (*www.altavista.com*) was created in 1995 by Digital Equipment Corporation and was originally designed to index the entire Internet. AltaVista is a very powerful search engine that contains one of the largest Web databases.

AltaVista allows users to choose the most appropriate search mode for the level of search assistance they require. It offers two search engines: general and advanced. General searching works well if you know some general keywords related to the information you are seeking but do not have details. Advanced searching is intended for experienced searchers who know the information they want and the way to get it quickly.

To ensure the most current database contents, AltaVista uses a Web spider program to routinely search every Web page. Pages that do not change often are checked for updates less frequently than pages that do change often.

Like many search engines, AltaVista returns your results in terms of accuracy, with the highest likely returns posted first. The results are influenced by a combination of the following events:

- The keywords or search strings you specify are found in the title, or in page text near the beginning of the document, or in the HTML page's <meta> tag.

- The Web document contains additional keywords or strings.

- The Web document contains keywords or strings that have been assigned a high priority by the search engine.

The AltaVista home page is shown in Figure 4-8.

Figure 4-8: AltaVista home page

To perform a keyword search, type the keyword(s) in the search box, then click the Find button. When specifying keywords, try to use nouns. Verbs and modifiers can be too variable to be useful, and many search engines ignore them. Articles and prepositions such as "the," "an" or "with" are also too common to be useful for a search.

You can also use more than one keyword in a search. Using several keywords can help narrow the search results to yield hyperlinks that are more pertinent to your topic. Some search engines assume when you list multiple keywords that you want the results to contain either one or the other of the keywords. However, some search engines, such as Google, assume that you want the results to contain all keywords. Check a search engine's Help section to determine the logic that is used by default.

To further narrow your search, specify a search string by using quotation marks to combine words that must appear together in the specified order. Because results are restricted to exact matches, using quotation marks will treat "information technology" as a single phrase and you will receive only hyperlinks to Web pages that contain both words in that order.

In the following lab, you will perform a keyword search. Suppose you are an IT manager and have been asked by the human resources department to provide IT compensation estimates for various job roles in your geographic region. You know that the Information Technology Association of America (ITAA) conducts periodic surveys that may provide the information you need. How would you quickly find the ITAA home page on the Internet?

OBJECTIVE:
1.11.2: Common search engine operators

OBJECTIVE:
1.11.3: Keyword searching

Lab 4-2: Performing a keyword search using AltaVista

In this lab, you will use AltaVista to perform a keyword search.

1. Start **Internet Explorer**. Click anywhere in the **Address** box, type *www.altavista.com*, then press **ENTER**. The AltaVista search engine home page will display.

2. In the Search box, type ***information technology***, then click the **Find** button. You will see hyperlinks to all Web pages containing the keyword "information" or the keyword "technology" or both. Notice that each hyperlink is accompanied by a description of the Web site. Notice also that AltaVista found tens of millions of sites using these keywords.

3. Click one of the hyperlinks and determine the relevance of this site to your search and your needs.

4. In the browser toolbar, click the **Back** button to return to the list of search results.

5. In the Search box, add quotes before and after the existing text so that it reads ***"information technology"***, then click the **Find** button. You will see hyperlinks to all Web pages containing the keywords "information technology" in the order specified. Notice that the number of Web sites found, or hits, is still in the millions but is dramatically smaller than in your first search.

6. In the Search box, change the search string to ***"information technology association of America"***, then click the **Find** button. Notice that the number of hits has again been reduced and now is in the low thousands.

7. Click the **Information Technology Association of America Website** link to display the site.

8. In the toolbar, click the **Back** button four times to return to the AltaVista home page.

Notice that finding the ITAA Web site is only a two-step process using a keyword search (Steps 6 and 7 in this example), a shorter process than a directory search.

Google

The Google search engine (*www.google.com*) has become extremely popular. Like other sites, Google's Web search engine is designed to rank the relevance of a particular site according to the keywords entered by the user. However, Google's system also uses an additional technique: It determines a site's relevance based upon the number of links that point to it. Essentially, Google determines a site's popularity according to the number of other sites that link to it.

The Google search engine is also capable of giving weight to particular links. For example, if both the *New York Times* Web site and a simple user-based site from Yahoo! link to a particular site, the *New York Times* Web site will receive more weight. This is because Google's developers have created statistics-based applications that, in effect, count each link from one page to the next as a "vote." Visit *www.google.com/technology* to learn more about Google's search and voting functions.

Lycos

The Lycos search engine (*www.lycos.com*) is one of the largest and most complete Internet databases. Originally maintained and funded by Carnegie Mellon University in Pittsburgh, Pennsylvania, United States, Lycos became a publicly traded company in April 1996. Similar to Excite, Lycos offers both keyword and directory searching. As with AltaVista, Lycos uses a spider program to validate all links, which ensures only current, existing pages are contained within the Lycos database.

WebCrawler

WebCrawler (*www.webcrawler.com*) was started in 1994 as a private project to offer free searching to Internet users. WebCrawler is a much smaller database than Lycos, and its search results do not supply the same amount of detail, but it is fast, simple and reliable. WebCrawler is a good search engine to use when searching for a broad topic, such as travel, sports, entertainment, and so forth.

Excite

The Excite search engine (*www.excite.com*) offers a completely different way to search the Web. Like other search engines, it allows keyword searches. However, the Excite database also contains cross-referencing fields for conceptual searches. The Excite database knows that one word or phrase may have the same meaning as another, and it will return those related results as well.

Site rankings

Many search engines, such as Google, conduct statistical analyses on Web sites in order to return a ranked list of sites. Such search engines have become very popular because they help the user differentiate between popular and unpopular sites.

Manipulating search engine results

Web users have learned the methods that search engines, such as Google, use to create their vote-based systems. Users have created automatic applications that spoof links to Web pages, making the statistical analysis applications return inaccurate rankings. As a result, it is even more important to evaluate the results of your searches. You should not necessarily trust the most popular sites simply because a Web search engine ranks them highly.

OBJECTIVE:
1.11.1: Boolean operators

Boolean operator
A symbol or word used in Internet searches to narrow search results by including or excluding certain words or phrases from the search criteria.

Boolean Operators

Just as standard mathematics uses addition, subtraction, division and multiplication, Boolean logic uses the AND, OR and NOT operators. **Boolean operators** enable users to narrow their Internet search results by requiring or excluding keywords from the search criteria.

When you use the OR operator between two keywords, results will contain one keyword or the other or both. The more terms you combine with an OR operator, the more results you retrieve.

When you use the AND operator between two keywords, results must contain both keywords. The more terms you combine using the AND operator, the fewer results you retrieve.

When you use the NOT operator with a keyword, you are specifying that the results cannot contain the keyword that follows the operator.

For example, if you were searching for laser printers, a standard search using the keyword *printers* may yield millions of Web sites. These documents will include printing companies, ink jet printers, dot matrix printers and many other types of printers, whether they are relevant to your search or not.

To limit your search results, you could use a combination of keywords and Boolean operators, such as *printers AND laser NOT ink jet*. By adding *AND laser*, you are requiring your results to contain the words *laser* and *printers*. By further narrowing your results with the NOT operator, you will exclude all pages that contain the words *ink jet*. This method will narrow your search results dramatically. By using additional Boolean operators to exclude other keywords irrelevant to your needs, such as *NOT dot matrix*, you can narrow your search even further.

Many search engines allow the use of the plus sign (+) to signify the AND operator and the minus sign (-) to signify the NOT operator.

You can also use parentheses to combine Boolean phrases. This strategy identifies single concepts and indicates the order in which the relationships should be considered.

Most operators are interchangeable among search engines. However, not all search engines recognize the same operators, or they may use commands other than Boolean operators. Table 4-2 lists some common Boolean operators and the actions they perform.

Table 4-2: Boolean operators

Boolean Operators	Action Performed
AND, &	Results must include both words.
OR, |	Results must include at least one of the words.
+ (plus sign does not work in advanced search)	Results must include the word specified after the operator.
NOT, !, - (minus sign does not work in advanced search)	Results must exclude the word specified after the operator.
NEAR, ADJ (adjacent), FAR, BEFORE	Two keywords on a page must be within a certain proximity to each other (near or far).
" "	Keywords must appear in phrases in the order specified.
( ), < >, [ ], { }	Boolean operator phrases must be performed in the order specified.
* (Example: *color** will return *color, colors, colorize, Colorado*, etc.)	The root word can include variations in spelling. This Boolean operator is called a wildcard character.
. (Example: *color.* will return only *color*, not *colors, colorize, Colorado*, etc.)	The root word cannot be expanded.

 Boolean operators in Excite are case-sensitive; in Lycos and AltaVista they are not. Some search engines allow user-defined variations of the Boolean operators. For more information, view the Help files at each site.

In the following lab, you will use Boolean operators to narrow Web search results. Suppose that the IT manager has asked you train the new sales interns to quickly access information on the Internet by narrowing their search results to a manageable number. Which Boolean operators would you teach them about first?

 Lab 4-3: Using the plus sign (+) and minus sign (-) operators in AltaVista

OBJECTIVE:
1.11.2: Common search engine operators

In this lab, you will use the plus sign (+) and minus sign (-) operators in AltaVista.

1.   First, you will use the plus sign operator to search for Web pages that contain the search string "database administrator" and the keyword "network." Open the **AltaVista** home page.

2. In the Search box, type **"database administrator"**, then click the **Find** button. You will see hyperlinks to all Web pages containing the keywords "database" and "administrator" in the order specified. Notice that the number of sites found is in the tens of thousands.

3. Change the text in the Search box so it reads **"database administrator" +network**, then click the **Find** button. You will see hyperlinks to all Web pages containing the original search string and "network." Notice that the number of sites is still in the tens of thousands but is dramatically smaller than in your first search.

    Note: In most search engines, the plus sign (+) or minus sign (-) must directly precede the keyword it requires or excludes; do not add a space between them.

4. Next, you will use the minus sign operator to narrow the search. Change the text in the Search box so it reads **"database administrator" +network -server**, then click the **Find** button. You will see hyperlinks to all Web pages containing the original search string and "network," but excluding pages that contain the word "server." Notice that the number of sites found has again been reduced.

5. Use the plus sign and minus sign operators to perform your own Web search. Do you find these operators helpful in narrowing your search results to display more relevant hyperlinks?

Note: The plus sign and minus sign operators do not work when conducting an advanced search in AltaVista, which you will do in the next section.

Movie Time!

Insert the CIW Foundations Movie CD to learn even more about this topic.

Searching on the Web (approx. playing time: 07:30)

All movie clips are © 2004 LearnKey, Inc.

Advanced Web Searching Techniques

A basic search using a keyword or a search string is sufficient when a simple, distinguishable topic is requested. However, for more complex subjects, or to narrow the results of a standard search, you should use advanced search techniques. Some search engines use a separate interface for advanced searches, whereas others allow you to use Boolean operators in the standard search interface.

In this section, you will learn about the advanced search features of AltaVista, Excite and Lycos.

Advanced searching in AltaVista

AltaVista's advanced search features enable users to narrow search results from a standard search to specific criteria. You can use Boolean operators to include or exclude certain keywords.

Figure 4-9 shows the AltaVista Advanced Web Search page.

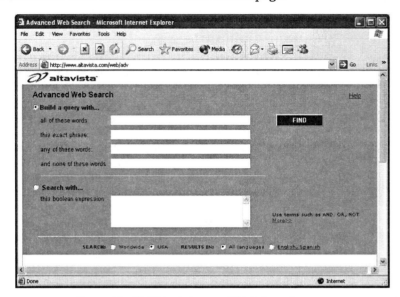

Figure 4-9: AltaVista Advanced Web Search page

When you conduct a standard search, results are generally ranked by the frequency of keywords, as well as whether they are placed in the title of the linked page. However, when you use the AltaVista Advanced Web Search page and enter search criteria only in the Search With This Boolean Expression field, the results will appear in random order.

In the following lab, you will use Boolean operators to perform an advanced search. Suppose the sales interns at your company are familiar with basic keyword search techniques. What other search techniques can you show them to make their Internet searches as efficient as possible?

Lab 4-4: Performing an advanced search in AltaVista

OBJECTIVE:
1.11.2: Common
search engine
operators

In this lab, you will perform an advanced search in AltaVista.

1. First, you will use the AND and OR operators to search for information about specific project management phases. Display the **AltaVista** home page.

2. Click the **Advanced Search** hyperlink to the right of the Find button. The AltaVista Advanced Web Search page will appear.

3. Click anywhere in the **Search With This Boolean Expression** box, type *"project management"*, then click the **Find** button. Notice that approximately 2 million sites are found.

4. Change the text in the Search With This Boolean Expression box so that it reads *"project management" AND (planning phase or implementation phase)*, then click the **Find** button. The search results will include only those Web pages containing the original search string plus either "planning phase" or "implementation phase" but not necessarily both. Notice that the number of sites found is fewer than 1 million.

5. Next, you will use the NOT and NEAR operators to search for Web sites that contain information about database administration and related software. Select the text in the **Search With This Boolean Expression** box and press DELETE to delete the text.

6. In the Search With This Boolean Expression box, type *"database administration"*, then click the **Find** button. Notice that more than 200,000 sites about database administration are found.

7. Change the text in the Search With This Boolean Expression box to read *"database administration" NOT software*, then click the **Find** button. Most sites that focus on database administration software are removed from the results. Notice that the number of sites found is dramatically reduced.

8. Replace NOT with NEAR so that the text in the Search With This Boolean Expression box reads *"database administration" NEAR software*, then click the **Find** button. Web pages that contain the words "database administration" and "software" within 10 words of each other are displayed. The search will find Web sites about database administration software, but probably a minimal number of sites about other types of software or other database administration topics. Notice that the number of sites found has increased from the previous search.

9. Next, you will combine the NEAR and NOT operators to find Web sites that contain information about non-Microsoft database administration software. Add ***NOT Microsoft*** to the end of the text in the Search With This Boolean Expression box so that the text reads *"database administration" NEAR software NOT Microsoft*. Click the **Find** button. Hyperlinks to Web pages about database administration software other than Microsoft software are displayed. Notice that the number of sites found is considerably smaller than in the previous search.

10. Capitalize the first letters of *database* and *administration* so that they read *"Database Administration"*, then click the **Find** button. The search will retrieve only Web pages in which the first two keywords are capitalized. How did this change affect the number of sites found?

Advanced searching in Excite

The Excite search engine (*www.excite.com*) allows conceptual searches that will return results related to the keyword(s) you enter, as well as sites that exactly match the keyword(s).

For example, if you entered the keywords *small business tax forms*, Excite would find sites that exactly match the keywords. Expanding on exact matches, the database also knows that a relationship exists between tax forms and government, and would also return sites that discuss the concept of taxes and small businesses.

Excite supports the Boolean operators AND, OR and NOT, as well as parentheses. If you use these operators, Excite will automatically disable its conceptual search mechanism. Therefore, the results will display only documents containing your exact keywords.

Advanced searching in Lycos

Lycos has a feature for advanced searches (*http://search.lycos.com/adv.asp*) that enables you to control the types of keyword matches, number of hyperlinks (or hits) returned per page, content of the results, and other useful search criteria. To access the Lycos advanced search, you can also click the Advanced Search link under the search field on the Lycos home page (*www.lycos.com*).

Using Web Searches to Perform Job Tasks

OBJECTIVE:
1.11.9: Internet searches for job tasks

As you have seen, you can conduct Web searches to find information about any subject imaginable. You can use any search engine to find any type of data you need from the Internet. This vast resource can help you perform tasks at your job, regardless of what your job may be.

For example, many jobs require employees to perform research periodically. Search engines can help researchers find the information they seek or the correct resource to provide that information. If you are performing research on the job, you need only specify keywords about the topic being researched, then analyze the resulting references and choose the best sources of information.

Search engines can help you find other online services that can assist you in your job. You can accomplish many tasks quickly with instant access to maps, travel services, product comparisons, couriers, supply ordering and delivery, Web hosting services, yellow pages, news, weather reports, people searches, and much more.

Whatever tasks your job requires you to perform, using the Internet can often save time and money by providing fast, convenient access to a vast amount of information and services.

In the following lab, you will use the Internet to perform a job task. Suppose you are novice network engineer and your company is setting up a branch office in an area outside the city. The IT director has asked you to research various kinds of transmission media with which to connect the network equipment. The current equipment is old and the IT director wants to upgrade the equipment in the new office. She has also asked you to research building wiring standards to ensure that the cabling in the new office is in compliance with commercial building wiring standards. How can you use the Internet to perform this job task?

 Lab 4-5: Using the Internet to perform job tasks

In this lab, you will use Google to access Internet resources to perform the job task assigned to you in the previous scenario.

1. Click anywhere in the Internet Explorer **Address** box, type *www.google.com*, then press **ENTER**. The Google search engine home page will display (Figure 4-10).

Figure 4-10: Google home page

2. In the Search box, type **"network cabling"**, then press **ENTER**. Notice that more than 100,000 links are found containing the keywords you specified. However, several links on the first page appear to be very helpful.

3. Click on several links in the first page to determine if they provide information about transmission media.

4. In the Search box, type **"network cabling" AND "building wiring standards"**, then press **ENTER**. Notice that only a few pages of links are found containing the keywords you specified.

5. Click on several links in the first page to determine if they provide information about building wiring standards.

6. In the Search box, replace *cabling* with *wiring* so that the text reads **"network wiring" AND "building wiring standards"**, then press **ENTER**. Notice that even fewer links are found during this search.

7. Click on several links in the first page to determine if the information you find is more helpful than any of the previous sites you visited. Notice that subtle changes in keywords can yield different results. When you are conducting Internet searches, you should try various keyword combinations in order to retrieve information as closely related as possible to the job task you are trying to complete.

8. Close the browser window.

Unexpected Web Search Results

OBJECTIVE:
1.11.4: Search sites
vs. information
portals

Search engines sometimes yield unexpected results such as an error page, an alternative search engine or an advertisement instead of the topic for which you were searching.

Error pages most commonly occur when you enter erroneous search criteria, click a dead link or try to access a busy server. In many cases, when an error page displays, you can click the browser's Back button to return to the previous screen, wait a few seconds, then click the link again. Provided that the link is not a dead link and you entered the search criteria correctly, the site you are trying to access should display.

Unexpected Web pages and advertisements most commonly display when you click a link for a site that was added to a search engine's database by its spider program. Spider programs can inadvertently add unrelated sites to a search engine's database if links to that site exist on the Internet.

You may remember that Web sites are added to information portal databases manually. Because you commonly search for data in information portals by clicking subtopic links to reach a specific site, it is much less likely that you will encounter unexpected results. However, if you conduct keyword searches in search engines or information portals, unexpected results can occur if unrelated Web sites are encountered.

In the following lab, you will access a Web site that yields unexpected results. Suppose the sales interns at your company try to access a certain Web site to sign up for sales training, and an error page displays instead. As the help desk technician, what would you recommend they do to obtain the information they need?

 Lab 4-6: Retrieving unexpected Web search results using Google

In this lab, you will use Google to search keywords that retrieve unexpected results.

1. Open the **Google** search engine home page.

2. In the Search box, type *official netbus home page*, then press **ENTER**. You will see links to Web pages containing the specified keywords.

3. Click the **Official NetBus Homepage** link. Instead of seeing the NetBus home page as you would expect, you receive an error message indicating that the page you requested could not be found, and you see an advertisement for Angelfire, which includes its own search engine. This unrequested page is an example of an unexpected Web search result. You wanted to find information about NetBus, but were instead directed to an advertisement and a search engine.

4. In the browser toolbar, click the **Back** button to return to the Google search page.

5. Close the browser window.

Web Search Strategies

Before beginning any search, think about the information you are seeking. If you want to browse the Web just to see the types of information available, start with an index on a site such as Yahoo! If you are looking for specific information, use a major keyword search engine such as AltaVista, Google, Lycos or Yahoo! If you want as much information as you can find about a topic, try your search on several search engines.

Check the default settings for each search engine you use. Some automatically insert a Boolean AND between keywords, whereas others automatically insert a Boolean OR.

Consider the following tips when you enter keywords in search engines:

- Use keywords that are specific, and try to use nouns rather than verbs.

- Put the most important keywords first in your keyword list.

- Use the plus sign (+) before each keyword to ensure that it is included in the result.

- Whenever possible, combine keywords into phrases by using quotation marks to indicate exact wording, and limit your search results by using the Boolean operator AND.

- Use all uppercase letters when typing Boolean operators in search engines (for example, AND). Some engines will accept both lowercase and uppercase operators, but all will accept uppercase. Conversely, you should use all lowercase letters when typing keywords so that all variations of the keywords (whether they appear in lowercase or uppercase in the Web pages) will be found.

- Use parentheses to combine Boolean phrases in order to identify single concepts and to indicate the order in which the relationships should be considered.

Web search relevancy

OBJECTIVE:
1.11.6: Meta search engines

Search engines display results in a similar manner, generally a list of hyperlinks to Web pages containing the information that most closely matches the keyword(s) you entered. Each database uses its own scoring system. Some engines, such as Lycos, are useful for deciding whether the information is current; others, such as Excite, offer ways to sort results. The more searches you conduct, the better you will become at reading and quickly navigating through the results.

A ranking system, or relevancy, is used to help you determine how closely a site matches the topic for which you are searching. The more frequently your specified keywords are found in a particular document, the higher the relevancy score that document receives. The more powerful search engines use both the words you enter and their synonyms to perform a search, which yield more relevant Web pages.

Usually, a scoring system ranks sites from 0.000 to 1.000 (1.000 being the highest probability of a match), but other variations are used. If you find that one site has the highest score of all the results displayed, you should still look at other results. Because these scoring systems used by search engine databases are based on programming instructions, savvy Web developers sometimes construct Web pages with many keyword references. Thus, you might not always find the best information on the first site you visit.

Evaluating Web site information

OBJECTIVE:
1.11.10: Evaluating online sources

After you have found the information you need on the Web, you must still evaluate its accuracy and value. The fact that you found it on the Internet does not make it true or reliable. You can expect to find all sorts of resources on the Web: personal pages, reference sources, white papers, hoaxes, advertisements, scientific papers and personal opinions. How can you decide whether information is reliable or factual?

Web pages are not overseen or controlled by a central authority. You must determine whether the pages are objective or biased, accurate or inaccurate. Ask yourself the following questions when determining the accuracy and value of information you find on the Internet:

- **Who owns the Web site?** Always consider the source of the information. Remember that you can often learn a lot about a site from the URL. Does your information come from a commercial organization? An institution of higher learning? A nonprofit organization? Information you find on a *.gov* or *.edu* site will probably be accurate because these institutions do not publish sites with the goal of making money. You may need to verify information you find on a *.net, .org* or *.com* site because these types of sites generally present material favorable to their own agendas, services or goods.

- **Who created the Web site?** Are the author's name and e-mail address available? Is the Web site owner's information available?

  ○ Look for links with names such as About Us, Our Mission, Our Philosophy or Background. Are the site owners willing to say who they are and what they stand for?

  ○ Can the author or host be contacted? If an author seems elusive, you may want to carefully investigate the information. Most reputable Web sites will provide a link for questions and comments.

  ○ If the author's credentials are not listed on the site, try to contact the author to verify them.

- **When was the Web site last updated?** Sometimes the information you need must be current. At other times, the timeliness is less important.

- **Whose links can be found on the site?** The Web site owner's associations may tell you a lot about the owner. Which organizations or individuals allow their links to be listed on the Web site? (Web site developers should ask for permission prior to linking to another Web site because such a link usually implies a business relationship or endorsement.) If they are well-known and reputable, the Web site contents are probably reputable as well.

OBJECTIVE:
1.11.5: Hard-copy resources

- **How does the information found on the site compare with information found in print?** Remember that hard-copy resources, such as professional journals, scholarly writings and reference books, contain accurate and current information that you can use to corroborate the information you find during Web searches. If hard-copy reference materials refute your Web search findings, you may want to search further or use the reference materials as your basis of information.

- **How was the Web site's rank determined?** If a search engine ranks the site highly, this may or may not indicate reliability. Was this ranking the result of legitimate links, sponsor preference, or manipulation by a person or group of people?

Citing Copyrighted Web Site References

OBJECTIVE:
1.11.8: Reference citation standards

It is important to properly cite information that you obtain from an Internet search to avoid plagiarizing someone else's work. Plagiarizing information you obtain from the Internet is the same as plagiarizing someone else's printed work and could constitute copyright infringement. When using information from any medium, you must cite the source to give appropriate credit to the creator.

Style manuals, such as the *MLA Handbook for Writers of Research Papers* and *The Chicago Manual of Style*, are good sources for determining the way to properly cite Internet-based information. The citation for an Internet source should be the same as that for a print source.

According to the *MLA Handbook for Writers of Research Papers*, a reference to Internet-based information should be cited as follows:

- Ramirez, Holly, and Michelle Meyer. "Project Management: Is It Right for You?" Certification Magazine. March 2004. <http://www.certmag.com/articles/templates/cmag_feature.asp?articleid=622&zoneid=9>.

In this example, the authors are Holly Ramirez and Michelle Meyer; the title of the article is "Project Management: Is It Right for You?"; the source of the article is *Certification Magazine*; and the issue date was March 2004. Notice that the first author's last name is displayed first, and that name is used to sequence this entry in an alphabetical list of citations.

The Chicago Manual of Style uses the following format for citing Internet-based information:

- Holly Ramirez and Michelle Meyer, "Project Management: Is It Right for You?" *Certification Magazine*, March 2004, http://www.certmag.com/articles/templates/cmag_feature.asp?articleid=622&zoneid=9 (accessed June 25, 2004).

In this example, the components of the entry are the same as in the first example. However, the first author's last name is not displayed first, and the date on which the Web site was accessed is displayed parenthetically after the Web site reference.

Either citation method is acceptable, although you should choose one standard and use it consistently. Most organizations designate standard style manuals or conventions for company publications.

Remember that any published work or expression is protected by copyright. You cannot copy and use someone else's work for your own site or publication without express written permission. Always check copyright notices on any site you want to borrow from. In many cases, the copyright owner may only require proper credit and citation for you to use the material, but sometimes you must pay a fee. The copyright owner sets the terms. Always observe fair use of others' copyrighted material. Copyright infringement is a punishable offense.

Case Study
Is This a Valid Theory?

Ellen is an anthropologist who has been working at Olduvai Gorge in Tanzania for the past six months. She has been conducting research on the Internet. She finds a Web site with an article that proposes a revolutionary theory regarding human migration patterns from east-central Africa that may have occurred about 150,000 years ago. Ellen wants to determine whether the information is valid before she presents it to her fellow anthropologists for consideration.

Ellen performs the following tasks:

- She obtains information about the organization on whose Web site the article was presented. Based on the domain name, Ellen determines that the organization is an educational institution, rather than a commercial entity that may be promoting its own agenda. She believes the information is reliable because it is posted on a site hosted by an educational institution.

- She researches other organizations that link to the Web site containing the article by following some of the links. She finds that the sites are hosted by trustworthy sources known in her field.

- She checks the credentials of the author and determines that he is a known professional in anthropology who has published reputable works.

- She accesses current scholarly writings and professional journals and finds that this new and exciting theory has the support of other anthropologists.

Ellen feels comfortable presenting the information she found to her fellow anthropologists because she knows it is valid.

*   *   *

As a class, discuss other ways Ellen can evaluate the information presented in the article to determine its legitimacy.

Lesson Summary

Application project

Each search engine has advantages and disadvantages for different types of Internet searching. Now that you have used several search engines, which do you think will work best for your needs?

Your company wants to open a branch office in Athens, Greece, or Lisbon, Portugal. Locate commercial real estate in Athens and Lisbon for your new office using an advanced search with Boolean operators and wildcard characters as needed. Use AltaVista, Excite and Lycos for your advanced search (remember that your results will vary). Attempt to narrow your search as much as possible, using only one search entry. Which search engine provided the most useful information? Attempt to locate the rates per square meter of available office space in both cities. What results would you report back to your company?

Skills review

In this lesson, you learned about database components, relational databases, database table keys and relationships, database queries using SQL, and common database vendors.

You also learned about search engines and Web searches, registering a Web site with a search engine, and the types of Web searches you can perform. You learned common basic and advanced search techniques, and the Boolean operators that can help you narrow the scope of your search results.

Finally, you learned how to conduct Web searches to perform job tasks, and you learned the reasons you may sometimes encounter unexpected search results. You also learned about Web search strategies, evaluating Web search relevancy and Web site information, and citing Web site information when you use it in your own work.

Now that you have completed this lesson, you should be able to:

✓ Define databases and database components.

✓ Define relational database concepts.

✓ Define Web search engines and explain Web search types.

✓ Register a Web site with a search engine.

✓ Conduct basic and advanced Web searches.

✓ Define Boolean operators.

✓ Use Web searches to perform job tasks.

✓ Explain Web search strategies and unexpected Web search results.

✓ Identify Web search relevancy.

✓ Evaluate Web site information and cite copyrighted Web site information as a resource.

Lesson 4 Review

1. Briefly describe a relational database.

    _____

    _____

2. What is a search engine?

    _____

    _____

3. What is the function of a <meta> tag?

    _____

    _____

4. List three types of search engine indexing methods.

    _____

5. List at least three standard Boolean operators.

    _____

6. What is the purpose of a search engine ranking system?

    _____

    _____

    _____

Lesson 5:
E-Mail and Personal Information Management

Objectives

By the end of this lesson, you will be able to:

- ✦ Explain the way that electronic mail (e-mail) works.

- ✦ Configure an e-mail client.

- ✦ Identify e-mail components.

- ✦ Create and send e-mail messages.

- ✦ Receive and view e-mail messages.

- ✦ Identify ways to use e-mail effectively in the workplace.

- ✦ Identify e-mail problems and solutions.

- ✦ Identify the functions of personal information management (PIM) software.

Pre-Assessment Questions

1. What feature provided with many e-mail programs can store information for commonly accessed e-mail contacts?

    a. Import tool
    b. Address book
    c. Autoresponder
    d. Attachment

2. What is an e-mail signature?

    a. A digital display of one's handwritten signature
    b. Proof of one's identity for security purposes
    c. A closing remark that is manually attached to an e-mail message
    d. Text that appears automatically at the bottom of an e-mail message

3. Name the protocol used to send e-mail over the Internet, and name one of two protocols that can be used to receive e-mail over the Internet.

    to send: SMTP Simple Mail Transfer Protocol

    to rcv: POP3 - Post-Office Protocol

    " Internet Message Access Protocol (IMAP)

snail mail
Slang term for the standard postal service.

Introduction to Electronic Mail (E-Mail)

Electronic mail, or e-mail, has revolutionized the way people communicate with each other and has been widely embraced in corporate communication. Never before has our global society been able to send and receive information so quickly. The commonplace use of electronic mail has given rise to the term **snail mail**, which is a slang term for the standard postal service.

How E-Mail Works

Whether your e-mail system is configured for you at work or you set up your own system at home with a modem and an e-mail program installation CD-ROM, the basic function of e-mail is simple: You use it to send electronic messages from one computer to another.

For messages to be sent from one computer to another, the computers must be linked, or networked. You may have a physical connection (such as a cable) between the two computer stations, or the computers may each connect to a local server that relays the messages, or the computers may use the Internet to relay messages.

Internet communication is made possible by TCP/IP software. Remember that TCP enables two computers to establish a communication link and exchange packets of data, while IP configures the format and addressing scheme of the packets. TCP/IP software sends information to the computer with which you are connected, which then passes it on to other computers until it reaches the destination.

IP address
A unique numerical address assigned to a computer or device on a network.

Every device on the Internet has a unique **IP address**, just as every house and business has a street address. An IP address is a series of numbers divided into four sections, each separated by a period, or dot. IP addresses are also called "dotted quads."

Local area networks (LANs) and wide area networks (WANs) use IP addresses to identify each user on the network, whether or not the network has access to the Internet. When you log on to the company network, you enter a user name that the network associates with your IP address. Some companies devise their own internal IP address scheme and never connect to the Internet. These companies use TCP/IP across leased lines and establish an internal network.

E-mail is available to anyone who has an IP address either on an internal network or on the Internet. When you use e-mail at work, your IT department assigns you an IP address and user name by which the company network recognizes you. Usually when you log on to a company network, you must also enter a password. IT departments generally assign a generic password to a new account, which you can later change. When you purchase Internet service through an ISP or a commercial online service, your provider assigns an IP address to you. Your provider uses that IP address to recognize you, and you can send and receive e-mail using that address.

When you are logged on to the network or connected to the Internet, you can create an electronic message using an e-mail program, and send your message across the network (or the Internet) using a specific address for your intended recipient. The network delivers your message, and your recipient receives and reads your message using an e-mail program.

E-mail protocols

As you learned earlier in this course, e-mail involves two mail servers: outgoing and incoming. You can use separate servers for outgoing and incoming e-mail, or a single server for both tasks. The outgoing and incoming servers use various protocols to send, receive and store e-mail messages.

You send e-mail to others with an outgoing server using Simple Mail Transfer Protocol (SMTP). SMTP is the Internet standard protocol for transferring e-mail messages from one computer to another. It specifies how two e-mail systems interact. SMTP is responsible solely for sending e-mail messages, and is part of the TCP/IP suite.

Message Transfer Agent (MTA)
A messaging component that routes, delivers and receives e-mail.

An outgoing mail server runs a **Message Transfer Agent (MTA)**, also called a mail transport agent, which routes, delivers and receives messages, usually via SMTP. A **Mail Delivery Agent (MDA)** receives the messages delivered by the MTA and then delivers the messages to their proper destination (or mailbox), where a user can pick them up.

Mail Delivery Agent (MDA)
An e-mail server program that receives sent messages and delivers them to their proper destination mailbox.

As you have learned, you receive e-mail from an incoming mail server using Post Office Protocol version 3 (POP3) or Internet Message Access Protocol (IMAP). POP3 and IMAP are used to store and access e-mail messages.

POP3 servers receive and hold incoming e-mail messages in the appropriate mailbox on the server until users log on (authenticate themselves with a user name and password) and download their mail. Once messages are downloaded, they are removed from the server. Because messages are downloaded immediately, you do not need a constant connection with the server in order to work with your e-mail, which is beneficial for people who have dial-up connections. POP3 is also referred to as a "store-and-forward" service.

An IMAP server receives and holds your messages. When you log on with your user name and password, you can read a message on the server, or you can view just the heading and the sender of the message and decide whether to download it. Messages are not downloaded automatically as they are with a POP3 server. Recent e-mail clients, including Netscape Mail & Newsgroups, Eudora Pro and Microsoft Outlook Express, support IMAP and allow you to specify multiple IMAP accounts.

Using IMAP, you can create and manipulate mailboxes or folders directly on the server, and the messages remain on the server until you delete them. IMAP can be thought of as a remote file server. If you are working remotely, you must have a constant connection with the server, and IMAP is more widely used by people who maintain a constant connection, for example through DSL or cable. Users who want to work with their e-mail files locally must download their messages.

E-mail addresses

To send and receive messages, you need an e-mail address. E-mail addresses use the following format:

> *username@domain*

user name
A unique name or number that identifies you when logging on to a computer system or online service. In an e-mail address, the part before the @ symbol.

All e-mail addresses contain the @ symbol between the **user name** and the domain. The @ symbol means "at." The following is a typical e-mail address format:

> student1@class.com

The part of the address before the @ identifies the user within a domain. The user name is also known as an e-mail account. When you purchase Internet service or when you join a company that has e-mail, you choose (or you are assigned) a user name. Because the rules for creating user names are flexible, conventions vary. Typically, the user name is related to the person's name or job function, and may include periods, underscores or numbers in addition to letters, as shown in the following examples:

> jsmith@company.net
> johns@company.net
> john.smith@company.net

domain name
An IP address represented in words.

The part of the address after the @ is the **domain name** of the organization or company that issues the e-mail account. The domain name portion of your e-mail address identifies your location on the Internet (or on the company network) so that you can receive mail.

Your e-mail address, like your home address, is unique; no one else can have the same address within the same domain. For example, different individuals can have the addresses johndoe@fed.gov, johndoe@fed.com and johndoe@fed.mil because the user name is not duplicated within the same domain. This arrangement is similar to having a 1234 Main Street in various U.S. cities.

E-mail services and programs

e-mail client
An e-mail program that is independent of any specific Web browser, and that you can use to send e-mail messages.

Many types of e-mail services are available. You can use an **e-mail client** to send messages over the Internet if you have an account with an ISP. Eudora is a popular e-mail program on the Internet because it can run on multiple platforms, such as Macintosh and Windows. E-mail clients are for e-mail purposes only. You cannot use them to browse Web pages or search for information. An e-mail client is also referred to as a **Mail User Agent (MUA)**.

Mail User Agent (MUA)
A messaging component used as a stand-alone application by the user.

You can also use **browser e-mail** programs. Browsers, such as Netscape Navigator and Microsoft Internet Explorer, come with e-mail programs. When you install Internet Explorer, you can also install Outlook Express. Netscape Navigator provides Netscape Mail & Newsgroups, a complete e-mail program you can use to exchange messages with individuals and newsgroups.

browser e-mail
E-mail programs such as Netscape Mail & Newsgroups or Outlook Express that come bundled with a Web browser and with which they may be integrated.

Commercial **online service e-mail** programs are also available. Online services, such as America Online (AOL) and CompuServe, offer custom e-mail programs. Before you use the online service e-mail program, you must download and install it, and you must learn how to address and send messages. The formats for addressing e-mail messages may vary among services.

online service e-mail
An e-mail program that is part of an online service's software.

You can also use **Web-based e-mail** services. Several such services are available, including Yahoo! Mail, Hotmail, RocketMail (now part of Yahoo.com), Netscape Mail and Mail.com. Web-based e-mail is free, offers e-mail accounts that are accessible from any computer with Internet access, and permits family members who share a single Internet account to have separate e-mail addresses. However, you must have Internet access through a service provider before you can use Web-based e-mail, or you can use a public computer that offers Internet access, such as a computer at a public library.

Web-based e-mail
Free e-mail service from a provider such as Hotmail or Yahoo! in which you request a user name. You can access your e-mail from any computer that has access to the Internet.

Web-based MUAs store e-mail messages on their HTTP servers, and users access their e-mail through a Web page. In many cases, you can use an e-mail client to download mail from a Web-based account. For example, Outlook Express has built-in settings for downloading mail from Hotmail. Some Web hosts, such as Yahoo! Mail, may charge a fee for making a Web-based account POP-enabled.

When you create a Web-based e-mail account, you request a user name (e-mail address), and the hosting service will accept or deny your request depending upon whether that name is already in use within that domain.

E-mail over the Internet

Because your e-mail address is unique within a domain, and because your user name and domain constitute a unique address on the Internet, anyone who knows your address can send you e-mail. The computers to which you connect on the Internet use TCP/IP to deliver your message at your specific address.

The people sending you messages need not be in the same domain, nor does it matter which e-mail programs they use. Your unique Internet address ensures that the message will be delivered to you. Gateways between e-mail systems allow users on different e-mail systems to exchange messages. A gateway is a computer that connects two networks that have different protocols.

Gateways enable you to send and receive e-mail between all Internet mail services over the Internet because they enable different networks to communicate. For example, if you have an account with AOL, you can send an e-mail message to your brother in another state, who has an account at his university. He in turn can forward your message to your cousin in another country, who has an account with her employer.

E-mail on a network

E-mail works on a network much as it does over the Internet. Each user has a specific IP address within the company's domain, and messages are routed from one user to another via the network server, which uses TCP/IP to transfer messages to specific IP addresses.

However, LANs may use proprietary protocols to send messages to people within the LAN, and use SMTP to send e-mail to recipients outside the LAN, such as remote employees or business associates.

Some networks may be self-contained; they will use only proprietary protocols to send messages to people within the LAN. You may be unable to connect to the global Internet from within your company's network. In such cases, you can send and receive messages to and from your co-workers, but you cannot exchange messages with anyone outside the network.

MIME, S/MIME, PGP and GPG

OBJECTIVE:
1.6.2: MIME, S/MIME
and PGP/GPG

Multipurpose Internet Mail Extensions (MIME)
A protocol that enables operating systems to map file name extensions to corresponding applications. Also used by applications to automatically process files downloaded from the Internet.

Multipurpose Internet Mail Extensions (MIME) is a protocol that was developed as an extension of SMTP. MIME allows users to exchange various types of data files over the Internet, such as audio, video, images, applications, and so forth.

MIME is a system that identifies attached files by type. MIME types are classified under broad headings (text, image, applications, audio and video) and then subclassified by specific type. For example, a QuickTime video is identified as a video/quicktime MIME type.

header
A block of information attached to a piece of data. The first part of a network packet. Can contain network addressing information or additional information that helps computers and applications process data.

Servers insert a MIME definition inside the HTTP **header** at the beginning of any Web transmission so that your browser (or e-mail client or any other Internet client) can select the appropriate player (whether built-in or plug-in) for the type of data indicated in the header.

Modern e-mail clients support MIME, allowing users to receive various types of files as attachments to e-mail messages. When a user opens the attachment, the appropriate application (as specified by the attachment's MIME type) is opened and the attachment can be viewed, heard or otherwise experienced, assuming that the client computer has the appropriate application installed.

Secure MIME (S/MIME)
Secure version of MIME that adds encryption to MIME data.

Secure MIME (S/MIME) is a new version of the MIME protocol that provides a secure method of sending e-mail. S/MIME supports encryption (based on the RSA algorithm) and the use of digital certificates in e-mail. RSA Security, which licenses the algorithm, owns the RSA encryption system and charges a fee for using it. (Encryption will be discussed in detail in a later lesson.)

MIME controls the way that messages and attachments are organized and distinguished from one another, whereas S/MIME controls the way that encryption information and digital certificates can be included as part of an e-mail message. The latest versions of Internet Explorer and Navigator both support S/MIME.

Pretty Good Privacy (PGP)
A method of encrypting and decrypting e-mail messages. It can also be used to encrypt a digital signature.

An alternative to S/MIME is **Pretty Good Privacy (PGP)**, a method developed by Philip Zimmerman for encrypting and decrypting e-mail messages. PGP is available in a free version and a low-cost commercial version. The free version (Diffie-Hellman version) uses non-patented encryption algorithms, whereas the commercial version (RSA version) uses a patented RSA algorithm. PGP was once an open-code product (anyone could read the code), before Network Associates bought PGP and closed the code. Closed code cannot be read unless the company that owns it allows someone to do so. Anyone reading closed code must sign a nondisclosure agreement before looking at the code.

PGP uses the public-key encryption system. Each user has a publicly known encryption key, which is used to encrypt messages, and a private key (known only to that user), which is used to decrypt messages. When you encrypt a message intended for your recipient, you encrypt it using his or her public key. When the recipient receives the message, he or she decrypts it with his or her private key.

To use PGP, you download (or purchase) it and install it on your computer. Then you register the public key that your PGP program gives you with a PGP public-key server. This process enables people with whom you exchange messages to find your public key and use it for encrypting messages they send you.

The free version can be used only for private (non-commercial) exchanges. For commercial exchanges, you must use the RSA version. The free version and the commercial version of PGP are not compatible with each other because they use different algorithms.

PGP runs on BeOS (an operating system designed specifically to support multimedia applications), Macintosh, MS-DOS, OS/2, UNIX and Windows 3x/9x/200/Me/XP operating systems. You can download the free version from *www.pgpi.org/*.

After Philip Zimmerman put PGP in the public domain, the U.S. government brought a lawsuit against him because he made an effective encryption tool available to anyone (including potential enemies of the United States). The lawsuit was eventually dropped, but it is illegal to use PGP in many other countries.

Gnu Privacy Guard (GPG), also known as GnuPG, is an open-source version of PGP that does not use patented algorithms. It is free and can be used, modified and distributed under the terms of the GNU Public License. The GNU General Public License guarantees a developer's freedom to share and change free software and to ensure the software is free for all users. GnuPG is available for Linux/UNIX, as well as for Macintosh and Windows operating systems. Visit *www.gnupg.org/download/* to download GnuPG.

PGP and GnuPG encrypt the e-mail message and its attachments. However, neither encrypts the authentication session (that is, your user name and password for signing on and receiving and sending mail) or the e-mail's Subject field. When you use these encryption tools, you should not include sensitive information in the Subject field.

E-Mail Configuration Requirements

Before a user can send and receive e-mail, an e-mail client must be installed and configured. To configure an e-mail client, you must identify yourself and provide the names of the mail servers used by your ISP. Most e-mail clients allow you to set up and configure multiple accounts.

Configuring Outlook Express

Microsoft Outlook Express is an e-mail program provided with Internet Explorer, so it is installed when you install Windows XP. Outlook Express requires the same configuration information as most e-mail clients: the e-mail address, the name of the outgoing (SMTP) mail server, the name of the incoming (POP3) mail server, a POP3 account name and a POP3 account password.

Note: You can also specify an IMAP or HTTP server as the incoming mail server. HTTP servers are used for Web-based e-mail accounts.

You use the General and Servers tabs of the Properties dialog box to specify these settings in Outlook Express. Use the General tab of the Properties dialog box (Figure 5-1) in Outlook Express to specify your user name and e-mail address.

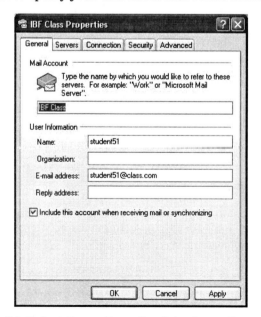

Figure 5-1: Outlook Express Properties dialog box — General tab

When you log on to your e-mail account, your user name and password are sent to the POP server for authentication. You can download your messages only after you have supplied a valid user name and password.

You use the Servers tab of the Properties dialog box (Figure 5-2) in Outlook Express to specify the names of your incoming and outgoing mail server(s). You also use this tab to specify your account name and password.

Figure 5-2: Outlook Express Properties dialog box — Servers tab

Notice that the Outgoing Mail Server section of the Properties dialog box contains an option that reads My Server Requires Authentication. This option is available in most e-mail clients. Some system administrators configure their SMTP servers to require a user name and password in order to send e-mail as well as to receive it. When you select this option, you enable your e-mail client to send your user information each time you send an e-mail message.

OBJECTIVE:
1.6.6: SMTP
authentication

System administrators may require authentication before sending mail in an effort to curtail the illicit use of their SMTP servers for sending unsolicited junk mail, or spam (which will be discussed later in this lesson). One of the drawbacks of requiring SMTP authentication is that the transmission of the user name and password are not encrypted by default, therefore the requirement increases the chances that a hacker can use a packet sniffer (software that monitors network activity) to obtain a valid user name and password.

Configuring Netscape Mail & Newsgroups

The Netscape Navigator 7.1 Web browser includes an integrated e-mail program called Netscape Mail & Newsgroups. To specify e-mail configuration settings in Netscape, you use the Mail & Newsgroups Account Settings dialog box.

To specify your identity (your name and e-mail address), you use the Account Settings panel. To specify your incoming server information, you use the Server Settings panel. To specify your outgoing server settings, you use the Outgoing Server (SMTP) Settings panel. Figure 5-3 shows the Account Settings panel, which you use to specify your account name, your name and your e-mail address.

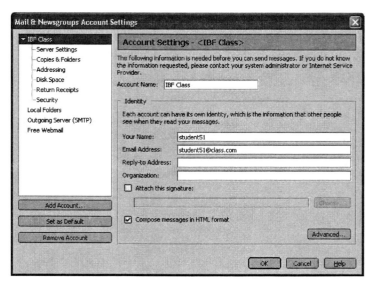

Figure 5-3: Mail & Newsgroups Account Settings dialog box — Account Settings panel

Figure 5-4 shows the Server Settings panel, which you use to specify the name of your POP3 server.

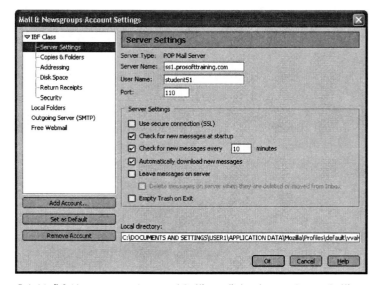

Figure 5-4: Mail & Newsgroups Account Settings dialog box — Server Settings panel

Figure 5-5 shows the Outgoing Server (SMTP) Settings panel, which you use to specify the name of your SMTP server.

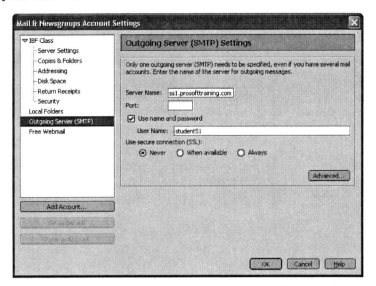

Figure 5-5: Mail & Newsgroups Account Settings dialog box — Outgoing Server (SMTP) Settings panel

Remember that service patches and updates for e-mail clients become available periodically. Check the vendor sites frequently for updates. Consider that some functions for e-mail messages, such as printing, may be configured outside the client. For example, you must configure Microsoft Internet Explorer to print before you can print correctly from within Outlook Express.

In the following lab, you will configure Outlook Express as an e-mail client. Suppose the personnel manager of your company requests a laptop with Outlook Express set up as the e-mail client. You can configure Outlook Express to access the corporate e-mail servers so that the manager can use the laptop to access her company e-mail.

 Lab 5-1: Configuring Outlook Express as your e-mail client

In this lab, you will configure Microsoft Outlook Express as your e-mail client for this class.

1. First, you will configure the mail client. From the Windows Desktop, select **Start | All Programs | Outlook Express**.

    *Note: If you are asked whether you want Outlook Express to be your default e-mail program, click **No**.*

2. If Outlook Express has never been configured, the Internet Connection Wizard may appear. Click **Cancel**, then click **Yes** to verify your cancellation of the wizard. You will access the wizard later in this lab.

3. The Outlook Express Import window, which allows you to import e-mail configurations from other e-mail clients on your computer, may display. Select **Do Not Import At This Time**, click **Next**, then click **Finish**. The Outlook Express window will open (Figure 5-6). You may have a Welcome e-mail message from Microsoft.

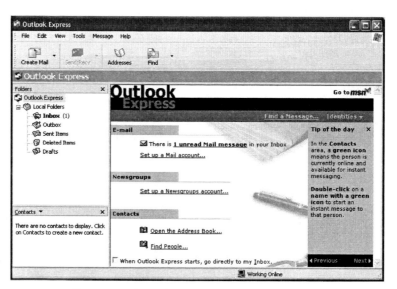

Figure 5-6: Microsoft Outlook Express main window

4. Select **Tools | Accounts**, then click the **Mail** tab.

5. Click **Add**, then click **Mail** in the pop-up menu to launch the Internet Connection Wizard and display the Your Name screen.

6. In the Display Name text box, type the user name that will appear on your account, such as *studentX* (where *X* is your assigned student number). Then click **Next** to display the Internet E-Mail Address screen in the wizard.

7. In the E-Mail Address text box, type your e-mail address, such as *studentX@class.com* (where *X* is your assigned student number). Then click **Next** to display the E-Mail Server Names screen. The mail server dedicated for this class currently has user accounts for student1 through student120; the domain is class.com. Therefore, the available e-mail addresses are student1@class.com through student120@class.com.

Tech Tip: The student accounts in the class.com domain are valid only for communicating with other student accounts in the class.com domain. These accounts do not function outside the ss1.prosofttraining.com mail server and are incapable of sending or receiving any correspondence outside the domain.

8. In the Incoming Mail (POP3, IMAP or HTTP) Server text box, type **ss1.prosofttraining.com** to specify the POP3 server name, then press **TAB**.

9. In the Outgoing Mail (SMTP) Server text box, type **ss1.prosofttraining.com** to specify the name of the SMTP server, then click **Next** to display the Internet Mail Logon screen.

10. In the Account Name text box, type your POP3 account name if necessary (*studentX*, where *X* is your assigned student number), then press **TAB**.

11. In the Password text box, type **password**. Verify that the **Remember Password** check box is selected, then click **Next** to display the final screen in the wizard.

12. Click **Finish** to close the Internet Connection Wizard. This step also displays the Internet Accounts dialog box, as shown in Figure 5-7.

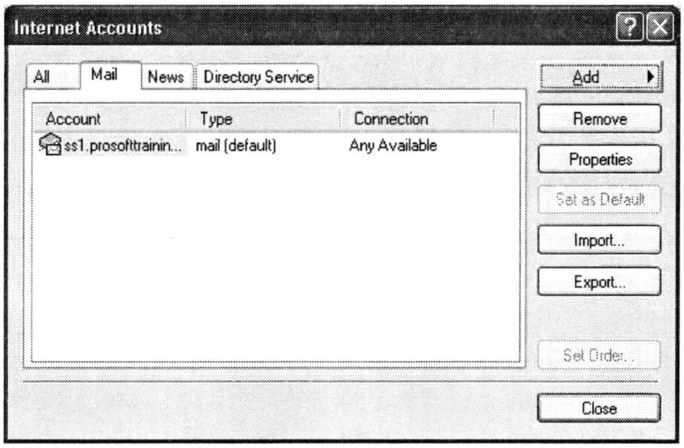

Figure 5-7: Configured e-mail account in Outlook Express

13. Next, you will review the settings. Click the account you just set up, then click the **Properties** button to display the General tab of the Properties dialog box. Notice that you can specify a name for the account.

14. Type **IBF Class** in the Mail Account text box to specify a name for the new account.

15. Click the **Servers** tab to review the server information, then click **OK** to close the Properties dialog box for the new mail account. Notice that the account now displays the *IBF Class* account name in the Internet Accounts dialog box.

16. Close the **Internet Accounts** dialog box, then close **Outlook Express**.

OBJECTIVE:
1.6.1: E-mail clients

Web-based e-mail

You can set up Web-based e-mail, such as Hotmail or Yahoo! Mail, while you are online. You set up an account by registering a Web-based e-mail address with the provider. In many cases, an e-mail message confirming your request for an account will be mailed to your new Web-based e-mail address, and you must respond to the message to activate your account.

Web-based e-mail is advantageous for many reasons. You can log on and check your e-mail from any computer that has Internet access. In theory, this eliminates the need to purchase Internet service from an ISP, although most users choose to purchase Internet service so that they do not have to use a public computer to check their e-mail. You can also set up multiple accounts, and you can send attachments (if your browser supports them).

After your Web-based account is set up, you can access your e-mail using the provider's Web page. You may also be able to download messages in an e-mail client such as Outlook Express. Search your Web host's help menus for information or instructions about configuring your e-mail client. Some Web hosts may charge a fee for enabling it for POP.

In the following lab, you will configure a Web-based e-mail account using Hotmail. Suppose the marketing director of your company wants an e-mail account that he can use while traveling and asks you to set up an account that will be free and accessible from any location. You can set up a free Hotmail account for the marketing director that he can access from any computer that is connected to the Internet.

Lab 5-2: Configuring a Web-based e-mail account using Hotmail

In this lab, you will set up a Web-based Hotmail account.

1. Start **Microsoft Internet Explorer**, and then enter the URL *www.msn.com* to go to the MSN home page.

2. Click the link for **Hotmail** to display the logon page. The first step will be to sign up for a new account.

3. Click the **New Account Sign Up** link to display the Registration page.

4. In the Profile Information section, enter your personal information. Your profile contains information that identifies you, such as your name and address, birth date and gender. You can click the **What Does Passport Do With My Information** link at the top of the registration form to read about the ways your personal information is used.

5. In the Account Information section, type the name you would like to use for your e-mail address, such as *ITProfessional2003x*. When you sign up for a new account, you are requesting a user name at the Hotmail.com domain. The e-mail address you request must be unique within the domain.

6. Enter and re-enter a password that is at least six characters and does not contain spaces.

7. Display the **Secret Question** drop-down list, and select a question that you would like Hotmail to use to prompt you for an answer in the event that you forget your user name or password.

8. Type the answer to the question you selected in Step 7.

9. Type the characters that display in the picture to demonstrate that a person (not an automated program) is completing the registration form.

   Tech Note: Automated programs are sometimes used to register large numbers of accounts with Web services for purposes such as sending spam or slowing down the service by signing in to multiple accounts simultaneously. Usually, automated registration programs cannot recognize the characters in the picture.

10. Scroll down the page and read the agreement, then click the **I Agree** button to submit your registration information. When your account has been successfully set up, a Registration Is Complete dialog box, such as the one shown in Figure 5-8, will display.

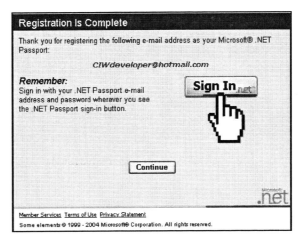

Figure 5-8: Hotmail account registration

Note: If you specified an e-mail address that is already in use at the Hotmail domain, you will be asked to choose a different address. Hotmail will suggest several alternatives to the one you originally submitted. You may choose one of those or create a new one.

11. Write your new Web-based e-mail address and your password in the space provided.

_____

The remaining steps in this lab will complete your account configuration. You can specify which free newsletters and featured offers (if any) you would like to receive in your Inbox.

12. Click the **Continue** button to display the Hotmail page, and then click the **Free E-Mail** link at the bottom of the page to specify that you want the free Hotmail account. This step displays a page of free newsletters you can opt to receive.

13. Scroll to the bottom of the page and click the **Continue** button to display the next page of advertising.

14. Scroll to the bottom of the page and click the **Continue** button to display the MSN Hotmail page. The mailbox usage graph should display near the top of the page.

15. Click the **Sign Out** button at the top of the Web page to sign out of Hotmail and return to the MSN home page.

16. Close the **Internet Explorer** window.

E-Mail Message Components

OBJECTIVE:
1.6.7: Blind copying (BCC)

Although e-mail programs may differ, all messages have the same basic components. Table 5-1 describes the typical elements of an e-mail message.

Table 5-1: E-mail message components

Component	Description
To (address) field	Contains the e-mail address(es) of primary recipient(s). The address(es) you enter here are displayed in the e-mail message header.
Cc (carbon copy) field	Contains the e-mail address(es) of additional recipient(s) to whom you want to send the message. The address(es) you enter here are displayed in the e-mail message header.
Bcc (blind carbon copy) field	Contains the e-mail address(es) of additional recipient(s) to whom you want to send the message. The address(es) you enter here are not displayed in the e-mail message header. Recipients designated in the To and Cc fields will not be able to see recipients you specified in the Bcc field.
Subject field	Contains a brief description of the message content.
Attachment field	Indicates a file or files that are attached and sent with the message.
Message field	Contains the body of the message. You type your message directly into the message area.
Signature field	Contains a few lines of text that appear at the bottom of each message you send. A signature generally consists of the sender's contact information.

The To, Cc, Bcc, Subject and Attachment components constitute the e-mail message header. The e-mail message header contains information about the message (such as its author, its intended recipients, its general content and whether separate files are attached), but is separate from the body of the message. The e-mail message header generally displays in a portion of the message window separate from the body of the message.

At the very least, an e-mail message must include one address in the To field. Outlook Express will prompt you if you attempt to send a message without a Subject line, although you can choose to send the message anyway. It is also possible to send an e-mail message that contains no body text, but doing so would have no purpose.

attachment
A file that is sent with an e-mail message.

Attachments are separate files that you add to e-mail messages. When you attach a file using Outlook Express, a file icon, along with the name of the attached file, displays in the e-mail message header. (Other e-mail clients may display attachments differently.) When you receive a message that contains an attachment, an attachment icon displays to the left of the message subject in your Inbox. You can download and read the attachment, save the attachment to your hard drive or other storage location, or you can delete it. You will attach files to messages and open attachments in an upcoming lab.

Creating and Sending E-Mail Messages

Toolbar buttons and display windows vary among e-mail clients, but generally, the steps required to create and send an e-mail message are the same. To create an e-mail message, you click the command to create a new message, enter an address in the To field, enter a Subject line, type the message, attach any necessary files, then click the command to send the message.

Creating messages in Outlook Express

To create messages in Outlook Express, you select Message | New Message to display the New Message window. Type the recipient's e-mail address in the To field. Type the subject of your message in the Subject field, then click in the message area of the window to type your message. When your message is complete, click the Send button to send the message immediately.

Alternately, you can select File | Send Later in the New Message window to move your message to the Outbox folder, where it will be queued to be sent at a later time. By default, Outlook Express saves a copy of every message you send in the Sent Items folder. E-mail client folder structure will be discussed at length later in this lesson.

In the following lab, you will create and send e-mail messages using Outlook Express. Suppose your manager has assigned you the task of configuring Outlook Express on four systems. You have configured the client on each system, and now you can test each client by sending and receiving e-mail messages.

 Lab 5-3: Creating and sending e-mail messages using Outlook Express

In this lab, you will create a new e-mail message in Outlook Express.

1. Start **Outlook Express**. In the Folders pane, click **Inbox** to display your Inbox.

2. Select **Message | New Message** to display the New Message window. Notice that the To, Cc and Subject fields display in the header.

    *Note: The Bcc field does not display by default. To display it, select **View | All Headers** in the New Message window.*

    *Note: You can also click the **Create Mail** button in the toolbar to display the New Message window.*

3. In the To field, type your own e-mail address (**studentX@class.com**, where *X* is your assigned student number) to address the message to yourself.

4. Press **TAB** twice to move the cursor to the Subject box, then type **Test Message** as the subject.

5. Press **TAB** to move the cursor to the message area of the window, then type **This is a test message.** This step enters the message text. Your message should resemble the one shown in Figure 5-9.

Figure 5-9: Creating message in Outlook Express

6. Click the **Send** button to send your message to the mail server.

7. Minimize the **Outlook Express** window.

Creating messages in Hotmail

To create messages in Hotmail, sign in to your account, then click the Mail tab to display your Inbox. Click the New button to display a blank new message form in the browser window, as shown in Figure 5-10.

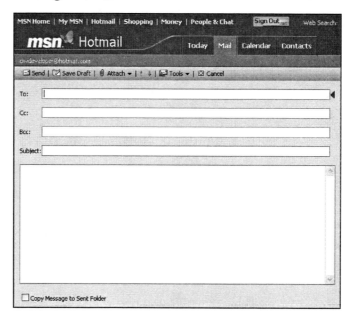

Figure 5-10: Creating message in Hotmail

Notice that in Hotmail, the Bcc field displays by default. Notice also that you must select Copy Message To Sent Folder to save a copy of the message. Most Web-based e-mail accounts give you limited server space, and saving copies of sent messages takes up space.

Type the recipient's e-mail address in the To field. Type the subject of your message in the Subject field, then click in the message area of the window to type your message. When your message is complete, click the Send button to send the message.

In the following lab, you will create and send e-mail messages using Hotmail. Suppose you have set up a Hotmail account for the marketing director of your company. You can test the account by using it to send and receive e-mail messages.

 Lab 5-4: Creating and sending e-mail messages using Hotmail

In this lab, you will use Hotmail to send an e-mail message to a classmate and send a blind carbon copy to yourself.

Start **Internet Explorer**, go to *www.msn.com*, then click the **Hotmail** link.

1. In the .NET Passport Sign-in box, enter your Hotmail e-mail address and password, then click the **Sign In** button to display the Today tab of the Hotmail Web page.

*Note: If your e-mail address displays automatically, select **Do Not Remember My E-Mail Address For Future Sign-In**. It is not advisable to allow your e-mail address to display by default if you are using a public computer. However, on a home or work computer, having the address display by default is convenient.*

2. Click the **Mail** tab to display your Inbox, then click the **New** button to open a blank message form.

3. In the To field, type your classmate's e-mail address.

4. Press **TAB** twice to move to the Bcc field, then enter your own e-mail address.

5. Press **TAB** to move to the Subject field, then type ***A Brief Message From Me***.

6. Press **TAB** to move to the message area, then type a brief message.

7. Click the **Send** button to send your message. Hotmail displays a confirmation such as the one shown in Figure 5-11 to show that your message was sent.

Figure 5-11: Delivery confirmation in Hotmail

8. Click the **Return To Inbox** link to redisplay your Inbox. Notice that the message you sent was also delivered to you, because you specified your own address in the Bcc field.

9. Minimize the **Internet Explorer** window.

Creating e-mail signatures

An e-mail signature consists of a few lines of text that appear at the bottom of each of your messages. A signature might identify your position, the department in which you work or both. Typical signatures include the sender's name and e-mail address. Your signature can also include the name of your company, a Web address and a phone number. The signature is a reminder to your recipients of your identity or the identity of your company. Following is a sample signature:

J.Q. Student, IT Professional
Putting the Internet to Work
Student51@class.com
(800) 555-0162

In Outlook Express, you can use the Signatures tab of the Options dialog box to create custom signatures that are automatically added to your e-mail messages. You can create several signatures in Outlook Express, but only one can be designated as the default signature at a time. You can also create an external signature file and link to that file from Outlook Express.

Most Web-based e-mail programs also include options for creating and attaching signatures automatically. Some also allow you to format the text in your signature.

In the following lab, you will create e-mail signatures in Outlook Express and Hotmail. Suppose the marketing director has asked if it is possible to automate the process of adding his signature line to all outgoing messages. You can create an e-mail signature in each e-mail client to automate this process for him.

OBJECTIVE:
1.6.3: E-mail signatures

 Lab 5-5: Creating e-mail signatures in Outlook Express and Hotmail

In this lab, you will create e-mail signatures in Outlook Express and Hotmail.

1. First, you will create a signature in Outlook Express. Restore the **Outlook Express** window, then select **Tools | Options** to display the Options dialog box.

2. Click the **Signatures** tab, then click the **New** button to create a new signature named Signature 1.

3. In the Edit Signature text box, create a signature with your name, title, company name and phone number.

4. In the Signature Settings section, select **Add Signatures To All Outgoing Messages**. This step specifies that the signature will automatically be added to the bottom of every message you create. It also displays an option which (by default) specifies that your signature should not be added to replies and forwards.

5. Click the **Apply** button, then click the **OK** button. This step applies the new setting, then closes the Options dialog box.

6. Click the **Create Mail** button to open a new message window. Notice that the new message includes your signature.

7. Close the **New Message** window, then minimize the **Outlook Express** window.

8. Next, you will create a signature in Hotmail. Restore the **Internet Explorer** window.

9. Click the **Options** link in the upper-right corner of the Web page, then click the **Personal Signature** link to display the Personal Signature page.

10. Type your signature again, entering your name, title, company name and phone number.

11. Select **Show The Rich-Text Toolbar** to display a toolbar that will allow you to format your signature text.

12. Apply formatting to your signature, such as bold or italic type, different fonts, and so forth.

13. Click the **OK** button to save your signature, then click the **Mail** tab to return to your Inbox.

14. Click the **New** button to display a new message form. Notice that the new message includes your signature.

15. Click the **Cancel** button to return to your Inbox.

16. Minimize the **Internet Explorer** window.

Using e-mail address books

E-mail programs include address books that allow you to store names and information for your frequently accessed e-mail contacts. Address books can contain e-mail addresses, names or aliases, phone numbers, street addresses and other relevant data. You can select a name from the address book list instead of typing an e-mail address each time you want to send a message.

Address books vary among e-mail clients, but all serve the same purpose, and many include features that will allow you to import contact names from other address books in other applications.

Using an address book to insert e-mail addresses is fast, convenient and accurate. Users do not need to remember or type addresses and can select several recipients at once. Most company e-mail systems include a global address book that contains the e-mail addresses of all company employees.

<table>
<tr><td>

OBJECTIVE:
1.6.14: Sharing files
via e-mail

</td></tr>
</table>

Attaching files to e-mail messages

You can attach almost any kind of file to an e-mail message. The ability to attach files (such as word processor documents, presentations, spreadsheets and images) to your messages makes e-mail a powerful tool and allows users to share files and documents within their organization or with users in other organizations. Compression utilities (which will be discussed in a later lesson) enable you to compress large files into smaller sizes to send them efficiently across the Internet. E-mail clients use MIME to identify attached files by their file type.

Most e-mail clients display attachments in the e-mail message as separate links, such as a paper-clip icon. However, some display text attachments as additional text directly within the e-mail message. Older e-mail clients detach files from your e-mail messages upon arrival and automatically place the files into an attachment directory instead of leaving them attached to the message. These legacy e-mail clients do not indicate that an attachment is included, and some may not receive attachments properly. Therefore, it is advisable to use an up-to-date e-mail client, such as the ones used in this class.

The recipient of a message with an attachment can open and edit the attached file in the appropriate application if that application is installed on his or her computer. To avoid frustrating your recipient, verify that he or she has the software necessary for viewing or editing the attached file before you send it.

E-mail attachments and the server

Your organization's e-mail server may scan or even block e-mail attachments. Attachment scanning always takes place at the server, usually just after the message has been received via SMTP. Attachments are scanned because they may contain malicious code that can be used to damage or infiltrate systems. E-mail attachments are sometimes blocked completely for various reasons. Some companies block them to increase security. Others block attachments because they are deemed unnecessary or because they occupy too much bandwidth.

In the following lab, you will add attachments to e-mail messages. Suppose your supervisor is working from home and asks you to send her several files that are located on her office computer. You can attach the requested files to an e-mail message and send them to her.

Lab 5-6: Attaching files to e-mail messages

OBJECTIVE:
1.6.13: E-mail
attachments

In this lab, you will attach files to e-mail messages using Outlook Express and Hotmail.

1. First, you will attach a file in Outlook Express. Restore the **Outlook Express** window.

2. Display the **New Message** window, and address the new message to your class e-mail account.

3. Type ***Benefits Overview Information*** in the Subject box to indicate the subject of the message.

4. As the body of the message, type the following:

    Attached please find a Benefits Overview document. Please review this document before attending the Benefits presentation.

5. Resize the **New Message** window to display all 12 buttons in the toolbar.

6. Click the **Attach** button in the toolbar to display the Insert Attachment dialog box.

7. Navigate to the **C:\CIW\Internet\LabFiles\Lesson05** folder.

8. Click **Benefits Overview.pdf**, press and hold CTRL, click **Benefits Overview.doc**, release CTRL, and then click the **Attach** button to attach the files. This step also closes the Insert Attachment dialog box.

9. Click the **Send** button to send the e-mail message with the attachment.

10. Minimize the **Outlook Express** window.

11. Next, you will attach a file in Hotmail. Restore the **Internet Explorer** window.

12. Create a new message and address it to your Hotmail account.

13. Type ***Benefits Overview Information*** in the Subject box to indicate the subject of the message.

14. As the body of the message, type the following:

    Attached please find a Benefits Overview document. Please review this document before attending the Benefits presentation.

15. Click the **Attach** button, then click **File** to indicate that you want to attach a file. This step displays a Web page for attaching files.

16. Click the **Browse** button to display the Choose File dialog box.

17. Navigate to the **C:\CIW\Internet\LabFiles\Lesson05** folder.

18. Click **Benefits Overview.pdf**, and then click **Open** to attach the selected file. This step also closes the Choose File dialog box.

19. Click the **OK** link in the Hotmail window to return to your message. Notice that an Attachments link now displays in the e-mail message header and that the name and size of the attached file also display.

20. Click the **Send** button to send the message with the attachment.

21. Minimize the **Internet Explorer** window.

Movie Time!

Insert the CIW Foundations Movie CD to learn even more about this topic.

Using E-Mail (approx. playing time: 06:55)

All movie clips are © 2004 LearnKey, Inc.

Receiving and Viewing E-Mail Messages

Most e-mail programs contain all the tools you need for composing, sending and receiving messages. The e-mail client's folder structure provides tools for viewing, storing and organizing items.

Although the folder names and order may vary from one client to the next, most e-mail programs include an Inbox folder, a folder for sent messages, a folder for deleted items and a folder for drafts. Outlook Express and others also include an Outbox folder, which can contain messages that are queued for sending. This feature was designed for users with dial-up accounts, allowing them to work offline and accumulate messages, then connect to the Internet for a few minutes to send all their queued messages at once, and then log off again.

The Outlook Express window is divided into five major sections:

- The Outlook **toolbar** contains shortcuts to the most frequently used e-mail tools.

- The **Folders** pane displays the e-mail client's organizational structure.

- The **Contacts** pane displays the contents of the Address Book.

- The **Message** list displays the messages in your Inbox (or any folder in the structure that you choose to display).

- The **Preview** pane displays the text of any message you select in the Message list.

Figure 5-12 shows the sections of the Outlook Express window.

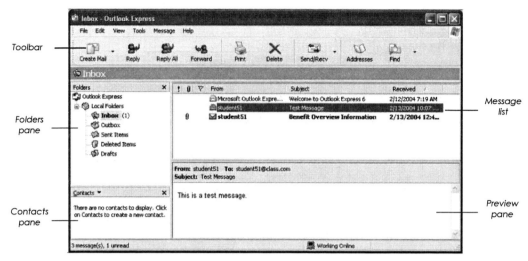

Figure 5-12: Outlook Express window sections

Receiving e-mail messages

Most e-mail clients, including Outlook Express, can be configured to check the incoming mail server at regular intervals so that you can receive mail continuously while you are online. You can also check your incoming mail server at any time using the Send/Recv button in the Outlook Express toolbar. To check for incoming messages in a Web-based e-mail application, click the Inbox link in the folder structure or click some other appropriate link to check the server.

When you send and receive mail, any messages stored in your Outbox are sent, and a copy of each message is stored in the Sent Items folder. Incoming messages are routed to your Inbox.

Viewing e-mail messages

When you display the Inbox folder, information about each message displays in the Message list. A Message list usually displays the name of the sender, the subject of the message and the date received for each message. (If you display the Sent Items folder, the Message list displays recipient names, message subjects and sent dates.) The Message list also features columns that indicate the priority of a message, whether a message has been flagged, and whether a message includes an attachment.

Unread messages are usually represented by a closed-envelope icon. In Outlook Express, the header information of unread messages also displays in bold. The header information of messages that have been read or previewed displays in unbolded type with an open-envelope icon. Outlook Express also allows you to use a Preview pane in which the text of the currently selected message displays below the Message list. Not all e-mail clients support message previewing.

Double-click a message in the Message list in Outlook Express to open it in a separate window. In a Web-based e-mail program, click the link for the message to open it.

In the following lab, you will receive and view e-mail messages, and you will save attachments to your computer. Suppose your supervisor has sent you a draft of a contract in an e-mail attachment and has asked you to complete various portions. You can save the attachment to your system, work on the document, save your changes, and then send the amended version as an e-mail attachment back to your boss.

Lab 5-7: Receiving and viewing e-mail messages

In this lab, you will receive and view e-mail messages and attachments using Outlook Express and Hotmail.

1. First, you will receive and view mail in Outlook Express. Restore the **Outlook Express** window.

2. In the toolbar, click the **Send/Recv** button to send and receive all messages.

3. In the Folders pane, click **Inbox** to display the Message list. Notice that the text of the first selected message is displayed in the Preview pane.

4. Click the message with the attachment to display its contents in the Preview pane.

5. Next, you will view and save attachments in Outlook Express. Double-click the message with the attachment to display its contents in a separate window. Notice that Outlook Express has removed access to the Benefits Overview.doc file, but allows you access to the Benefits Overview.pdf file.

   *Tech Note: Outlook Express 6.0 contains a default setting that will not allow a user to open an attachment that may contain a virus, including executable files, spreadsheets and Word documents. If you want to receive and open attachments using Outlook Express, select **Tools | Options**, then click the **Security** tab. Deselect the **Do Not Allow Attachments To Be Saved Or Opened That Could Potentially Be A Virus** option, click the **Apply** button, then click **OK**.*

6. Close the message window to return to the Message list.

7. In the Preview pane, click the attachment icon to display a drop-down menu. You can open the Benefits Overview.pdf attachment by clicking its file name, or you can save it to your hard drive without opening it. Notice that Benefits Overview.doc is listed, but it is unavailable. If you want access to blocked attachments, you must change the Outlook Express security setting.

8. In the attachment drop-down menu, click **Benefits Overview.pdf** to launch Adobe Reader and view the document.

9. Close the **Adobe Reader** window.

10. In the Preview pane, click the attachment icon, then click **Save Attachments** to display the Save Attachments dialog box. You can specify to save attachments to any location you choose.

11. Click the **Browse** button in the Save Attachments dialog box to display the Browse For Folder dialog box.

12. Scroll up the directory tree, click **Desktop**, then click **OK**. This step specifies to save the attachment to your Desktop, and redisplays the Save Attachments dialog box.

13. Click the **Save** button to save the attachment to your Desktop.

14. In the Message list, click the **Benefits Overview Information** message to select it, if necessary, then press **DELETE** to move the message to the Deleted Items folder. Moving a message to the Deleted Items folder is equivalent to placing a file in your computer's Recycle Bin — it will remain there (and can be restored) until you empty the Deleted Items folder.

15. Minimize the **Outlook Express** window.

16. Next, you will receive and view messages in Hotmail. Restore the **Internet Explorer** window.

17. Click the **Return To Inbox** link to download any new messages from the mail server.

18. Click the link for the message with the subject **A Brief Message From Me** to display it in a separate message page.

19. Click the **Inbox** link at either the top or the bottom of the message page to return to the Inbox.

20. Select the check box to the left of the Benefits Overview Information message to mark the message, then click the **Delete** button to move the message to your Trash Can folder. You can click the **Empty** button (which is visible when you view the contents of your Trash Can folder) to empty the trash. Hotmail automatically empties the trash several times a week. Messages in the Hotmail Trash Can folder do not count toward your account limit.

    Tech Note: Other Web-based e-mail services, such as Yahoo!, keep messages in your Trash folder until you manually empty it. Some Web-based e-mail services count messages in your Trash folder (or its equivalent) toward your account limit.

21. Click the **Sign Out** button to sign out of your Hotmail account.

22. Close the **Internet Explorer** window.

E-Mail in the Workplace

OBJECTIVE:
1.6.10: E-mail in the workplace

E-mail is used in today's workplace for accomplishing a wide variety of tasks. Employees use e-mail to communicate with one another, to share files across the company or with other organizations, and to document and track the progress of projects. Some e-mail clients, such as Microsoft Outlook, also include calendar features that allow you to schedule meetings and send reminders via e-mail.

The following sections will describe the options available for responding to e-mail messages, and it will discuss some guidelines for keeping e-mail professional in the work environment.

Responding to e-mail messages

OBJECTIVE:
1.6.8: E-mail forwarding and replying

E-mail clients offer several options for responding to messages. You can reply to the sender, you can reply to everyone addressed in the message, or you can forward the message to another user. Table 5-2 describes the result of each action.

Table 5-2: E-mail response options

E-Mail Response Command	Result
Reply	Displays a message window that automatically inserts the address of the original sender, the subject and a copy of the original message. The subject line is prefaced by the letters RE: indicating that this message is a response.
Reply All	Displays a message window that automatically inserts the addresses of the original sender and all other recipients copied on the original message; the subject; and a copy of the original message. The subject line is prefaced by the letters RE: indicating that this message is a response.
Forward	Displays a message window with a copy of the original message. The original subject line is automatically inserted and the subject line is prefaced by the letters FW: or FWD: indicating that this message is a forwarded copy of someone else's message.

When responding to e-mail messages that you have received, if you want to address only the original sender of the message, click the Reply button. If you want to address everyone copied on the original message, click the Reply All button.

When you click Reply or Reply All, the text you type is distinguished from the text of the original message. In the Microsoft Outlook e-mail client, your text displays in blue (by default) and flush with the left margin. The original text of the message, which is generally included by default, appears indented and is preceded by a divider reading -----Original Message-----. In Outlook Express, text from the original message is marked by a thick vertical line in the left margin and is also preceded by ----Original Message----. In both e-mail clients, the address of the original sender and recipient(s) displays in the text from the original message. The subject line is prefaced by the letters RE: indicating that the message you are sending is a response.

If you want to send the message to a user who did not receive the original, click the Forward button.

When you forward a message to another recipient, the text you type is distinguished from the text of the original message in the same manner that it is distinguished from the original text of the message to which you have replied. The subject line is prefaced by the letters FW: or FWD: indicating that the message you are sending is forwarded.

Some e-mail clients precede each line of forwarded text with a right-pointing angle bracket (>).

Professional communication via e-mail

E-mail is a unique communication medium that combines the formality of a letter with the informality of a telephone call. Although e-mail is not a new form of communication, it may still be new to many users. The tendency in the busy work environment is to quickly send brief e-mail messages with little thought. Many individuals regret these hasty actions later. You should treat e-mail messages as you would treat any other written communication. The term netiquette has been coined to encourage common sense and politeness, and to establish general rules for Internet etiquette.

The workplace environment is usually professional. Professional communication via e-mail should follow the same guidelines as professional correspondence via standard mail, including the use of proper grammar and correct spelling. Ideas should be communicated clearly and concisely to keep messages reasonably short.

When possible, respond immediately to e-mail messages addressed to you. Most people expect more immediate responses with e-mail than they do with other forms of business communication. Responding within 24 hours makes a good impression. However, think clearly about your responses, and answer messages only when you have gathered all your information.

OBJECTIVE:
1.6.9: E-mail
etiquette

Avoid typing messages in all capital letters; this practice connotes shouting or anger. Remember also that for business communication it is important to be as clear as possible. Although acronyms and abbreviations such as LOL (Laughing Out Loud) or TIA (Thanks In Advance) may be familiar to you, they may not be familiar to everyone. Using acronyms and expecting them to be understood introduces the possibility of miscommunication.

emoticon
A combination of characters that you read sideways that helps convey emotion in an e-mail message.

Also remember that your reader does not have the benefit of facial clues and tone of voice to help understand your message's intended meaning. Some people use **emoticons** in e-mail messages to give the recipient an idea of the intended tone, but this practice is not professional and is best reserved for personal communication. For these reasons, be judicious when attempting to convey humor or sarcasm. In most cases, it is best to remain businesslike.

Permanence of e-mail

E-mail is permanent because it is written. Messages can be printed or forwarded to other people. This permanence can be helpful or detrimental in a business environment. Remember that after you click Send, the message cannot be retrieved.

When crafting e-mail messages, consider that the time, date and address are added to your message automatically. Choose an appropriate subject line for your message. Remember also that the subject line is usually visible from the Inbox view, and that your subject lines should remain professional and inoffensive.

OBJECTIVE:
1.6.4: E-mail threads

E-mail threads

In business communication, it is a good practice to include information from an original e-mail message in a response, generating what is known as an e-mail thread. E-mail clients usually include the original message when you click Reply or Forward. Most e-mail clients automatically format original message text in a manner that distinguishes it from the text of a reply or forward message, and most users recognize text preceded by an angle bracket (>) in the left margin to be text from an original message.

Including an e-mail thread in a continuing discussion reminds the recipients of all the previous details, and provides a record or history of an issue. Some issues may take weeks to resolve, and having a full thread of discussion may be helpful. However, if messages become too long, they can be tiresome to read. If new issues pertaining to the task at hand arise, consider beginning a new e-mail thread that will address only the new issues.

Reply vs. Reply All

Use the Reply All option judiciously to avoid sending unnecessary communications. If an original e-mail message was addressed to 18 people, and only you and the original sender need to pursue an issue further, use Reply instead of Reply All. You will save the other 17 recipients from unnecessarily reviewing your discussion with the original sender, and you may save the original sender embarrassment. Work out your issue with the person who sent the message. If a clarifying communication needs to be sent later to the other 17 recipients, it can be done when all the issues are resolved.

Avoid sending unnecessary attachments. If you send an attachment, make sure the recipient wants it and has the ability to open it. Remember that large attachments can take a long time to download.

E-mail privacy

OBJECTIVE:
1.7.11: Network
communications
privacy

An employer has legal ownership of everything an employee creates while on the job, including personal messages. Your employer has the right to read e-mail you send using company equipment and Internet connections. Your employer can also read e-mail sent to you from other sources — business acquaintances, friends, mailing lists, perhaps individuals you do not even know. If you are given an e-mail address for company business, should you use that address to conduct private conversations as well? And if so, should you expect this correspondence to be truly private? After all, your employer is paying for the Internet connection, the software, the browser, the operating system, and so forth. If you send an e-mail message to a co-worker about another employee (perhaps discussing a promotion or a performance appraisal), is there a chance that the other employee will be able to read that message? Although many companies now have written employee policies that address these questions, they often remain unanswered.

Out-of-office messages

OBJECTIVE:
1.6.12: E-mail
autoresponder
services

Because people expect a fairly immediate response to e-mail messages, it is important to provide notification to those sending you e-mail when you will be out of the office for an extended period of time (such as for a vacation or a business trip). People may get irritated if they send an e-mail message and get no response for a prolonged period with no explanation.

Some e-mail programs, such as Microsoft Outlook, include an autoresponder, or automatic reply, feature that allows you to configure and send an automated response to e-mail messages that are received while you are away. Generally, the same automated response is sent to every user who sends you a message. Some Web e-mail clients support this feature with their free e-mail, and others include it only as part of a premium package for which they charge a fee. Fastermail.com (*www.fastermail.com*) offers this service as part of its free e-mail package.

An autoresponder feature in an e-mail client automatically sends a specified response to anyone who sends e-mail to your address. The feature does not interfere with any e-mail that you receive; those messages are stored in your Inbox as usual. When you compose your automatic reply message, you should specify the period of time you will be unavailable, and when you expect to respond to e-mail and phone messages received during your absence. You may want to include information about ways you can be reached while you are away, or specify the name and contact information of a co-worker who can handle issues on your behalf. Always keep automatic reply messages brief and professional.

For example, you can create an automatic reply message similar to the following:

> *I will be out of the office February 16 through February 20. During that time, I will not be accessible by phone or e-mail. I will return to the office February 23 and will respond to your e-mail message at that time. If you need assistance while I am away, please contact Stephanie Miller at smiller@company.com or (800) 555-0114, extension 5555.*

Some people also create and enable automatic reply messages to provide information to customers or contacts when they leave a job. Following is an example of such a message:

My last day as Contracts Manager will be July 7. For contract issues after that date, please contact Stephanie Miller at smiller@company.com or (800) 555-0114, extension 5555. It has been a pleasure working with you.

The automatic reply feature must be enabled manually before the absence period and manually disabled upon return. In Outlook, this feature is called AutoReply. To use AutoReply in Outlook, select Out Of Office Assistant in the Tools drop-down menu. Select the I Am Currently Out Of The Office option. Create your own automatic reply message, then click OK. AutoReply is now enabled. To test the AutoReply feature before you leave, send an e-mail message to yourself. You should receive your automatic reply to the message you sent, and you will also receive the message.

Once you return to your office, remember to turn off the AutoReply feature. Failure to do so can generate confusion and make you seem irresponsible. Outlook will prompt you when you launch the program after enabling AutoReply. However, you must open Out Of Office Assistant and select the I Am Currently In The Office option to manually disable AutoReply.

E-Mail Problems and Solutions

Although e-mail has many advantages, its widespread use has inherent problems. Several points should be considered in order to use e-mail wisely.

OBJECTIVE:
1.6.11: Common e-mail issues

For example, e-mail content has contributed to several human resources-related issues, including sexual harassment, offensive language and the disclosure of confidential information.

Sending jokes via e-mail is a popular practice. However, think carefully before using company e-mail as an arena to spread humor. You might not know who will take offense to something you find funny. And consider that one of your recipients may forward your message to others who might take offense. Remember that your name and e-mail address are on the original.

It is also important to know when not to use e-mail. Confidential information (such as salary or hiring information) should be exchanged either in person or over the phone, or via the standard postal service. As previously discussed, e-mail is not private within an organization.

Also, some situations call for "live" communication (a phone call or face-to-face meeting). E-mail can be too impersonal or slow to satisfy some types of discussions, especially those involving emotionally charged issues.

OBJECTIVE:
1.6.5: Spam and filters

spam
Unsolicited and unwanted e-mail messages; the online equivalent of junk mail.

Spam

Just as junk mail can fill your mailbox at home, junk e-mail can clutter your Inbox. Such unsolicited mail is called **spam**. Spam is unsolicited e-mail sent to multiple users and is often made to appear as if it came from a trusted source.

The people who send the messages, called spammers, are the Internet equivalent of telemarketers, and many commercial organizations purchase e-mail address lists for this purpose. Like a listed telephone number, your e-mail address is available through online directories. Spammers can also get e-mail addresses from newsgroups and chat rooms, and use Internet tools to search the Web and e-mail servers for valid addresses.

spam filter - spam-bayes

Spammed messages are often used for the following purposes:

- To generate sales for various services and products
- To spread malicious viruses and worms
- To spread virus hoaxes

Sending e-mail is virtually free (the only charge is for Internet service), so spam is free advertising for anyone who sends it. As with other types of marketing, the more messages that are sent, the more money an advertiser can make. Spamming can be a lucrative enterprise, especially if messages are sent in bulk.

Spammers often use automated registration programs to create large numbers of Web-based e-mail accounts. They use these accounts to send spam or to slow down a service by signing in to multiple accounts simultaneously.

OBJECTIVE:
1.7.11: Network communications privacy

Many spammers use automated tools to search the Internet for open relays, then use the open relays to send large amounts of spam. An open relay (also called a third-party relay or an insecure relay) is an SMTP server that allows third-party relay of e-mail messages. Open relays are frequently used to support mobile users or to support multiple domains within an organization. The relay feature is part of all SMTP-based servers. System administrators must turn off the relay option to protect their servers from illicit users.

Combating spam

The battle against spam takes place on both the server (host) side and the client (user) side.

Completely Automated Public Turing Test to Tell Computers and Humans Apart (CAPTCHA)
A test that uses a word-verification graphic designed to differentiate humans from automated senders during online transactions.

You have already encountered a **Completely Automated Public Turing Test to Tell Computers and Humans Apart (CAPTCHA)** when you signed up for a Web-based e-mail account. A CAPTCHA is a test designed to detect the automated systems used by spammers for registering e-mail accounts. A CAPTCHA is one way administrators attempt to control spam at the server.

blackhole list
A published list of IP addresses known to be sources of spam.

Administrators can also block mail from IP addresses known for sending spam. A **blackhole list** (also known as a blacklist) is a published list of IP addresses known to be sources of spam. Administrators can use the list to filter out the offending IP addresses. The traffic that is filtered out simply disappears, as if sucked into a black hole.

Another server-side method for trying to control spam is the use of SMTP authentication, in which a valid name and password must be provided each time a message is sent. SMTP authentication can prevent a spammer from illicitly using your mail server to send spam.

OBJECTIVE:
1.6.6: SMTP authentication

On the client side of the equation, you can take several actions to reduce the amount of spam you receive:

spam filter
An e-mail client program that identifies and filters out spam messages before they reach the e-mail Inbox.

- You can set up **spam filters**, or rules, in your e-mail client. A spam filter deletes (or otherwise diverts from your Inbox) e-mail messages based on the text in the Subject line, the To and From fields, and even the body of the message.

- Many Web-based e-mail clients such as Hotmail include spam filters you can configure to look for specific words. Many e-mail clients feature buttons or links that allow you to mark specific messages as spam. Hotmail also has a folder called Junk E-mail designed to receive messages the server recognizes as spam. You can select from three levels of junk-mail filtering. Sign in to your Hotmail account and click the Junk E-mail folder to review your options.

- You can use a third-party spam filter to help control the problem. A popular spam filter is MailShield Desktop (*www.mailshield.com*). This product was formerly known as SpamDetective. Such third-party filters have the ability to store e-mail in a database or queue, then scan it for offending items (for example, inappropriate language). The application deletes spam and forwards legitimate e-mail to its destination. Such technology is often called store-and-forward technology.

- You can contact your ISP or systems administrator regarding spam; these parties may have or pursue solutions.

When you set up rules for controlling spam in your e-mail client, consider the following points:

- Specifying multiple conditions for the same rule means that all conditions must be met before a message becomes subject to the instructions in the rule.

- Specifying a condition that is too broad may result in false positives. A false positive is a situation in which a legitimate e-mail message is filtered out.

- Spammers often find ways to evade spam filters.

In the following lab, you will create a spam filter in Outlook Express. Suppose the personnel director is receiving several spam e-mail messages a day regarding free credit reports. You can set up a spam filter for her in Outlook Express to automatically delete messages that contain the words "free credit report" in the Subject line.

 Lab 5-8: Setting up a spam filter in Outlook Express

In this lab, you will create a spam filter in Outlook Express.

1. Restore the **Outlook Express** window.

2. First, you will set up a rule that will filter spam. Select **Tools | Message Rules | Mail** to display the New Mail Rule dialog box, as shown in Figure 5-13.

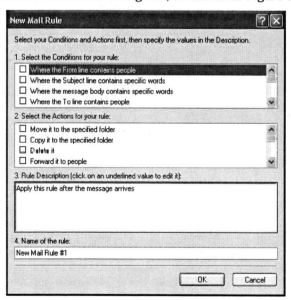

Figure 5-13: New Mail Rule dialog box

3. In the Select The Conditions For Your Rule section, select **Where The Subject Line Contains Specific Words**. This step specifies the condition for the rule. An incoming message must meet this condition before Outlook Express will take any action.

4. In the Select The Actions For Your Rule section, select **Delete It**. This step specifies that when Outlook Express encounters a message that meets the specified conditions, it will divert the message to your Deleted Items folder.

5. In the Rule Description (Click On An Underlined Value To Edit It) section, click the **Contains Specific Words** link to display the Type Specific Words dialog box, shown in Figure 5-14.

Figure 5-14: Specifying words for spam filter in Outlook Express

6. In the Type Specific Words Or A Phrase And Click Add box, type the word ***Free***, then click the **Add** button to add the word to the Words text box.

7. Click in the **Type Specific Words Or A Phrase And Click Add** box, type ***Loan***, then click the **Add** button to add the word to the Words text box.

8. Click in the **Type Specific Words Or A Phrase And Click Add** box, type ***No Carbs***, then click the **Add** button to add the phrase to the Words text box.

9. Click **OK** to redisplay the New Mail Rule dialog box. The Rule Description box now specifies that all messages containing the words "Free" or "Loan" or "No Carbs" in the Subject line will be diverted to your Deleted Items folder.

10. Click **OK** twice. This step saves the new rule and closes the Message Rules dialog box.

11. Next, you will test your spam filter. Choose a partner with whom to perform the remainder of this lab. Create a new e-mail message and address it to your partner.

12. In the Subject line, type the following: ***I have a great recipe for pizza with no carbs!***

13. Send the message, and be sure that your partner sent the same message to you.

14. Click the **Send/Recv** button to check the POP server for incoming mail. Notice that no new messages display in your Inbox. You received the message sent by your lab partner, but it was automatically sent to your Deleted Items folder.

15. Click the **Deleted Items** folder to verify that the message has been diverted.

16. Close **Outlook Express**.

Storing e-mail messages

Most e-mail clients have a default folder structure that includes an Inbox folder, a folder for sent messages, a folder for drafts and a folder for deleted messages. Outlook and Outlook Express include an Outbox folder, in which they store messages that are queued for sending but have not yet been sent. You can also create and arrange additional folders for organizing your messages, and you can move and copy messages to any of your folders.

OBJECTIVE:
1.6.11: Common
e-mail issues

Outlook Express writes all e-mail folders to your local hard drive. The specific location of stored messages varies by operating system. In Windows XP, Outlook Express stores your mail folders in the Documents and Settings\<user name>\ Local Settings\Application Data\Identities\Microsoft\Outlook Express folder. This folder contains a file for each of your mail folders, and each of these files has a .dbx file name extension.

Writing e-mail folders to files on a local disk makes your e-mail easily transportable. If you set up Outlook Express on a new computer, you can copy the DBX folders from your old computer to the new one, and keep all your old e-mail.

For interesting information and tips on using and managing Outlook Express, visit www.insideoe.tomsterdam.com/.

E-mail file storage space may be limited if you use an IMAP server or a Web-based e-mail account, because your messages are stored on the server. Web-based e-mail accounts allot limited storage space on the server, and once that space is used, you must either delete some of your stored messages or purchase additional storage space. You can also use Outlook Express to write all of your Web-based e-mail messages to your local hard drive.

In organizations that use proprietary LAN protocols for handling e-mail within the network, messages may also be stored on the server rather than on the user's computer. Many e-mail clients, such as Microsoft Outlook, allow you to archive your e-mail messages. Archiving your mail folders removes them from the server and writes them to your local hard drive. Archived Outlook files have a .pst file name extension. Storing files on your hard drive frees space on the mail server, and having local access to e-mail messages can be useful when the mail server is down.

OBJECTIVE:
1.6.15: Web-based
and IMAP-based
e-mail

Having local access to e-mail messages may be especially important for those who use IMAP servers. If a network problem occurs, IMAP server users may not have access to messages for a while unless they have archived messages locally. Remember that IMAP servers do not download messages to your computer automatically. The messages are stored, read and managed on the server unless you choose to download them. People who use IMAP servers should download their messages so that they have backup copies of important information stored on their computers.

When you use Web-based e-mail, your user name and password reside on a third-party server. If someone hacks into the server, the hacker will have your personal information. Web-based e-mail clients do not download messages to your hard drive. Some do not even save a copy of sent messages in your Sent folder unless you indicate that you want to save a copy. To save a copy of your mail folders on your local computer, use an e-mail client such as Outlook Express to read (and download) messages from your Web-based account.

OBJECTIVE:
1.12.2: PIM
productivity tools

**personal information
management (PIM)
program**
A tool used to
schedule
appointments and
meetings, store
contact information,
and manage tasks.

Personal Information Management (PIM)

You can use a **personal information management (PIM) program** to schedule appointments and meetings, store contact information, and manage tasks. Examples of PIM programs are Microsoft Outlook, Lotus Organizer, CorelCENTRAL and ACT!

You can also find freeware versions of PIM software on the Web, but not all versions are stable. Aethera is a freeware PIM package that will run on UNIX, Windows Me and Windows XP operating systems. To learn more about Aethera and download the package, visit *www.thekompany.com/projects/aethera/*.

Typical uses for PIM

You can use a PIM program to keep track of appointments and meetings by scheduling them on an electronic calendar. You can schedule recurring appointments and reminders, which sound an alarm or display a dialog box. You can also use a PIM program to track tasks. Figure 5-15 shows a sample calendar containing scheduled appointments.

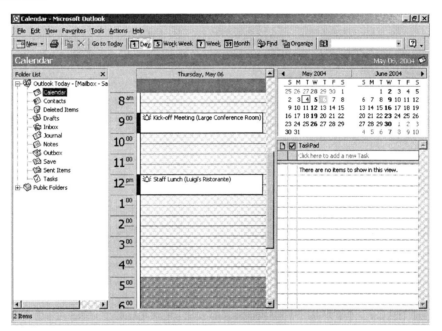

Figure 5-15: PIM calendar entries in Outlook

You can also use a PIM program to store contact information (such as names, addresses, telephone numbers and other pertinent information) for people you call or communicate with via e-mail frequently. Some PIM programs, such as Microsoft Outlook, also provide e-mail capabilities you can use to send and receive messages over an intranet or the Internet. Figure 5-16 shows sample contact information in Outlook.

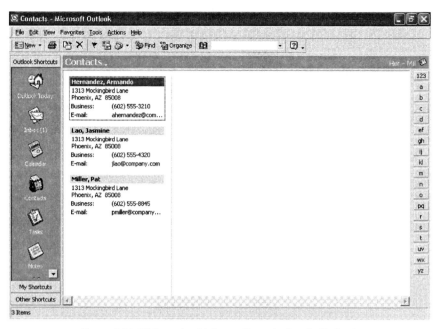

Figure 5-16: PIM contact information window in Outlook

OBJECTIVE:
1.12.1: Calendar
and scheduling
software

Using a centralized electronic calendar to schedule meetings and reserve resources (such as a meeting room or projector) can streamline office events and prevent scheduling conflicts. Scheduling Webinars or Webcasts on a centralized calendar also informs employees about the upcoming event and can alert to IT personnel, who may be called upon to troubleshoot any difficulties.

IT personnel can also examine a centralized calendar to identify the best time to schedule activities, such as installing updates or patches, that might take services offline. An IT department can also publish the scheduled date for such activities and send reminders or notifications to employees if certain services may be unavailable for a period of time.

PIM and Personal Digital Assistants (PDAs)

Personal Digital Assistant (PDA)
A small, handheld computer used for personal information management.

Personal Digital Assistants (PDAs) are small, handheld computers that were originally designed for storing contact information, taking notes and keeping track of appointments. Modern PDAs can perform complex calculations, play games, download music, browse the Web and check e-mail.

OBJECTIVE:
1.12.2: PIM
productivity tools

PDAs store basic programs such as the operating system, address book, calendar and memo pad in a read-only memory (ROM) chip. As you enter or change data, your changes are saved automatically in your PDA's random access memory (RAM), which remains intact even after you turn off the unit.

PDAs come in handheld and palm-sized versions. Handheld versions use miniature keyboards for inputting information, whereas palm PDAs use their 4-inch screens as input and output devices. The LCD screen on a palm PDA displays data, and users input information by using a plastic stylus on the touch screen layer (which resides on top of the LCD). Users can enter data by writing with the stylus and by tapping on the touch screen.

All PDAs include some kind of PIM software for performing PIM tasks. These tasks include storing contact information, making lists, taking notes, writing memos, tracking appointments, setting reminder alarms, planning projects, performing calculations and tracking expenses. However, not all PDAs support all of these functions.

OBJECTIVE:
1.12.3: Wireless-device-to-network interfacing

PDAs are designed to work in tandem with traditional desktop or laptop computers. The information you enter into your PDA must be synchronized with the data you enter into your PIM software on your desktop or laptop system if you want to use both your PDA and your computer effectively. Many PDAs include PIM software you can install on your computer. You can also use a mainstream PIM package that supports data synchronization, such as Lotus Organizer or Microsoft Outlook, to keep both your PDA and your computer up to date.

Data can be synchronized between a PDA and a computer using a serial port or USB port. Many PDAs also have an infrared communication port that beams information to a computer using infrared light. Many PDAs use wireless technology to transfer files to and from a computer or computer network.

Wireless Application Protocol (WAP)

Wireless Application Protocol (WAP)
A standard protocol that wireless devices use to access the Internet.

Wireless handheld devices, such as mobile phones or PDAs, are commonly used to browse the Web and check e-mail. These devices use a protocol called **Wireless Application Protocol (WAP)**. WAP provides text-based Web browsing and secure e-mail services to wireless handheld devices.

WAP supports TCP/IP, so your wireless device can support most Web and e-mail Internet services. Provided that your carrier supports WAP, you can access the Internet from any location where WAP service is provided.

Wireless Markup Language (WML)
A markup language that presents the text portions of Web pages to wireless devices.

Instead of using HTML to present Web pages, WAP-enabled devices use **Wireless Markup Language (WML)**. WML presents only the text portion of Web pages. If developers of traditional Web sites want to make their sites available to wireless devices, they must implement WML in their Web page code. Because the wireless industry is currently experiencing rapid growth, WAP-enabled sites are becoming more common.

Advantages of WAP

WAP enables wireless access to the Internet for Web content and e-mail from anywhere that WAP support and service are available. WAP is designed to work on any of the existing wireless services.

Disadvantages of WAP

Handheld device screens are small and difficult to read, and content is available in text format only. Most end users want the full Internet experience they are accustomed to on their computers, so they are not satisfied with text-only versions.

Also, no e-mail attachment support exists for WAP at this time. In addition, mobile phone text entry is limited to the phone's keypad, and transmission rates are slow: Most wireless devices (such as cellular phones) and Web-enabled PDAs have data transfer rates of 14.4 Kbps or less (which is much slower than a typical 56 Kbps modem). Also, very little content is currently available. Most Web designers do not want to take the time to implement WML in their pages.

Finally, Most Web pages are designed for a resolution of 640 x 480 pixels, but most wireless devices have a display screen that is about 150 pixels wide. Therefore, users have to scroll horizontally to read.

Small-Screen Rendering (SSR)

Small-Screen Rendering (SSR)
A browser technology developed for wireless devices that reformats Web pages to display on 176-pixel-wide cellular phone display screens.

Opera Software developed the **Small-Screen Rendering (SSR)** technology in 2002 and is including it in its Opera version 7.0 browser. Small-Screen Rendering performs a client-side transformation of a Web document to size it to a 176-pixel-wide cellular phone screen. The content is stacked vertically, eliminating the need for horizontal scrolling. Because this is a client-side transformation, all Web content can be viewed on the cellular phone screen, instead of only pages that use WML.

Nokia, Sony Ericsson and Motorola are among the cellular phone manufacturers that are including the Opera browser on their new smart phones (smart phones are wireless phones with computer capabilities such as e-mail, Web browsing, LAN connectivity, PIM, and so forth).

Case Study

My Outlook Express Is Broken!

A new employee called the IT department complaining that his Outlook Express was not working. He said he could read and send e-mail, but he could not open attachments or print messages.

The IT help desk technician first considered the new user's security settings. By default, the security settings in Outlook Express do not allow a user to open or save any attachments that may be harmful. So the help desk technician directed the user to select **Tools | Options**, click the **Security** tab, and deselect **Do Not Allow Attachments To Be Saved Or Opened That Could Potentially Be A Virus**. She reminded the user to be sure to click the **Apply** button, then click **OK**.

The help desk technician then considered the user's printing problem. All printing in Outlook Express is handled by the settings specified in Internet Explorer. Because the employee is new, it is possible that Internet Explorer has not yet been configured to print. So the help desk technician directed the user to start Internet Explorer and check the print settings in the browser (**File | Print**). She reminded the user to be sure that the correct printer is selected, and to print a page in Internet Explorer as a test, then reopen Outlook Express and print the mail messages.

The user followed these directions and found that Outlook Express now worked as expected.

*   *   *

As a class, discuss the e-mail functions that needed troubleshooting in this scenario.

*   What do you think are the best security settings for e-mail applications in the workplace? What are the advantages and disadvantages of each?

*   How might the technician troubleshoot the printing problem differently in another e-mail program, such as Outlook or Hotmail?

Lesson Summary

Application project

After having used two e-mail clients, which do you prefer? Which one would you recommend for your company? As with browsers, many companies choose a standard e-mail client for all employees to reduce help-desk calls and potential problems.

Suppose you are telecommuting and want your e-mail client at home to be configured for both your work and personal e-mail accounts. To accomplish this task, configure either Outlook Express or Netscape Mail & Newsgroups with two e-mail accounts. If you conduct this Application Project during class, use the e-mail account information you used in this lesson's labs for your work account. Create a second account on the e-mail client using an additional student account, or obtain a free e-mail account from Yahoo! Mail (*www.yahoo.com*), MSN Hotmail (*www.msn.com*) or Juno (*www.juno.com*). Your free e-mail account will be available to you after class, but you should record the configuration information. After you finish, delete both accounts from your e-mail client, and be sure to download and delete all messages.

Skills review

In this lesson, you learned the functions of e-mail, and you configured and used various e-mail clients. You identified common e-mail components; created, sent, received and viewed messages and attachments; and identified ways to use e-mail effectively in the workplace. You also identified modern e-mail problems and solutions, and you discussed the functions of personal information management (PIM) software.

Now that you have completed this lesson, you should be able to:

✓ Explain the way that electronic mail (e-mail) works.

✓ Configure an e-mail client.

✓ Identify e-mail components.

✓ Create and send e-mail messages.

✓ Receive and view e-mail messages.

✓ Identify ways to use e-mail effectively in the workplace.

✓ Identify e-mail problems and solutions.

✓ Identify the functions of personal information management (PIM) software.

Lesson 5 Review

1. Name the three elements of an e-mail address.

    NAME @ domain

2. You can receive e-mail, but you cannot send it. What type of e-mail server may be causing the problem?

    ~~attachment~~ _Smtp problem_

3. What is the best method for sending a word processor document to another person via e-mail?

    Attachment

4. Define the term netiquette.

    E-Mail Etiquette

5. Why would an alarm feature be useful in PIM software?

    Reminder of events

Lesson 6:
Internet Services
and Tools

Objectives

By the end of this lesson, you will be able to:

- ⚐ Use a news client.

- ⚐ Use Telnet.

- ⚐ Use FTP.

- ⚐ Manage downloaded files.

- ⚐ Use Virtual Network Computing (VNC) and Microsoft Terminal Services.

- ⚐ Use instant messaging applications.

- ⚐ Identify the functions of peer-to-peer networks.

- ⚐ Identify the functions of LDAP.

- ⚐ Identify the functions of Concurrent Versions System (CVS).

- ⚐ Troubleshoot Internet problems using TCP/IP tools.

Pre-Assessment Questions

1. Some FTP sites allow guests who do not have accounts to access the site. What are these sites called?

   anonymous FTP sites

2. Name at least four popular newsgroup categories.

   BIZ   _RAC_   _SOC_   _SCI_
   COMP   _NEWS_   _TALK_

3. What protocol encrypts transmissions, is command-line based, and allows a user to log on to a remote computer and operate the system as if he or she were sitting at that computer?

   a. Network News Transfer Protocol (NNTP)
   b. Secure Shell (SSH)
   c. File Transfer Protocol (FTP)
   d. Virtual Network Computing (VNC)

Internet Resource Tools

You can use the Internet to gather information in a variety of ways, in addition to the Web and e-mail. You can also use File Transfer Protocol (FTP), newsgroups and Telnet for research and collaboration. Virtual Network Computing (VNC) and Microsoft Terminal Services enable IT professionals to control computers from remote locations. Instant messaging enables users to communicate over the Internet in real time. Peer-to-peer networking maximizes the processing power of client computers. SMTP, POP3 and Lightweight Directory Access Protocol (LDAP) servers allow users to locate people and other resources on a network, and TCP/IP diagnostic tools help us troubleshoot and solve problems with all these technologies. All of these tools enable business users to complete their tasks more efficiently. You will learn to use each of these Internet resource tools in this lesson.

Newsgroups

Web pages are somewhat formal documents, produced at considerable expense by companies that sell products or services. Although most companies keep their Web pages current, it is difficult to modify them every day. By contrast, online newsgroup articles are generally unofficial, informal and rapidly updated sources of information. Much like traditional newspapers or television news, online newsgroups tend to provide timely, significant and often spirited content. However, most newsgroup articles are not news documents in the traditional sense: They are not usually about current events. Instead, newsgroup articles tend to focus on goods and services, events, people, pets, concepts, ideas, and so forth.

Purpose of newsgroups

Newsgroups are all loosely part of a huge distributed bulletin board system called Usenet (User Network). As you learned in an earlier lesson, Usenet is a public-access network consisting of newsgroups and group mailing lists. Usenet was created in 1979 at Duke University, and its original purpose was to house news postings. With the increase in Internet use, Usenet is now a repository of more than 50,000 newsgroups on nearly every subject imaginable.

Usenet has no central moderator; rather, it is a cooperative environment. Therefore, it can provide users with a rich variety of information. Newsgroups are usually excellent informal sources of information, and newsgroup content tends to be credible. Web users participate in newsgroups by choice, which helps to ensure that the subject of the newsgroup remains tightly focused.

The business world is striving to utilize this store of information. Companies are beginning to examine newsgroup resources and extract information that can be used for product design and development. Various corporate departments can use online newsgroups to their advantage. These departments include the following:

- Product development
- Planning
- Management
- Marketing

- Accounting
- Sales
- Service
- Graphic design

Both public newsgroups and, increasingly, intranet newsgroups are being sponsored by individual companies. Intranet newsgroups are created for employees of the sponsoring companies to provide a forum for discussion.

Newsgroup postings

Each newsgroup contains items that resemble e-mail messages. These items are the newsgroup content, known as articles. Although these postings may appear to be written to an individual about a specific subject, they are posted for all users to read.

Any user can post an article to a newsgroup by clicking a New Post button, then typing a message and clicking the Send button. You can reply to a newsgroup article in two ways: You can reply only to the person who posted the article by clicking the Reply button, or you can send your reply to the entire newsgroup by clicking the Reply Group button. When you use Reply Group, your response is posted as a newsgroup article below the article to which you are replying.

Why use newsgroups?

Researching a product before you buy it can be beneficial. The product vendor's Web site will give you information about its products, but the information will be biased. A business is not likely to post negative comments about its products or services, even if they are true.

Newsgroups can help you learn other Internet users' opinions of the product. For example, suppose you are considering buying Microsoft Visual Studio, which combines a number of compilers and utilities. Many programmers like it, but you wonder if it will meet your needs. You can visit the Microsoft Web site to learn about Visual Studio, but if you want to investigate it further, newsgroups can provide you with real users' opinions.

How to find newsgroups

Google Groups (*http://groups.google.com*) is one collection of newsgroup articles you can use to learn about Visual Studio or any other newsgroup topic. Google Groups provides access to the Usenet database and features a text box similar to that of search engines. Like many search services, Google Groups offers features to help you conduct your topic search.

Another benefit of newsgroups is the fact that articles are stored. For instance, Google Groups offers a 20-year archive of Usenet articles. This archiving makes newsgroups an excellent resource.

Like Web search engines, relevant newsgroups and messages are returned when you conduct a search. For example, when you conduct a search for Visual Studio .NET, two newsgroups appear in the Related Groups section. If you want to narrow your search from the more than 700,000 postings from all the newsgroups, you can refine your search to within one of these related newsgroups. You accomplish this by selecting the related newsgroup's link, such as comp.lang.basic.visual.misc. Enter Visual Studio .NET in the search field again and select the Search Only In comp.lang.basic.visual.misc radio button.

As Figure 6-1 shows, the comp.lang.basic.visual.misc newsgroup contains an enormous number of posts about Microsoft Visual Studio .NET. Some articles offer to sell copies of the product, some ask for opinions, and some request help with the product. To narrow your query, it is advisable to add more keywords to your search, such as words that describe the specific problems you are experiencing.

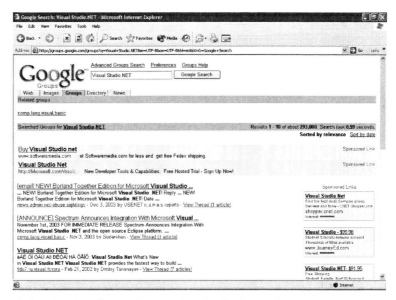

Figure 6-1: Hits for Visual Studio .NET in comp.lang.basic.visual.misc newsgroup on Google Groups

If you or your employer wanted to evaluate Visual Studio .NET before purchasing it, these articles would be helpful. You can also note the newsgroups that include a lot of Visual Studio .NET discussions and then visit those newsgroups regularly.

Newsgroup categories

Newsgroups make discussions among many people convenient. Tens of thousands of newsgroups discuss topics that range from serious subjects to chats about television shows. Newsgroups are arranged in a topical hierarchy to make it easier to find a group that meets your needs. The 10 top-level categories are carried throughout the Internet, and hundreds more narrowed categories feature discussions related to specific geographical areas, companies or organizations.

Following is a list of the 10 newsgroup categories common throughout the Internet:

- **biz** — commercial topics, such as sales announcements.
- **comp** — topics related to computers.
- **news** — topics related to Usenet news.
- **rec** — topics related to recreation, including sports, games and hobbies.
- **sci** — scientific topics such as medicine or linguistics.
- **soc** — social discussions, including cultural and religious topics.
- **talk** — discussions about controversial topics.
- **humanities** — topics in the humanities, such as Shakespeare or fine art.
- **misc** — topics not relevant to other newsgroup categories, including business discussions.
- **alt** — topics that have not been assigned a category, including controversial or adult-oriented subjects. This category has discussion areas that may be considered inappropriate for traditional business use and research.

A multitude of newsgroups exists in which businesspeople can learn valuable information about potential customers, rival companies and similar businesses. When you want to enter a newsgroup conversation, you simply post a response. Instantly, you become part of the discussion. Businesspeople can obtain free advice from experts, and perhaps create, build and maintain a positive public reputation for themselves or their companies.

Newsgroup structure

Newsgroups have a standard tree structure in which each branch leads the user to more focused information. Adjacent trees can also exist.

In newsgroup name syntax, a period is used to separate elements. Consider the following example:

comp.lang.java*

This newsgroup would contain discussions about the popular programming language Java. The group would represent a cross-section of Java programmers who have posted messages and responses about Java. The asterisk (*) tells the user that more branches of the tree follow.

Newsgroup names can be expanded to include more detail, such as the following:

comp.lang.java.databases

This newsgroup topic would discuss Java and databases.

In the following lab, you will use Outlook Express as a news client. Suppose you work for your company's legal department, and your manager has instructed you to locate a lawyer who can speak and write Greek. You can access Google Groups and subscribe to the *alt.greek-lawyer* newsgroup to inquire about Greek attorneys in your area.

 Lab 6-1: Configuring and using Outlook Express as a news client

OBJECTIVE:
1.7.1: News clients

You must configure a news client before you or other employees in your company can use newsgroups to learn about customers or rivals, or seek advice from experts. In this lab, you will configure and use Outlook Express as a news client.

1. First, you will configure Outlook Express as a news client. Start **Outlook Express**. Select **Tools | Accounts**, and then click the **News** tab.

2. Click the **Add** button, and then click **News** to display the Internet Connection Wizard.

3. Your assigned student name should automatically display in the Display Name field (the wizard uses your Outlook Express e-mail account information whenever possible). If not, enter your assigned student name, and then click **Next**. This step displays the Internet News E-Mail Address screen of the wizard.

4. Click **Next** to display the Internet News Server Name screen.

5. In the News (NNTP) Server field, type **ss1.prosofttraining.com**, and then click **Next**. This step specifies your news server and displays the final screen of the wizard.

    Tech Note: Throughout this class, the ss1.prosofttraining.com server will be your news, FTP and e-mail server. Each Internet service uses specific port numbers (for example, news uses port 119, FTP uses port 21, and mail uses ports 25 and 110). These agreed-upon standards allow computers to communicate with one another.

6. Click **Finish** to close the Internet Connection Wizard and redisplay the Internet Accounts dialog box.

7. Click **Close**. Because this is the first time you accessed the server, Outlook Express will prompt you to download all the newsgroups from the *ss1.prosofttraining.com* news server.

8. Next, you will use Outlook Express as your news client. Click **Yes** to download all newsgroups. This step displays the Newsgroup Subscriptions dialog box, shown in Figure 6-2.

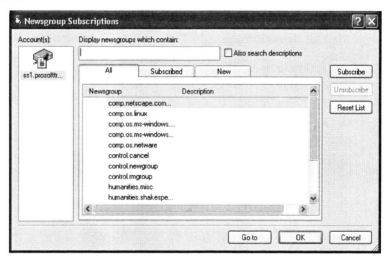

Figure 6-2: Newsgroup Subscriptions dialog box — Outlook Express

If you are not immediately prompted to download all newsgroups, return to the Outlook Express window, select the news account you created from the list of accounts on the left side of the screen, then click the Newsgroups button on the toolbar to download the newsgroups.

OBJECTIVE:
1.7.2: Newsgroup
articles

9. All newsgroups on the *ss1.prosofttraining.com* news server will appear. To access a newsgroup on the news server, you must subscribe to it. As a class, choose one newsgroup to which everyone will subscribe. After agreeing on a newsgroup to which all students will subscribe, select the newsgroup, and then click the **Subscribe** button.

10. Access that newsgroup by clicking the **Go To** button. You may be prompted to choose Outlook Express as your default news client. Select **Yes** or **No**, depending on your preference.

11. Posting, reading and replying to newsgroup articles will utilize the same skills you learned for working with e-mail messages. Now you will create a new post. Click the **New Post** button to display the New Message window. Type a subject and a brief message, then click the **Send** button to post your message. When the Post News dialog box displays informing you that your post might not appear immediately, click **OK**.

12. Press the F5 key to refresh your screen and view your message. (You may need to press F5 several times before your post displays.)

13. Next, you will read and respond to a newsgroup post. Find a newsgroup article that you want to read, then click the link to display its contents in the Preview pane. You can also double-click a news article link to display it in a separate window.

14. Select a newsgroup article posted by one of your classmates, and then click the **Reply Group** button to open a reply window. Type a response to the article, and then click the **Send** button. Outlook Express will prompt you to confirm that you want to send your response to the entire newsgroup. Click the **Yes** button to post your reply, and click **OK** if necessary.

15. Press **F5** until a plus sign (+) displays to the left of the article to which you replied. The plus sign indicates that the article includes responses.

16. Click the **plus sign** to display the posted response, and then click each response to read the text.

17. Exit **Outlook Express**.

Do you enjoy using newsgroups? Are they as easy to use as e-mail? How useful do you think they can be on the job?

For further practice, use Google Groups (*http://groups.google.com*) to examine various newsgroups that are relevant to your profession or employer, a hobby, or a new product or service. Not all newsgroups will be available on every Usenet server because the server administrator chooses the newsgroups that will be made available. If your company supports a Usenet news server and you need a specific newsgroup that is not available, contact your company IT department or the appropriate ISP.

Movie Time!

Insert the CIW Foundations Movie CD to learn even more about this topic.

Newsgroups (approx. playing time: 04:50)

All movie clips are © 2004 LearnKey, Inc.

OBJECTIVE:
1.7.6: Telnet
implementations

1.5.9: Browser
software

Telnet
The Internet
standard protocol
for remote terminal
connection service.

Telnet

Before access to the Internet was available through graphical user interfaces (GUIs), scientists, researchers and educators used computers with the UNIX operating system to retrieve information. Occasionally, they would use a protocol called Telnet.

A **Telnet** connection is a remote connection you can establish with a server, and then you can gather the information you need from that computer remotely. You are essentially logging on to the server and accessing information as if you were sitting at it. This process is possible because Telnet provides a login shell, which is an environment that allows you to issue commands (for example, run a text editor, list and transfer files, or start and stop services).

In Telnet, each command you type is usually echoed back to your screen after the host interprets it. The host — not your computer — is reading your input, running your commands and returning your requested information. Because much of the Internet is still UNIX-based (Web servers, FTP servers), a wide variety of information is still available through Telnet access. To use Telnet, you need an account and a password on the host computer. You can use Telnet to access some public servers, such as public libraries and government resources, using a generic user name.

In the following lab, you will use Telnet to access a library database. Suppose you are a research assistant and your supervisor asks you to find out if the University of California's library system contains any books about the NASA Mercury Probe program. You can use Telnet to access the library catalog.

 Lab 6-2: Accessing a library database using Telnet

In this lab, you will use Telnet to search for a book at a public library.

1. On the Desktop, click **Start**, click **Run**, then type **telnet** in the Open box. Press **ENTER** to open a command window and start the Telnet client.

2. Type **open rock.lib.asu.edu** and press **ENTER** to access the Arizona State University (ASU) library system. Notice that you are asked to log on.

3. Type **library** and then press **ENTER** to log on and display the main screen. No password is requested.

4. Notice that you can enter a number from 1 to 6, or E to exit. Each Telnet site usually has its own set of commands. The ASU site uses single-letter or single-number commands for accessing menus. Your screen may resemble Figure 6-3.

![Telnet window showing "The Arizona State University Libraries' Network" with menu options: 1> ASU Libraries' Catalog, 2> Encyclopedia Britannica Online - Go to http://search.eb.com, 3> Arizona Libraries, 4> Other Library Catalogs, 5> Library Information and help using the system, E> Exit. Choose one (1-6,E). You may also access the Libraries catalog on the web at: http://library.lib.asu.edu]

Figure 6-3: Accessing library database using Telnet

5. Type **1** to display the library catalog and a list of search method options.

6. Type **T** to search by title.

7. Type the title of your favorite book, and then press **ENTER** to submit the request. If your entry is found, it will display on the screen. If it is not found, the screen will display titles similar to the one you typed, with a placeholder indicating where in the list your title would be located if it were found.

8. Experiment with Telnet and explore the site.

9. When you are finished, type **N** to return to the search screen. Type **Q** to return to the catalog screen, and then type **E** to exit and disconnect from the library.

10. Close the command window.

Telnet continues to be widely used by UNIX administrators. Telnet allows them to remotely log on to a server, such as a Web server, and manage it from any location that has an Internet connection.

OBJECTIVE:
1.7.6: Telnet
implementations

Two versions of Telnet exist: standard Telnet and Microsoft Telnet. Standard Telnet uses a server that listens on TCP port 23, and this version of Telnet is supported by various vendors and distributors such as Microsoft, Red Hat, Sun Solaris and FreeBSD. Standard Telnet is universal and does not encrypt data transmissions, nor does it encrypt the authentication sequence.

Only Microsoft supports Microsoft Telnet. The server listens on TCP port 23, and both the authentication sequence and the ensuing data transmission are encrypted. The proprietary version is more secure and is the better choice for sending sensitive information. However, because the protocol is proprietary, a server that is running encrypted Microsoft Telnet can only be used with Microsoft clients. If you are using another operating system (for example, Linux or Macintosh), you may encounter problems logging on to the remote system.

OBJECTIVE:
1.7.7: Secure Shell
(SSH)

Secure Shell (SSH)   *Not on Exam*

Secure Shell (SSH)
A protocol and
command interface
that provides secure
access to a remote
computer.

Secure Shell (SSH), sometimes known as Secure Socket Shell, is a protocol and command interface that you can use to gain secure access to a remote computer and then execute commands to administer a system. In the past, SSH was used only on UNIX-based systems. However, it is possible to install an SSH server on any Windows platform.

SSH is similar in functionality to Telnet, and it supports clients from any operating system (for example, Macintosh, Windows or UNIX). SSH commands are encrypted and secure. Both the client and server are authenticated using public keys, and passwords are encrypted. The latest version of the SSH protocol is SSH2. SSH servers listen for connections on TCP port 22 by default. Figure 6-4 shows a typical SSH session.

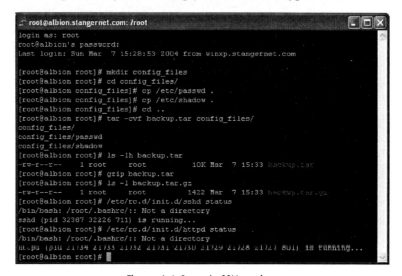

Figure 6-4: Sample SSH session

In the session shown in the figure, a user has logged on to a remote system named *albion.stangernet.com*. He logged on as root, then backed up important configuration files (including the /etc/passwd and /etc/shadow files, which contain user authentication information). The user then archived these files and compressed them using the gzip program. The user then checked the status of the SSH and HTTPD daemons (services).

Several utilities have been created based on the SSH and SSH2 protocols. Many users now use SSH rather than any form of Telnet. Table 6-1 lists the most relevant SSH-based utilities.

Table 6-1: SSH-based utilities

SSH utility	Description
Secure Shell (SSH)	Provides secure logon and authentication. Allows you to obtain a logon shell and execute commands on the server, assuming you have permissions to execute these commands. Also known as "slogin," which is short for secure login.
Secure Copy (SCP)	Provides a secure method of copying files between systems. SCP sessions are usually non-interactive; that is, you generally do not list files and issue other commands, as you would with SSH.
SSH File Transfer Protocol (S/FTP)	An interactive client that works much like standard FTP, but is encrypted.

You will learn more about Secure Copy (SCP) and SSH File Transfer Protocol (S/FTP) later in this lesson.

SSH, encryption and authentication

All sessions for SSH-enabled clients are encrypted. SSHv1 encryption is weaker than SSHv2. All SSH clients and the servers cooperate with each other to automatically exchange keys with each other when a first connection is made. These keys, which are generated through asymmetric-key encryption, enable all data to be encrypted. Asymmetric-key encryption, also called public-key encryption, uses two keys to encrypt and decrypt messages. You will learn more about asymmetric-key encryption in a later lesson.

By default, SSH servers require a user name and a password for a client to log on. Remember that authentication sessions are generally not encrypted. Authentication (the process of verifying a user's identity) is generally achieved through the transmission of a valid user name and password from the client to the server. By default, the user name and password are sent as plaintext, which means that a hacker could obtain a valid user name and password by using a packet-sniffing program.

Public keys can also be used to authenticate users. Using public keys for authentication is not the default for SSH clients. Enabling asymmetric-key authentication is a step further than using only the default asymmetric-key encryption, which encrypts only the exchanges that take place after authentication. Enabling asymmetric-key authentication requires additional configuration steps, which include the following:

- Generating your own key pair

- Exchanging public keys with a remote user

- Configuring your server to recognize your partner's public key

Note: In-depth knowledge about SSH authentication is not necessary to pass the CIW Foundations exam, and the subject is not discussed in detail in this course. Understand that SSH encrypts by default, but that by default, authentication occurs via user names and passwords. Asymmetric-key authentication occurs only if you take steps to enable it.

File Transfer Protocol (FTP)

OBJECTIVE:
1.7.3: FTP services

1.5.9: Browser
software

File Transfer Protocol (FTP) is a TCP/IP suite protocol that allows the transfer of files between two computers, or one server and one computer. FTP is a convenient way to transfer files and can be a good alternative to sending an e-mail attachment. For example, if you need to send a file to a remote co-worker and the file is too large to send via e-mail, you can upload the file to your company FTP server, and then your co-worker can download the file from the FTP server. Many corporate e-mail servers (and even firewalls) prevent sending and receiving executable files as e-mail attachments. However, you can upload and download such files using an FTP server.

 If you download executable files via FTP or any other file transfer method, be sure that you scan the files with a virus scanner before using them. Users who download executable files from the Internet often find that these files are not what they purport to be.

FTP and authentication

An FTP server can require user-based authentication, meaning that in order for the FTP server to allow uploading and downloading, it requires the user to provide a user name and a password. All FTP clients provide a place for you to enter authentication information. Even Web browsers allow authentication. Modern Web browsers allow you to authenticate via FTP (or HTTP) using the following syntax:

ftp://username:password@servername

So, if you wanted to log on as *ciwuser* with the password *ciwcertified* to a server named *ftp.ciwcertified.com*, you would issue the following command:

ftp://ciwuser:ciwcertified@ftp.ciwcertified.com

If you wanted to log on to a Web server on that same server that has enabled password protection, you would simply change the protocol in the preceding URL (for example, from *ftp://* to *http://*).

However, remember that standard FTP does not encrypt the authentication session. Malicious users will often attempt to obtain authentication information during FTP-based authentication sessions, so reconsider using sensitive information for FTP authentication.

As a result, some FTP site administrators allow guests to transfer files without requiring the system administrator to create a specific account for the user on the remote site. These sites are called anonymous FTP sites and are available to the public. Many major universities have reliable anonymous FTP servers on the Internet. However, these sites usually do not allow uploading of files. They only allow files to be downloaded, and only if downloading such files does not violate national and international laws

 FTP does not encrypt data transfer. If you are transferring sensitive data, consider a secure alternative to FTP, such as SSH (for example, S/FTP) or SSL/TLS-encrypted FTP (FTPS).

For logging on to public FTP sites, a user name of *anonymous, ftp* or *guest* is often used to gain immediate access to the FTP server. In most cases, the password is your e-mail address. The FTP client usually sends the user name and password automatically. Most private FTP sites require users to provide a specific user name and password that have been assigned by an FTP server administrator.

 FTP clients cannot change their own passwords. If a password must be changed, the user must contact the FTP administrator, who can change it.

Navigating an FTP server

Navigating an FTP server is similar to navigating the directory structure of a hard drive. You start at the top of the hierarchy by selecting a directory name that is close to the general topic in which you are interested. You then continue to select directory names that are more specific to the subject you are seeking, until you find the file you want. This navigation process may take you many levels into an FTP server's hard drive. Most FTP servers are structured similarly. When you become familiar with FTP servers, navigating their contents becomes easy.

FTP server contents

binary file
A file containing data or instructions written in zeros and ones (computer language).

FTP servers contain documents of various sizes and types. Two common types of resources available on Internet FTP servers include large text files and **binary files**. The large text files are usually application source files. Programmers use these files to customize and compile programs. Binary files are executable files, small software applications, images that require an association to open, or compressed files that require decompression. End users will probably download only binary files.

FTP servers often contain popular shareware and open-source freeware. Shareware is inexpensive; download it, and if you like it, send the vendor a payment. Freeware is free; it may be a beta version (in the process of being tested) or distributed by an unknown source, but there is no charge for it. Major software companies, such as Microsoft and Netscape, often distribute free program samples to help you get started, and more complete versions are available for a fee. Plug-ins (software to extend browser capabilities) and helper applications (which your browser opens to play or view multimedia files) are usually free, as well.

Large text documents, binary files and/or shareware can take a long time to download and read, depending on your connection speed. To accelerate this process, several compression utilities are available to reduce file size for the purpose of transmission. The files are then placed on FTP servers in a compressed format. Thus, after you download the compressed files, you must decompress them. Decompression restores the files to their original, readable states. Table 6-2 lists the file types commonly found on FTP servers.

Table 6-2: Popular file types found on FTP servers

File Name Extension	File Type
.txt	A basic text file; can be read by any word processor or text editor.
.zip	A WinZip or PKZIP compressed file; a popular form of compressed file for the personal computer (PC).
.exe	An executable file; typically, a self-extracting compressed file, sometimes found as an executable software program.
.asc	An ASCII text file. ASCII is a universally accepted standard text format for all computers.
.tar	A UNIX tape archive (tar) file; a form of compression used by UNIX operating systems.
.sea	A Macintosh Stuffit self-extracting compressed file.
.sit	A Macintosh Stuffit compressed file.
.rar	A platform-neutral compression standard, used by applications such as RAR (for UNIX) and WinRAR (for Windows).

You will manage downloaded files, decompress files and specify MIME types in labs later in this lesson.

Installing an FTP client

Most modern operating systems and Web browsers feature built-in FTP clients. You can also install an FTP client that suits your preferences. FileZilla is a free user-friendly FTP client.

In the following lab, you will install an FTP client. Suppose your company's publishing department needs to upload files to a printing company's FTP site. The department manager has requested that a particular user-friendly FTP client be installed on all systems.

 Lab 6-3: Installing the FileZilla FTP client

In this lab, you will download, install and set up the FileZilla FTP client.

1. Start **Internet Explorer**, go to ***http://filezilla.sourceforge.net***, and then click the **Download** link on the left side of the Web page.

2. Click the link for the latest version of the setup executable file, and then click the link for the closest mirror site.

3. Download the file to the **Class Downloads** folder you created in an earlier lesson.

4. Close your browser.

5. Access the **Class Downloads** folder, double-click the **FileZilla** setup executable file, then install the product using the default configuration.

6. Close any open windows.

Downloading files using FTP

To download files, the FTP client program uses the *get* command. For instance, after a user logs on to an FTP server, he or she enters the command *get filename.ext*, depending on the name and extension of the file to be downloaded. However, with most user-friendly FTP client programs, the *get* command is initiated when the user clicks on the file he or she wants to download. The client automatically uses the *get* command (invisible to the user) to download the file. The user must then identify the location to which the file should be downloaded. In the following labs, you will use various implementations of FTP.

Using command-line FTP

On Windows systems, you can use the MS-DOS prompt to access a command-line FTP client to upload files. You need to use the *open* command to access an FTP server, and you must use the *get* command to copy a file to your computer. You should also be familiar with DOS commands for navigation and file management.

Files are downloaded into the directory from which you enter the FTP commands. When you access the MS-DOS prompt, the DOS window opens in the Windows directory. To download files into a specific folder other than the Windows directory, create or navigate to the directory, then start the FTP session.

In the following lab, you will download files using command-line FTP. Suppose your company's human resources director, who rarely needs to download files, has been instructed to download archived personnel records from the corporate headquarters FTP site. Using command-line FTP, you can quickly download the files for her without having to install any additional software on her system.

 Lab 6-4: Downloading files using command-line FTP

In this lab, you will create a directory on your hard drive to receive FTP downloads. You will then use FTP from the command line to download a file from the FTP server into the directory you create.

1. First, you will access the command prompt and create a directory on the root directory of your hard drive for your FTP files. Click **Start**, click **Run**, type *cmd* in the Open box, and then press **ENTER** to open a command prompt window.

2. Maximize the command prompt window.

3. Type *cd*, and then press **ENTER** to move to the root directory of the hard drive.

4. Type *md ftp_files*, and then press **ENTER** to make a directory called *ftp_files*.

5. Type *cd ftp_files*, and then press **ENTER** to access the new directory.

6. Next, you will begin the FTP session, display the server's contents and download a file. Type *ftp*, then press **ENTER**.

7. Type *open ss1.prosofttraining.com*, then press **ENTER**.

8. Type *anonymous*, and then press **ENTER**.

9. Type your class-assigned e-mail address as a password, and then press **ENTER**.

10. Type *dir* and then press **ENTER** to see a listing of directories on the server.

11. Type *get FTP-readme.txt* and then press **ENTER** to copy the file FTP-readme.txt from the FTP server to the current directory (FTP_files) on your hard drive.

12. Next, you will close the FTP session and close the command prompt window. Type *bye* and then press **ENTER** to close the FTP session. Your screen should resemble Figure 6-5.

Figure 6-5: Using command-line FTP

13. Type *exit* and press **ENTER** to close the command prompt window.

What is your opinion of command-line FTP? Was it easy or difficult to use? Would you like to use it for all of your FTP activities?

Using a Web browser's built-in FTP client

OBJECTIVE:
1.7.4: FTP-based vs.
HTTP-based retrieval

Although FTP sites do not usually look like Web pages, accessing them and copying content from them is very similar to saving Web site content with your browser. Generally, you right-click the file you want to copy, select the Copy command, and then specify a destination location on your hard drive.

In the following lab, you will use the Internet Explorer built-in FTP client. Suppose the accounting manager at your company needs to download a file from the company FTP site. However, he does not have time to learn to use an FTP client. You can demonstrate to him how to use his Web browser to download the file without having to learn any FTP commands.

 Lab 6-5: Downloading files using the Internet Explorer FTP client

In this lab, you will use the Internet Explorer built-in FTP client to download files.

1. Start **Internet Explorer**.

2. In the Address box, type **_ftp://ss1.prosofttraining.com_** and press **ENTER** to display the contents of the ss1 FTP site. Your screen should resemble Figure 6-6.

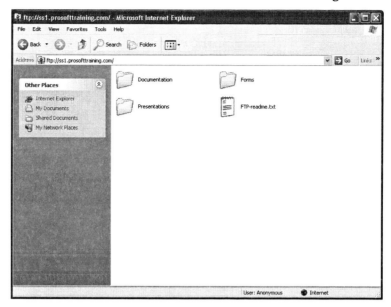

Figure 6-6: Using Internet Explorer FTP client

3. Double-click the **Documentation** folder, right-click **Command_Prompt_FTP.txt**, and then click **Copy To Folder** to display the Browse For Folder dialog box.

4. Navigate to the **C:\FTP_files** folder, and then click **OK** to copy the selected file to your hard drive.

5. Close **Internet Explorer**.

How does Web browser FTP compare with command-line FTP? Was it easier to see what was available? Did you prefer it to command-line FTP?

In the following lab, you will use the FileZilla FTP client. Suppose your company's marketing department has asked you to recommend for a user-friendly FTP client. You can demonstrate the free FileZilla client to the department personnel so that they can evaluate it.

 Lab 6-6: Downloading files using the FileZilla FTP client

In this lab, you will use the FileZilla FTP client to download files from the ss1 FTP server.

1. Select **Start | All Programs | FileZilla | FileZilla** to start the FileZilla FTP client, then maximize the FileZilla window.

2. In the Address box, type **_ss1.prosofttraining.com_**, then press **ENTER** to access the FTP site and display its contents. Your screen should resemble Figure 6-7.

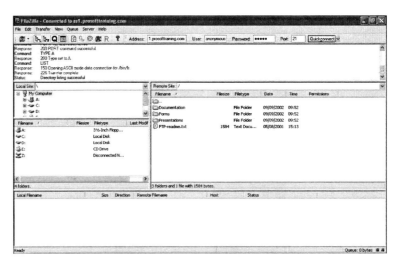

Figure 6-7: Using FileZilla FTP client

3. Notice that you are automatically logged on as an anonymous user. Notice also that the window is divided into several panes. Take some time to explore the FileZilla interface. You use the Local Site pane to select a directory on your local system. You use the Remote Site pane to navigate the FTP server. Notice that FileZilla includes a Site Manager, which saves logon and address information for the FTP sites you access. FileZilla also includes a queue for files to be uploaded or downloaded so that you can process all of your file transfers at one time.

4. In the Local Site pane, navigate to the **C:\ftp_files** folder to specify the location to which downloaded files will be copied.

5. In the Remote Site pane, double-click the **Presentations** folder to access the folder contents, and then right-click **Colossus.txt** to display the shortcut menu.

6. Notice that you have several options, including downloading and adding the file to the queue. Some of the other options may or may not be available depending on the permissions you have to the FTP folder. Offering read-only permissions to anonymous users is standard; however, the system administrator decides which permissions to allow.

7. In the shortcut menu, click **Add To Queue** to add the file to the queue for downloading.

8. Right-click **An Interesting File.wow**, and then click **Add To Queue** to add the file to the queue for downloading. Notice that this file has a unique file name extension. You will learn more about this file name extension later in this lesson.

9. In the Remote Site pane, double-click the folder icon at the top of the tree to return to the previous directory.

10. In the menu bar, select **Queue | Process Queue** to download all files in the queue to the C:\ftp_files folder on your hard drive.

11. In the menu bar, select **File | Disconnect** to disconnect from the server.

12. Close the **FileZilla** FTP client window.

OBJECTIVE:
1.7.4: FTP-based vs. HTTP-based retrieval

What is your opinion of this FTP client? Did you find the interface intuitive and easy to use? How does it compare to using a Web browser's FTP client?

Uploading files using FTP

Uploading to an FTP site requires an FTP client program, which can be embedded within other applications, such as a Web browser or Web publishing program. It also requires permission, which is usually provided by the FTP server administrator. If an FTP server allowed anonymous users to upload files, the server would be unmanageable and would quickly be depleted of hard drive space.

To upload files, an FTP client uses the *put* command. For instance, after a user logs on to an FTP server, he or she enters the command *put filename.ext*, depending on the name and extension of the file to be uploaded. Similar to downloading FTP files, most user-friendly FTP client programs initiate the *put* command when the user clicks the Upload button or chooses Upload from a menu and then identifies the file to upload. The client automatically uses the *put* command (invisible to the user) to upload the file.

In the following lab, you will use FileZilla to upload files to an FTP server set up on your instructor's computer. Suppose that your company's publishing department has asked you to demonstrate how to use FileZilla to upload files to a printing company's FTP site.

 Lab 6-7: Uploading files to an FTP site using FileZilla

In this lab, you will use FileZilla to log on to an FTP site on your instructor's computer using a password, and upload files to that site. In this lab, you have full permissions to the FTP folder. However, in most cases, permissions to an FTP folder are tightly controlled.

1. Start **FileZilla**.

2. In the **Address** box, type the name of your instructor's computer. Your instructor will provide this information.

3. Press **TAB** and type *ciwuser* to specify the user name. Press **TAB**, type *ciwcertified* as the password, then press **ENTER** to connect.

4. In the Remote Site pane, right-click the folder icon, then click **Create Directory** to display the Enter Directory Name dialog box.

5. Type your name, then press **ENTER**. This step creates a new folder on the FTP site.

6. In the Remote Site pane, double-click the new folder you created.

7. In the Local Site pane, navigate to your **ftp_files** folder, right-click **FTP-readme.txt**, then click **Upload** to transfer the file to your folder on your instructor's computer.

8. Choose **File | Disconnect** to disconnect from the server, and then close **FileZilla**.

9. Turn your attention to your instructor's monitor. Look at the files displayed. What do you think happens when FTP site administrators allow anonymous users to upload files, create directories or delete files? It is up to the site administrator to assign permissions to users. An anonymous user may have permissions to read, write, append and copy files and folders, as well as delete files and folders.

10. Your instructor will now demonstrate how to restrict permissions on an anonymous account. As a class, choose permissions for anonymous users. Your instructor will assign the chosen permissions.

11. After your instructor has changed the permissions for anonymous users, restart **FileZilla**.

12. In the Address box, type the name of your instructor's computer. Your instructor will provide this information.

13. If necessary, delete the entries in the User and Password fields, then press **ENTER** to log on as an anonymous user.

14. Attempt to upload files and create directories. Do you have the same access as you did when you logged on with a user name and password?

15. Disconnect from the server, then close **FileZilla**.

OBJECTIVE:
1.7.3: FTP services

Secure Copy (SCP), SSH File Transfer Protocol (S/FTP) and SSL/TLS-enabled FTP (FTPS)

As you have learned, FTP is used for transferring files from one computer to another. However, because security is a growing concern for all aspects of computing, including FTP, many companies and public entities are implementing secure forms of file transfer.

Secure Copy (SCP)
A program used with Secure Shell (SSH) to transfer files between systems.

SSH File Transfer Protocol (S/FTP)
A file transfer protocol that allows the encryption of transmissions using the Secure Shell (SSH) protocol.

SSL/TLS-enabled FTP (FTPS)
FTP that runs on an SSL/TLS-secured connection.

Secure Copy (SCP) is a program used to securely transfer files between systems. SCP is used primarily on UNIX/Linux systems (command-line interface), although versions are available for Windows (graphical user interface). SCP uses an SSH-secured connection, and it is quickly becoming a replacement for FTP. All SCP transmissions use 128-bit encryption, and SCP allows quick transfer of large files. SCP adds file transfer capability to SSH, and each file transfer constitutes a discrete session.

SSH File Transfer Protocol (S/FTP) is a secure version of File Transfer Protocol (FTP), performing file transfer operations over a connection secured by SSH. S/FTP is very similar to SCP, although it allows longer sessions. That is, you can perform several file transfers in one session.

SSL/TLS-enabled FTP (FTPS) is FTP that runs on an SSL/TLS-secured connection. FTPS differs from SCP and S/FTP in that it relies on SSL/TLS for encryption, whereas SCP and S/FTP rely on SSH for encryption.

SCP, S/FTP and FTPS all offer secure methods of transferring files, and all three are encrypted by default. That is, all user name and password information transfers are encrypted as they are sent across the Internet.

Figure 6-8 shows WinSCP (a Windows-based SCP program). Notice the similarities to a regular FTP client. However, remember that SCP is most often used as a command-line client.

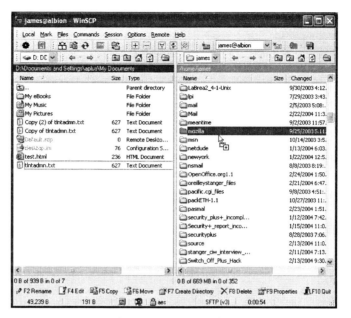

Figure 6-8: WinSCP client

Managing Downloaded Files

As you already know, waiting for large files to download or upload can be tedious. Most files that you download arrive in a compressed format and are decompressed (usually automatically) after they are copied to your system. You may also download files that your system does not know how to open. The following sections will examine compression utilities, and you will learn to define MIME types for unknown files.

OBJECTIVE:
1.13.1: MIME file types

Defining MIME types

Occasionally, you may encounter files that your system does not know how to open. For example, in an earlier lab in this lesson, you downloaded a file named *An Interesting File.wow*. This file is a plain text file, but the file name extension has been changed from *.txt* to *.wow*. The .wow file name extension is not one that will be recognized by your system, and when you attempt to open this file in the following lab, Windows XP will display the dialog box shown in Figure 6-9.

Figure 6-9: File with undefined MIME type

Windows does not know how to open the file because it does not recognize the file name extension or the file's MIME type. As you learned in a previous lesson, MIME types are used to identify a document type and the application required to open it.

MIME types are standardized and are created by the Internet Assigned Numbers Authority (IANA). Visit www.iana.org/assignments/media-types/ to view a list of the defined types.

You can use the options in the dialog box to define a MIME type, or you can define a MIME type on the File Types tab of the Folder Options dialog box, as shown in Figure 6-10.

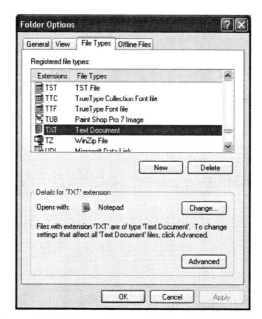

Figure 6-10: File Types tab — Folder Options dialog box

In the following lab, you will define a MIME type for a file. Suppose a co-worker has asked for your help because she downloaded a file from the corporate FTP site that she cannot open. You can add a MIME-type definition to her system and enable her to open files of this type in the future without problems.

 Lab 6-8: Defining MIME types

In this lab, you will examine a MIME type definition and then define a MIME type for a file that you downloaded in a previous lab.

1. Open **Windows Explorer**, select **Tools | Folder Options**, then click the **File Types** tab. This step displays the file types currently defined in your system.

2. Scroll down the list box and click **TXT Text Document**. This step displays the details for the text document file type. Notice that text documents are opened with Notepad by default.

3. Close the **Folder Options** dialog box, navigate to the **ftp_files** folder, and then double-click **An Interesting File.wow**. This step displays a message box informing you that Windows does not know how to open the file.

4. Click the **Cancel** button to close the message box.

5. Select **Tools | Folder Options**, and then click the **File Types** tab.

6. Click the **New** button, then type *wow* in the File Extension box. Click the **Advanced** button.

7. Click the arrow to display the **Associated File Type** drop-down list, then click **Text Document** to specify that any file with the .wow file name extension should be treated as a text document and opened with a text editor.

8. Click **OK**, then click **Close** to close the Folder Options dialog box. Notice that *An Interesting File.wow* now displays with a Notepad icon.

9. Double-click **An Interesting File.wow**. This step opens the file in Notepad because you have modified your system's MIME settings.

10. Close the **Notepad** window.

The MIME type definitions set in Windows XP are used by all applications running on the system. That is, once you define a type in the Folder Options dialog box, all programs will use that definition. However, you can also define MIME types in Navigator. Any definitions you create in Navigator will be used only by Navigator, and will not be accessible to other applications.

You can define a MIME type in Navigator by performing the following steps:

1. Select Edit | Preferences, then click Helper Applications in the Category list box.

2. Click the New Type button, specify the MIME type (in this case, text/plain) and the file name extension.

3. Specify the application you want Navigator to use to open the file, then click OK twice.

In most cases, installing the latest version of a browser, or installing any available upgrades, will eliminate the need to define a MIME type for files that you download from Web sites.

OBJECTIVE:
1.13.2: MIME vs. S/MIME

You learned in a previous lesson that S/MIME provides a secure method of sending e-mail. Whereas MIME controls how messages and attachments are organized and distinguished from one another, S/MIME controls how encryption information and digital certificates can be included as part of an e-mail message.

OBJECTIVE:
1.13.3: Compression utilities

Compression utilities

To reduce transfer time, most files you download from the Internet arrive in a compressed (or "zipped") format, and the compressed files must be decompressed on your system. Windows XP contains a built-in utility that decompresses zipped files.

Most compression utilities (such as WinZip, BitZipper, PKZIP, bzip2, gzip and RAR/WinRAR) allow you to create archives. An archive is a file that contains several files that have been compressed and bundled together. Archive files simplify the process of distributing all the files that are necessary for a particular application. When compressed files are extracted from an archive file, you have two files: the compressed file and the folder with the extracted files.

Generally, you should compress files that you want to send as e-mail attachments to reduce transfer time and to conserve space on your recipient's hard drive. On your own system, you can compress files that you use infrequently in order to save space.

Table 6-3 describes several popular compression applications.

Table 6-3: Compression applications and common file name extensions

Application	File Name Extension (MIME)	Comments
Zip/unzip	.zip	Includes the PKZIP and WinZip applications, as well as all variants. You can obtain free command-line versions of zip at *http://sourceforge.net/projects/gnuwin32.*
Bzip2/bunzip2	.bz2	You can obtain free command-line versions of bzip2/bunzip2 at *http://sourceforge.net/projects/gnuwin32.*
Bzip/bunzip	.bz	You can obtain free command-line versions of bzip/bunzip at *http://sourceforge.net/projects/gnuwin32.*
Gzip/gunzip	.gz	Many times, archives of files and directories are created using the tar application, then compressed using gzip. If this is the case, the file will often have a .tgz or .tar.gz file name extension.
Compress/uncompress	.Z	Many times, archives of files and directories are created using the tar application, then compressed using gzip. If this is the case, the file will often have a .tar.Z or .tZ file name extension.
RAR/WinRAR	.rar	You can obtain versions of RAR/WinRAR at *www.rarlab.com* and *http://sourceforge.net/projects/sevenzip.*

Compressing files, especially word processor files, can save a considerable amount of hard disk space. However, some formats (such as PNG, GIF and JPG) are already compressed. Compressing these files does not significantly reduce file size.

Bzip2 is a free compression utility that you can use to compress files and create archives. In the following lab, you will compress a file, and compare its size with the size of the decompressed file.

Suppose your project manager has given you the task of compressing thousands of image files that are currently stored and downloaded from the corporate server. You can improve system performance and use bandwidth more efficiently by compressing these files.

 Lab 6-9: Compressing and decompressing files using bzip2 and bunzip2

In this lab, you will use the bzip2 and bunzip2 applications to compress and decompress files.

1. First, you will copy the necessary files to your hard drive. Copy the contents of the **C:\CIW\Internet\LabFiles\Lesson06\bzip2** directory to the **C:\windows** directory.

   Note: This step is essential. Placing these files into the C:\windows\ directory will also place them into the Windows path, which means that you will be able to execute the files from a command prompt, regardless of the directory you are currently using.

2. Copy the file **image.tiff** from the **C:\CIW\Internet\LabFiles\Lesson06** directory to your Desktop, and then close any open windows.

3. On the Desktop, double-click **image.tiff** to open it. Notice that you can view the image.

4. Close the **Windows Picture And Fax Viewer** window.

5. Right-click **image.tiff**, then click **Properties**.

6. How large is this file? Write its uncompressed size in the space provided:

   _____

7. Close the **Properties** dialog box.

8. Next, you will compress the file image.tiff. Click **Start**, then click **Run**. Type *cmd* in the Open box, and then press **ENTER** to open a command prompt.

9. Type *cd desktop*, then press **ENTER**. This step navigates to the Desktop directory.

10. Type *bzip2 image.tiff* and then press **ENTER**. This step compresses the file.

11. If necessary, drag the command prompt window out of the way so that you can view the Desktop.

12. Notice that the image file name has changed to image.tiff.bz2. The file name has changed because it has been compressed using the bzip2 application.

13. On the Desktop, right-click **image.tiff.bz2**, then click **Properties**. Notice that the file size has changed significantly. Write the new file size in the space provided:

   _____

14. Close the **Properties** dialog box.

15. On the Desktop, double-click **image.tiff.bz2**.

16. Notice that Windows does not know how to open this file. You cannot view the image because the file has been compressed.

17. Close the message box.

18. Finally, you will decompress the file. At the command prompt, type *bunzip2 image.tiff.bz2* and then press **ENTER**. This step decompresses the file.

19. Close the command prompt window, then double-click **image.tiff**. Notice that you can view the image again.

20. Check the file size of the image. Notice that it has returned to its original size.

21. Close all open windows.

   Note: Many image file formats (such as PNG, GIF and JPG) already have compression enabled, so compressing them further using bzip2, zip or WinRAR will not significantly reduce their file sizes.

**Virtual Network
Computing (VNC)**
A program that
allows you to
control a computer
at a remote
location.

Virtual Network Computing (VNC) and Microsoft Terminal Services

Virtual Network Computing (VNC) is a program that allows you to control a computer at a remote location as if you were sitting in front of it. VNC is similar to applications such as pcAnywhere by Symantec (*www.symantec.com*) and NetOp by Danware Data A/S (*www.netop.com*). VNC consists of two components: the server and the viewer. The server listens on a specific port (for example, TCP 5800 on Windows systems) and allows clients to connect. The server also allows authenticated users to log on and see the same display they would see if they were sitting in front of the (server) computer. Unlike Telnet or SSH, VNC provides a full GUI display. The VNC viewer allows users to see the remote system's logon environment. The server and the viewer do not need to be running the same operating system.

VNC can be used in a variety of ways. In an office, a system administrator can use VNC to diagnose and solve problems on an employee's computer, or access and administer servers without going to the server room. Newer versions of VNC promise a proprietary file transfer program that allows VNC the functionality of programs such as pcAnywhere and NetOp.

Help desk personnel might also use VNC to troubleshoot computer problems for remote employees, or to install software on remote systems.

In the following lab, you will use VNC. Suppose you work in the IT department at your company, and the security manager has tasked you with updating the virus definition files on all corporate systems. You can use VNC to update the systems without leaving your desk.

 Lab 6-10: Using the TightVNC remote administration application

In this lab, you will install and use TightVNC. TightVNC is a version of VNC that is available free of charge under the GNU General Public License (GPL). A lab partner is required for this lab. One partner's system will function as the server (the computer that will be controlled), and the other will function as the client (the computer from which commands will be issued). Decide the role each of you will take.

1. Copy the file *tightvnc-1.2.9-setup.exe* from the **C:\CIW\Internet\LabFiles\Lesson06** folder to your Desktop, and install it using the default configuration.

2. On the server computer, select **Start | All Programs | TightVNC | Launch TightVNC Server**. This step displays the WinVNC Current User Properties dialog box, shown in Figure 6-11. You use this dialog box to specify settings for the server side of the VNC connection.

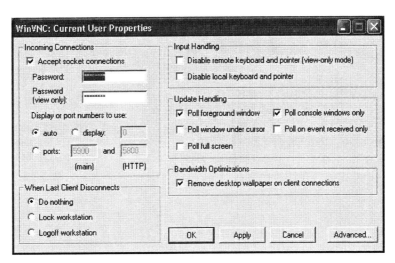

Figure 6-11: WinVNC Current User Properties dialog box

3. Type **password** in the Password box, press **TAB**, then type **password** in the Password (View Only) box. WinVNC will not accept incoming connections without a password due to security risk. You must specify a password in order to proceed.

4. Click **OK**. This step closes the WinVNC Current User Properties dialog box. Notice that a WinVNC icon displays in the status bar.

5. On the server computer, double-click **image.tiff** on the Desktop to display the image file in the Windows Picture And Fax Viewer.

6. On the client computer, select **Start | All Programs | TightVNC | TightVNC Viewer (Best Compression)** to display the Connection Details dialog box (Figure 6-12).

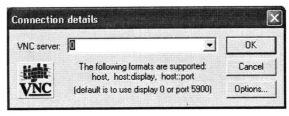

Figure 6-12: Connection Details dialog box

7. In the VNC Server box, enter the IP address of the server computer, then click **OK** to display the VNC Authentication dialog box.

    Note: You can display the IP address of the server computer by positioning the mouse pointer over the VNC icon in the status bar.

8. Type **password** in the Session Password text box, then click **OK** to start the VNC session. The screen on the client computer will display the Desktop of the server computer, as shown in Figure 6-13. Notice that the name of the server displays in the window title bar.

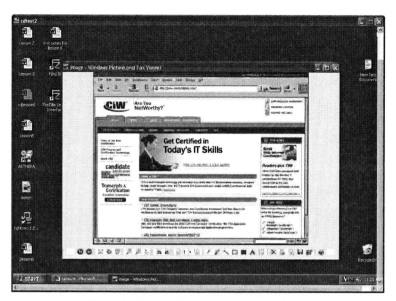

Figure 6-13: VNC display on client computer

9. On the client computer, scroll down to display two taskbars. The upper taskbar controls the server computer, whereas the lower taskbar controls the client computer.

10. On the client computer, click the **Close** button in the Windows Picture And Fax Viewer window to close the image file on the server computer. You can control the server computer from the client computer. You can even restart the server computer.

11. On the server computer, double-click **image.tiff** on the Desktop to redisplay the image. Notice that while using VNC, the server computer can still function normally.

12. On the server computer, right-click the **VNC** icon in the status bar, then click **Kill All Clients** to close the connection. This step displays a *Connection Closed* message on the client computer. Notice that the VNC viewer window closes on the client computer.

13. On the client computer, click **OK** to close the message box.

14. On the server computer, right-click the **VNC** icon in the status bar, then click **Close VNC**. This step makes it impossible for any clients to connect.

15. On the server computer, close the **Windows Picture And Fax Viewer** window.

In this lab, you used VNC to gain remote access to another computer. When using VNC, both the viewer (client) and the server have control over the server computer.

Microsoft Terminal Services is a suite of tools that enables computers to function as dedicated clients to a server running Windows. In Windows XP, you can use Remote Desktop Connection for the remote administration capability of Terminal Services.

In the following lab, you will use Remote Desktop Connection. Suppose that the IT manager has instructed you to defragment the hard drives of several corporate systems. You can use Remote Desktop Connection to gain control of those computers and defragment them while sitting at your desk.

Lab 6-11: Using Remote Desktop Connection

In this lab, you will use Remote Desktop Connection to control a remote computer. A lab partner is required for this lab. One partner's system will function as the server (the computer that will be controlled), and the other will function as the client (the computer from which commands will be issued). Decide the role each of you will take.

1. On the client computer, select **Start | All Programs | Accessories | Communications | Remote Desktop Connection** to display the Remote Desktop Connection dialog box, shown in Figure 6-14.

Figure 6-14: Remote Desktop Connection dialog box

2. In the Computer box, enter the IP address of the server computer, and then click the **Connect** button to display the Log On screen of the server computer.

3. Log on to the server computer with the user name and password your instructor provides.

4. You should be able to see the Desktop of the server computer, and its IP address should display in the Remote Desktop tab across the top of your screen. Notice that the tab contains Minimize, Maximize/Restore and Close buttons. You can click the Minimize button in the tab to see the display from your own (client) system.

5. Notice that an Unlock Computer screen displays on your lab partner's monitor. When you establish a remote desktop connection and log on to the server computer, all control of that computer is passed to you.

6. On the (server) Desktop, double-click **image.tiff** to open the Windows Picture And Fax Viewer.

7. Click the **Minimize** button in the Remote Desktop tab. This step minimizes the display of the server computer and displays your own Desktop.

8. Click the **Remote Desktop** button in the taskbar to redisplay your partner's Desktop.

9. Click the **Close** button in the Remote Desktop tab to disconnect the Remote Desktop Connection session.

10. Click **OK** to end the session.

11. Direct your lab partner to log back on.

12. Direct your lab partner to close the **Windows Picture And Fax Viewer** window.

You have now used VNC and Remote Desktop Connection (a part of Microsoft Terminal Services) to control a remote computer. How do these programs compare with each other? Which was easier to use? Which gives you more control?

Instant Messaging

instant messaging (IM)
A computer-based method of communication in which users can type and view messages sent to one or more recipients, and view the responses immediately.

Instant messaging (IM) is a computer-based method of communication in which users can type and view messages sent to one or more recipients, and view the responses immediately. Unlike e-mail, which can be sent whether the recipient is online or not, instant messages can be sent only to contacts who are currently online (that is, signed in to an instant messaging service).

Instant messaging can also be used to send files, view photos, send Web links, and talk to contacts (if your computer is equipped with a microphone and sound card).

Instant messaging is very popular in the workplace, allowing employees to "chat" without leaving their desks or using their telephones. You can also save long-distance telephone charges by sending instant messages to remote employees rather than calling. Because most instant messaging services allow for conversations among more than two people, you can in effect hold a conference via instant messages.

To use instant messaging, you must install an instant messaging client on your system and then sign up for service. Instant messaging allows you to specify a list of contacts (often called a buddy list or a contact list) with whom you want to communicate. When you log on to your instant messaging service, the status (online or not) of each of the contacts in your list will display. To open an instant messaging session, you specify an online contact and open a window in which you and your contact can type messages that both of you can see.

Instant messaging became extremely popular in 1996 when a company called Mirabilis introduced a free instant messaging utility called ICQ. When you sign in to your instant messaging service, your client communicates with an ICQ server, sending it your IP address and the port number on your computer that is assigned to the ICQ client. Your client also sends the names of everyone in your contact list to the ICQ server. The ICQ server then creates a temporary file with the connection information for you and your contacts.

The server also checks to see whether your contacts are currently logged on. If so, the server sends a message back to your ICQ client with the connection information for your online contacts and displays their status as "online." The server also sends a message to your online contacts notifying them that you are online.

Today, there are several IM services, clients and servers in use. Yahoo!, MSN and AOL use their own proprietary protocols and clients. Instant messaging clients are available from a variety of sources, including the following:

- AOL Instant Messenger (*www.aim.com/*)
- Netscape AOL Instant Messenger (click the AIM icon in the Netscape Navigator toolbar)
- Yahoo! Messenger (*http://messenger.yahoo.com/*)
- MSN Messenger (*http://messenger.msn.com/*)
- Windows Messenger (included with Windows XP; uses the same protocol as MSN Messenger)
- ICQ Instant Messenger (*http://web.icq.com/*)

triallian

Gaim is a multi-protocol instant messaging application for Linux, BSD, Mac OS X and Windows operating systems. It is compatible with AIM, ICQ, MSN Messenger, Yahoo!, Internet Relay Chat (IRC), Jabber, Gadu-Gadu and Zephyr clients. Gaim allows you exchange instant messages with users on various other clients (such as AOL, Yahoo! and MSN) simultaneously. You can download Gaim for Windows at *http://sourceforge.net/*.

OBJECTIVE:
1.7.11: Network communications privacy

It is important to note that instant messaging is not a secure method of communication. You should never transmit sensitive information (credit card numbers, user names and passwords, etc.) in an instant messaging session. It is equally important to note that, like company e-mail, instant messaging conducted at work may be considered company property. Instant messages display in pop-up boxes on the status bar (unless a recipient has turned off that option). Is it realistic to expect that instant messaging conducted on the job will be private?

Following are some instant messaging services that include security features:

- J.I.M. or JXTA Instant Messenger (*http://jxtaim.sourceforge.net/*) is a server-free instant messaging system that features encrypted messaging.

- The NNIM project (*http://nnim.sourceforge.net/*) supports multiple IM protocols and offers encrypted messaging.

spim
Spam that is delivered through instant messaging.

Instant messaging has also given rise to **spim**, which is spam delivered through IM rather than through e-mail. Because instant messaging is immediate, users are more likely to click links, making IM an effective channel for spammers. Because instant messaging bypasses antivirus software and firewalls, it is also an easy way to spread viruses. You can protect yourself against spim by blocking messages from anyone not on your contact list.

In the following lab, you will create a Windows Messenger instant messaging account, add a contact and send instant messages. Suppose the members of your department are located in various parts of your office building. You can use instant messaging to communicate in real time with co-workers who do not work near you, and you can communicate without others overhearing your conversations.

Lab 6-12: Using the Windows Messenger instant messaging client

OBJECTIVE:
1.7.9: Instant messaging

In this lab, you will sign up for Windows Messenger, create a contact list and send instant messages. A lab partner is required for this lab. You need a .NET Passport account to use Windows Messenger. Because you created a Hotmail e-mail account in a previous lesson, you already have a passport.

1. First, you will sign up for Windows Messenger. Select **Start | All Programs | Windows Messenger** to display the Windows Messenger window, then click the **Click Here To Sign In** link. This step displays the .NET Passport Wizard.

2. Click **Next** three times, then enter your Hotmail e-mail address and password. Click **Next**, then click **Finish**. This step uses your .NET Passport as a sign-in name and signs you in to the Windows Messenger service.

3. If you are prompted to install a newer version, select **Yes**, click **OK**, and follow any necessary steps to install and run the new version. When installation is complete, you will be signed in to Windows Messenger. Your Windows Messenger window should display as shown in Figure 6-15.

Run: stts services

Figure 6-15: Signing in to Windows Messenger

4. Next, you will create a contact list. In the **I Want To** section of the Windows Messenger window, click **Add A Contact** to launch the Add A Contact Wizard.

5. Click **Next**, then type your lab partner's Hotmail e-mail address. Click **Next**, then click **Finish**. These steps add your lab partner as a contact. Notice that your contact appears to be offline.

6. A message box such as the one shown in Figure 6-16 should display on your screen.

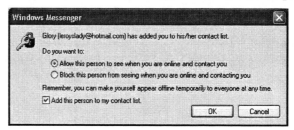

Figure 6-16: Adding Windows Messenger contact

7. If a message box does not display on your Desktop, check your taskbar for a second Windows Messenger button, then click the button to display the message box. Notice that you have the ability to block people from seeing when you are online, and you can indicate yourself as offline at any time.

8. Click **OK** to specify that you want your status to appear as online. A pop up window should display informing you that your lab partner is now online. Your lab partner's status should also show as online in your Windows Messenger window.

9. Next, you will send instant messages. In the Windows Messenger window, double-click your online contact, type a brief message, and then click the **Send** button (or press **ENTER**).

10. When you receive the message from your lab partner, Windows Messenger will play a sound, display a pop-up box on the status bar that contains the text of the message, and flash a message button in the taskbar. Your Desktop should appear similar to the one shown in Figure 6-17.

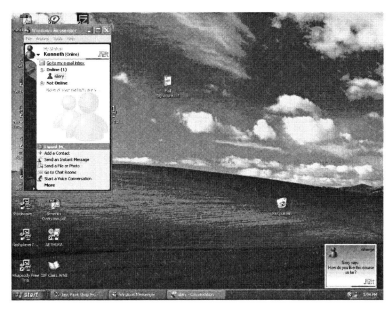

Figure 6-17: Receiving instant message

11. Click the **Conversation** button in the taskbar to open a Conversation window that displays the message. Type a response, and then click the **Send** button. This step sends a reply to your lab partner.

12. Experiment with Windows Messenger. Add other classmates as contacts. Click **Tools | Options** in the Windows Messenger window to see the options you can specify for the ways instant messaging will function on your system.

13. Close any open **Conversation** windows.

14. In the Windows Messenger window, select **File | Sign Out** to log off the instant messaging service.

15. Close the **Windows Messenger** window.

What is your opinion of instant messaging? Can you see the ways it can be used in a business setting? Is it easy to use? Would you prefer to use instant messaging or the telephone?

Windows Remote Assistance

OBJECTIVE:
1.7.8: Terminal
services clients

Windows Remote Assistance is a service that allows a user to seek assistance from another person in a remote location. This service involves allowing a trusted person at the remote location to connect to your computer and view your screen. Remote Assistance is used in conjunction with Windows Messenger (or e-mail), enabling the remote person to offer real-time assistance via instant messaging. When you accept a connection from a remote assistant, your Desktop displays on the remote computer. The remote person can send you messages with directions for performing a task, you can perform the task, and the results will display on both your computer and the remote station, allowing for instant feedback. Your remote partner can request to take control of your computer. However, you are free to decline any and all help. Even if you allow your remote partner to take control, you can halt remote control at any time by pressing the ESC key. Both computers must be running Windows XP in order to use Remote Assistance.

OBJECTIVE:
1.7.10: Peer-to-Peer
(P2P) services

**peer-to-peer
network**
A network in which
each computer has
both server and
client capabilities.

P2P
A peer-to-peer
network on the
Internet.

Peer-to-Peer Networks

By now you should be familiar with the client/server architecture used in networks. The client/server model is also used on the Internet. The client sends a request to the server, which processes that request and delivers the information. In a **peer-to-peer network**, however, each computer has both client and server capabilities. That is, each computer has the same capabilities as any other member of the network, and each one can open a communication session with any other member of the network.

On the Internet, a peer-to-peer (referred to as **P2P**) network allows a group of users to connect with each other and directly share files among their hard drives. P2P is advantageous because it is very inexpensive and allows all the users to share their bandwidth. That is, you can share the load of distributing files among all the members of the network.

Sharing MP3 files

You have probably heard of Napster, a service that allowed free file sharing. Napster is a P2P application, developed in 1999 by then-19-year-old Shawn Fanning, that enabled millions of users to share music (in MP3 format) across the Internet. Users installed the Napster application on their computers, which enabled the computers to act as miniature servers that allowed users to obtain files from other Napster users. As users logged on to the Napster Web site, they would indicate which MP3 files were available on their own systems. The central servers at Napster created and maintained a vast directory of song files and the IP addresses at which they were available.

Napster created a public controversy over the legality of file sharing because shared MP3 files contained copyrighted music, for which permission to use, borrow or share was never sought. Owners of the songs were not paid for access to them. A court order handed down in March 2001 forced Napster to halt sharing of more than 100,000 copyrighted songs. Napster now charges a nominal per-song fee to download MP3 files.

Other Web-based applications for sharing MP3 files include Gnutella, Napigator, Wrapster, Gnapster (open source) and Macster (for Macintosh).

The major difference between Gnutella and Napster is that instead of maintaining a central database, users on the Gnutella network find songs using a distributed query. Using Gnutella, you type the name of a song you want to find (query), and you enter the IP address of at least one other computer on the Gnutella network. Your query is sent to that computer, that computer searches its hard drive for the file, then sends the query to another computer on the network, and so on. The query is thereby distributed among thousands of users on the network. A Napster peer-to-peer network uses a server to direct requests, whereas a Gnutella network is server-free.

Peer-to-peer networks in business

P2P power is not limited to sharing music files. Corporations are beginning to consider P2P as a way for employees to share files directly, eliminating the cost and maintenance associated with a centralized server. P2P allows companies to utilize the otherwise dormant processing power of each employee's computer. P2P also allows businesses to exchange information with each other directly, without having to maintain servers to provide FTP access.

OBJECTIVE:
1.7.11: Network
communications
privacy

IBM, Intel and Hewlett-Packard are currently exploring ways to standardize and commercialize peer-to-peer technology. In order to protect privacy and sensitive materials, companies will be able to control access to information, and will be able to password-protect files.

Many large corporations (such as Intel, Amerada Hess and Boeing) have been using peer-to-peer technology to maximize processing power and even eliminate the need for mainframes. Many universities and research organizations have been using peer-to-peer networks for years.

BitTorrent is a P2P application used for downloading huge files (more than a gigabyte). Red Hat Linux uses it so that users can download files faster (*http://torrent.dulug.duke.edu*). Red Hat runs it on Linux, but a Windows version is also available. One of the interesting features of BitTorrent is that it has a built-in mechanism to ensure that people who participate share their bandwidth and the files they download. That is, it prevents people from merely taking advantage of the system. You can read about BitTorrent at *http://bitconjurer.org/BitTorrent.*

OBJECTIVE:
1.7.13: LDAP

Lightweight Directory Access Protocol (LDAP)

Lightweight Directory Access Protocol
A protocol that allows a network entity to access a directory service listing.

Lightweight Directory Access Protocol (LDAP) is an Internet protocol that allows users to locate organizations, people or other resources on a network, whether that network is a corporate intranet or the public Internet.

LDAP is a simplified version of Directory Access Protocol, which is part of the X.500 standard. The X.500 standard defines the structure of global directories in a network. The X.500 standard is too complex to be supported over the Internet or on desktop computers. LDAP, which supports TCP/IP, makes global directory service available to everyone.

An LDAP directory, which can be distributed among a collection of servers called Directory System Agents, contains contact information (name, address, e-mail, public keys, and so on). You can use an LDAP directory to locate people. For example, you can search for all people in the city of Detroit with the first name Margaret who have e-mail addresses.

You can access large public LDAP servers such as Infospace (*www.infospace.com*) and Bigfoot (*www.bigfoot.com*) on the Internet to find people, organizations and e-mail addresses. Universities and corporations may also use large LDAP servers. Smaller LDAP servers can be set up for workgroups. LDAP allows organizations to keep a centralized, up-to-date address book that anyone can access.

Modern e-mail clients such as Outlook, OS X Mail, Eudora, Netscape, QuickMail Pro and Mulberry are capable of searching an LDAP directory.

OBJECTIVE:
1.7.5: Concurrent
Versions System
(CVS)

Concurrent Versions System (CVS)

Concurrent Versions System (CVS)
A tool that allows programmers to control different versions of the pieces of a program as those pieces are developed.

Concurrent Versions System (CVS) is a popular development tool for programmers working on Linux or other UNIX-based systems. CVS is also known as a version control system.

CVS is a tool that allows programmers to control different versions of the pieces of a program as those pieces are developed. CVS maintains a single copy of each piece of source code, and also keeps a record of all the changes that have been made. The code is kept in a repository. A developer can specify which version is desired, and CVS will reconstruct that version using the recorded changes.

CVS is usually used to track each developer's work individually, but it can also be used to manage and merge the work of a team of developers into a common repository. Each developer exclusively accesses a piece of code (as one would check out a library book), works with the code, and then returns it to the repository. Changes to the code can be made through the use of a *commit* command.

In a rapid software development environment, CVS allows developers to use the latest (debugged) versions of their co-workers' code while developing their own portions, allowing a large program to be developed in a much shorter period of time than it would take if Developer D had to wait for Developer C's part to be completed, and Developer C had to wait for Developer B, and so on.

Communicating Effectively over the Internet

Just as there are various guidelines for using e-mail in a professional and productive manner, there are points to consider when using other Internet services.

OBJECTIVE:
1.8.1: Etiquette for Internet-based communication

Netiquette

As you learned in a previous lesson, netiquette encourages common sense and politeness, and establishes general rules for Internet etiquette. The guidelines you learned for e-mail etiquette apply to all forms of Internet-based communication. Those guidelines include the following:

- Use business language in all work-related messages.
- Messages or posts have permanence and may be printed or forwarded to other people.
- Check your spelling and proofread your message before sending or posting it.
- Typing in all capital letters connotes shouting or anger.
- Readers do not have the benefit of tone of voice and facial clues to help understand the intended meaning or tone of your messages.
- Instant messages can display in pop-up boxes on the status bar. Messages should be kept professional and appropriate while at work.
- Respond immediately to messages and posts sent to you, and think clearly about what you write.
- Using emoticons in e-mail messages or newsgroup postings is not considered a professional practice.
- Common Internet acronyms and abbreviations, such as LOL (Laughing Out Loud) or BRB (Be Right Back), may be unfamiliar to some people.

OBJECTIVE:
1.8.2: Ethical issues for Internet-based communication

Internet ethics

Internet technology allows us to communicate on a personal level with people we may not know. The ethical issues that apply to face-to-face communication also apply to Internet-based communications.

- Online chat and instant messaging sessions are not secure. Never send credit card or password information to another user.

- Instant messaging and chat rooms make communication easy and anonymous. Remember that when you are in an online chat room with other users whom you do not know personally, you only know what they choose to tell you (which may be true or false). Do not provide personal information, such as your Social Security number or your address, to unknown sources.

- You should not ask other users to divulge personal information via these sessions.

- Some people like to adopt online personalities that are different from the way they act face-to-face. If you are in a chat session, are you required to tell only the truth? Are you required to be yourself?

- Parents or older siblings should warn children carefully about the dangers of online chat. Predators lurk on the Internet. Children should never disclose their full names, ages, addresses or school names to people they do not know.

As you have also learned in this lesson, you can use various Internet services to download freeware, shareware and other files from FTP servers and personal systems in peer-to-peer networks. You should consider the following points when using these Internet services:

- Shareware is not free. You can download it for free and try it; if you like it and intend to keep using it, you are expected to forward the indicated fee.

- Copyright laws protect original works of authorship online as well as in print. Works of authorship include literary works (including computer programs); musical works; pictorial, graphical and sculptural works; motion pictures and other audiovisual works; sound recordings; and architectural works. Downloading songs and movies from the Internet or a peer-to-peer network is an illegal use of copyrighted information.

- Plagiarizing online content (copying someone else's written work and presenting it as your own) is illegal and unethical, just as it is with printed books. Using information that you find on the Web in research papers is permissible if you cite the work properly, just as you must do with material you find in a printed publication.

- If you publish your own Web page or otherwise make information available via the Internet, be careful about its content. Any writing or picture that you publish that subjects another person to public contempt or ridicule can be considered libel and may make you vulnerable to a lawsuit or prosecution.

Avoiding harassment

OBJECTIVE: 1.8.3: Sexual harassment

Sending threatening e-mail or instant messages is illegal, just as if the threats were made via telephone. Use good judgment when composing a message. E-mail is permanent, and the text of an instant message can also be saved to a file.

Sometimes harassment is not as obvious as sending a threat. Some people may take offense at material you think is humorous. Think carefully before forwarding jokes or cartoons. Remember that your recipients may forward your jokes non-judiciously to others, who in turn might take offense.

Sending instant messages to someone who does not want to be contacted can also be considered a form of harassment. Although users can set their status to offline and block messages from certain people, not all users know how to use these options. Some IM programs, such as AOL Instant Messenger, provide tools for recipients to issue warnings to users who send unwanted correspondence. Receiving warnings can inhibit your ability to use instant messaging services.

Although sending jokes via e-mail is generally an accepted practice, remember that not everyone wants to receive multiple forwarded jokes a day from you. Ask your intended recipients whether they want to receive such communications regularly. If not, be courteous and respect requests that you do not send such messages.

Creating effective messages

When sending e-mail or instant messages, or posting messages to newsgroups, be sure to create messages that are pertinent, appropriate and brief. Be certain that you have communicated your ideas clearly and concisely. Sending a lengthy message takes up other people's time, and many recipients find long messages irritating and difficult to follow.

Including an e-mail thread (a record of the discussion) can be helpful when sending messages back and forth. If the information in the thread is no longer applicable, consider starting a new thread to continue a discussion.

Blogging

A Web log, or **blog**, is a collection of personal thoughts posted on a public Web site. A blog is essentially an electronic journal or public diary. The act of adding to a blog is known as blogging.

blog
A collection of personal thoughts posted on a public Web site. Blogging is the act of adding entries to a blog.

The following are attributes of a common blog entry:

- It consists of brief, informal thoughts focused on a specific topic.

- It reflects the personality of the author in a unique way.

- It can contain links to other authors or sites.

Some individuals add to their blogs daily, whereas others add to blogs only when moved by a particular event or issue.

Personal and group blogs

Although blogging began as an expression of private feelings and events, community blogs have also become popular. In a community blog, all participants express their perspectives without any attempt at coming to a consensus.

Many people look forward to reading the next installment of a blog. Blogs have become a form of intellectual stimulation as well as entertainment. Many blogs provide an opportunity to collaborate and interact with the participants on the Web site.

Blog sites

Blog sites are becoming more popular and numerous. As of the time of this writing, more than 11,000 Web logs were registered at *http://globeofblogs.com* alone. While blogs are personal, many are dedicated to professional interests, art, literature, and so on.

You can search for blogs using Web search engines such as Google or Yahoo!, or you can explore Web log directories such as the ones in the following list. These sites are search engines dedicated to finding blogs of various individuals and groups:

- *http://portal.eatonweb.com*

- *www.weblogs.com*

- *www.blogit.com/Blogs*

Blog directories are becoming available all over the Web, and many categorize blogs by subject matter, similar to the way newsgroups are categorized. Some blog sites you might want to visit include:

- **Blogger** (*www.blogger.com*) — a common blog site sponsored by Pyra Labs, the most famous purveyor of blogger software.

- **Slashdot** (*www.slashdot.org*) — a news site that also allows users to post reactions to stories collected by its editor, Rob Malden.

Troubleshooting Using TCP/IP Tools

OBJECTIVE:
1.9.5:
Troubleshooting
connectivity issues

Now that you have used various Internet services, you should be familiar with a few basic tools for troubleshooting problems with your Internet clients. All Internet communications are handled through TCP/IP, and certain diagnostic tools use IP addresses to discover information within a TCP/IP network. You can use the following TCP/IP commands and tools to assist with basic troubleshooting:

- ipconfig
- ping
- tracert

The *ipconfig* command

The Windows XP ipconfig utility (Internet protocol configuration) is used to display your system's IP configuration. To use this command, type *ipconfig* at the command prompt and then press ENTER to display your system's IP address. You can use this command when you are using remote control services and need to enter the IP address of the system you want to control.

The *ping* command

The ping utility (Packet Internet Groper) tests connectivity between source and destination systems. To use this command, type *ping ip_address* (where ip_address is the IP address of the destination computer) at the command prompt and then press ENTER. If a reply is received, then a connection exists between your computer and the computer at the IP address you specified. You can use this command to ensure connectivity between two systems.

The *tracert* command

The Windows tracert utility can determine the path between a source and destination system. That is, it will display all the IP addresses between your system and the destination system, and it will locate failures along the path that may interrupt service. The *tracert* command also displays information about the travel time for each stage of the path from the source to the destination. To use this command, type *tracert ip_address* at the command prompt and then press ENTER. You can also use this command with a host name.

In the following lab, you will use TCP/IP diagnostic tools to test connectivity. Suppose that your co-worker is unable to connect to the CIWcertified Web site. You can use these diagnostic tools to test her computer's connectivity.

Lab 6-13: Using TCP/IP diagnostic tools

In this lab, you will use the ipconfig, ping and tracert utilities to test for basic connectivity.

1. Select **Start | Run**. Type *cmd* in the Open box, then press **ENTER** to open a command window.

2. At the command prompt, type *ipconfig*, and then press **ENTER**. Write your IP address in the space provided:

   _____

3. Exchange IP addresses with a classmate and write your classmate's IP address in the space provided:

   _____

4. At the command prompt, type *ping ip_address* (where ip_address is the IP address of your classmate's computer) and then press **ENTER**. Were you able to successfully ping your classmate's computer?

5. At the command prompt, type *tracert 12.42.192.73* and then press **ENTER**. How many hops were required to reach the *www.CIWcertified.com* site? Your display should resemble Figure 6-18.

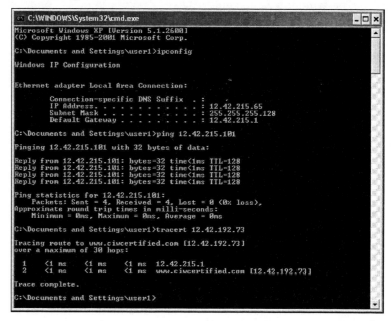

Figure 6-18: Using TCP/IP diagnostic tools

6. Close the command window.

Case Study

These Are Sensitive Files

The contracts manager at a company needs to make a large legal document available to an overseas customer. However, the document contains sensitive information, it is too large to send via e-mail, and the manager is expecting an amended document in return.

The contracts manager must make the document available in electronic format to only himself and the customer.

- First, the contracts manager sets up an FTP account that requires user names and passwords. He gives these user names and passwords to the customer and instructs her not to divulge the account information to anyone. He reveals authentication information to the customer only across a secure channel (or in person).

- Next, the contracts manager sets up a folder on the company FTP site into which the sensitive document may be uploaded. He ensures that only users with specific permissions can access the folder.

- The contracts manager now gives the customer permissions to upload and download files to and from this folder.

*   *   *

As a class, consider that the information is extremely sensitive. Suppose someone may try to gain access by "sniffing" the FTP passwords during authentication. How could you further secure this file? Could you use S/FTP to secure the file? Could you use FTPS?

Lesson Summary

Application project

Now that you have used several methods for downloading files from FTP servers, which did you find to be the easiest? How does downloading files through an FTP client compare with retrieving files from a Web server using HTTP? Is FTP faster? Is it more difficult to use? Do you think that FTP is the best way to get information from your computer onto the Internet? What other options are available?

Suppose your company is considering changing its current e-mail client, Microsoft Outlook Express, to Microsoft Outlook 2003. Your manager has asked you to report on other Outlook 2003 users' opinions about the product. Use Google Groups (*http://groups.google.com*) to find and access a newsgroup forum about Microsoft Outlook 2003. What would you report to your manager?

Skills review

In this lesson, you used a news client, you used Telnet, and you used FTP to transfer files to and from your computer. You also managed downloaded content by defining MIME types and using compression utilities. You used VNC and Microsoft Terminal Services to control a remote computer, and you used instant messaging to communicate with your lab partner. You discussed the function of peer-to-peer networks, LDAP and CVS, and reviewed methods for communicating effectively over the Internet. You also used TCP/IP tools to troubleshoot connection problems.

Now that you have completed this lesson, you should be able to:

✓ Use a news client.

✓ Use Telnet.

✓ Use FTP.

✓ Manage downloaded content.

✓ Use Virtual Network Computing (VNC) and Microsoft Terminal Services.

✓ Use instant messaging applications.

✓ Identify the functions of peer-to-peer networks.

✓ Identify the functions of LDAP.

✓ Identify the functions of Concurrent Versions System (CVS).

✓ Troubleshoot Internet problems using TCP/IP tools.

Lesson 6 Review

1. How are FTP servers structured, and how do you navigate them?

   _____

   _____

   _____

   _____

2. What FTP command do you use to place files on an FTP server?

   _____

3. Which types of files are not significantly reduced in file size by compression utilities?

   _____

   _____

4. How can using peer-to-peer networks save company resources?

   _____

   _____

   _____

5. What is a blog?

   _____

   _____

Lesson 7:
Internet Security

Objectives

By the end of this lesson, you will be able to:

- Identify the three types of encryption.
- Identify ways that authentication provides Web security.
- Identify ways that firewalls provide Web security.
- Identify malware (malicious software).
- Identify ways to detect and prevent virus attacks.
- Define spyware.
- Define patches and updates.
- Identify ways that screen savers provide workstation security.
- Define list servers and listserve groups.
- Identify security-related ethical and legal issues faced by IT professionals.

Pre-Assessment Questions

1. What is the most secure method for sending information over the Internet?

    a. Using encryption
    b. Using passwords
    c. Using patches
    d. Using spyware

2. Firewalls prevent unauthorized access to or from:

    a. the Internet.
    b. the World Wide Web.
    c. private networks.
    d. public networks.

3. What is malware?

    _____

    _____

    _____

Introduction to Internet Security

The Internet is a network of shared information and resources. The connectivity that makes the Internet possible also makes systems vulnerable to unwanted activity. This lesson will identify Internet security issues that IT professionals must be familiar with in order to protect their companies' systems.

Encryption   *32, 64, 128 bit*

OBJECTIVE:
1.10.1: Major encryption types

1.10.2: Authentication, digital certificates, encryption, firewalls

1.10.3: Data confidentiality, data integrity, non-repudiation

Most business Web pages encourage you to subscribe to, register for or purchase products or services over the Internet. These pages usually solicit personal or confidential information. If you submit information in a Web form, such as the form in Figure 7-1, how do you know that your personal data will be securely transmitted? Will a credit card number be stolen? Will a home address be exploited? Sending sensitive information across the Internet may seem unsafe. However, Web transactions are at least as secure as traditional transactions in which consumers give their credit cards to waiters in restaurants or supply credit card numbers to vendors over the phone. What prevents a waiter or a phone vendor from stealing the credit card number?

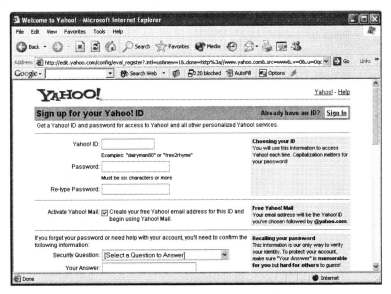

Figure 7-1: Web page personal information form

In an effort to make online transmission of sensitive data more secure, many businesses use encryption. As you have learned, encryption is the process of converting data into an unreadable form of text. Encryption is the primary means of ensuring data security and privacy on the Internet. For e-commerce businesses, the mere presence of encryption increases consumer confidence.

key
A variable value, such as a numeric code, that uses an algorithm to encrypt and decrypt data. Some applications encrypt and decrypt with the same key, whereas other applications use a pair of keys.

Encryption applications dramatically reduce the risk of information theft by scrambling the information using mathematical algorithms. Encrypted data is referred to as ciphertext; unencrypted data is referred to as plaintext.

Encrypted text cannot be read without the correct encryption **key**. Only the intended recipient of the information has the key to decrypt, or decipher, the data you supply. Because encrypted text is unreadable by anyone who does not possess the correct key, data encryption helps secure online transactions by ensuring the confidentiality and integrity of the data supplied by the customer.

       Version 1.0

Three types of data encryption exist: symmetric-key encryption, asymmetric-key encryption and hash encryption.

Symmetric-key (secret-key) encryption

symmetric-key encryption
An encryption method in which the same key is used to encrypt and decrypt a message.

Symmetric-key encryption (also called symmetric encryption or secret-key encryption) is an encryption method in which the same key is used to encrypt and decrypt a message. The message sender uses a key (generated by an encryption application) to encrypt the message; the sender forwards a copy of the key to the message recipient, who uses the same key to decrypt the message. It is critical that the secrecy of the key be maintained by the sending and receiving parties in order for symmetric encryption to be effective. If the key is acquired by a malicious third party (such as during the key exchange between sender and recipient), the third party can use the key to decrypt the message and even pretend to be the message sender.

When you want to use symmetric-key encryption to communicate with your intended recipients, you should use asymmetric encryption (presented in the next section) to send the key.

For all encryption types, the 128-bit encryption standard is considered to be high-level encryption, although much more powerful keys exist (for example, 512-bit key standard).

Asymmetric-key (public-key) encryption

asymmetric-key encryption
An encryption method in which two keys (the private key and public key) are used to encrypt and decrypt a message.

Asymmetric-key encryption (also called asymmetric encryption or public-key encryption) refers to an encryption method in which two keys are used to encrypt and decrypt a message: a private key and a public key. The public key is known to all sending and receiving parties involved in the communication, whether via Web browsers, e-mail or instant messaging. The private key is used by the recipient to decrypt the message. Therefore, the private key must be kept secret.

The sending and receiving parties must share a public key in order to use asymmetric-key encryption. For example, when Sarah wants to send a secure message to Tina, Sarah uses a shared public key to encrypt the message. When Tina receives the message, she must use her own private key to decrypt the message. As long as Tina keeps her private key secure, only Tina will be able to decrypt her messages. When Tina wants to send a secure message to Sarah, Tina uses a shared public key to encrypt the message. When Sarah receives the message, she must use her own private key to decrypt the message.

In asymmetric-key encryption, the public and private keys are mathematically related so that only the public key can be used to encrypt messages, and only the corresponding private key can be used to decrypt them. Asymmetric-key encryption provides a high level of data confidentiality because it is nearly impossible for a malicious third party to decipher the private key, even if the third party knows the public key. Asymmetric-key encryption also provides a high level of data integrity because as long as the private key remains private, a malicious third party cannot alter the data before it reaches the intended recipient.

The RSA algorithm

RSA is the most common asymmetric encryption algorithm. It was developed in 1977 by Ronald Rivest, Adi Shamir and Leonard Adleman. RSA is included in the Microsoft Internet Explorer and Netscape Navigator Web browsers, as well as in Lotus Notes, Intuit Quicken and many other products. RSA Security (*www.rsasecurity.com*), which owns the encryption algorithm, licenses the algorithm technologies. RSA has evolved into the standard for Internet encryption, and is included in existing and proposed Internet, Web and computing standards.

Hash (one-way) encryption

hash encryption
An encryption method in which hashes are used to verify the integrity of transmitted messages.

hash
A number generated by an algorithm from a text string.

Hash encryption (also called one-way encryption) is an encryption method in which hashes are used to verify the integrity of transmitted messages. (You learned about data integrity and data confidentiality in a previous lesson.) A **hash** (also called a message-digest) is a number generated by an algorithm from a string of text. The generated hash value is smaller than the text itself, and is generated in such a way that it is nearly impossible for the same hash value to be generated from some other text. The hash is as unique to the text string as fingerprints are to an individual.

Hash algorithms are often used to encrypt and decrypt digital signatures (presented later in this lesson), which are used to authenticate message senders and recipients. The hash algorithm transforms the digital signature into a hash value. When a sender transmits a message, both the digital signature and the hashed digital signature are sent to the recipient, along with the message (which itself should be encrypted using symmetric or asymmetric encryption). Using the same hash algorithm that the sender used, the recipient decrypts the digital signature to derive another hash value, and then compares it with the hashed value that was sent by the sender. If the hashed values are the same, the recipient can be confident that the message integrity remained intact. The hash algorithm verifies that the digital signature was not secretly decrypted, altered and re-encrypted during transit from sender to receiver.

Another use for hash encryption is to protect passwords from disclosure. A malicious third party cannot re-engineer the hash through a hash algorithm to decrypt a password. When a user enters a password to access a secure Web site or intranet, the password is encrypted and compared to the stored hashed password in the Web server. If the values match, then access is permitted. Once the password is hashed, the process cannot be reversed. Thus, hashing is always a one-way operation. Hash encryption is not useful for data confidentiality, because the encrypted data cannot be decrypted.

Hash algorithms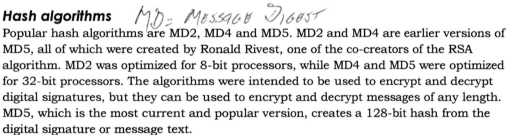

Popular hash algorithms are MD2, MD4 and MD5. MD2 and MD4 are earlier versions of MD5, all of which were created by Ronald Rivest, one of the co-creators of the RSA algorithm. MD2 was optimized for 8-bit processors, while MD4 and MD5 were optimized for 32-bit processors. The algorithms were intended to be used to encrypt and decrypt digital signatures, but they can be used to encrypt and decrypt messages of any length. MD5, which is the most current and popular version, creates a 128-bit hash from the digital signature or message text.

Another popular hash algorithm is the Secure Hash Algorithm (SHA), which creates 160-bit hashes. Because SHA produces longer hashes than those produced by MD5, it is more secure from attacks than MD5.

Movie Time!

Insert the CIW Foundations Movie CD to learn even more about this topic.

Encryption (approx. playing time: 05:30)

All movie clips are © 2004 LearnKey, Inc.

Authentication

OBJECTIVE:
1.10.2:
Authentication,
digital certificates,
encryption, firewalls

As you learned in a previous lesson, authentication is the process of verifying the identity of a user who logs on to a computer system, or the integrity of transmitted data. Authentication is usually performed through the use of digital certificates, and user names and passwords.

User names and passwords

Requiring user names and passwords is the most common way to authenticate users on private and public computer networks, including the Internet. User names and passwords provide a measure of Web security because the user must enter the correct user name and password to gain access to the Web server. However, user names and passwords can often be forgotten, intercepted, or accidentally revealed, which diminishes their reliability. For this reason, digital certificates are likely to become the standard authentication method on the Internet.

digital certificate
A password-protected, encrypted data file containing message encryption, user identification and message text.

Digital certificates

A **digital certificate** is a password-protected, encrypted data file that verifies the identity of the sender of a message. It is attached to an electronic message and guarantees that the data has not been compromised during transmission. A digital certificate must be signed by a certificate authority to be valid. Digital certificates provide data integrity.

digital signature
An electronic stamp added to a message that uniquely identifies its source and verifies its contents at the time of the signature.

Digital certificates are issued by a certificate authority (CA) or internal security administrators. A CA is a trusted third party that verifies the identity of the person or company that submitted a certification request (CR). A digital certificate contains the requestor's name, a serial number, expiration date, a copy of the requestor's public key and the digital signature of the CA (so the requestor can verify that the certificate is legitimate). A **digital signature** is an electronic stamp that identifies a message's source and its contents. A digital signature can be used with any kind of message, whether it is encrypted or not.

non-repudiation
The security principle of providing proof that a transaction occurred between identified parties. Repudiation occurs when one party in a transaction denies that the transaction took place.

To verify your identity, you can attach your own digital signature to any message or data you send over the Internet. Digital signatures do not provide data confidentiality because they do not encrypt the data; they simply verify the integrity of the data and the identity of the sender. However, digital signatures enforce **non-repudiation**, which is the ability to prove that a transaction occurred. Sending data with a digital signature proves that the message was both sent and received. Neither party can repudiate the transaction.

Firewalls

OBJECTIVE:
1.10.2:
Authentication,
digital certificates,
encryption, firewalls

A **firewall** is a security barrier that prevents unauthorized access to or from private networks. Businesses use this combination of hardware, software and corporate policies to prevent Internet users outside the business from accessing proprietary data on the business's networks that are connected to the Internet, as well as private intranets. Firewalls are also used to control employee access to Internet resources.

firewall
A security barrier that controls the flow of information between the Internet and private networks. A firewall prevents outsiders from accessing an enterprise's internal network, which accesses the Internet indirectly through a proxy server.

The most common business firewall technique uses a firewall server in conjunction with a proxy server to screen packets of data. All data entering or leaving an organization passes through the firewall. The firewall examines each packet and determines whether to forward it to its destination, based on security policies set up by the firewall administrator or IT department. The proxy server replaces the network IP address with another, contingent address. This process effectively hides the network IP address from the rest of the Internet, thereby protecting the network.

When you connect your computer to the Internet, you are potentially connecting to all the computers on the Internet. This relationship works in reverse as well: All other computers on the Internet are connected to yours, and perhaps to all the computers on your corporate LAN.

Some LANs feature Web servers or FTP servers that provide confidential or proprietary files to users on the LAN. If the LAN is on the Internet, anyone outside the business who knows the domain name or IP address of the server could access these files. Often, these files have no encryption or password protection because the administrators of the Web or FTP servers did not know the LAN was accessible to the Internet.

By connecting to the Internet through firewalls, no computer on the LAN is actually connected to the Internet, and any requests for information must pass through the firewall. This feature allows users on the LAN to request information from the Internet, but to deny any requests from outside users for information stored on the LAN.

Firewalls can be inconvenient for business users who are protected by them. For example, users may be unable to access an external e-mail provider or to upload files to external servers. Some standardized Internet plug-ins, such as RealAudio, cannot function through firewalls. Some of the new video plug-ins used on news Web sites are also unable to operate through firewalls. If your employer's firewall interferes with work you need to conduct on the Internet, you should work with your IT department's firewall administrators to achieve a level of protection that allows you to access necessary resources.

Security policies are a vital part of any firewall strategy. The policies created by firewall administrators govern who will be allowed external access, what information employees will have access to, how often passwords must be changed, and so forth. Hardware and software alone cannot protect information from employees determined to hurt the company, but hardware, software and sensible security policies can protect proprietary data and internal communications from malicious outsiders.

Firewalls can be considered the first line of defense against LAN security breaches because they provide data confidentiality. Firewalls do not ensure data integrity or non-repudiation because they do not encrypt or authenticate data.

Desktop firewalls

Desktop firewalls are available for individual client workstations. Also known as personal firewalls, they offer protection for an individual system instead of an entire network. Tools such as Symantec Norton Personal Firewall (*www.symantec.com*), Zone Labs ZoneAlarm Pro (*www.zonelabs.com*) and BlackICE PC Protection (*http://blackice.iss.net*) can detect and respond to attacks on your computer system. Desktop firewalls offer many firewall features, such as inspection of all incoming transmissions for security threats. When a firewall is used in conjunction with antivirus software (which will be presented later in this lesson), a personal computer is very secure, provided that the user updates the antivirus and desktop firewall software frequently.

Native desktop firewall software

Increasingly, operating system vendors are providing native desktop firewall software. For example, Windows XP includes a native desktop firewall that is disabled by default. You can enable the firewall and customize your desktop firewall settings.

UNIX and Linux systems often provide applications that allow you to block connections, such as the following examples:

- **iptables** — found on newer UNIX and Linux systems

- **ipchains** — found on older UNIX and Linux systems

Desktop firewall features
Some desktop firewalls include the following features:

- **Logging** — You can determine when a connection was made, as well as its source. You can also discover the protocol and/or port a remote user used to make the connection.

Internet Control Messaging Protocol (ICMP)
A subset of Internet Protocol that is most often used to determine whether a computer can communicate with the rest of the network.

- **Blocking protocols** — You can block various protocols, including Transmission Control Protocol (TCP), User Datagram Protocol (UDP), **Internet Control Messaging Protocol (ICMP)** and Internet Protocol (IP). If blocking TCP and UDP, you can select any port to allow or disallow. ICMP is an especially common protocol to block, because attackers often use it to flood network connections. However, blocking this protocol may cause problems when troubleshooting your computer's connectivity to the network, because ICMP is most often used to test whether a system is able to communicate on a network.

Default desktop firewall stances
Desktop firewalls can be configured in one of the following ways:

- **Default open** — allows all traffic except that which is explicitly forbidden

- **Default closed** — denies all traffic except that which is explicitly allowed

Blocking incoming and outgoing traffic
Desktop firewalls can also be configured to block incoming and outgoing traffic. Most desktop firewalls block incoming traffic (for example, traffic from the Internet to your computer). Most desktop firewalls can also be configured to block traffic from your computer to computers on the network. If you are experiencing connection difficulties specific to one protocol on your local network, consider that a desktop firewall might be blocking transmissions.

In the following lab, you will explore the options to consider when enabling a desktop firewall. Suppose you are the security administrator for a bank. The bank manager has asked you to protect employees' computers by restricting access to Internet resources. How would you configure the desktop firewalls to offer appropriate protection but still allow employee access to relevant Internet resources?

 Lab 7-1: Enabling your desktop firewall

In this lab, you will enable your desktop firewall.

1. Minimize any open windows so that the Windows XP Desktop is visible.

2. Click the **Start** button, right-click **My Network Places**, then click **Properties**. This step displays the Network Connections window (Figure 7-2). The Local Area Connection icon that displays represents your system's network interface card (NIC).

*Note: If My Network Places does not display in the Start menu, open **Windows Explorer** and right-click **My Network Places** in the Folders pane, then click **Properties**.*

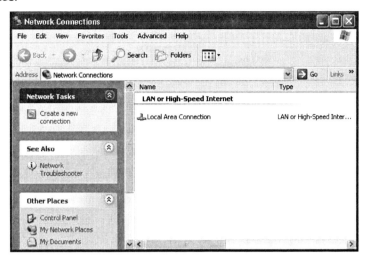

Figure 7-2: Network Connections window

3. Right-click the **Local Area Connection** icon, click **Properties** to display the Properties dialog box, then click the **Advanced** tab.

4. Select **Protect My Computer And Network By Limiting Or Preventing Access To This Computer From The Internet**, then click the **Settings** button. This step enables your desktop firewall and displays the Advanced Settings dialog box (Figure 7-3). You can use the tabs in this dialog box to customize the firewall settings.

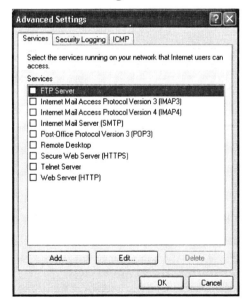

Figure 7-3: Advanced Settings dialog box

5. Click each tab in the Advanced Settings dialog box. Notice that in the Services tab, you can specify the services running on your network that Internet users can access. In the Security Logging tab, you can specify logging options. In the ICMP tab, you can specify the Internet requests to which your computer will respond.

6. Click the **Cancel** button twice to close the dialog boxes without enabling your desktop firewall, then close the Network Connections window.

Malware (Malicious Software)

Malware, or malicious software, refers to programs or files whose specific intent is to harm computer systems. Malware is an electronic form of vandalism that can have global implications. IT professionals must be aware of malware to be able to detect and remove malicious code before it causes harm to systems and networks. Malware includes computer viruses, worms, Trojan horses and illicit servers, each of which will be discussed in this section.

Viruses

OBJECTIVE:
1.10.4: Computer virus attacks

A **virus** is a malicious program designed to damage computer systems, from stand-alone computers to entire networks. Specifically, a virus is a program that assumes control of system operations, and damages or destroys data. Viruses are loaded onto your computer without your knowledge and run without your consent. All computer viruses are man-made and are often designed to spread to other computer users through networks or e-mail address books.

virus
A malicious program that replicates itself on computer systems, usually through executable software, and causes irreparable system damage.

Viruses can be transferred via e-mail attachments, program or file downloads, and disk or CD swapping. In most cases, the creator or user of the source media containing the virus is unaware of its presence. For example, a virus might have written itself onto every floppy disk that you used. If you pass an infected disk to a colleague, that colleague's system can also be infected. Similarly, a colleague might inadvertently send you an e-mail attachment infected by a macro virus. If you attempt to open or print the file, the virus will engage. E-mail attachments have become the most effective way to spread viruses.

Viruses that reside within the text of an HTML-formatted e-mail message are particularly virulent because the user need only receive the virus for it to cause damage. The next time the virus recipient starts the computer, the virus runs and is sent to everyone in the recipient's address book.

A simple virus can:

- Display harmless messages on the screen.

- Use all available memory, thereby slowing or halting all other processes.

- Corrupt or destroy data files.

- Erase the contents of an entire hard disk.

More dangerous viruses can have devastating effects on a global scale. For example, the Chernobyl (CIH) virus infected 32-bit Windows 95/98 and Windows Server executable files, which caused computers to lose their data. In Korea, it affected approximately 1 million computers and caused more than US$250 million in damage. The VBS Love Letter virus overwrote Windows files with common file name extensions (such as .gif and .ini) on remote and local drives, replaced the files' contents with the source code of the virus, and appended the .vbs extension to the files. All infected files were destroyed. The Melissa virus infected Microsoft Word documents and was sent to the first 50 people in the recipient's Microsoft Outlook Address Book. The virus inserted text into infected documents once every hour after the number of minutes corresponding to the date had passed (if the document was opened or closed at the appropriate time).

Table 7-1 describes types of computer viruses.

Table 7-1: Computer virus types

Virus Type	Description
Boot sector virus	Moves boot sector (an area of a disk that stores essential files needed by the computer during startup) data to another part of the disk and replaces it with its own code. Whenever the computer starts up, the boot sector virus executes.
Bomb	Resides on the hard disk and is activated when a particular event occurs, such as a date change, a file change or a user or program action.
Cluster virus	Makes changes to a disk's file system. Any program run from an infected disk causes the virus to run, giving the impression that the virus infects all programs on the disk.
File-infecting virus	Infects program files on a disk. When the infected program is run, the virus also runs.
Macro virus	Infects a specific type of document file that can include macros (codes, commands, actions or keystrokes that produce a result), such as Microsoft Word or Excel files. When a document containing a macro is opened, the virus runs.
Stealth virus	Resides in the computer's memory and conceals changes it makes to files, hiding the damage from the user and the operating system.

Worms

OBJECTIVE:
1.10.10: Virus vs. worm

worm
A self-replicating program or algorithm that consumes system resources.

A **worm** is a self-replicating program or algorithm that consumes system resources. The difference between a worm and a virus is that a worm does not alter files; it resides in active memory and replicates itself until an entire disk is full. Worms can spread to all computers connected to a network and are commonly spread over the Internet via e-mail attachments.

For example, the PE_Nimda.A-O worm was spread as an executable file attachment in e-mail messages. The PE_Nimda.A-O worm did not require a user to open the e-mail attachment; it exploited a weakness in Microsoft e-mail clients and executed the file automatically. As this worm has shown, TCP/IP networks are particularly vulnerable to worm attacks. Worms rely on specific software implementations. For example, Win32/Melting.worm attacks only Windows systems running Microsoft Outlook. This worm can spread by itself and can disable any type of Windows system, making it permanently unstable.

Trojan horses

Trojan horse
A program disguised as a harmless application that actually produces harmful results.

A **Trojan horse** is a program that appears to be harmless but actually produces harmful results. Trojan horses contain code that produces malicious or harmful results within applications that appear benign, such as computer games. Unlike worms and viruses, Trojan horses do not replicate themselves or copy themselves to other files and disks. A Trojan horse may be spread as part of a computer virus.

One of the most sinister Trojan horse types is a program that claims to find and destroy computer viruses, but introduces viruses into your system instead.

Illicit servers

illicit server
An application that installs hidden services on systems. Illicit servers consist of "client" code and "server" code that enable the attacker to monitor and control the operation of the computer infected with the server code.

An **illicit server** is an application that installs hidden services on systems. Many illicit servers, such as NetBus and Back Orifice (a play on Microsoft's Back Office), are remote control or remote access programs.

Illicit servers differ from Trojan horses in that they consist of "client" code and "server" code. The client (the malicious third party that is attacking a system) can send the server code as an unsolicited file attachment via e-mail, Internet chat and newsgroup messages to users, hoping that they will open the file and install the application. If the users who receive the server code install the application (intentionally or otherwise) and connect to the Internet, the attacker can use the client code's remote control capabilities to monitor and control the operation of the infected computers.

An illicit server can be made to look like a patch or a program fix (which will be presented later in this lesson), so that recipients think they have received a legitimate file. Attackers can use illicit servers to perform malicious operations on infected computers, such as:

- Creating custom startup messages.

- Editing the Windows registry files.

- Sending messages.

- Changing the Desktop display.

- Playing sounds.

- Switching off the display screen.

- Disabling keyboard keys.

- Hiding the mouse cursor.

- Hiding the taskbar.

- Stealing passwords.

- Monitoring keystrokes.

- Restarting the computer.

- Locking up the computer.

- Executing applications.

- Viewing the contents of files.

- Transferring files to and from the computer.

Virus Detection and Prevention

Corporate IT departments are often the first line of defense against computer viruses. Generally, the IT department will receive warnings about viruses that are being spread, and will have time to prepare for virus detection and subsequent disinfection.

Common ways that computer viruses are contracted include:

- Receiving an infected disk from someone else and reading it from your disk drive.

- Downloading an infected file or program to your computer from a network computer, an intranet or the Internet.

- Downloading an illicit server attachment from a malicious source.

- Copying to your hard disk a document file infected with a macro virus.

OBJECTIVE:
1.10.4: Computer
virus attacks

Following are some actions you can take to protect your systems from contracting viruses:

- Do not open e-mail messages or attachments from unknown senders.

- Configure the security settings for your e-mail program and Web browser to the highest possible levels.

- Use an antivirus software program to periodically scan e-mail attachments, files, programs, software or disks (even new software from a trusted source) before you open or use them on your computer.

- Use an antivirus software program to scan your disks and files if you use them on another computer.

- Use an antivirus software program to scan all files and programs you download from the Internet.

- Keep your antivirus software current by downloading virus signature updates as they become available.

- Stay informed about the latest virus threats so that you recognize an e-mail virus before you open and unleash it.

- Make backup copies of important files and store them on separate disks so that the files will be unaffected if you contract a virus.

Antivirus software

antivirus software
Software that scans
disks and programs
for known viruses
and eliminates
them.

The best protection against a virus is to know the origin of each program or file you install on your computer, or open from your e-mail or instant message client. Because this is difficult, you should use **antivirus software** to scan e-mail attachments and files for known viruses, and eliminate any it finds.

In general, viruses can be detected when they modify parts of your system in order to pass themselves along. When a virus has been detected, you must use antivirus software to disinfect your system. Antivirus software that is kept current knows the signature of the virus, and works by scanning the infected file or program for the identifying signatures. If the virus is found, your hard drive can often be disinfected immediately so that the virus cannot infect other files or cause more damage. Most antivirus programs download signature profiles of new viruses automatically so that the program can check for the new viruses as soon as they are discovered.

If your company has an IT department, it will probably provide and update antivirus software for you. If you work for a company without an IT department, you can download antivirus software from many Web sites. Trend Micro (*www.trendmicro.com*), Network Associates (*www.networkassociates.com*) and Panda Software (*www.pandasoftware.com*) are three providers of antivirus software. Another antivirus software company, Symantec (*www.symantec.com*), provides the Symantec Security Response page (*www.symantec.com/avcenter/*), which identifies the latest virus threats. You can also obtain information about virus threats at the Trend Micro Security Information page (*www.trendmicro.com/vinfo*). All of these Web sites are excellent sources of information about current viruses.

Unexpected attachments

OBJECTIVE:
1.10.6: Unexpected
e-mail attachments

Because e-mail is the most common method for spreading viruses, you should be wary of any unexpected attachments you receive with e-mail or instant message transmissions.

Following are some actions you can take if you receive an attachment you did not expect or do not recognize:

- Do not attempt to open the attachment.

- Try to contact the message sender and determine whether the attachment is legitimate.

- If you are unable to contact the sender or the sender is unaware of the attachment, delete the attachment from the message.

- Open your Deleted Items folder and delete the attachment from it to permanently remove the attachment from your system.

Virus attacks

If your computer is attacked by a virus, do not panic. Most viruses can be removed without permanent damage to your system, and most viruses can be halted even after they commence an attack.

OBJECTIVE:
1.10.7: Suspected
attacks

Following are some actions you can take if you suspect a virus attack:

- Use antivirus software to remove the virus immediately.

- If the virus is active in memory and you are not able to launch the antivirus software, turn off your computer and reboot from a known clean system disk. This procedure will start the system without the virus in memory. You should then be able to launch the antivirus software and begin the disinfection process.

- Check all your disks and backup files with the antivirus software, and remove the virus from them if necessary.

- If files or programs are damaged or altered by the virus, you will need to replace them with backup copies or reinstall programs from original installation media.

- Because viruses can self-replicate, you must find and remove all copies of the virus in your system. Use the antivirus software to scan your entire system and disks for the virus and remove it.

- If damage is widespread, you may be forced to reformat your hard disk and reload all your programs and files. However, this technique should be used as a last resort because most antivirus software is very effective at disinfecting systems, even for difficult-to-remove viruses.

OBJECTIVE:
1.10.11: Spyware

Spyware

spyware
A software
application secretly
placed on a user's
system to gather
information and
relay it to outside
parties, usually for
advertising
purposes.

Spyware (or adware) is a software application that is secretly placed on a user's system to gather information and relay it to outside parties, usually for advertising purposes. Many Internet-based applications contain spyware. Companies with both good and bad reputations have included spyware code in their software. Spyware can also be placed on a user's system by a virus or by an application downloaded from the Internet. Once installed, spyware monitors the user's activity on the Internet and conveys the information to the spyware originator. The originator can then gather Web site usage, e-mail and even password information from the user, then use it for advertising purposes or malicious activities.

Spyware is analogous to the Trojan horse in that it is installed automatically without the user's knowledge or consent. Legitimate data-collecting programs that are installed with the user's knowledge are not considered spyware, as long as the user provides consent, and knows the type of data being collected and to whom it is being conveyed. For example, cookies are data-collecting programs that store information about Internet use and reside on users' systems. Users generally know about cookies and their functions, and users can disable outside access to cookie information.

Spyware can also affect the efficiency and stability of computer operations by consuming memory resources and bandwidth. Because spyware is an independent executable program, it has the ability to:

- Scan files on hard drives.

- Read cookies.

- Monitor keystrokes.

- Install other spyware applications.

- Change the default home page in Web browsers.

- Automatically send information to the spyware developer.

Removing spyware helps ensure privacy by preventing companies from tracking your Internet activity and collecting your personal information.

Detecting and blocking spyware

You can detect the presence of spyware by obtaining a spyware detection application. Such applications work much like antivirus applications in that they scan a computer's hard drive, memory and network connections, and look for suspicious activity. These applications can be updated, just like an antivirus application can be updated.

Network and systems administrators can detect the presence of spyware by doing the following:

- Using a network analyzer to capture and study network transmissions for suspicious packets.

- Using the netstat application to review all ports. (Netstat is a TCP/IP utility that reads network data structures.) If the administrator finds a suspicious port open on your system, he or she can conduct a Web-based search on that port. The administrator may discover that it is a port used by spyware installed on your system.

You can combat spyware by:

- Deleting the application that contains the spyware.

- Using a desktop firewall to block transmissions between your system and the spyware vendor.

Spyware detection applications and false positives

Spyware detection applications use the following strategies:

- They contain lists of known spyware.

- They contain programming that can detect suspicious activity, which includes Windows registry entries that are out of place, suspicious network connections, and applications that behave suspiciously.

Spyware detection applications can report false positives, wherein legitimate applications are incorrectly categorized as spyware. As you use a spyware detection application, ensure that you examine the results carefully so that you do not remove legitimate applications.

In the following lab, you will install the Ad-aware spyware detection software. Suppose you are the IT administrator for a small family-run business. Several employees have complained that their default Web browser home pages have been changed without their input, and their computers have been running more slowly than they usually do. You suspect that they are victims of spyware, so you install spyware detection software to find and remove the spyware applications.

 Lab 7-2: Installing and using spyware detection software

In this lab, you will install and use Ad-aware spyware detection software.

1. Open **Windows Explorer** and navigate to the **C:\CIW\Internet\LabFiles\Lesson07** folder.

2. Double-click **aaw6.exe** to display the Ad-aware 6 Personal Installation Wizard.

3. Follow the installation instructions in the wizard to install Ad-aware 6 Personal on your system.

    Note: If you do not have access to the aaw6.exe binary in the data folder, complete the following steps to install Ad-aware 6 Personal on your system:

    - *Start your browser.*

    - *Type the URL **www.lavasoft.de/support/download** in the Address box, then press ENTER. This step accesses the Lavasoft Download Web page.*

    - *Scroll down the page and click a link for a site that accesses the Ad-aware 6 installation binary.*

    - *You will be forwarded to an external site, with a link to the software. Download the Ad-aware installation binary to your Desktop.*

    - *Display the Windows XP **Desktop**, double-click the installation binary (**aaw6.exe**) and follow the instructions to complete the installation.*

4. Display the Windows XP **Desktop**, then double-click the **Ad-aware 6.0** shortcut to launch the application and display the Ad-aware 6.0 Personal window (Figure 7-4.)

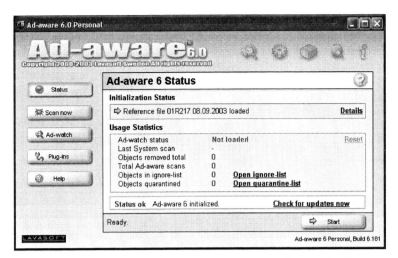

Figure 7-4: Ad-aware 6.0 Personal spyware detection application

5. Click the **Start** button, then click **Next** to perform an initial scan, which will look for spyware applications and suspicious activity.

    Note: The scan may take several minutes, depending upon the size of your hard drive and speed of your system.

6. When the scan is finished, click the **Show Logfile** button to display the list of spyware that the scan found on your system.

7. Scroll through the log file. Notice that some legitimate applications were marked as spyware. In these cases, you are probably viewing false positives.

8. Close the log file, then click **Next** to display the scanning results.

9. Double-click each entry and read it. Take note of any software that might be spyware.

    *Note: Do **NOT** click **Next**, as this would remove all apparent spyware applications. You do not want to remove these applications unless you are absolutely certain they are spyware.*

10. Close the Ad-aware 6.0 Personal window and the Windows Explorer window.

11. As a class, answer the following questions:

    •   Did you find any false positives?

    •   What spyware did you find?

    •   How can removing spyware improve privacy?

    *Note: For additional information about how to use Ad-aware (including technical support), access the **www.lavasoftsupport.com/index.php** Web page.*

OBJECTIVE:
1.10.5: Client
software patches
and updates

update
A file or collection of
tools that resolves
system liabilities and
improves software
performance.

patch
Programming code
that provides a
temporary solution
to a known
problem, or bug.

Updates and Patches

An **update** is any file or collection of software tools that resolves system liabilities and improves software performance. A **patch** is a file of programming code that is inserted into an existing executable program to fix a known problem, or bug. Patches are designed to provide an immediate solution to a particular programming problem and can often be downloaded from the Web site of the software vendor. However, patches are intended to be only temporary solutions until problems can be permanently repaired.

Generally, a software vendor will provide permanent solutions to program bugs in later product releases, known as updates. Updates are released periodically when deemed necessary by the vendor. A major update with significant software improvements is often marketed as a new release.

Patches and updates should never be applied to all system units without applying them to test computers first. In fact, many security policies require an extensive testing process before an update is installed onto any systems. If the patches or updates do not address the problems your system is experiencing, or if there would be no performance gain by applying them, you should not install them. Patches and updates can cause incompatibility issues among system resources or applications, and can even introduce new security issues. However, if your system is vulnerable to a security problem, you may need to install the patches or updates as soon as possible.

Make sure that you obtain patches or updates from trusted sources, especially if the program is an open-source upgrade. Verify hashes and signatures before installing upgrades to avoid installing a virus onto your system.

Antivirus program updates

Antivirus program updates generally refer to files containing virus signature profiles that have become known since the last program update. Updates are important because even the best antivirus program will not protect you if its signature profiles are outdated.

Antivirus software uses signature profiles to recognize patterns that indicate viruses. Because new viruses are created so rapidly, manufacturers update these signature profiles frequently. Most antivirus software will download the latest profiles automatically.

Encryption levels and Web browsers

Software applications and Web browsers support various encryption levels. Many Web sites require that your browser use 128-bit encryption for added security. The latest versions of both Internet Explorer and Navigator support 128-bit encryption. If you are using earlier versions of either browser, you can download updates to support 128-bit encryption.

Desktop security

It is important to maintain the security of individual computers, particularly because most computers in the workplace are connected to corporate networks, intranets and the Internet. Computers running older operating systems (such as Windows 95/98 or Windows NT) may no longer be supported with security patches, thereby leaving them vulnerable to intrusion. For newer computers (2000 or later), it is important to apply regular operating system patches and updates supplied by software vendors to minimize security breaches.

E-mail clients

As you have already learned, e-mail is the most common way to spread viruses. You should keep your e-mail client current, and install necessary security patches and updates to minimize security breaches. Additionally, many e-mail clients default to 40-bit encryption levels. You can install updates to support 128-bit encryption.

Screen Savers

OBJECTIVE:
1.10.9: Workstation
screen saver
security

A **screen saver** is a utility program that displays images or animation on your monitor when no keystrokes or mouse actions have occurred for a specified duration. You can use screen savers to hide your work while you are away from your desk, providing a measure of security. Some system screen savers allow you to password-protect your screen saver. If you configure this feature, then once your screen saver activates to hide your Desktop, your specified password must be entered to deactivate the screen saver.

screen saver
A graphic or moving image that appears on your screen when your computer is idle.

In Windows XP, you use the Screen Saver tab of the Display Properties dialog box (Figure 7-5) to specify a screen saver and the amount of time your computer is to remain idle before the screen saver activates.

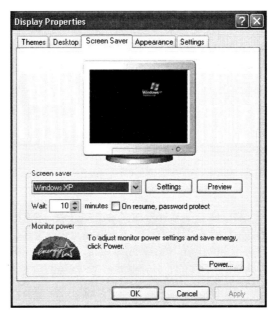

Figure 7-5: Display Properties dialog box — Screen Saver tab

In the following lab, you will activate a screen saver. Suppose you are an IT administrator and you want to update computer security measures in your company. One of the first tasks you perform is instructing employees to set their screen savers to display no longer than five minutes after their computers are idle. Would you recommend that users password-protect their screen savers for additional security? For which types of job roles are password-protected screen savers appropriate?

Lab 7-3: Activating a screen saver

In this lab, you will specify a screen saver and the amount of time your computer needs to remain idle before the screen saver appears on your Desktop.

1. Right-click a blank area of the Windows XP **Desktop**, click **Properties** to display the Display Properties dialog box, then click the **Screen Saver** tab.

2. Display the **Screen Saver** drop-down list, then click a screen saver of your choice.

3. Double-click the contents of the Wait text box, type *1*, then click **OK**. This step specifies that the screen saver will display when your computer has been idle for one minute.

4. Do not press any keys or move the mouse for at least one minute. The screen saver you selected should display on your screen.

5. When the screen saver displays, move the mouse to redisplay the Desktop.

6. Right-click a blank area of the Windows XP **Desktop**, click **Properties** to display the Display Properties dialog box, then click the **Screen Saver** tab.

7. Display the Screen Saver drop-down list, then click **Windows XP**. This step specifies the default operating system screen saver.

8. Double-click the contents of the Wait text box, then type *10*. This step specifies that 10 minutes is the amount of time your computer needs to remain idle in order for the screen saver to activate.

9. Click **OK** to close the dialog box and restore the screen saver to its default settings.

List Servers and Listserve Groups

OBJECTIVE:
1.10.8: E-mail
listserve groups

list server
A server that collects and distributes information from an authorized group of participants, called a listserve group.

listserve group
Users who subscribe to an e-mailing list through a list server.

A **list server** is a server that automates the collection and distribution of messages from an authorized group of participants, allowing collaboration among multiple users. A list server differs from a mail server, which handles incoming and outgoing e-mail for Internet users.

A group of users that subscribes to a mailing list is called a **listserve group**. Participants must send an e-mail to the list server to join a specific group. Once subscribed, they are placed on a mailing list of users authorized to receive messages from the list server. When a list server receives messages from listserve group participants, it stores the messages, then distributes them to its mailing list.

A user who wants to join a listserve group simply sends an e-mail message to the list server. This request is often a blank e-mail message with a simple request in the Subject field. A request can be worded as follows:

subscribe ciw

Some list servers request that the same command also be placed in the body of the e-mail message. If the list server is configured to allow a particular user to join, the list server then sends a confirmation e-mail to the subscriber. Occasionally, users will attempt to subscribe other people to listserve groups. To prevent this practice, list servers often require the user to confirm the subscription before he or she is added to the mailing list.

List servers typically forward e-mails, announcements, newsletters or advertising to group members on a regular schedule or as events occur.

Three of the most popular list servers are LISTSERV (*www.lsoft.com*), which is a product of L-Soft; Majordomo (*www.greatcircle.com/majordomo*), which is hosted by Great Circle Associates and is freeware; and Lyris (*www.connectweb.net/newfiles/lyris.html*). List servers forward e-mail messages that are addressed to their mailing lists to the list's respective listserve group.

A number of Web sites are devoted to mailing lists, such as Topica (*http://lists.topica.com*) and Yahoo! Groups (*www.yahoogroups.com*). You can use these sites to find mailing lists that you want to join. Topica and Yahoo! Groups are not list servers; they simply search for and provide links to mailing lists. The mailing lists themselves are hosted by list servers.

In the following lab, you will explore LISTSERV. Suppose you are the marketing director for a company. You want to distribute timely information to customers about your company's products. You purchase LISTSERV to create your own mailing list server so that you can distribute messages to all subscribers on your list (your customers) quickly and efficiently.

 Lab 7-4: Exploring LISTSERV

In this lab, you will access the LISTSERV Web page and explore various links to obtain information about LISTSERV.

1. Start **Microsoft Internet Explorer**.

2. Click anywhere in the **Address** box, type *www.lsoft.com*, then press **ENTER**. This step displays the L-Soft home page (Figure 7-6).

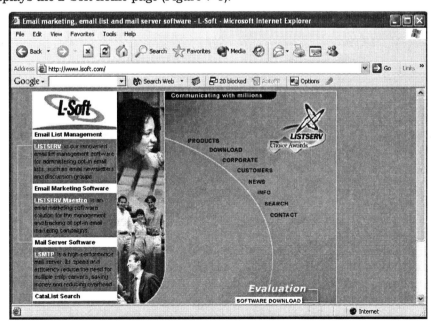

Figure 7-6: L-Soft home page

3. In the left pane, click the **LISTSERV** link to display the LISTSERV page.

4. Click the various links to obtain information about LISTSERV. If time permits, click the **Web Demo** link to display a demonstration of the LISTSERV Web interface. Click various links in the Demo page to obtain information about the latest product interface.

5. Close the **Web Demo** window and redisplay the browser window.

6. If time permits, click the **Free Download** link on the LISTSERV page to download one of the products. To use it, you will need to configure the software with the following information:

   • Full Internet host name by which the LISTSERV server will be known

   • All Internet domain names to which LISTSERV should respond

   • Full Internet host name of the computer through which Internet mail will be delivered

   • E-mail address of the user who will be in charge of operating the server

   • Password that will be used to validate special postmaster-only commands

   • Name of your organization

In the following lab, you will explore the Topica Web site. Suppose you are an IT project manager and you want to join mailing lists that pertain to project management topics so you can keep your skills current. You search the listings provided by Topica to determine which lists might be the most worthwhile for you to join.

Lab 7-5: Exploring Topica

In this lab, you will access the Topica Web site to find mailing lists about project management.

1. Click anywhere in the **Address** box, type *lists.topica.com*, then press **ENTER**. This step displays the Topica home page (Figure 7-7).

Figure 7-7: Topica home page

2. Scroll down to display the Search text box. Click anywhere in the box, type *project management*, then click the **Search** button. This step displays a page of mailing list links related to project management.

3. Click a project management link, then follow any additional links that display until you access a project management mailing list. Follow any instructions that grant you access to the e-mails that have been posted, then read several of them. How would you subscribe to the mailing list? How would you post a message to the mailing list?

4. Close the browser window.

Security-Related Ethical and Legal Issues

The main function of IT professionals in any organization is to provide network and Internet-related services, and to protect system resources from unauthorized entry, malicious attackers and malware. IT professionals are also faced with ethical and legal issues related to the security of network and individual computer use by employees. In addition, the Internet has brought about new challenges to copyright, trademark and licensing law enforcement. Because the Internet spans numerous countries and each government has its own set of rules, new enforcement techniques must be applied. This section discusses privacy concerns, copyright issues, licensing issues, trademark issues and encryption policies.

Privacy concerns

OBJECTIVE:
1.14.1: Privacy issues

1.14.2: Appropriate use issues

1.14.3: Personal privacy vs. company resources

One of the major drawbacks of networked computing and Internet use is that your computer activities and personal information are no longer private. For example, online businesses collect information from users who make purchases on the Internet, and may sell the information for advertising or marketing purposes.

Along with susceptibility to infection by malware, you may also be the recipient of junk e-mail (spam). Because spam is sent to you uninvited, it can be considered an invasion of privacy, even though it generally has no harmful effects on computer systems. However, reviewing and deleting spam may hinder your productivity.

Some actions you can take to minimize the spam you receive include the following:

- **Avoid adding yourself to unwanted mailing lists** — When you submit any type of online form, choose to not be added to a mailing list (unless you want to be added to the list). If such an option is not available, consider not submitting the form.

- **Conduct online transactions through secure Web sites** — Before you purchase anything over the Internet, ensure that the transaction is secure. Current Internet Explorer and Navigator versions will inform you whether a site is secure when you access the site. Remember that a URL beginning with *https://* ensures that your Web session is managed by a secure protocol, which encrypts and decrypts the information you send and receive during the course of the transaction.

- **Do not assume that only the intended recipient will read your e-mail messages** — Assume that whatever you write in an e-mail message could be seen by other people, particularly if you work for a company that routinely monitors its employees' e-mail. Even if your company does not monitor e-mail, the person to whom you send an e-mail message may forward it to others with your original message intact.

- **Be selective when posting information to newsgroups** — Remember that many newsgroups and chat rooms are unsupervised. When you post a message to a newsgroup, your e-mail address becomes available to all those who have access to the newsgroup or chat room at that moment, which can make you vulnerable to unwanted solicitations or virus attacks. Before posting any messages, monitor the newsgroup to determine whether the users seem trustworthy.

Some organizations monitor their employees' e-mail messages and restrict their access to certain Web sites. Employers sometimes adopt such a policy because they consider all information carried by the company's communication system to be company property, just as the network, communication equipment and software used by the employees are company property. However, by restricting access to certain Web sites, companies may be denying employees legitimate Internet resources that may help them do their jobs.

Reasons that some companies elect to monitor employees' e-mail messages or restrict Internet access include the following:

- To protect proprietary information

- To prevent users from viewing or downloading undesirable data or malware

- To ensure that resources are being used solely for business purposes

Network administrators can also audit the contents of employee hard drives. Cached files from the Internet (as well as personal document files you have created) may be subject to examination. Therefore, you should use your home computer to keep personal data and send personal e-mail messages, and use company resources only for work-related activities. For example, you may be trying to help a family member find a job. You may modify and format his or her résumé on your company computer, and spend time surfing the Web for employment-related sites. Are you using the resources provided to you for their intended purposes? Are you being paid to use company resources for personal business? Could the time you spend helping your family member be better spent on work-related tasks, which in turn help the business?

Copyright issues

OBJECTIVE:
1.14.4: Copyright
issues

As you learned in a previous lesson, copyright laws protect original works of authorship that are fixed in a tangible medium of expression. According to copyright law, the basic elements are:

- Expression.

- Originality.

An Internet user who uses an unauthorized copy of someone else's work is violating the copyright owner's rights. Remember that although copying text or images from a Web site is easy, the ability to do so does not make it legal to use someone else's work for your own purposes. Copyright infringement is a punishable crime.

Contrary to popular belief, an international copyright does not exist. To protect your copyright of your original material, you must contact the government agency that handles copyrights in the country in which you reside. For instance, in the United States, you would contact the Library of Congress Copyright Office. You can request the forms (depending on your specific work) by phone, or download forms at *www.loc.gov/copyright*. In Canada, you would contact the Canadian Intellectual Property Office (*http://cipo.gc.ca*).

If you or your company holds a copyright on your Web site material, you should place the copyright symbol (©) and year at the bottom of each page that contains the copyrighted material. Copyright symbols are not required but are highly recommended because they are often the first line of defense against copyright infringement.

Information Infrastructure Task Force (IITF)

The Information Infrastructure Task Force (IITF) was formed in 1993 to codify copyright law as it applies to digital information. The IITF in turn established the Working Group On Intellectual Property Rights to examine the intellectual property implications of combining the existing infrastructures of radio, television, telephones, fax machines and computers into one information infrastructure of all communication mediums. The group's mission was to make recommendations for changes to U.S. intellectual property law and policy.

In 1994, the Working Group On Intellectual Property Rights published the "Green Paper," a preliminary report on intellectual property rights. The group recognized the need to review current copyright laws in light of the fact that copying and disseminating information is extremely easy in the digital age.

World Intellectual Property Organization (WIPO)

The World Intellectual Property Organization (WIPO) is a specialized United Nations agency formed to protect intellectual property worldwide. Intellectual property consists of industrial property (trademarks, inventions) and copyrighted works. WIPO attempts to enforce copyright laws through cooperation among countries. More than 170 countries are currently members of WIPO.

If you register a copyright for a book in the United States, and someone reproduces and sells it in Germany without your permission, you would be able to prosecute that person in both the United States and Germany because both countries have signed copyright agreement documentation. The WIPO site (*www.wipo.org*) lists the copyright administration office for each member country.

Precedent copyright law and Internet cases

The following court cases have precedent-setting implications with respect to copyright laws and the Internet.

*   **Sega Enterprises Ltd. vs. MAPHIA** — In *Sega Enterprises Ltd. vs. MAPHIA,* Sega Enterprises brought suit against MAPHIA, an electronic bulletin board system (BBS). Sega Enterprises claimed that MAPHIA copied Sega games to its BBS and made them available for user downloads. The court found that MAPHIA sometimes charged users a direct fee for downloading privileges, or bartered for the privilege of downloading the Sega games. Because Sega's games are protected by copyright, MAPHIA violated Sega's copyright by obtaining unauthorized copies of Sega's games and placing them on storage media of the BBS to be downloaded by unknown users. The courts found in favor of Sega Enterprises.

*   **Playboy Enterprises vs. Frena** — In *Playboy Enterprises vs. Frena,* Playboy brought a lawsuit against the defendant George Frena, an independent BBS operator. Playboy claimed that Frena distributed unauthorized copies of Playboy's copyright-protected photographs from his BBS. Frena's BBS was available to anyone for a fee. Frena admitted that he did not obtain authorization from Playboy to copy or distribute the photographs. The courts found evidence of direct copyright infringement, and stated that the fact that Frena may not have known he was committing copyright infringement was irrelevant.

- **Recording Industry Association of America (RIAA) vs. Napster** — This copyright-infringement case was filed by the RIAA to contest the distribution of copyrighted music files over the Internet using a popular program called Napster. As you have learned, Napster allowed users who had installed the Napster software on their computers to share MP3 music files with other users who had the Napster software. No fee was charged for copying files from one user's computer to another. The RIAA wants artists and record companies to receive royalty payments from users who swap copyrighted files. Napster argued that, because the MP3 files were transferred from user to user and were never in Napster's possession, Napster did not act illegally. The courts ruled in favor of the RIAA and required Napster to halt its services. Napster (*www.napster.com*) is still operating but now charges a per-track or per-album fee. Record companies such as Bertelsmann Music Group (BMG) have since joined with technology developers to create subscription services that will allow users to share copyrighted MP3 files while observing a permission agreement. These arrangements allow artists and record companies to receive payment for their copyrighted music.

Licensing issues

If you want to license someone else's copyright-protected material, you must contact the copyright owner and ask for permission. This task might involve contacting the legal department of a large organization, a copyright specialist at a small to midsize organization, or even an individual.

If you are granted permission to use copyrighted work, the copyright holder dictates the terms of use. For example, there may be no cost but you may be required to credit the owner for the work. In most cases, you must license the work from the owner under the terms of an agreement. The agreement usually determines the way the work may be used (limited or unlimited reproduction) and the payment arrangement (royalties or one lump payment).

Trademark issues

A trademark is any word, slogan, symbol, name, package design or device (or any combination thereof) that marks and distinguishes a product from other products in trade. For instance, AltaVista and Rolls Royce are both trademarks. Trademarks are protected worldwide by participating WIPO countries.

To register a trademark, you must contact the government agency in your country that handles trademarks. For example, in the United States, you would contact the U.S. Patent and Trademark Office. You can request the forms by phone, or download forms online from *www.uspto.gov*. In Canada, you would contact the Canadian Intellectual Property Office at *http://cipo.gc.ca*.

Encryption policies

OBJECTIVE:
1.14.5: Company encryption policies

As you have learned, encryption is a very effective safeguard, but the amount of protection it offers varies based on the type of encryption used and the size of the key. Smaller keys, such as 40-bit keys, are easier to break than 128-bit or 256-bit keys. However, longer keys require more computational power to encrypt and decrypt data, which can slow transmission. It is imperative that companies protect their encryption keys to ensure secure transmissions.

Many businesses encrypt network transmissions in order to:

- Protect data.

- Prevent data from being intercepted by malicious outsiders.

- Deter hackers.

- Respond to customer or competitor pressure for increased security.

- Comply with government requirements regulating the security of Internet data transmissions.

Even if data transmissions do not warrant encryption, network administrators may still need to protect the privacy of e-mail messages, which often contain information of a proprietary or confidential nature. As you have learned, Web browsers such as Microsoft Internet Explorer and Netscape Navigator include S/MIME, which is based on RSA's asymmetric encryption algorithm. S/MIME describes the way that encryption information and a digital certificate can be included as part of the message body. Each e-mail message includes a digital signature, which the recipient must receive in order to decrypt the message.

Companies that conduct business internationally must be aware of the encryption laws in various countries. Some countries do not allow large encryption keys to be exported, which forces network administrators to implement encryption solutions that fall within legal guidelines.

When establishing company encryption policies, network administrators must determine the risk of sending unencrypted data based on the nature of the data and its risk to the company if it were obtained by unauthorized users. Encrypting data slows data communication because each packet of data must be encrypted and decrypted. If the data is proprietary or sensitive in nature, then encrypting transmissions becomes critical. If not, network administrators need not encrypt their transmissions.

Case Study
Protecting Networks

Roberto is the network administrator for an international law firm with offices and customers in North America, South America, Africa and the Middle East. The lawyers frequently contact each other via e-mail, use the Internet to research cases, and use listserve groups to discuss recent cases and developments in international law. Roberto wants to protect the company's network from malicious invasions, and limit the lawyers' access to the Internet and newsgroups.

Roberto performs the following tasks:

- He ensures that firewalls are in place to prevent outsiders from accessing proprietary data on the law firm's private network, and to prevent access to specific Internet resources.

- He installs antivirus software on all computers and prepares a maintenance schedule to periodically update the software with the most recent virus signature profiles.

- He assigns user names and passwords that the lawyers must use to access the network.

- He configures Web browsers and e-mail clients to reject incoming file attachments that do not have digital signatures or digital certificates.

- He educates the lawyers on the steps to take to prevent malware infection.

- He establishes encryption policies for sending sensitive information via e-mail.

                            *   *   *

As a class, discuss other ways Roberto can protect the law firm's network resources from outside attack. Which protective measures do you consider too restrictive? Discuss your reasons.

Lesson Summary

Application project

Some computer viruses have received worldwide attention because of the damage they have inflicted. The PE_Nimda.A-O and the infamous W97M.Melissa.A worms spread globally because they were contained in executable e-mail and newsgroup article attachments.

Access the Symantec Security Response page at *www.symantec.com/avcenter* or the Trend Micro Security Information page at *www.trendmicro.com/vinfo,* and research the PE_Nimda.A-O or W97M.Melissa.A worm or a more recent virus. For each virus, identify precautionary measures that you can take to prevent your company's network from becoming infected.

Skills review

In this lesson, you learned about symmetric-key, asymmetric-key and hash encryption. You studied the way user names and passwords, as well as digital certificates and firewalls, can provide Web security and ensure secure online transactions. You learned about viruses, worms, Trojan horses, illicit servers and spyware, and you studied methods you can employ to protect computers and networks from the harmful effects of viruses. You learned ways to protect your computer from virus attacks, steps to take when an attack is suspected, and steps to take when you receive an unexpected or unexplained file attachment.

You learned about patches and updates and their functions with regard to antivirus programs, Web browser encryption levels, desktop security and e-mail clients. You also learned the ways that screen savers can provide a measure of workstation security.

Finally you learned about list servers and how to manage your participation in listserve groups. You also learned about the privacy concerns, copyright issues, licensing issues and trademark issues facing IT professionals, as well as the need to encrypt company transmissions and establish company encryption policies.

Now that you have completed this lesson, you should be able to:

- ✓ Identify the three types of encryption.
- ✓ Identify ways that authentication provides Web security.
- ✓ Identify ways that firewalls provide Web security.
- ✓ Identify malware (malicious software).
- ✓ Identify ways to detect and prevent virus attacks.
- ✓ Define spyware.
- ✓ Define patches and updates.
- ✓ Identify ways that screen savers provide workstation security.
- ✓ Define list servers and listserve groups.
- ✓ Identify security-related ethical and legal issues faced by IT professionals.

Lesson 7 Review

1. What is the difference between symmetric-key encryption and asymmetric-key encryption?

_____

_____

_____

2. What is a digital certificate?

Password protected data file

_____

_____

3. What is a firewall?

Security barrier

_____

4. What is the difference between a virus and a worm?

virus damages files
worm replicates & fills available space

_____

5. What is the difference between malware and spyware?

malware harms systems
secretly placed on system to gather & send
info

6. What is the difference between a patch and an update?

Patch - fixes particular problem - temporary
updt - could include patch & other info

_____

7. Describe the purpose of a list server.

bulk email

_____

_____

Lesson 8:
IT Project
Management

Objectives

By the end of this lesson, you will be able to:

- ↯ Identify project management fundamentals.
- ↯ Identify project management skills.
- ↯ Identify the five project management phases.
- ↯ Define the project triangle.
- ↯ Identify the value of project management software.
- ↯ Create a project schedule.
- ↯ Identify the value of documenting projects.
- ↯ Identify the value of planning and scheduling meetings.
- ↯ Identify the value of reviewing projects.
- ↯ Identify quality assurance techniques.
- ↯ Identify the business implications of IT decisions.
- ↯ Identify project management certifications and resources.

Pre-Assessment Questions

1. What is scope creep?

    Changes from the orig plan that "creep" into the scope of the project

2. Why do the executing phase and the controlling phase of a project usually overlap?

    _____

    _____

    _____

    _____

    _____

3. What is the project triangle?
    a. The relationships among project scope, time and money.
    b. The relationships among the planning, executing and controlling phases of project management.
    c. The relationships among project tasks, resources and assignments.
    d. The relationships among the planning skills, organizational skills and communication skills needed by good project managers.

Overview of IT Project Management

Business and project management skills are becoming increasingly important for IT professionals to master. Failed IT projects can put significant strain on business resources and can adversely affect an organization's bottom line. Poor project management is one of the primary reasons for IT project failure.

Businesses are starting to realize that successfully managed IT projects increase productivity, yield a greater return on investment, increase profits, and improve customer service and satisfaction. In fact, many organizations are starting to require project management skills for IT job advancement.

IT projects differ from other projects in one significant way. The IT department manages a business's data, which may include proprietary product data, customer and vendor data, financial data, personnel data, and so forth. Therefore, IT projects may involve several different systems. As an IT project manager, you must be able to work with these various systems and the individuals involved with them. IT projects can include hardware and software installations and upgrades, network security implementations, process improvements, training and support, and so forth.

This lesson will discuss project management fundamentals, and the importance that project management concepts and skills are gaining in IT job roles, particularly IT project leadership positions.

Project Management Fundamentals

project management
The practice of applying skills and processes to activities in order to meet deadlines and achieve desired results.

Project management is the practice of applying knowledge, skills and processes to activities in order to meet deadlines and achieve desired results. Project management skills can be applied to all industries and job roles. Whether you are creating a Web site, installing services and clients on your organization's computers, or creating courseware, the same basic project management techniques apply.

You have probably applied project management skills and techniques to projects you have undertaken. For example, before you purchase a new photocopy machine for your company, you assess the need for a new machine and the time frame within which you want it; you determine the brand and model that will best meet your company's needs; and then you contact vendors via telephone for price estimates. You then make the purchase. After the new photocopy machine is put to use, you may evaluate the decisions you made, as well as employees' level of satisfaction with the new machine.

Even though the steps involved in making such a purchase seem obvious, the relationships, phases and processes you use can be applied to all projects, large and small.

Defining project management terms

project
A sequence of tasks that must be accomplished within a certain time frame to achieve a desired result.

A **project** is a sequence of tasks that must be accomplished within a defined time frame in order to achieve a desired result. Projects differ from ongoing work operations in that projects are temporary and unique. A project has a start date and an end date, and it produces a specific deliverable, or end product. For example, the photocopy machine purchase project began when you were given the task of buying a new machine, and ended when you finalized purchase arrangements. Even if you purchased a new photocopy machine every year, each purchase cycle would be a temporary, unique, separate and distinct project.

task
A unit of work that must be accomplished during the course of a project.

resource
A person, department or device needed to accomplish a task.

assignment
The appointment of a specific resource to a specific task.

OBJECTIVE:
1.15.3: Project scope/scope creep

scope
The goals and tasks of a project, and the work required to complete them.

A **task** is a unit of work that must be accomplished during the course of a project. In the photocopy machine purchase scenario, tasks include determining the type of machine you need and contacting vendors for price estimates. A **resource** is a person, department or device needed to accomplish a project task. In the scenario, you, the vendor and your telephone can all be considered resources. An **assignment** is made when a resource is given a specific task to perform.

As a project manager (IT or otherwise), you will usually manage project elements such as:

- Schedules.
- Costs.
- Performance risks.

You use project management skills and techniques to control these project elements. You begin the project management process by creating realistic objectives and establishing the scope of the work to be completed.

Scope and scope creep

The end product or ultimate goal of a project, along with the tasks required to achieve that goal, constitute the project **scope**. In the photocopy machine purchase scenario, all the work required to research and make the purchase is included in the scope of the project.

Project scope varies depending on the complexity of the project and the number of tasks required to complete it. For example, developing a Web site is a project of greater scope than designing a company newsletter. You must consider the project's scope when planning a project of any size.

A common problem associated with project management is the tendency for the project's scope to increase over time. Any changes in the schedule, cost or performance required to complete the project can affect its scope. Issues often arise during the project that were not initially considered. You may be able to contain the scope of the project, but only by introducing subprojects, which also must be managed.

scope creep
Gradual increases in project scope that can undermine the success of a project.

Changes in project scope tend to occur in small increments, and therefore might seem negligible. However, small increases in scope will add up. These gradual increases are called **scope creep**. If you do not adequately manage scope creep, the success of your project may be compromised.

Project Management Skills

To effectively manage a project, you must have strong planning, organizational, communication and problem-solving skills. If you are a novice project manager, managing a part of a project is a good way to start. As you gain experience, you can manage bigger pieces and, eventually, take on the role of project manager for an entire IT project.

Earning project management certification can strengthen your project management skills. Two of the most recognized certifications are:

- The Project Management Professional (PMP) certification from the Project Management Institute (*www.pmi.org/info/PDC_CertificationsOverview.asp*).
- The IT Project+ certification from CompTIA (*www.comptia.org/certification/itproject/default.asp*).

The Project Management Professional (PMP) certification is the more widely known of the two and is geared toward various professions. The IT Project+ certification is geared specifically for IT professionals.

Planning skills

To plan a project well, you must be able to identify the tasks that constitute the project, understand the ways in which tasks are dependent upon one another, and know the ways that project dependencies will affect the project as a whole.

You must also make the most effective use of the people involved with the project, which includes the following:

stakeholder
A person or group with an interest in a project and the power to exert influence (either positive or negative) over the project and affect results.

- **Identifying the project stakeholders** — Stakeholders are people or groups that can exert influence over the project and affect results. Stakeholders include the project manager, the project team, the sponsors and the customers.

- **Acquiring the right staff for the project** — Projects require employees with varied skills, backgrounds and job roles. You must be able to recognize the needs of the project and staff it with the right people.

- **Developing and managing teams** — Projects often involve temporary processes and disparate groups of people. For example, individuals may be brought together who work in different departments or are at different levels within the organization. You must be able to bridge departmental boundaries and individual skill levels in order to accomplish the goal. You must also be able to impart ownership to project participants by holding them accountable for the completion of their tasks, and by soliciting their input and incorporating it into project processes.

Organizational skills

As a project manager, you must have the ability to control how and when individual tasks are completed throughout the course of the project. Managing a project is like conducting an orchestra. Whereas a conductor must be able to follow a score, cue the musicians to play at the correct time and conduct multiple sections at once, a project manager must be able to follow a project plan, ensure that each resource begins and completes tasks at the proper time, and manage a variety of tasks simultaneously.

You must be able to help project participants organize and prioritize their tasks to stay within the project scope. You can accomplish this by identifying and assigning project roles and responsibilities and reporting relationships. That is, you must define the organizational structure for the project.

Communication skills

Before you begin a project, you must gather information from the customers to ensure that the end product will meet their needs. Failure to determine goals at the outset can hinder project success.

As a project progresses, you must be able to evaluate the condition of the project and communicate project data effectively. You are responsible for keeping project participants informed in order to keep the project running smoothly. Regular communication helps manage scope creep and determine whether costs are exceeding the budget. Understanding the status of a project can also help participants focus on areas that need immediate attention.

Problem-solving skills

As a project manager, you must be able to quickly identify problems (real or potential) and propose solutions. Problem-solving skills will help you implement solutions without affecting project scope. You must have the ability to make appropriate decisions in a timely manner to prevent problems from adversely affecting the project.

Project Management Phases

Five project management phases constitute the project life cycle:

- Initiating phase

- Planning phase

- Executing phase

- Controlling phase

- Closing phase

Each phase is marked by the completion of one or more deliverables. The conclusion of each project phase usually includes a review of performance to date and a decision about whether to proceed to the next phase.

Project management phases often overlap. Typically, the executing and controlling phases of a project occur simultaneously. It is also important to note that some phases may occur more than once throughout the project life cycle.

Initiating a project

The initiating phase sets the foundation for the project. This phase defines the project scope, the project goals and the tasks required to accomplish those goals. The initiating phase of a project consists of the following tasks:

- Conducting a needs analysis

- Determining project objectives, assumptions and constraints

- Developing a Statement Of Work (SOW)

OBJECTIVE:
1.15.2: Needs analysis

needs analysis
Determining a customer's needs by acquiring information, processing and evaluating the information, then creating a plan of action to address the needs.

Needs analysis

A critical first step in the initiating phase is to conduct a **needs analysis**, which will help identify the goals of the project. A needs analysis identifies the problems or needs that the project must resolve or address. You can then translate the results of the needs analysis into the requirements that the project must meet.

Conducting a needs analysis consists of learning the customer's needs. The customer is the person, department or company for whom you are performing a project. You must elicit needs information, such as the problem the customer is experiencing, the time frame for solving the problem, and the budget for solving the problem. You must get as much information as possible from the customer, and from all systems and individuals that will be affected by the project; process and evaluate the information you receive; and turn it into a cogent plan of action.

The needs analysis will help you clearly define the project objectives. The success of a completed project can be judged by how closely each objective was met.

Project objectives, assumptions and constraints

A project objective should be specific and measurable. Objectives can include a list of project deliverables, deadlines for both the final deliverable and intermediate tasks, quality criteria for the deliverables, and cost limitations for the project. All stakeholders must understand and agree to the project objectives.

assumption
A factor that is considered to be real or certain for planning purposes.

During this time, you should also define any project assumptions. An **assumption** is any factor that is considered to be real or certain. For example, if you need to utilize resources from other departments, who will manage those resources? When, and for how long, will those resources be available to you? Assumptions should be clearly defined so that others will know what is expected of them.

constraint
A factor, such as budget or time, that limits a project manager's options.

You should also try to determine project **constraints** at this time. Constraints are factors that limit your options. Generally, a constraint is a restriction. A project may be constrained by a fixed budget or a deadline. One task may need to end by a specific date so another task that is reliant on the first task can begin.

The three major constraints on any project are:

- Schedule (time).

- Resources (money, people, equipment).

- Scope.

OBJECTIVE:
1.15.8: Statement Of Work (SOW)

Statement Of Work (SOW)

Finally, you and all stakeholders should define the ways that project success will be measured. At the end of the initiating phase, you should complete a **Statement Of Work** before you proceed to the next phase. The SOW outlines the requirements for each project task to ensure that the project objectives are met. The SOW should contain clearly defined goals and an agreed-upon plan to achieve them.

Statement Of Work (SOW)
A contract to initiate a project; the contract contains project goals and specifies how those goals will be met.

The SOW can be created between individuals, between departments, between individuals and departments, and so forth. If the SOW is completed between your organization and an outside organization or individual, the payment structure can be included in the SOW.

By determining the customer's needs during the initiating phase, you can create a project that meets those needs, and you can determine the tasks, time and cost required to complete the project.

Planning a project

The planning phase addresses project details. Project planning involves identifying all the tasks required to achieve the project goals, the people who will perform those tasks, and the resources that will be required. Planning also involves estimating the time each task will take to complete and determining project tasks that are dependent upon one another.

The project schedule

project schedule
A document that lists the planned dates for performing tasks and meeting goals defined in a project plan.

During the planning phase, you must develop a **project schedule**. A project schedule lists the planned dates for performing tasks and meeting goals identified in the project plan. To develop a project schedule, you should meet with the entire project team to determine the time and money required to complete each task. You should then outline the required tasks and assign resources to each.

The project team

Project teams can (and often do) consist of individuals from different departments. For example, your project may consist of IT professionals from within your department, as well as individuals from the Web development, marketing and accounting departments. Each person offers a different perspective and perhaps a different set of priorities. Consider the following examples:

- The person from the accounting department may be primarily concerned with project costs and may have authority over budget constraints.

- The person from the marketing department may be concerned with the project's effect on customers' perceptions of the products or company, or on promotional or advertising functions.

- The Web designer may be concerned with Web site content or design changes as a result of the project.

- The IT department members will probably be most concerned about the tasks required to meet the project goals and the time constraints imposed on them.

As the project manager, you will be responsible for satisfying these disparate priorities as you seek to complete the project schedule within the project constraints.

At the completion of the planning phase, you should have a schedule outlining tasks, responsibilities, budgets and deadlines. However, remember that planning is a constantly evolving process that lasts throughout most of the project life cycle.

Executing and controlling a project

During the executing and controlling phases of a project, project work is performed (executed), and progress is monitored and corrective action is taken as needed (controlled). At the start of the executing phase, you coordinate people and other resources to carry out the project plan. As work progresses, you must delegate or reassign tasks and resolve conflicts as necessary.

The executing phase continues as work progresses. Meanwhile, you begin the controlling phase. This phase includes coordinating project activities, detecting disruptions, taking corrective measures, troubleshooting problems, updating team members about project status and driving the project forward. Thus, during these concurrent phases, you ensure through regular monitoring that all objectives are being met. By comparing actual data to the original estimates determined during the planning phase, you can identify variations and take corrective action when necessary. Corrective action might involve replacing or assigning additional resources, changing tasks, or adjusting the budget.

Finally, to successfully execute and control a project, you must produce action plans and status reports to keep everyone apprised of the project's progress. Controlling your project can be especially challenging when your project team consists of cross-departmental members whose reporting structures differ. Figure 8-1 illustrates an organizational structure in which various project team members report to different company officers.

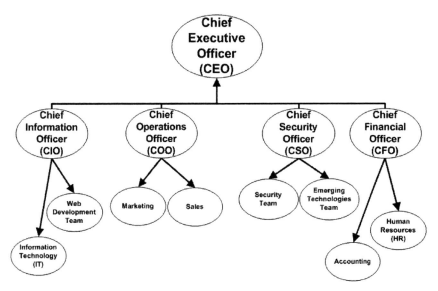

Figure 8-1: Organizational structure — project team members

OBJECTIVE:
1.15.6: Information
flow and reporting
models

The organizational structure shown in the figure is for a relatively large company (350 or more employees). Of course, not all companies and organizations follow this model exactly. However, all companies and organizations should create a model that ensures accountability among departments and reduces conflicts of interest.

Understanding conflicts of interest

Project team members will probably forward action plans and status reports to others within their departments. Each department will have a different reaction to project plan modifications, particularly if the modifications affect them directly. Following are examples of conflicts of interest that can develop among the various departments represented in your project:

- The Chief Financial Officer (CFO) may veto a proposed change due to the extra costs involved.

- The Chief Information Officer (CIO) may resist changes that require additional personnel who cannot be spared or additional tasks that adversely affect the project timeline.

- The Chief Operations Officer (COO) may determine that the returns on certain phases of the project are not worth the risk, and may seek to eliminate or modify certain tasks.

- The Chief Security Officer (CSO) may determine that the tasks involved in certain phases of the project pose too great a security risk to the company's data or network, and may seek to eliminate the tasks from the project.

Adjusting the project plan

If situations such as the ones in the previous list occur, you must make appropriate recommendations and adjust the project plan accordingly without losing sight of the project's ultimate goal. In a worst-case scenario, departmental differences may become untenable and put the entire project at risk. In some cases, the appropriate course of action may to terminate the project if it simply will not justify the investment required. Terminating unprofitable projects helps the bottom line.

Remember that as the project manager, you are the owner of the project. You must accept final responsibility for all project decisions and outcomes.

Closing a project

The final phase of a project is the closing phase. During the closing phase, your team should evaluate the project schedule, budget, scope, resources and assignments to determine the aspects of the project that worked well and the changes that should be implemented in the future. A project is deemed a success when it is completed within the budget and time frame specified, and the finished product meets quality standards.

At the end of the closing phase, you should receive a formal acceptance of the project deliverable from the customer, a documented history of the project, and recommendations for revising the project plan for future projects.

The Project Triangle

OBJECTIVE:
1.15.1: Project
triangle

Three factors — time, money and scope — affect every project, and they form what is sometimes referred to as the project triangle. When any one of these elements is adjusted, the other two are also affected. For example, if you decrease the budget on a project, you may need to limit its scope as well. Or if you add more time to a schedule, you may be able to reduce costs by eliminating overtime expenses.

All three of these elements are important, but typically one will have a greater impact on a project than the others. The relationship among these three elements will determine the kinds of problems that may arise during a project, as well as the solutions you can implement.

A fourth element — quality — is at the center of the project triangle. It is not a factor in the triangle, but changes you make to the other three factors will most likely affect quality. For example, if you have extra time in your schedule, you may be able to increase the project's scope, which may result in a higher level of quality. If you need to cut costs, you may need to decrease scope, and a lower level of quality may result. Therefore, as you optimize a project's schedule, consider the ways that adjusting one element of the triangle might affect the other two, and how overall quality will be affected.

Movie Time!

Insert the CIW Foundations Movie CD to learn even more about this topic.

Project Management Concepts (approx. playing time: 08:15)

All movie clips are © 2004 LearnKey, Inc.

Project Management Software

As you can see, project management is a balancing act. Although experience is the best way to become an excellent project manager, project management software can help you with the details. Most project management software stores your schedule information in a database. This database might be proprietary (for example, part of a project management program). In many cases, you can export information to a database application (for example, Microsoft Access or MySQL).

Scheduling information

Project management software stores the following schedule information:

- A project start date
- A project calendar
- Necessary tasks and their durations
- Project resources and their costs

As you establish relationships among project tasks, project management software calculates the length of time required to complete the tasks, as well as resource availability. As you adjust the schedule, the software recalculates the finish dates and adjusts the project calendar.

Tracking project progress and status

As you post progress information to the database, you can use project management software to compare the actual performance to the planned performance, and display variations. The software can alert you if your project is behind schedule or over budget, as well as inform you when you are ahead of schedule. These features can help you to increase quality and reduce costs. Finally, most project management software enables you to produce charts and reports to communicate project status.

Using a successful project as a template

After closing a project, if you decide that the project was well planned and executed, you can save the old project as a template and use it as a starting point for future projects of a similar nature.

In the following lab, you will install a free project management application called GanttProject. You will also install Java (also free) because GanttProject requires Java in order to run. Suppose you are the IT administrator at your company. A new project manager will be joining your department next week, and you want to prepare the project manager's computer so that she has all the resources necessary to be immediately productive.

 Lab 8-1: Installing Java and the GanttProject project management tool

In this lab, you will install Java and the GanttProject project management software application.

1. First, you will install Java. Open **Windows Explorer** and navigate to the **C:\CIW\Internet\LabFiles\Lesson08** folder.

2. Double-click **j2re-1_4_2_03-windows-i586-p.exe** to display the Java Installation Wizard.

3. Follow the instructions to install Java on your system. Ensure that you specify a **Typical** installation when given the choice between a Typical or Custom installation.

4. When prompted, restart your system to complete the installation.

5. Next, you will install GanttProject. Open **Windows Explorer** and navigate to the **C:\CIW\Internet\LabFiles\Lesson08** folder.

6. Double-click **ganttproject-1.9.10-setup.exe** to display the GanttProject Installation Wizard.

7. Follow the instructions to install GanttProject on your system.

8. When the installation is complete, close **Windows Explorer**.

Now you are ready to use GanttProject to create and manage a project, which you will do in the next section.

Creating Project Schedules

OBJECTIVE:
1.15.4: Project
software, charts and
timelines

Once you have completed the initiating phase of a project, you are ready to begin the planning phase and create the project schedule. When you start this phase, you should have clearly defined goals and objectives in mind, as well as the tasks necessary to achieve them. You should also know the approximate length of time each task will take, the order in which tasks should be performed and the employees who will perform them. You can then create a project schedule to determine the project timeline.

Gantt charts

Gantt chart
A horizontal bar
chart that
graphically displays
project tasks and
durations.

Project management software often contains **Gantt charts** that graphically display the project tasks and task durations. A typical Gantt chart is shown in Figure 8-2. In a Gantt chart, each task is represented by a separate bar. The top of the Gantt chart displays dates in increments of days, weeks or months, depending on the length of the project. The task duration is represented by the length of the horizontal bar. The left end of the taskbar marks the task start date, and the right end marks the task completion date. Tasks may be performed concurrently, they may overlap, or they may run sequentially if the start of one task is dependent on the completion of another.

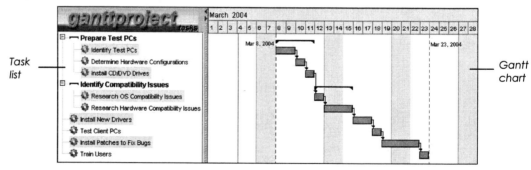

Figure 8-2: Sample Gantt chart

Henry Gantt, an American engineer and pioneer in the field of scientific management, developed Gantt charts in 1917 as a tool for scheduling production work for military projects. In addition to the basic elements of the Gantt chart shown in the figure, most project management software can enhance the chart to display the following information:

• A vertical marker that represents the current date.

• The progression of each task, indicated by shading the portion of the task that is completed. Shading completed tasks or portions of tasks provides a visual representation of the status of the project.

• Sequential relationships among tasks to illustrate task dependencies, usually in the form of link arrows.

- The resources assigned to each task.

- Project milestones, which mark major events during the course of the project.

In the following lab, you will use GanttProject to create a project schedule. Suppose your company's IT department wants to upgrade the operating system on all company computers. The department first wants to upgrade the operating system on test computers, or PCs, to ensure the upgrades will work properly. You are a new IT project manager, and the IT administrator has asked you to create a project schedule to organize the tasks necessary to complete the upgrades on the test PCs.

 Lab 8-2: Creating a project schedule

In this lab, you will use GanttProject to create a project schedule. The project for which you are creating a schedule is upgrading the operating system on test computers, or PCs, in preparation for upgrading computers throughout the company.

1. First, you will list the tasks and subtasks necessary to upgrade the operating system on test computers. Minimize any open windows to display the Windows XP Desktop.

2. Double-click the **GanttProject** icon to display the GanttProject application window (Figure 8-3).

   *Note: If a Tips Of The Day message box displays, click the **Close** button to close it.*

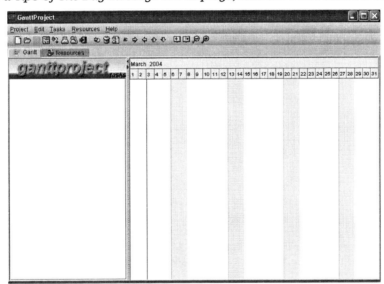

Figure 8-3: GanttProject application window

The GanttProject toolbar buttons are labeled in Figure 8-4.

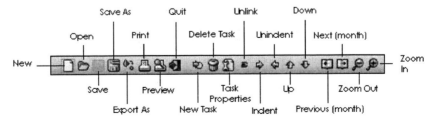

Figure 8-4: GanttProject toolbar

3. In the toolbar, click the **New Task** button to add a task to the Tasks pane.

4. In the Tasks pane, double-click the task to display the Properties dialog box (shown in Figure 8-5).

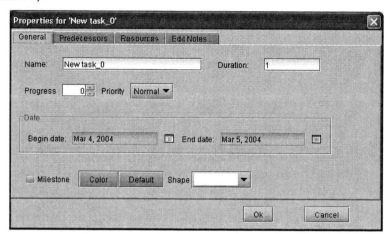

Figure 8-5: GanttProject Properties dialog box for task

5. Select the text in the Name text box, then type **_Prepare Test PCs_** to specify the task name.

6. Click the **Choose A Date** button next to the Begin Date box, click the first Monday following the current week, then click **OK** twice. This step specifies the project start date.

    *Note: If the first Monday following the current week resides in the following month, click the **Next** (month) button in the GanttProject toolbar to view the Gantt chart changes in the following steps.*

7. With the first task selected, click the **New Task** button to add a second task to the Tasks pane. Notice that it is indented and displays as a subtask of the first task.

8. Double-click the subtask, specify a name of **_Identify Test PCs_** and a duration of **_2_** days, then click **OK**. In the Gantt chart, notice that the bar for the first task has been replaced by a thick black line, which indicates that the first task is a top-level task that will be defined by its subtasks.

9. Click **Prepare Test PCs**, then click the **New Task** button. This step adds a second subtask to the first top-level task group.

10. Double-click the second subtask, specify a name of **_Determine Hardware Configurations_** and a duration of **_1_** day, then click **OK**.

11. Add a third subtask under *Prepare Test PCs* with the name **_Install CD/DVD Drives_** and a duration of **_1_** day.

12. Click anywhere in an empty area of the Tasks pane to deselect any tasks, then click the **New Task** button. Notice that the new task is not indented as a subtask under *Prepare Test PCs*

13. Double-click the new top-level task, specify a name of **_Identify Compatibility Issues_**, then click **OK**.

14. With Identify Compatibility Issues still selected, click the **New Task** button to create a subtask for the top-level task.

15. Double-click the subtask, specify a name of ***Research OS Compatibility Issues*** and a duration of ***1*** day, then click **OK**.

16. Click **Identify Compatibility Issues**, click the **New Task** button, double-click the new subtask, then specify a name of ***Research Hardware Compatibility Issues*** and a duration of ***1*** day.

17. Add the top-level tasks and durations specified in the following table to the project schedule.

Top-Level Task	Duration
Install New Drivers	2 Days
Test Client PCs	1 Day
Install Patches to Fix Bugs	2 Days
Train Users	1 Day

18. Review the display of the data you entered in the application. Your task list and Gantt chart should resemble Figure 8-6.

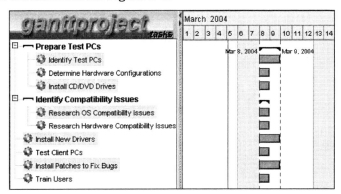

Figure 8-6: Task list and Gantt chart

19. Next, you will specify task dependencies. In the Gantt chart, click and hold the Gantt bar for Identify Test PCs, drag it to the Gantt bar for Determine Hardware Configurations, then release the mouse button. This step specifies that the start of the second subtask is dependent on the completion of the first, and moves the start date of the second subtask forward two days.

20. Click and hold the Gantt bar for **Determine Hardware Configurations**, drag it to the Gantt bar for **Install CD/DVD Drives**, then release the mouse button. This step specifies that the start of the third subtask is dependent on the completion of the second, and moves the start date of the third subtask forward one day.

21. Continue to link the remaining Gantt bars so that the start of each task (or subtask) is dependent upon the completion of the previous task (or subtask). Notice that the scheduled start dates for the Research Hardware Compatibility Issues and Install New Drivers tasks occur on the weekend.

22. Change the duration for **Research Hardware Compatibility Issues** from *1* to *3* days, then change the duration for **Install Patches to Fix Bugs** from *2* to *4* days. This step shifts the task start dates so that all tasks are scheduled during the work week. Your task list and Gantt chart should now resemble Figure 8-7.

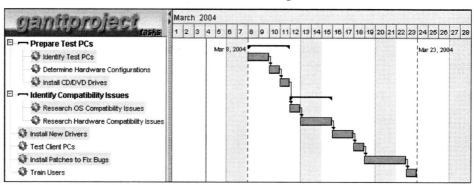

Figure 8-7: Task list and Gantt chart — final

23. Exit **GanttProject** without saving the project schedule.

You now know how to use a project management software application to create a project schedule and display it using a Gantt chart.

Documenting Projects

OBJECTIVE:
1.15.12: Project documentation

After the planning stage, you should be able to identify the tasks that are most important and the tasks that can be delayed without affecting the completion of other tasks or the overall project. Being aware of critical tasks will help you make adjustments to ensure that the project is completed on time.

Paper trail

During the executing and controlling phases of a project, you should document project tasks to provide a paper trail, or record, of the team members who worked on tasks, and the dates they started and completed them. Team members should sign and date the document to confirm that they completed the tasks. By documenting the project as it advances, you can track its progress by determining whether tasks are starting and finishing on time, and whether tasks are being completed within the budget. By tracking these factors while the project is still in progress, you can solve problems as they occur and make necessary adjustments. Documenting a project promotes team member accountability and enables stakeholders to monitor various stages of the project.

Issues log

You should also keep an issues log in which you document problems that need to be escalated to managers or executives outside the project team for resolution. Issues often arise during the course of a project that require authoritative decisions in order for the team to complete tasks and keep the project on track. You can use the issues log as backup documentation to support any time, resource or cost changes that may accrue due to circumstances beyond the project team's control.

Planning and Scheduling Meetings

Also during the executing and controlling phases of a project, you need to meet with team members regularly to discuss progress, and to respond to project issues and unanticipated developments. Any variations from the project plan should also be identified and addressed. Proactively anticipating and responding to potential project deviations will help you avoid a crisis later. Meeting with team members provides opportunities to present new ideas to improve workflow, solve problems, inform team members of project status and make decisions.

You should also periodically meet with stakeholders and management to keep them apprised of project progress and to handle issues they bring up that may affect the scope of the project. You may want to schedule meetings with stakeholders and management around project milestones. You can also prepare a Project Status report to review specific highlights or achievements, stages of task completion, cost status of the project, and so forth. This is also a good time to solicit information from management that you need in order to respond to problems.

Meetings and scope creep

Scheduled meetings are also an excellent way to manage scope creep. A few minor scope increases may not significantly affect the project. However, major or frequent requests that were not part of the original Statement Of Work can derail the project if they are not properly managed. Regular meetings to review and discuss requests will help to manage change requests and eliminate those that are not crucial to the success of the project.

Reviewing Projects

During the closing phase of every project, the project manager should perform a formal project review with the project team. The project review provides an opportunity for the following:

- **Testing the product** — The customer has the opportunity to evaluate and test the deliverable, and formalize acceptance of it. If the product does not meet expectations, the customer can reject the product and request modifications before granting final approval. If the product is approved, it can be implemented.

- **Evaluating performances** — You can review team members' performances and determine the individuals and departments that contributed most to the project's success. If the project exceeded its initial constraints or yielded an unacceptable end product, team members can determine the mix of resources that would have yielded a high-quality product within time and budget constraints.

- **Documenting lessons learned** — Team members can document the processes that worked well, as well as modifications to improve processes that did not work as well as expected. Team members should identify aspects of the project that contributed to time, cost or scope overruns. Documenting the lessons learned can help team members (and others) improve their performances or resolve similar issues in future projects.

Quality Assurance

OBJECTIVE:
1.15.13: Separation
of duties

1.15.15: Quality
management and
assurance

As a project manager, you are not only concerned with the components of the project triangle. You must also consider the quality of the product. If the product does not meet the customer's quality standards, it will not be accepted, and the project will probably be considered a failure.

You can employ several techniques to manage and assure the quality of the product, including the following:

- **Separation of duties (also called segregation of duties)** — Project teamwork can help ensure quality by providing independent verification that project tasks were completed correctly. One team member can check the work of another, and vice versa. If one team member misses a crucial step, the other will probably notice it and complete the task properly. This type of teamwork helps ensure the quality of the product.

- **Adherence to ISO 9000 standards** — ISO 9000 standards (introduced in the next section) are an international benchmark for systemizing processes to help organizations create products and services that meet the quality standards set by customers and government regulations. By complying with ISO 9000 standards, organizations are implementing a best-practices approach to managing projects and processes to ensure high-quality deliverables.

International Organization for Standardization (ISO) 9000

The International Organization for Standardization (ISO) is a grouping of national standards bodies from 148 countries. ISO develops technical specifications for intellectual, scientific, technological and economic activities worldwide. ISO is not an acronym; the name is derived from the Greek *isos*, which means equal. You can learn more about ISO at *www.iso.org*.

ISO offers a family of management system standards called ISO 9000. ISO 9000 details the steps recommended to produce high-quality products and services using a quality-management system that maximizes time, money and resources. ISO 9000 outlines a systematic approach to managing business processes so that they consistently deliver quality products.

IT Business Implications

Many IT projects have a direct effect on a company's bottom line. The risk and business value of each project must be considered relative to each other to determine the projects that should be authorized and the projects that should not. This section will discuss the effects of organizational rules and policies on IT projects; IT rights and responsibilities; the effects of IT projects on employee productivity; and the ways that business concerns determine the IT projects to pursue and the IT functions that receive the endorsement of upper management.

Organizational rules and policies

OBJECTIVE:
1.15.7: IT issues in
organizational
policies

IT project initiation and implementation are bound by the rules and policies that govern an organization. IT professionals must consider the ways that the rules and policies will affect their ability to fulfill customer requests, particularly when the customer is an individual or department within the organization.

For example, suppose that you are managing the installation of new server equipment and a new e-mail client. Organizational rules and policies that you may have to consider include the following:

- **Change request forms** — You can initiate a project only when formally requested to do so by a requestor who must submit a form, such as a change request form. This form details the specific problem or need, and requests IT time and resources to resolve it. You can use the form as the basis for your needs analysis and Statement Of Work to determine the project goals and objectives.

- **Employee overtime** — During the changeover of server equipment, the existing equipment must be disengaged, resulting in server downtime. If equipment downtime is significant, will employees need to work overtime to remain on schedule with their own tasks? If the company is reluctant to grant overtime for non-IT personnel, you may have to schedule the installations at off-peak times, such as evenings or weekends.

- **Employee training** — If your organization has a sales or customer service staff, will business be affected if phones are not covered? You may have to stagger software installations or e-mail client training so that not all employees are away from their phones at one time.

- **Project documentation** — Company policy may dictate that all project managers document their activities to provide a formal tracking process. IT project documentation can be used to confirm which employee requested the service or product, the tasks and objectives that were agreed upon, the project start and end dates, the testing or acceptance criteria, and final project sign-off. For example, if the project involved updating the company Web site, documentation can be used to identify specific Web page changes, the person who made them and the reasons they were made. Such a tracking process ensures accountability so that Web site changes are not made without proper authorization. Documentation provides a vehicle for problem resolution if the changes require further modification.

IT rights and responsibilities

OBJECTIVE:
1.15.7: IT issues in organizational policies

IT professionals have certain rights, and they also have responsibilities to the organization. For example, IT professionals must have access to the tools needed to perform their jobs, such as the hardware, software and security access required to perform tasks. They also have the right to receive clear, detailed objectives and instructions so that they can provide the appropriate services and products to their customers.

IT professionals have the responsibility to provide services and products in a timely, cost-effective, secure manner that satisfies customer needs without compromising the integrity or security of the data or processes with which they work. They also have the responsibility to plan service and product installations and conduct training in a manner that minimizes workflow interruption and hardware or network downtime.

Effects of IT projects on productivity

OBJECTIVE:
1.15.9: Implications of technical changes

IT projects often impact an organization's bottom line because systems upon which employees rely to perform their job duties are affected. Employees and stakeholders will respond to IT professionals based on the way IT projects are conducted and managed. As an IT project manager, you must always strive to minimize workflow interruptions to avoid negatively affecting an organization.

When IT projects affect systems that employees use, you should:

- Inform employees about the systems that will be affected, and the date and duration that the systems will be inaccessible.
- Provide alternative ways to complete tasks when systems are offline.
- Perform tasks during off-peak hours to minimize distractions.
- Provide training and support so that users assimilate the new systems as quickly as possible.
- Provide support to answer questions and solve problems while employees learn the new systems.

When IT projects are managed properly:

- Employee productivity loss is minimized, which minimizes the negative impact to the company's bottom line.
- Employee transition from old to new systems occurs more swiftly and smoothly.
- Fewer problems occur, which will result in less IT support time.
- Good will will be fostered among departments because users will view IT as a service organization that is responsive and sensitive to their wants and needs.

When IT projects are mismanaged:

- Employees may become frustrated and angry because their ability to work is unnecessarily hindered.
- Employee productivity and perhaps morale may be adversely affected because of an inordinate amount of system downtime.
- Project tasks may take longer to complete, which may waste company resources and money.
- Animosity among departments may occur because users will view IT as a department that hinders their ability to get their jobs done.

Following are some examples of how IT projects affect employee productivity.

Upgrading a firewall
How does installing a firewall affect employee productivity? Suppose that IT is upgrading the firewall to no longer allow certain types of file attachments (for example, .doc, .bat or .exe files) to pass through the e-mail server. If employees routinely exchange these types of files via e-mail, productivity may be diminished because employees must find alternative methods of transmitting this information.

Employees may have to use a VPN or FTP server to transfer files, which may involve training. If productivity is adversely affected, the organization's bottom line may be adversely affected, particularly in a large company in which hundreds or thousands of employees can be affected at once.

Restricting Internet access
As part of the firewall upgrade, certain Web sites that employees may have routinely accessed are now rendered inaccessible. What are the implications to employee productivity? If the Web sites contained information instrumental to their job functions, employees may lose productivity until they find comparable information from another easily accessible source.

As an IT professional, you must weigh the increase in firewall security against the deterrent to employee productivity, and make decisions accordingly.

Changing user names and passwords

Another common IT function is to periodically change user names and passwords for network access as an extra security precaution. If employees are unaware of or unprepared for the change, they may become frustrated and confused when they try to log on to the network and are denied access.

As an IT professional, you must notify employees in advance of the change, specify the date on which the new user names and passwords will take effect, and give employees instructions regarding the new user names and passwords. Sending reminders and giving employees instructions in advance will increase their comfort level with the change.

Changing e-mail protocols

How does changing e-mail protocols affect employee productivity? Suppose that IT is switching the company e-mail protocol from POP3 to IMAP4. Upgrading the protocol software will involve user downtime while IT installs and tests the software on the e-mail server. Users may experience unanticipated problems or conversion incompatibilities. IT must reconfigure the firewall and provide training and support in order for employees to use the new e-mail protocol. As stated in the other examples, a proactive approach by IT can minimize productivity loss.

Return On Investment (ROI) and IT projects

OBJECTIVE:
1.15.10: Return On
Investment (ROI)

Return On Investment (ROI) in the context of IT projects refers to the profit earned as a result of a project relative to the value of the resources required to complete the project. Before starting a project, an IT project manager must determine the benefits of spending the money to create the product or service. As a project manager, you will be held responsible for the project's ROI and be required to justify the project's benefits relative to its costs. You must be able to determine the risk and business value of each project to justify which projects to preserve and which projects to eliminate.

**Return On
Investment (ROI)**
Profit earned as a
result of a project
relative to the value
of resources
required to
complete it.

For example, IT may receive a request to replace one software suite with another throughout the company. As the IT project manager, you must determine whether the costs of switching suites (including ramifications such as installation time, end-user training, and so forth) can be justified relative to the benefits afforded by the new suite. If the cost of upgrading is high and no measurable increase in productivity or sales will result from it, the ROI considerations would probably lead you to reject the request.

By contrast, IT may receive a request to add information to the company Web site that research has indicated may dramatically increase sales. If you determine that it would take a Web developer less than a week to update the Web site and test the new links, the potential ROI may be well worth the investment.

Proving ROI

An ROI concern exists for technical IT functions relative to the company's bottom line. The IT department can decide to undertake various projects, from changing e-mail clients to installing a firewall to creating a company intranet. Before any of these projects gains upper-management approval, the IT department will probably have to convince management that the end products or services will produce a positive ROI; that is, that the money spent will be more than offset by the savings or productivity gains resulting from the new products or services.

For example, the Web team may request updated Web development software, which they claim will enable them to enhance the company Web site design for greater visual impact

OBJECTIVE:
1.15.14: Information
systems and
business concerns

and functionality. Upper management will need answers to the following questions before approving the purchase:

- Will the new software yield a significantly improved Web site?

- Will the upgraded Web site attract more customers?

- Will the upgraded Web site translate into greater sales?

- Will the investment in the software upgrade increase the bottom line?

Unless the Web team can provide evidence that the new software will produce a positive ROI, upper management probably will not approve the purchase.

Project Management Institute (PMI)

Many resources exist to help expand your knowledge of project management concepts and principles. A key resource is the Project Management Institute (PMI), which is a nonprofit membership organization that publishes standards and offers education in the project management profession. PMI sets ethical and professional project management standards, and offers the Project Management Professional (PMP) certification program.

Project Management Body of Knowledge

The Project Management Body of Knowledge (PMBOK) identifies nine topic areas that define project management. Each topic area provides a set of principles and techniques to help you manage projects, and is explained in a book published by PMI titled *Guide to the Project Management Body of Knowledge*. The nine topic areas are as follows:

- **Project Integration Management** — ensuring that all project elements are properly coordinated by developing and executing the project plan

- **Project Scope Management** — defining the tasks and resources needed to meet project objectives, and identifying the budget constraints

- **Project Time Management** — defining task durations and developing the project schedule to ensure that a project is completed by the deadline.

- **Project Cost Management** — controlling expenses to ensure that a project is completed within the approved budget

- **Project Quality Management** — incorporating appropriate quality assurance and product testing techniques to ensure that project deliverables satisfy project goals and meet customer needs

- **Project Human Resource Management** — assessing and coordinating resource allocations to assign appropriate individuals to project tasks to maximize the efficiency of the project team

- **Project Communications Management** — communicating project status and distributing information to team members and stakeholders in a timely manner to address issues as they arise and manage deviations from the project plan

- **Project Risk Management** — analyzing and identifying project risks relative to ROI to determine which projects should proceed and which should be terminated

- **Project Procurement Management** — obtaining the necessary resources to meet project goals

To learn more about the Project Management Institute and to purchase copies of *Guide to the Project Management Body of Knowledge*, visit PMI online at *www.pmi.org*.

Case Study

We Need an Intranet!

Mary Kate is a project manager in the IT department for a university. She has been asked to manage a project to create a faculty intranet. The university has multiple campuses in various locations, and professors and other faculty need to be able to easily post questions, schedules and other documents to share in a secure environment.

Mary Kate performed the following steps to begin the intranet project.

- She performed a needs analysis. Mary Kate interviewed the university faculty to determine their needs for an intranet and the uses they foresee for it. She discovered that several of the professors were working on a research project and wanted to use the intranet to facilitate group discussions, as well as to host periodic Webinars for professors at other universities.

- She chose the project team. Mary Kate enlisted members of the IT department for the project, including someone to install firewalls so users have access to the Internet through the firewall server, and someone to set up the site to host Webinars.

- She determined the project constraints. Mary Kate determined when the intranet needed to be live. She considered how long she would have the services of the various team members, how long team members could work on this project before being assigned to other tasks, and when the first Webinar was scheduled. Once she gathered all of this information, she was able to determine the project scope and constraints.

- She created the project schedule. Mary Kate worked with the project team to outline the tasks and task relationships required to complete the project. She assigned resources to specific tasks so that each person was aware of his or her role in the overall project plan.

- She scheduled weekly meetings for the duration of the project. Mary Kate included the CIO, project team members, faculty members and all other stakeholders in the meetings.

- She created a Project Status report and an issues log. Mary Kate used these documents in each meeting to apprise stakeholders of the project status and to introduce any problems or issues that had arisen since the last meeting.

Once Mary Kate had performed all these tasks, she was ready to begin the executing phase of the project.

*   *   *

As a class, discuss the management of this project. How might scope creep occur? How could it be managed?

Lesson Summary

Application project

Several free project management software applications are available for download from the Web. Use any of the search engines that have been introduced in this course to search for free project management software that can be downloaded (use search keywords such as "project management software," "Gantt chart software," and so forth). Download an application to your Desktop.

Pair up with a partner or friend and create a Statement Of Work for a simple IT project, such as the installation of software upgrades and services on the computers within a particular department. List specific tasks that must occur during the various stages of the project in order to meet your project objectives. Be sure to include at least one task for each of the five project management phases.

Use project management software to enter the tasks, task durations and milestones to create a Gantt chart of the project schedule.

Skills review

In this lesson, you learned about the fundamentals of project management, project management skills, and the five project management phases that constitute the project life cycle: initiating, planning, executing, controlling and closing a project. You also learned that the project triangle — time, money and scope — affects every project and impacts the quality of the project deliverables.

You learned about the benefits of project management software and used a freeware application to create a project schedule and develop a Gantt chart of tasks, task durations and task dependencies.

You learned the value of documenting and reviewing projects, planning and scheduling meetings, and applying quality assurance techniques.

You learned about the impact of IT decisions on organizations and vice versa, such as the impact organizational rules and policies have on IT projects, IT rights and responsibilities, the impact of IT projects on employee productivity, and the ROI implications of IT decisions.

Finally, you learned about the Project Management Institute (PMI), which is a key resource for project management concepts and principles.

Now that you have completed this lesson, you should be able to:

✓ Identify project management fundamentals.

✓ Identify project management skills.

✓ Identify the five project management phases.

✓ Define the project triangle.

✓ Identify the value of project management software.

✓ Create a project schedule.

✓ Identify the value of documenting projects.

✓ Identify the value of planning and scheduling meetings.

✓   Identify the value of reviewing projects.

✓   Identify quality assurance techniques.

✓   Identify the business implications of IT decisions.

✓   Identify project management certifications and resources.

Lesson 8 Review

1. Name the primary way that IT projects differ from other projects.

    Deals with DATA

2. Define project management.

3. What is the term for a unit of work that must be accomplished during the course of a project?

    task

4. What is the term for a person or group that has an interest in the outcome of a project and can affect its results?

    stake holder

5. List the five phases of the project management life cycle. *IPECC*

    init, plng, exec, contl, closing

6. How does the customer participate in the closing phase of a project?

    eval, acceptance, reception

7. Name some responsibilities that an IT professional has when working on a project that affects other departments in an organization.

    timing
    cost effective
    secure

Appendixes

Appendix A: Objectives and Locations*
Appendix B: Resources*
Appendix C: Works Consulted*

* Appendix found on Supplemental CD-ROM

CIW Foundations Glossary

absolute URL — A URL that gives the full path to a resource.

account lockout — A legitimate practice in which a user account is automatically disabled after a certain number of failed authentication attempts.

active partition — A logical partition that contains the files necessary to boot an operating system. This partition is read first at boot time. If no active partition exists, or if the operating system files are corrupted or missing, the computer will report error messages.

ActiveX — An open set of technologies for integrating components on the Internet and within Microsoft applications.

adapter — A device that provides connectivity between at least two systems.

Advanced Research Projects Agency (ARPA) — A U.S. Department of Defense agency that created the first global computer network.

Advanced Research Projects Agency Network (ARPANET) — A computer network, funded by ARPA, that served as the basis for early networking research and was the backbone during the development of the Internet.

antivirus software — Software that scans disks and programs for known viruses and eliminates them.

applets — Small programs written in Java, which are downloaded as needed and executed within a Web page or browser.

application programming interface (API) — A set of universal commands, calls and functions that allows developers to communicate with an application or operating system.

Application Service Provider (ASP) — A company that provides applications and services (over the Internet) to individual or enterprise subscribers that would otherwise need to provide those applications and services on their own servers.

application-level gateway — A firewall component that inspects all packets addressed to a user-level application; uses proxies to control and filter traffic on a connection-by-connection basis. Also provides authentication.

assignment — The appointment of a specific resource to a specific task.

assumption — A factor that is considered to be real or certain for planning purposes.

asymmetric-key encryption — An encryption method in which two keys (the private key and public key) are used to encrypt and decrypt a message.

attachment — A file that is sent with an e-mail message.

attenuation — The weakening of a transmission signal as it travels farther from its source.

AU — Audio file format used by UNIX servers, the majority of Web servers. Most Web browsers can read AU.

Audio Interchange File Format (AIFF) — High-quality audio format developed by Apple Computer.

Audio Video Interleave (AVI) — Standard Windows file format for video files.

authentication — The process of verifying the identity of a user who logs on to a system, or the integrity of transmitted data.

back end — A series of systems that fulfill requests made by a client. Back-end systems can include mainframes and servers containing information databases.

backbone — The highest level in the computer network hierarchy, to which smaller networks typically connect.

bandwidth — The amount of information, sometimes called traffic, that can be carried on a network at one time. The total capacity of a line. Also, the rate of data transfer over a network connection; measured in bits per second.

baseline — A recording of network activity, obtained through documentation and monitoring, that serves as an example for comparing future network activity.

bastion host — A computer that houses various firewall components and services and is connected to a public network, such as the Internet.

binary file — A file containing data or instructions written in zeros and ones (computer language).

blackhole list — A published list of IP addresses known to be sources of spam.

block-level element — A markup element that affects at least an entire paragraph.

blog — A collection of personal thoughts posted on a public Web site. Blogging is the act of adding entries to a blog.

Boolean operator — A symbol or word used in Internet searches to narrow search results by including or excluding certain words or phrases from the search criteria.

bottleneck — A point in network communication at which information is processed more slowly. Also, any element (a hard drive, I/O card or network interface card) that slows network connectivity rates.

browser e-mail — E-mail programs such as Netscape Mail & Newsgroups or Outlook Express that come bundled with a Web browser and with which they may be integrated.

buffer — A cache of memory used by a computer to store frequently used data. Buffers allow faster access times.

bus — An electronic pathway that conducts signals to connect the functional components of a computer.

business logic — The coding (usually in SQL) necessary to create relationships in the data stored in a database.

business-to-business (B2B) — An e-commerce model in which a Web-based business sells products and/or services to other businesses.

business-to-consumer (B2C) — An e-commerce model in which a Web-based business sells products and/or services to consumers or end users.

byte — A measurement of memory needed to store one 8-bit character.

cable modem — A device that allows computers to communicate over a network by modulating and demodulating the cable signal into a stream of data.

callback — A process in which a remote access server returns a call to a remote client that has logged on in order to authenticate that client.

Carrier Sense Multiple Access/Collision Avoidance (CSMA/CA) — The LAN access method used by the IEEE 802.11 wireless specification and Apple LocalTalk.

Carrier Sense Multiple Access/Collision Detection (CSMA/CD) — The LAN access method used by Ethernet. Checks for network access availability with a signal.

Cascading Style Sheets (CSS) — A technology that allows greater style definition and formatting control of HTML elements. Formatting can be placed within the HTML or called remotely from an external style sheet.

channel — The cable or signal between two network nodes that enables data transmission.

character set — The group of symbols used to render text on a page.

circuit-level gateway — A firewall component that monitors and transmits information at the transport layer of the OSI model. It hides information about the network; a packet passing through this type of gateway appears to have originated from the firewall.

client — An individual computer connected to a network. Also, a system or application that requests a service from another computer (the server), and is used to access files or documents (such as a Web browser or user agent).

client-side script — Code embedded into an HTML page and downloaded by a user; resides on the client and helps process Web form input. Common client-side scripting languages include JavaScript and VBScript.

cluster — A group of sectors used as the basic unit of data storage.

clustering — The ability for multiple systems to act as a single host. Allows organizations to ensure high availability of data and to balance loads in busy networks.

coax — High-capacity two-wire (signal and ground) cable; inner wire is the primary conductor, and the metal sheath serves as the ground.

codec — A compression/decompression algorithm used by modern video and audio player plug-ins.

common field — A field contained in two or more database tables that forms a connection between the tables.

Common Gateway Interface (CGI) — A program that processes data submitted by the user. Allows a Web server to pass control to a software application, based on user request. The application receives and organizes data, then returns it in a consistent format.

Completely Automated Public Turing Test to Tell Computers and Humans Apart (CAPTCHA) — A test that uses a word-verification graphic designed to differentiate humans from automated senders during online transactions.

Concurrent Versions System (CVS) — A tool that allows programmers to control different versions of the pieces of a program as those pieces are developed.

constraint — A factor, such as budget or time, that limits a project manager's options.

cookie — A text file that contains information sent between a server and a client to help maintain state and track user activities. Cookies can reside in memory or on a hard drive.

customs — National departments responsible for controlling items entering and leaving the country.

daemon — A UNIX program that is usually initiated at startup and runs in the background until required.

data — Information being stored, usually in a database.

data source name (DSN) — A text string that is used to reference the data source by application programs.

database — A collection of data that can be sorted and searched using search algorithms.

database administrator — An individual responsible for the maintenance and security of an organization's database resources and data.

database management system (DBMS) — A program used to store, access and manipulate database information.

dead link — A hyperlink that, when clicked, sends a Web site visitor to a page or resource that does not exist on the server.

decryption — The process of converting encrypted data back to its original form.

deep URL — A URL that includes a path past the domain into the folder structure of a Web site.

demand priority — The LAN access method used by 100VG-AnyLAN networks. By prioritizing transmissions, hubs specify how and when nodes can access the network.

dictionary program — A program specifically written to break into a password-protected system. It has a relatively large list of common password names it repeatedly uses to gain access.

digital certificate — A password-protected, encrypted data file containing message encryption, user identification and message text. Used to authenticate a program or a sender's public key, or to initiate SSL sessions. Must be signed by a certificate authority (CA) to be valid.

digital signature — An electronic stamp added to a message that uniquely identifies its source and verifies its contents at the time of the signature.

Digital Subscriber Line (DSL) — A high-speed direct Internet connection that uses all-digital networks.

direct memory access (DMA) — A process that allows devices to bypass controllers and directly access memory.

disk cache — Storage space on a computer hard disk used to temporarily store downloaded data.

dithering — The ability for a computer to approximate a color by combining the RGB values.

document type declaration (<!DOCTYPE>) — A declaration of document or code type embedded within an HTML, XHTML, XML or SGML document; identifies the version and nature of code used. Denoted by the <!DOCTYPE> tag at the beginning of the document.

Document Type Definition (DTD) — A set of rules contained in a simple text file that defines the structure, syntax and vocabulary as it relates to tags and attributes for a corresponding document.

domain name — An IP address represented in words.

domain name server — A server that resolves domain names into IP addresses.

domain name space — The three-level domain name hierarchy (root-level, top-level and second-level domains) that forms the DNS.

Domain Name System (DNS) — A system that maps uniquely hierarchical names to specific Internet addresses.

dynamic — Always changing.

Dynamic HTML (DHTML) — A combination of HTML, script, styles and the Document Object Model (DOM) that provides Web page interactivity.

electronic commerce (e-commerce) — The integration of communications, data management and security capabilities to allow organizations and consumers to exchange information related to the sale of good and services.

Electronic Data Interchange (EDI) — The inter-organization exchange of documents in a standardized electronic form directly between participating computers.

e-mail client — An e-mail program that is independent of any specific Web browser, and that you can use to send e-mail messages.

emoticon — A combination of characters that you read sideways that helps convey emotion in an e-mail message.

emulator — A type of software that imitates a computer then allows non-native software to run in a foreign environment. Sometimes also a hardware device.

Encapsulated PostScript (EPS) — File format used for importing and exporting graphics.

encryption — A security technique to prevent access to information by converting it to a scrambled (unreadable) form of text.

event handler — A line of code that allows a language to respond to a specific event or user input.

event-driven — Reacting to particular user actions or the browser's completion of a specific task.

Extensible Hypertext Markup Language (XHTML) — The current standard authoring language used to develop Web pages and other electronically displayed documents. XHTML requires stricter code syntax than HTML.

Extensible Markup Language (XML) — A markup language that describes document content, instead of adding structure or formatting to document content. A simplified version of SGML.

Extensible Stylesheet Language (XSL) — A style language that provides formatting instructions for XML documents.

extranet — A network that connects enterprise intranets to the global Internet. Designed to provide access to selected external users.

field — A category of information in a database table.

File Transfer Protocol (FTP) — An Internet protocol used to transfer files between computers.

firewall — A security barrier that controls the flow of information between the Internet and private networks. A firewall prevents outsiders from accessing an enterprise's internal network, which accesses the Internet indirectly through a proxy server.

fixed-width font — A font in which every character, including the space character, has equal width. In proportional-width fonts, letters such as I and J have less width than M or B.

foreign key — A field in a related database table that refers to the primary key in the primary table.

frame — 1: A scrollable region of a Web page in which other pages can be displayed; a single element of a frameset. Each frame has its own URL.
2: Data passed between a system that contains addressing and link control information. Like all network protocols, IPX/SPX encapsulates its communications into frames.

frameset document — A Web page that defines a set of adjacent frames in which other Web pages are displayed.

front end — A client that acts as an interface to a collection of servers (for example, mainframes or PC-based servers). A Web browser is a typical front-end client.

fully qualified domain name (FQDN) — The complete domain name of an Internet computer, such as *www.CIWcertified.com.*

Gantt chart — A horizontal bar chart that graphically displays project tasks and durations.

gateway — A node on a network that serves as a portal to other networks.

Gnu Privacy Guard (GPG) — An open-source version of PGP, used for encrypting and decrypting e-mail messages, that does not use patented algorithms.

graphical user interface (GUI) — A program that provides visual navigation with menus and screen icons, and performs automated functions when users click command buttons.

hacker — An unauthorized user who penetrates a host or network to access and manipulate data.

hash — A number generated by an algorithm from a text string.

hash encryption — An encryption method in which hashes are used to verify the integrity of transmitted messages.

header — A block of information attached to a piece of data. The first part of a network packet. Can contain network addressing information or additional information that helps computers and applications process data.

help desk technician — An individual responsible for diagnosing and resolving users' technical hardware and software problems.

hexadecimal — A base-16 number system that allows large numbers to be displayed by fewer characters than if the number were displayed in the regular base-10 system. In hexadecimal, the number 10 is represented as the letter A, 15 is represented as F, and 16 is represented as 10.

home page — The first Web page that displays when you access a domain.

hop — One link between two network devices; the number of hops between two devices is considered a hop count.

host — A computer that other computers can use to gain information; in network architecture, a host is a client or workstation.

hosts file — A file that contains mappings of IP addresses to host names.

hub — A device used to connect systems so that they can communicate with one another; a repeater or a bridge.

hyperlinks — Embedded instructions within a text file that link it to another point in the file or to a separate file.

hypertext link — Highlighted or underlined text in a Web page that, when clicked, links the user to another location or Web page.

Hypertext Markup Language (HTML) — The traditional authoring language used to develop Web pages for many applications.

Hypertext Transfer Protocol (HTTP) — The protocol for transporting HTML documents across the Internet.

I/O address — A memory location that allows resources to be allocated to a system device.

illicit server — An application that installs hidden services on systems. Illicit servers consist of "client" code and "server" code that enable the attacker to monitor and control the operation of the computer infected with the server code.

image map — A set of coordinates on an image that creates a "hot spot," which acts as a hyperlink when clicked.

index — A catalog of the contents of a database. Each entry identifies a unique database record.

Information Technology (IT) — The management and processing of information using computers and computer networks.

infrared — A spectrum of light used for communication between various network-enabled devices.

inline images — Images rendered in a Web page.

instant messaging (IM) — A computer-based method of communication in which users can type and view messages sent to one or more recipients, and view the responses immediately.

Integrated Services Digital Network (ISDN) — A communication standard for sending voice, video or data over digital telephone lines.

interactive — The characteristic of some hardware and software, such as computers, games and multimedia systems, that allows them to respond differently based on a user's actions.

interface — A communication channel between two components.

Internet — A worldwide network of interconnected networks.

Internet Control Messaging Protocol (ICMP) — A subset of Internet Protocol that is most often used to determine whether a computer can communicate with the rest of the network.

Internet Message Access Protocol (IMAP) — A protocol that resides on an incoming mail server. Similar to POP, but is more powerful. Allows sharing of mailboxes and multiple mail server access. The current version is IMAP4.

Internet Protocol (IP) — The data transmission standard for the Internet. Every computer connected to the Internet has its own IP address, which enables a packet of data to be delivered to a specific computer.

Internet Service Provider (ISP) — An organization that maintains a gateway to the Internet and rents access to customers on a per-use or subscription basis.

interoperability — The ability of one computer system to communicate with another; often refers to different operating systems working together.

intranet — An internal network based on TCP/IP protocols, accessible only to users within a company.

interrupt request (IRQ) — A hardware line over which devices can send interrupt signals to the processor.

IP address — A unique numerical address assigned to a computer or device on a network.

IP Security (IPsec) — An authentication and encryption standard that provides security over the Internet. It functions at Layer 3 of the OSI/RM and can secure all packets transmitted over the network.

Java — An object-oriented programming language developed by Sun Microsystems that is fully cross-platform functional.

Java Virtual Machine (JVM) — The artificial computer that runs Java programs and allows the same code to run on different platforms.

JavaScript — An interpreted, object-based scripting language developed by Netscape Communications that adds interactivity to Web pages.

junction table — A database table containing foreign-key fields that refer to the primary-key fields from the primary tables in a many-to-many relationship.

Kerberos — A proprietary key management scheme between unknown principals who want to communicate securely. Uses symmetric algorithms and acts as a trusted third party that knows the identities of the organizations asking to communicate, but does not reveal them.

kernel — The essential part of an operating system; provides basic services; always resides in memory.

key — A variable value, such as a numeric code, that uses an algorithm to encrypt and decrypt data. Some applications encrypt and decrypt with the same key, whereas other applications use a pair of keys.

keyword — A word that appears on a Web page and is used by search engines to identify relevant URLs. Some words, such as "the" or "and," are too common to be used as keywords.

Layer 1 switch — A device that connects individual systems; a Layer 3 switch connects networks.

legacy model — A model that, because of its age, may not support modern technologies without manipulation or upgrades.

Lightweight Directory Access Protocol (LDAP) — A protocol that allows a network entity to access a directory service listing.

list server — A server that collects and distributes information from an authorized group of participants, called a listserve group.

listserve group — Users who subscribe to an e-mailing list through a list server.

LiveScript — The Netscape-developed scripting language that was the predecessor to JavaScript.

local area network (LAN) — A group of computers connected within a confined geographic area.

lossless compression — A type of data file compression in which all original data can be recovered when the file is decompressed.

lossy compression — A type of data file compression in which some file information is permanently eliminated.

Mail Delivery Agent (MDA) — An e-mail server program that receives sent messages and delivers them to their proper destination mailbox.

Mail User Agent (MUA) — A messaging component used as a stand-alone application by the user.

mailing list server — An e-mail server that regularly sends e-mail messages to a specified list of users.

malware — Abbreviation for malicious software. Malware is software designed to harm computer systems.

many-to-many relationship — In databases, a relationship in which one record in Table A can relate to many matching records in Table B, and vice versa.

markup language — A series of commands used to format, organize and describe information on a Web page.

media — Any material that allows data to flow through it or be stored on it; includes hard and floppy disks, wire, cable, and fiber optics.

Media Access Control (MAC) address — The hardware address of a device connected to a network.

Message Transfer Agent (MTA) — A messaging component that routes, delivers and receives e-mail.

meta search engine — A search engine that scans Web pages for <meta> tag information.

metalanguage — A language used for defining other languages.

MIME type — Identifies the contents of a file in the MIME encoding system using a type/subtype format; examples are image/jpg and text/plain.

modem — Abbreviation for modulator/demodulator. An analog device that enables computers to communicate over telephone lines by translating digital data into audio/analog signals (on the sending computer) and then back into digital form (on the receiving computer).

motherboard — The main circuit board in a computer, on which the microprocessor, physical memory and support circuitry are located.

Moving Picture Experts Group (MPEG) — High-quality video file compression format.

MPEG-1 Audio Layer-3 (MP3) — Compression standard for audio files; maintains original sound quality.

MPEG-2 — Current video compression standard.

Multipurpose Internet Mail Extensions (MIME) — A protocol that enables operating systems to map file name extensions to corresponding applications. Also used by applications to automatically process files downloaded from the Internet.

Multistation Access Unit (MAU) — The network device that is the central connection point for token-ring networks.

municipal area network (MAN) — A network used to communicate over a city or geographic area.

Musical Instrument Digital Interface (MIDI) — A standard computer interface for creating and playing electronic music. It allows computers to re-create music in digital format for playback.

narrowband — A specific set of frequencies established for wireless communication (usually for voice). Communicates at lower rates than broadband.

National Science Foundation (NSF) — An independent agency of the U.S. government that promotes the advancement of science and engineering.

needs analysis — Determining a customer's needs by acquiring information, processing and evaluating the information, then creating a plan of action to address the needs.

network — A group of two or more computers connected so they can communicate with one another.

Network Address Translation (NAT) — The practice of hiding internal IP addresses from the external network.

network engineer — An individual responsible for managing and maintaining a network infrastructure.

network interface card (NIC) — A circuit board within a computer's central processing unit that serves as the interface enabling the computer to connect to a network.

Network News Transfer Protocol (NNTP) — The Internet protocol used by news servers that enables the exchange of Usenet articles.

network operating system (NOS) — An operating system that manages network resources.

newsgroup — On Usenet, a subject or other topical interest group whose members exchange ideas and opinions. Participants post and receive messages via a news server.

node — Any entity on a network that can be managed, such as a system, repeater, router, gateway or firewall. A computer or other addressable device attached to a network; a host.

non-repudiation — The security principle of providing proof that a transaction occurred between identified parties. Repudiation occurs when one party in a transaction denies that the transaction took place.

object — An element on a Web page that contains data and procedures for how that item will react when activated. On a Web page, an object is typically a multimedia presentation.

object-based — Similar to object-oriented programming languages, but does not allow for inheritance from one class to another.

object-oriented — A style of programming that links data to the processes that manipulate it.

object-oriented programming (OOP) — Programming concept based on objects and data and how they relate to one another, instead of logic and actions; C++ and Java are OOP languages.

OCx — Optical carrier levels; defines the transmission speeds used in SONET/SDH.

one-to-many relationship — In databases, a relationship in which a record in Table A can have multiple matching records in Table B, but a record in Table B has only one matching record in Table A.

one-to-one relationship — In databases, a relationship in which each record in Table A can have only one matching record in Table B, and vice versa.

online service e-mail — An e-mail program that is part of an online service's software.

Open Buying on the Internet (OBI) — An open-technology standard used by organizations to exchange data in a common format; an alternative to EDI.

open source — Characterized by providing free source code to the development community at large to develop a better product; includes Apache Web server, Netscape Communicator and Linux.

Open Systems Interconnection (OSI) reference model — A layered network architecture model of communication developed by the International Organization for Standardization (ISO). Defines seven layers of network functions

order tracking — The ability to determine progress on delivery of a product. Businesses often provide order-tracking support to end users via Web browsers and e-mail clients.

P2P — A peer-to-peer network on the Internet.

packet — Data processed by protocols so it can be sent across a network.

packet sniffing — The use of protocol analyzer software to obtain sensitive information, such as user names and passwords.

password sniffing — A method of intercepting the transmission of a password during the authentication process. A sniffer is a program used to intercept passwords.

patch — Programming code that provides a temporary solution to a known problem, or bug.

patch panel — A group of sockets that manually switches data between inbound and outbound transmissions.

PC repair technician — An individual responsible for installing, modifying and repairing personal computer (PC) hardware components.

peer-to-peer network — A network in which each computer has both server and client capabilities.

peripheral port — A socket on a computer in which a peripheral device is connected.

permission bit — A file or directory attribute that determines access. Permission bits include read, write and execute permissions.

permissions — Instructions given by an operating system or server (or a combination thereof) that restrict or allow access to system resources, such as files, user databases and system processes.

Personal Digital Assistant (PDA) — A small, handheld computer used for personal information management.

personal information management (PIM) program — A tool used to schedule appointments and meetings, store contact information, and manage tasks.

planned maintenance — Any scheduled maintenance procedures, including preventive maintenance.

plenum — Space between building floors; usually contains air and heating ducts, as well as communication and electrical wires.

plug-in — A program installed in the browser to extend its basic functionality. Allows different file formats to be viewed as part of a standard HTML document.

Point-to-Point Protocol (PPP) — A protocol that allows a computer to connect to the Internet over a phone line.

Point-to-Point Protocol over Ethernet (PPPoE) — A protocol that implements PPP over Ethernet to connect an entire network to the Internet.

Point-to-Point Tunneling Protocol (PPTP) — A protocol that allows users and corporations to securely extend their networks over the Internet using remote access servers. Used to create VPNs.

pop-under window — A small browser window that appears behind the browser window you are viewing.

pop-up window — A small browser window that appears in front of the browser window you are viewing.

port — A logical opening in an operating system or protocol stack that allows the transfer of information. Not the same as a TCP or UDP port.

Portable Document Format (PDF) — A file format that can be transferred across platforms and retain its formatting; designated by the file name extension .pdf.

Post Office Protocol (POP) — A protocol that resides on an incoming mail server. The current version is POP3.

power spike — A short-duration high-voltage condition.

presentation responsibilities — The forms in which the data and business logic are presented on your screen. Presentation responsibilities include XHTML and HTML forms, and application-specific interfaces such as Web browsers.

Pretty Good Privacy (PGP) — A method of encrypting and decrypting e-mail messages. It can also be used to encrypt a digital signature.

primary key — A field containing a value that uniquely identifies each record in a database table.

print queue — A mechanism that stores print requests until they are passed to a printing device.

project — A sequence of tasks that must be accomplished within a certain time frame to achieve a desired result.

project management — The practice of applying skills and processes to activities in order to meet deadlines and achieve desired results.

project schedule — A document that lists the planned dates for performing tasks and meeting goals defined in a project plan.

proxy server — A server that mediates traffic between a protected network and the Internet. Translates IP addresses and filters traffic.

PS/2-style connector — The six-pin mini-DIN connectors introduced with the IBM PS/2.

query — A question posed by a user to a database to request database information. The database returns the query results based on the criteria supplied by the user in the query.

QuickTime Movie (MOV) — Standard file format for Apple QuickTime; uses the .mov, .moov or .qt file name extension.

QuickTime — A plug-in developed by Apple Computer for storing movie and audio files in digital format.

record — A collection of information in a database table consisting of one or more related fields about a specific entity, such as a person, product or event.

relational database — A database that contains multiple tables related through common fields.

relationship — A connection between two or more database tables that is based on a field that the tables have in common.

relative URL — A URL that gives an abbreviated path to a resource using the current page as a starting position.

replay attack — An attack in which packets are obtained from the network or a network host, then reused.

Request for Comments (RFC) — A published document that details information about standardized Internet protocols and those in various development stages.

reseller — A company that adds some value to an existing, then sells it to the public or to another company.

resource — A person, department or device needed to accomplish a task.

resource conflict — A situation in which two or more devices share a configuration setting.

restore point — A snapshot of a computer's settings at a particular point in time. Also known as a system checkpoint.

Return On Investment (ROI) — Profit earned as a result of a project relative to the value of resources required to complete it.

Rich Text Format (RTF) — Portable text file format created by Microsoft that allows image insertion and text formatting; an almost universal format.

root directory — Topmost hard disk directory (folder).

root-level server — A server at the highest level of the Domain Name System.

router — A device that routes packets between networks based on network-layer address; determines the best path across a network. Also used to connect separate LANs to form a WAN.

RSA — A popular, proprietary public key encryption algorithm.

rule — 1: In page design, a graphical line or lines; the word is related to "ruler," a tool of measurement that can be used to draw straight lines. 2: In a style sheet, a format instruction that consists of a specified selector and the properties and values applied to it.

sans-serif — A font style that does not use decorative strokes at the tips of characters. Includes the Arial font family.

scope — The goals and tasks of a project, and the work required to complete them.

scope creep — Gradual increases in project scope that can undermine the success of a project.

screen saver — A graphic or moving image that appears on your screen when your computer is idle.

search engine — A powerful software program that searches Internet databases for user-specified information.

Secure Copy (SCP) — A program used with Secure Shell (SSH) to transfer files between systems.

Secure Electronic Transactions (SET) — An Internet protocol that uses digital certificates to secure financial transactions.

Secure MIME (S/MIME) — Secure version of MIME that adds encryption to MIME data.

Secure Shell (SSH) — A protocol and command interface that provides secure access to a remote computer.

Secure Sockets Layer (SSL) — A protocol that provides authentication and encryption, used by most servers for secure exchanges over the Internet. Superseded by Transport Layer Security (TLS).

security analyst/consultant — An individual responsible for examining an organization's security requirements and determining the necessary infrastructure.

security manager — An individual responsible for managing the security measures used to protect electronic data.

segment — Part of a larger structure; common term used in networking.

selector — In a style sheet, any element to which designated styles are applied.

serif — A font style that uses characters with small decorative additions at the outermost points of the characters, called strokes. Includes the Times and Times New Roman fonts.

server — A computer in a network that manages the network resources and provides, or serves, information to clients.

server administrator — An individual responsible for managing and maintaining network servers.

server-side script — Code that resides on a server to help process Web form input. Server-side CGI scripts are commonly written in Perl.

Service Advertising Protocol (SAP) — A protocol designed to provide file and print services for Novell NetWare networks.

servlet — A small Java application that runs on a server.

shared domain — A hosting service that allows multiple entities to share portions of the same domain name.

shell — A command-based interface that allows a user to issue commands.

Simple Mail Transfer Protocol (SMTP) — The Internet standard protocol for transferring e-mail messages from one computer to another.

site map — A brief, hierarchical representation of a Web site that enables visitors to quickly identify areas of the site and navigate to them.

Small-Screen Rendering (SSR) — A browser technology developed for wireless devices that reformats Web pages to display on 176-pixel-wide cellular phone display screens.

smart card — A credit card that replaces the magnetic strip with an embedded chip for storing or processing data.

snail mail — Slang term for the standard postal service.

socket — The end point of a connection (either side), which usually includes the TCP or UDP port used and the IP address. Used for communication between a client and a server.

spam — Unsolicited and unwanted e-mail messages; the online equivalent of junk mail.

spam filter — An e-mail client program that identifies and filters out spam messages before they reach the e-mail Inbox.

spim — Spam that is delivered through instant messaging.

spread spectrum — Technologies that consist of various methods for radio transmission in which frequencies or signal patterns are continuously changed.

spyware — A software application secretly placed on a user's system to gather information and relay it to outside parties, usually for advertising purposes.

SSH File Transfer Protocol (S/FTP) — A file transfer protocol that allows the encryption of transmissions using the Secure Shell (SSH) protocol.

SSL/TLS-enabled FTP (FTPS) — FTP that runs on an SSL/TLS-secured connection.

stakeholder — A person or group with an interest in a project and the power to exert influence (either positive or negative) over the project and affect results.

standard — A definition or format that has been approved by a recognized standards organization.

Standard Generalized Markup Language (SGML) — A metalanguage used to create other languages, including HTML and XHTML.

Statement Of Work (SOW) — A contract to initiate a project; the contract contains project goals and specifies how those goals will be met.

streaming audio and video — Audio and video files that travel over a network in real time.

streaming media — A continuous flow of data, usually audio or video files, that assists with the uninterrupted delivery of those files into a browser.

Structured Query Language (SQL) — A language used to create and maintain professional, high-performance corporate databases.

switch — A device used to connect either individual systems or multiple networks.

symmetric-key encryption — An encryption method in which the same key is used to encrypt and decrypt a message.

Synchronous Optical Network (SONET) — High-speed fiber-optic system used as a network and Internet backbone. The European counterpart is the Synchronous Digital Hierarchy (SDH).

T1 — A digital carrier that transmits data at a speed of 1.544 Mbps.

table — A collection of data about a limited topic, organized into rows and columns in a database.

Tagged Image File Format (TIFF) — Commonly used graphic file format, developed by Aldus Corporation; uses the .tif or .tiff file name extension.

tags — Pieces of code, enclosed in angle brackets, that tell the HTML interpreter how to process or display text.

task — A unit of work that must be accomplished during the course of a project.

Telnet — The Internet standard protocol for remote terminal connection service.

text-level element — A markup element that affects single characters or words.

token passing — The LAN access method used by token ring networks. A data frame, or token, is passed from one node to the next around the network ring.

top-level domain — The group into which a domain is categorized, by common topic (company, educational institution) and/or geography (country, state).

trace — Thin conductive path on a circuit board, usually made of copper.

transceiver — A device that transmits and receives digital or analog signals.

Transmission Control Protocol/Internet Protocol (TCP/IP) — A suite of protocols that turns data into blocks of information called packets, which are then sent across the Internet. The standard protocol used by the Internet.

Transport Layer Security (TLS) — A secure protocol based on SSL 3.0 that provides encryption and authentication.

Trojan horse — A program disguised as a harmless application that actually produces harmful results.

troll — A Web user who publishes comments or submits feedback simply to annoy or anger.

trouble ticket — A record of a problem related to a service provided by an ISP or ASP. Used to record receipt of a complaint and track resolution of the problem.

tunneling protocol — A protocol that encapsulates data packets into another packet.

Unicode — A universal character set designed to support all written languages, as well as scholarly disciplines (e.g., mathematics).

Uniform Resource Identifier (URI) — A standardized method of referring to a resource.

Uniform Resource Locator (URL) — A text string that specifies an Internet address and the method by which the address can be accessed.

uninterruptible power supply (UPS) — A power supply that uses a battery to maintain power during a power outage.

update — A file or collection of tools that resolves system liabilities and improves software performance.

Usenet (User Network) — A collection of thousands of Internet computers, newsgroups and newsgroup members using Network News Transfer Protocol (NNTP) to exchange information.

user agent — Any application, such as a Web browser, cell phone, PDA or help engine, that renders HTML for display to users.

user name — A unique name or number that identifies you when logging on to a computer system or online service. In an e-mail address, the part before the @ symbol.

vector graphics — Resizable images that are saved as a sequence of vector statements, which describes a series of points to be connected.

viewer — A scaled-down version of an application; designed to view and print files.

virtual domain — A hosting service that allows a company to host its domain name on a third-party ISP server.

virtual local area network (VLAN) — Logical subgroup within a LAN created with software instead of hardware.

Virtual Network Computing (VNC) — A program that allows you to control a computer at a remote location.

Virtual Private Network (VPN) — A secure network between two sites using Internet technology as the transport; an extended LAN that enables a company to conduct secure, real-time communication.

Virtual Reality Modeling Language (VRML) — A three-dimensional graphic authoring language.

virus — A malicious program that replicates itself on computer systems, usually through executable software, and causes irreparable system damage.

Visual Basic — The Microsoft graphical user interface (GUI) programming language used for developing Windows applications. A modified version of the BASIC programming language.

Visual Basic Script (VBScript) — Scripting language from Microsoft, derived from Visual Basic; used to manipulate ActiveX scripts.

Voice over IP (VoIP) — A technology that transmits voice in digital form as packets of data using Internet Protocol.

Waveform (WAV) — Windows standard format for audio files.

Web application developer — An individual who develops primarily server-side Web applications.

Web architect — An individual who is responsible for creating the overview plan of a Web site's development.

Web-based e-mail — Free e-mail service from a provider such as Hotmail or Yahoo! in which you request a user name. You can access your e-mail from any computer that has access to the Internet.

Web browser — A software application that enables users to access and view Web pages on the Internet.

Web page — An HTML document containing one or more elements (text, images, hyperlinks) that can be linked to or from other HTML pages.

Web site — A World Wide Web server and its content; includes multiple Web pages.

Web site analyst — An individual who analyzes Web site statistics to determine the site's effectiveness.

Web site designer — An individual responsible for the organization and appearance of a Web site.

Web site manager — An individual who manages a Web development team.

Webinar — An interactive Web-based seminar or training session.

What You See Is What You Get (WYSIWYG) — (pronounced whiz-ee-wig) A user-friendly editing format in which the file being edited is displayed as it will appear in the browser.

wide area network (WAN) — A group of computers connected over an expansive geographic area so their users can share files and services.

wideband — A large set of frequencies capable of carrying data at higher rates (for example, 1.544 Mbps). Usually carries digital signals. Includes DSL and cable Internet access.

wireless access point (WAP) — A device that enables wireless systems to communicate with each other, provided that they are on the same network.

Wireless Application Protocol (WAP) — A standard protocol that wireless devices use to access the Internet.

Wireless Markup Language (WML) — A markup language that presents the text portions of Web pages to wireless devices.

wizard — A tool that assists users of an application in creating documents and/or databases based on styles and templates.

World Wide Web (WWW) — A set of software programs that enables users to access resources on the Internet via hypertext documents.

worm — A self-replicating program or algorithm that consumes system resources.

X Window — A windowing system used with UNIX and all popular operating systems.

X.509 — The standard used by certificate authorities (CAs) for creating digital certificates.

xDSL — Collectively, the variations of Digital Subscriber Line (DSL), which include ADSL, RADSL and HDSL.

zone file — A file containing a set of instructions for resolving a specific domain name into its numerical IP address.

Index

3-D, 3-3
802.11 standard, 1-21
absolute URL, 2-7
active content, 2-41
ActiveX, 3-5
address book, e-mail, 5-21
address, Web, 2-6
addresses, e-mail, 5-4
Adleman, Leonard, 7-4
Adobe Acrobat, 3-20
Adobe PageMaker, 3-26
Adobe Photoshop, 3-26
Adobe Reader, 3-20
Adobe Systems Incorporated, 3-20
ADSL, 1-22
Advanced Research Projects Agency (ARPA), 1-16
Advanced Research Projects Agency Network
    (ARPANET), 1-16
adware, 7-14
AIFF, 3-24
AltaVista, 4-19
animation, 3-4
antivirus program updates, 7-18
antivirus software, 7-13
Apple QuickTime, 3-6, 3-14
applet, 3-4
Arachne, 2-15
ARPA, 1-16
ARPANET, 1-16
articles, newsgroup, 1-27
assignment, 8-4
assumption, 8-7
Asymmetric Digital Subscriber Line (ADSL), 1-22
asymmetric-key encryption, 7-4
attachment, 5-16
AU, 3-24
audio, 3-4
Audio Interchange File Format (AIFF), 3-24
authentication, 2-11, 7-6
authentication types, 2-11
authorship, 7-24
backbone, 1-16
bandwidth, 1-20
binary file, 6-13
blackhole list, 5-31
blacklist, 5-31
blog, 6-38
Bookmarks, 2-22
Boolean operator, 4-17
browser, 1-17
browser cache, 2-30
browser e-mail, 5-5
browser fonts, 2-26
browser functions, 2-3
browser, installation of, 2-3
C, 3-3
C++, 3-3
CA, 7-6
cable Internet, 1-22
cable modem, 1-22
cache, browser, 2-30
cache, disk, 3-7

CAPTCHA, 5-31
career model, IT, 1-13
Carnegie Mellon University, 4-16
case-sensitive, 4-13, 4-18
categories, newsgroup, 6-5
certificate authority (CA), 7-6
certification, project management, 8-4
CGI, 4-8
Challenge Handshake Authentication Protocol
    (CHAP), 2-12
channel, 1-19
CHAP, 2-12
Chernobyl virus, 7-10
Chicago Manual of Style, The, 4-27
ciphertext, 7-3
citing Web site references, 4-26
client, 1-14
client/server model, 1-14
closing phase, 8-10
codec, 3-8
common field, 4-3
Common Gateway Interface (CGI), 4-8
Completely Automated Public Turing Test to Tell
    Computers and Humans Apart (CAPTCHA), 5-31
compression, 3-8
compression utilities, 6-23
compression, lossless, 3-8
compression, lossy, 3-8
Concurrent Versions System (CVS), 6-35
constraint, 8-7
controlling phase, 8-2, 8-8
convergence technologies, 1-11
cookies, 2-35
copyright, 4-27, 7-24
copyright infringement, 3-26, 4-27, 7-24
copyright law, 7-25
CVS, 6-35
database, 4-3
database administrator, 1-10
database management system (DBMS), 4-7
DBMS, 4-7
dead link, 1-8
decompression, 3-8
decryption, 2-11
deep URL, 2-7
desktop firewall, 7-7
dial-up Internet connection, 1-19
dial-up Internet connection speeds, 1-20
digital certificate, 2-12, 7-6
digital signature, 2-12, 7-6
Digital Subscriber Line (DSL), 1-22
direct Internet connection, 1-20
direct Internet connection speeds, 1-23
directory search, 4-10
disk cache, 3-7
DNS, 1-27
document files, 3-25
domain, 5-4
domain name, 5-5
domain name server, 1-32
domain name structure, 1-28
domain name syntax, 1-28

Domain Name System (DNS), 1-27
domain, top-level, 1-29
DSL, 1-22
Duke University, 6-3
dynamic, 3-4
E1 line, 1-21
E3 line, 1-21
e-mail address book, 5-21
e-mail addresses, 5-4
e-mail client, 5-5
e-mail content, illicit, 5-30
e-mail protocols, 5-4
e-mail responses, 5-26
e-mail servers, 1-26
e-mail signature, 5-19
e-mail, workplace use of, 5-26
e-mail/groupware administrator, 1-11
emoticons, 5-28
Encapsulated PostScript (EPS), 3-26
encryption, 2-11, 7-3
encryption levels, 7-18
encryption policies, 7-26
encryption, asymmetric-key, 7-4
encryption, hash, 7-5
encryption, one-way, 7-5
encryption, public-key, 7-4
encryption, secret-key, 7-4
encryption, symmetric-key, 7-4
EPS, 3-26
EPSI, 3-26
event-driven, 3-4
Excite, 4-17
executing phase, 8-2, 8-8
extranet, 2-20
Favorites, 2-22
field, 4-3
File Transfer Protocol (FTP), 1-26, 6-12
files, document, 3-25
files, graphics, 3-25
files, sound, 3-24
files, video, 3-23
FileZilla, 6-17, 6-19
firewall, 7-6
firewall, desktop, 7-7
firewall, personal, 7-7
Flash, 3-10
fonts, browser, 2-26
foreign key, 4-5
FQDN, 1-29
Frena, George, 7-25
FTP, 1-26, 6-12
FTP over SSL (S/FTP), 2-14
FTPS, 6-20
fully qualified domain name (FQDN), 1-29
Gantt chart, 8-12
Gantt, Henry, 8-12
GanttProject, 8-11
gateway, 1-16
GIF, 3-4
Gnu Privacy Guard (GPG), 5-8
GnuPG, 5-8
Goldmine, 4-7
Google, 4-16
Google Groups, 6-4
GPG, 5-8
graphical user interface (GUI), 3-4
graphics files, 3-25
graphics-editing application, 3-26
Green Paper, 7-25

GUI, 3-4
Habitat for Humanity, 1-4
hash, 7-5
hash encryption, 7-5
HDSL, 1-22
header, 5-7
help desk technician, 1-12
hexadecimal, 1-25
High bit-rate Digital Subscriber Line (HDSL), 1-22
History folder, 2-28
home page, browser, 2-27
home page, Web site, 2-7
host, Web site, 1-28
hostile applets, 2-41
Hotmail, 5-14
HTML, 1-17
HTTP, 1-25
HTTP over Secure Sockets Layer (HTTPS), 2-13
HTTPS, 2-13
hyperlink, 1-17
hypertext link, 1-17
Hypertext Markup Language (HTML), 1-17
Hypertext Transfer Protocol (HTTP), 1-25
ICANN, 1-28
ICMP, 7-8
IEEE, 1-21
IETF, 2-13
IITF, 7-25
illicit server, 7-11
IM, 6-30
IMAP, 1-26, 5-4
index, 4-10
Information Infrastructure Task Force (IITF), 7-25
information portal, 4-10
Information Technology (IT), 1-3
initiating phase, 8-6
inline video, 3-4
instant messaging (IM), 6-30
Institute of Electrical and Electronics Engineers (IEEE), 1-21
Integrated Services Digital Network (ISDN), 1-19
interactive, 3-4
International Organization for Standardization (ISO), 8-18
Internet, 1-16
Internet connection speeds, dial-up, 1-20
Internet connection speeds, direct, 1-23
Internet connection, dial-up, 1-19
Internet connection, direct, 1-20
Internet Control Messaging Protocol (ICMP), 7-8
Internet Corporation for Assigned Names and Numbers (ICANN), 1-28
Internet Engineering Task Force (IETF), 2-13
Internet Explorer, 2-14
Internet History folder, 2-28
Internet Message Access Protocol (IMAP), 1-26, 5-4
Internet Protocol (IP), 1-24
Internet Protocol version 4 (IPv4), 1-24
Internet Protocol version 6 (IPv6), 1-25
Internet safety levels, 2-41
Internet Service Provider (ISP), 1-19
intranet, 2-20
IP, 1-24
IP address, 5-3
ipconfig, 6-39
IPv4, 1-24
IPv6, 1-25
ISDN, 1-19
ISDN Basic Rate Interface (BRI), 1-19

ISDN BRI, 1-19
ISDN PRI, 1-19
ISDN Primary Rate Interface (PRI), 1-19
ISO, 8-18
ISO 9000, 8-18
ISP, 1-19
issues log, 8-16
IT, 1-3
IT career model, 1-13
IT job roles, 1-3
IT projects, 8-3
IT projects, effects of, 8-19
Java, 3-3
JavaScript, 3-4
job roles, IT, 1-3
JPEG, 3-4
JScript, 3-5
junction table, 4-6
key, 7-3
key, private, 7-4
key, public, 7-4
keyword, 4-8
keyword search, 4-10
Konqueror, 2-15
LAN, 1-15
LDAP, 6-35
Lightweight Directory Access Protocol (LDAP), 6-35
link, 1-17
list server, 7-20
LISTSERV, 7-21
listserve group, 7-20
LiveScript, 3-5
LiveVideo, 3-23
local area network (LAN), 1-15
lossless compression, 3-8
lossy compression, 3-8
Lycos, 4-16
Lynx, 2-15
Macromedia Flash, 3-9
Macromedia Shockwave, 3-6, 3-9
Mail Delivery Agent (MDA), 5-4
mail transport agent, 5-4
Mail User Agent (MUA), 5-5
malware, 7-10
many-to-many relationship, 4-6
MAPHIA, 7-25
MDA, 5-4
Media Player, 3-17
meetings, 8-17
Melissa virus, 7-10
Message Transfer Agent (MTA), 5-4
message-digest, 7-5
meta search engines, 4-9
meta tag, 4-9
Microsoft Challenge Handshake Authentication
    Protocol (MS-CHAP), 2-12
Microsoft Excel, 3-4
Microsoft Internet Explorer, 2-14
Microsoft PowerPoint Viewer, 3-20
Microsoft Terminal Services, 6-28
Microsoft Visual Studio, 6-4
Microsoft Windows Media Player, 3-17
Microsoft Word, 3-4
MIDI, 3-7, 3-24
MIME, 5-6
MIME types, defining, 6-21
minus sign, 4-19
MLA Handbook for Writers of Research Papers, 4-27
modem, 1-19

Mozilla, 2-15
MP3, 3-24, 6-34
MPEG-1 Audio Layer-3 (MP3), 3-24
MS-CHAP, 2-12
MTA, 5-4
MUA, 5-5
Multilink Point-to-Point Protocol (MLPPP), 1-25
Multipurpose Internet Mail Extensions (MIME), 5-6
Musical Instrument Digital Interface (MIDI), 3-7
Napster, 6-34, 7-26
National Science Foundation (NSF), 1-16
Navigator, 2-14
needs analysis, 8-6
netiquette, 6-36
Netscape Mail & Newsgroups, 5-5
Netscape Mail & Newsgroups, configuration of, 5-9
Netscape Navigator, 2-14
network, 1-14
network engineer, 1-11
network interface card (NIC), 1-21
Network News Transfer Protocol (NNTP), 1-27
network server, 1-14
newsgroup articles, 1-27
newsgroup categories, 6-5
newsgroups, 1-27, 6-3
NIC, 1-21
NNTP, 1-27
node, 1-14
non-repudiation, 7-6
NSF, 1-16
NSFnet, 1-16
object, 3-3
object-based, 3-5, 3-6
object-oriented programming (OOP), 3-3
ODBC, 4-8
offline plug-in installation, 3-9
Ogg Vorbis, 3-24
one-to-many relationship, 4-5
one-to-one relationship, 4-5
one-way encryption, 7-5
online content design, 3-5
online plug-in installation, 3-9
online service e-mail, 5-5
on-screen element, 3-4
OOP, 3-3
Open Database Connectivity (ODBC) standard, 4-8
Open Group, The, 3-5, 4-8
Opera, 2-15
operators, Boolean, 4-17
Oracle Corporation, 4-7
Outlook Express, 5-5
Outlook Express, configuration of, 5-8
P2P, 6-34
packet, 1-17
page-layout application, 3-26
PageMaker, 3-26
PAP, 2-11
paper trail, 8-16
Password Authentication Protocol (PAP), 2-11
patch, 7-18
PC repair technician, 1-12
PDA, 5-36
PDF, 3-20
PE_Nimda.A-O worm, 7-11
peer-to-peer network, 6-34
personal computer (PC) repair technician, 1-12
Personal Digital Assistant (PDA), 5-36
personal information management (PIM) program, 5-35
PGP, 5-7

Photoshop, 3-26
PICT, 3-26
PIM, 5-35
ping, 6-39
plagiarism, 4-26
plaintext, 7-3
planning phase, 8-7
Playboy Enterprises vs. Frena, 7-25
plug-in, 3-6
plug-in appearance, 3-7
plug-in installation, 3-9
PMBOK, 8-22
PMI, 8-22
Point-to-Point Protocol (PPP), 1-25
Point-to-Point Protocol over Ethernet (PPPoE), 1-25
POP, 1-26
POP3, 5-4
pop-under window, 2-29
pop-up window, 2-29
Portable Document Format (PDF), 3-20
Post Office Protocol (POP), 1-26, 5-4
PostScript, 3-26
PowerPoint Viewer, 3-20
PPP, 1-25
PPPoE, 1-25
Pretty Good Privacy (PGP), 5-7
primary key, 4-5
privacy, 7-23
private key, 7-4
project, 8-3
project life cycle, 8-6
project management, 8-3
Project Management Body of Knowledge (PMBOK), 8-22
project management certification, 8-4
Project Management Institute (PMI), 8-22
project management phases, 8-6
project management software, 8-10
project review, 8-17
project schedule, 8-7, 8-12
project success, 8-7
project triangle, 8-10
protocols, e-mail, 5-4
protocols, secure, 2-13
proxy server, 2-44
public key, 7-4
public-key encryption, 7-4
QTVR, 3-14
query, 4-7
QuickTime, 3-14
QuickTime Movie (MOV), 3-14
QuickTime Virtual Reality (QTVR), 3-14
RADSL, 1-22
raster graphics, 3-10
Rate-Adaptive DSL (RADSL), 1-22
RealAudio, 3-13
RealNetworks, 3-13
RealOne, 3-13
RealPlayer, 3-13
real-time data feeds, 3-4
RealVideo, 3-13
record, 4-3
Recording Industry Association of America (RIAA) vs. Napster, 7-26
relational database, 4-3
relationship, 4-3
relative URL, 2-7
Remote Assistance, 6-33
Remote Desktop Connection, 6-28

Request for Comments (RFC), 2-13
resource, 8-4
responses, e-mail, 5-26
Return On Investment (ROI), 8-21
reverse DNS, 1-32
reverse Domain Name System (reverse DNS), 1-32
review, project, 8-17
RFC, 2-13
Rich Text Format (RTF), 3-26
Rivest, Ronald, 7-4
robot, 4-9
ROI, 8-21
root-level server, 1-29
router, 1-18
RSA algorithm, 7-4
RSA Security, 5-7, 7-4
RTF, 3-26
S/FTP, 2-14, 6-20
S/MIME, 5-7
scope, 8-4
scope creep, 8-4
SCP, 6-20
screen saver, 7-19
scripting, 3-5, 3-6
search engine, 4-8
search, directory, 4-10
search, keyword, 4-10
secret-key encryption, 7-4
Secure Copy (SCP), 6-20
Secure MIME (S/MIME), 5-7
secure protocols, 2-13
Secure Shell (SSH), 6-10
Secure Sockets Layer (SSL), 2-13
security analyst/consultant, 1-12
security manager, 1-12
security policies, 7-7
Sega Enterprises Ltd. vs. MAPHIA, 7-25
server, 1-14
server administrator, 1-10
server, domain name, 1-32
server, e-mail, 1-26
server, proxy, 2-44
server, root-level, 1-29
servers, types of, 1-15
Shamir, Adi, 7-4
shared domain, 1-32
Shockwave, 3-9
signature, e-mail, 5-19
Simple Mail Transfer Protocol (SMTP), 1-26, 5-4
Small-Screen Rendering (SSR), 5-38
SMTP, 1-26, 5-4
snail mail, 5-3
sound files, 3-24
SOW, 8-7
spam, 5-30
spam filter, 5-31
spider program, 4-9
spider search engines, 4-9
spim, 6-31
spyware, 7-14
spyware detection, 7-15
SQL, 4-7
SSH, 6-10
SSH File Transfer Protocol (S/FTP), 6-20
SSL, 2-13
SSL/TLS-enabled FTP (FTPS), 6-20
SSR, 5-38
stakeholder, 8-5
standard, 1-21

Stanford University, 4-13
Statement Of Work (SOW), 8-7
streaming audio, 3-3
streaming format, 3-13
streaming media, 3-7
streaming video, 3-3
Structured Query Language (SQL), 4-7
Sun Microsystems, 3-5
symmetric-key encryption, 7-4
T1 line, 1-21
T3 line, 1-21
table, 4-3
task, 8-4
TCP/IP, 1-17, 5-3
Telnet, 6-8
Terminal Services, 6-28
TIFF, 3-26
TLS, 2-13
Topica, 7-22
top-level domain, 1-29
tracert, 6-39
trademark, 7-26
Transmission Control Protocol/Internet Protocol
    (TCP/IP), 1-17
Transport Layer Security (TLS), 2-13
Trojan horse, 7-11
Uniform Resource Identifier (URI), 2-6
Uniform Resource Locator (URL), 2-6
update, 7-18
URI, 2-6
URL, 2-6
URL, absolute, 2-7
URL, deep, 2-7
URL, relative, 2-7
Usenet (User Network), 1-27, 6-3
user interaction, 3-4
user name, 5-4
user-interface controls, 3-4
VBS Love Letter virus, 7-10
VBScript, 3-6
vector graphics, 3-10
video files, 3-23
viewer, 3-20
virtual domain, 1-32
Virtual Network Computing (VNC), 6-26
Virtual Reality Modeling Language (VRML), 3-19
virus, 7-10
viruses, protection from, 7-13
Visual Basic, 3-6

Visual Basic Script (VBScript), 3-6
VNC, 6-26
VRML, 3-19
W3C, 2-36
WAN, 1-15
WAP, 1-21, 5-37
WAV, 3-24
Waveform (WAV), 3-24
Web address, 2-6
Web application developer, 1-7
Web architect, 1-7
Web browser, 1-17
Web browser functions, 2-3
Web browser, installation of, 2-3
Web conference, 2-21
Web page, 1-17
Web server administrator, 1-11
Web site, 1-17
Web site analyst, 1-7
Web site designer, 1-3
Web site host, 1-28
Web site information, evaluation of, 4-25
Web site manager, 1-9
Web, World Wide, 1-17
Web-based e-mail, 5-5
WebCrawler, 4-17
Webinar, 2-21
WebTV, 1-20
wide area network (WAN), 1-15
Win32/Melting.worm, 7-11
Windows Media Player, 3-17
Windows Messenger, 6-31
Windows Remote Assistance, 6-33
WIPO, 7-25
wireless access point (WAP), 1-21
Wireless Application Protocol (WAP), 5-37
Wireless Markup Language (WML), 5-37
wizard, 2-4
WML, 5-37
WordBasic, 3-4
Working Group On Intellectual Property Rights, 7-25
World Intellectual Property Organization (WIPO), 7-25
World Wide Web, 1-17
World Wide Web Consortium (W3C), 2-36
worm, 7-11
X.500 standard, 6-35
xDSL, 1-22
Yahoo!, 4-13

Supplemental CD-ROM Contents

The *Internet Business Foundations* supplemental CD-ROM contains the following files needed to complete the course labs:

💿 Internet_Student_CD

- Answers
- Appendix
- Handouts
- Lab Files

📂 Answers

- ANSWERS_Activity.pdf
- ANSWERS_CourseAssessment.pdf
- ANSWERS_OptionalLab.pdf
- ANSWERS_PreAssessment.pdf
- ANSWERS_Quiz.pdf
- ANSWERS_Review.pdf

📂 Appendix

- Appendix_A.pdf
- Appendix_B.pdf
- Appendix_C.pdf

📂 Handouts

- HANDOUTS_Activity.pdf
- HANDOUTS_CourseAssessment.pdf
- HANDOUTS_OptionalLab.pdf
- HANDOUTS_Quiz.pdf

📂 Lab Files

- Completed LabFiles
- Lesson01
- Lesson02
- Lesson03
- Lesson05
- Lesson06
- Lesson07
- Lesson08

📂 Lab Files\Completed Lab Files

- Lesson01
- Lesson08

📂 Lab Files\Completed Lab Files\Lesson01\Lab_1-1

- blitz
- blitz.html
- missing_image.txt
- SYBcollage.jpg

📂 Lab Files\Completed Lab Files\Lesson01\Lab_1-1\blitz

📄 ccbutton1.gif	📄 navbg_02.gif	📄 sybheaders_05.jpg
📄 ccyp.css	📄 navbg_04.gif	📄 sybheaders_06.jpg
📄 childbutton1.gif	📄 stylesheet.css	📄 sybheaders_07.jpg
📄 clear.gif	📄 syb_application.pdf	📄 sybheaders_08.jpg
📄 colchalbutton1.gif	📄 sybbutton1.gif	📄 sybheaders_09.jpg
📄 FWbutton1.gif	📄 sybheaders_01.jpg	📄 SYBSumRept03.pdf
📄 FWbutton2.gif	📄 sybheaders_02.jpg	📄 SYBSumReptCV.jpg
📄 HFHILogo.gif	📄 sybheaders_03.jpg	📄 valid-xhtml110.png
📄 Intlbutton1.gif	📄 sybheaders_04.jpg	

📂 Lab Files\Completed Lab Files\Lesson08

📄 CIWIBF_L8-2.gan	📄 CIWIBF_OL8-1.gan

📂 Lab Files\Lesson01

📁 Lab_1-1	📁 Lab_1-2

📂 Lab Files\Lesson01\Lab_1-1

📁 blitz	📄 missing_image.txt
📄 blitz.html	📄 SYBcollage.jpg

📂 Lab Files\Lesson01\Lab_1-1\blitz

📄 ccbutton1.gif	📄 navbg_02.gif	📄 sybheaders_05.jpg
📄 ccyp.css	📄 navbg_04.gif	📄 sybheaders_06.jpg
📄 childbutton1.gif	📄 stylesheet.css	📄 sybheaders_07.jpg
📄 clear.gif	📄 syb_application.pdf	📄 sybheaders_08.jpg
📄 colchalbutton1.gif	📄 sybbutton1.gif	📄 sybheaders_09.jpg
📄 FWbutton1.gif	📄 sybheaders_01.jpg	📄 SYBSumRept03.pdf
📄 FWbutton2.gif	📄 sybheaders_02.jpg	📄 SYBSumReptCV.jpg
📄 HFHILogo.gif	📄 sybheaders_03.jpg	📄 valid-xhtml110.png
📄 Intlbutton1.gif	📄 sybheaders_04.jpg	

📁 Lab Files\Lesson01\Lab_1-2

ctry_usage_200109.png	daily_usage_200206.png	hourly_usage_200309.png
ctry_usage_200110.png	daily_usage_200301.png	hourly_usage_200310.png
ctry_usage_200111.png	daily_usage_200302.png	hourly_usage_200311.png
ctry_usage_200112.png	daily_usage_200303.png	hourly_usage_200312.png
ctry_usage_200201.png	daily_usage_200304.png	hourly_usage_200401.png
ctry_usage_200202.png	daily_usage_200305.png	index.html
ctry_usage_200203.png	daily_usage_200306.png	usage.png
ctry_usage_200204.png	daily_usage_200307.png	usage_200109.html
ctry_usage_200205.png	daily_usage_200308.png	usage_200110.html
ctry_usage_200206.png	daily_usage_200309.png	usage_200111.html
ctry_usage_200301.png	daily_usage_200310.png	usage_200112.html
ctry_usage_200302.png	daily_usage_200311.png	usage_200201.html
ctry_usage_200303.png	daily_usage_200312.png	usage_200202.html
ctry_usage_200304.png	daily_usage_200401.png	usage_200203.html
ctry_usage_200305.png	hourly_usage_200109.png	usage_200204.html
ctry_usage_200306.png	hourly_usage_200110.png	usage_200205.html
ctry_usage_200307.png	hourly_usage_200111.png	usage_200206.html
ctry_usage_200308.png	hourly_usage_200112.png	usage_200301.html
ctry_usage_200309.png	hourly_usage_200201.png	usage_200302.html
ctry_usage_200310.png	hourly_usage_200202.png	usage_200303.html
ctry_usage_200311.png	hourly_usage_200203.png	usage_200304.html
ctry_usage_200312.png	hourly_usage_200204.png	usage_200305.html
ctry_usage_200401.png	hourly_usage_200205.png	usage_200306.html
daily_usage_200109.png	hourly_usage_200206.png	usage_200307.html
daily_usage_200110.png	hourly_usage_200301.png	usage_200308.html
daily_usage_200111.png	hourly_usage_200302.png	usage_200309.html
daily_usage_200112.png	hourly_usage_200303.png	usage_200310.html
daily_usage_200201.png	hourly_usage_200304.png	usage_200311.html
daily_usage_200202.png	hourly_usage_200305.png	usage_200312.html
daily_usage_200203.png	hourly_usage_200306.png	usage_200401.html
daily_usage_200204.png	hourly_usage_200307.png	webalizer.hist
daily_usage_200205.png	hourly_usage_200308.png	

📁 Lab Files\Lesson02

NSSetup-Full.exe

📁 Lab Files\Lesson03

AdbeRdr60_enu_full.exe

📁 Lab Files\Lesson05

AetheraInstallXp_1.0.2-040127.exe	Benefits Overview.pdf
Benefits Overview.doc	IBF Class.WAB

📂 **Lab Files\Lesson06**

📁 Bzip2	📄 Colossus.txt	📄 image.tiff
📄 An Interesting File.wow	📄 Command_Prompt_FTP.txt	📄 tightvnc-1.2.9-setup.exe
📄 basic_form.txt	📄 FTP-readme.txt	

📂 **Lab Files\Lesson06\Bzip2**

📄 bunzip2.exe	📄 bzegrep	📄 bzip2.exe
📄 bzcat.exe	📄 bzfgrep	📄 bzip2recover.exe
📄 bzcmp	📄 bzgrep	📄 bzless
📄 bzdiff	📄 bzip2.dll	📄 bzmore

📂 **Lab Files\Lesson07**

📄 aaw6.exe	📄 README.TXT

📂 **Lab Files\Lesson08**

📄 ganttproject-1.9.10-setup.exe	📄 j2re-1_4_2_03-windows-i586-p.exe

Version 1.0